American Foreign Policy
Since World War II

American Foreign Policy Since World War II

FOURTEENTH EDITION

JOHN SPANIER
University of Florida

STEVEN W. HOOK
Kent State University

CQ PRESS A DIVISION OF
CONGRESSIONAL QUARTERLY INC.

For
David and Lisa
Christopher, Emily, and Benjamin

Printed and bound in the United States of America.

Book and cover design: Kachergis Book Design, Pittsboro, North Carolina

Cover photo credits, clockwise from top right: Library of Congress, Reuters, R. Michael Jenkins, UPI/Bettmann, Reagan Presidential Library, National Archives. *Interior photo credits:* 1 Reuters, 22 National Archives, 51 Library of Congress, 83 UPI/Bettmann, 111 Reuters, 140 AP/Wide World Photos, 163 UPI/Bettmann, 187 The White House, 211 Reagan Presidential Library, 241 Reuters/Bettmann, 271 AP/Wide World Photos, 301 Reuters/ Corbis-Bettmann, 329 Reuters.

Library of Congress Cataloging-in-Publication Data

Spanier, John W.
    American foreign policy since World War II / John Spanier, Steven
W. Hook. -- 14th ed.
        p.   cm.
    Includes bibliographical references (p.   ) and index.
    ISBN 1-56802-317-0
    1. United States--Foreign relations--1945–1989. 2. United States-
-Foreign relations--1989–   I. Hook, Steven W., 1959–   .
II. Title.
E744.S8   1997
    327.73--dc21   97-18352

Contents

Contents

Maps

Preface

The United States approaches the twenty-first century as an uncertain world power. Despite the nation's unrivaled military strength, robust economy, and widely emulated system of government, political leaders and the general public remain divided about America's role in world politics. The Clinton administration's erratic response to regional crises and its bitter struggle against Congress over foreign policy are the most tangible symptoms of this national ambivalence.

To a large extent, this pattern of behavior represents a return to form. As in the days before the United States became a world power, many Americans today are openly questioning what obligations, if any, the United States has to the "outside world": whether domestic problems should take priority over transnational concerns, and whether American activism abroad threatens its own democratic values and institutions. Such fundamental questions were set aside during the two world wars, and they remained dormant for much of the Cold War, when the containment of communism served as a unifying thread for U.S. foreign policy makers.

It is by now a cliché that the "new world order" is far less orderly than was widely expected in the euphoria of the early 1990s. Ethnic violence has since erupted in many parts of the world, regional tensions formerly suppressed by the superpowers have been reignited, democratic reforms in many countries have been challenged, and efforts by the United Nations to expand its peace-keeping role and promote "sustainable development" have succumbed to the conflicting self-interests of its members.

At the same time, the global economy has become more integrated than ever before and technological advances have linked together the far reaches of the globe. Regional economic blocs have emerged, private investment has poured across state boundaries in record amounts, and the World Trade Organization has begun enforcing widely accepted rules of international commerce. Meanwhile, the Internet and the World Wide Web have made instantaneous contact possible among governments, corporations, and private citizens.

All these developments have sent mixed signals to American leaders.

Some believe that the "foreign entanglements" of the post–Cold War era should be allowed to run their own course, whatever the cost in human lives and material devastation, and that American foreign policy should be limited to "geoeconomics." Others assert that the United States should constructively exploit its global clout and take the lead in resolving regional conflicts, preserving democratic reforms, and tackling global problems such as environmental decay and population growth. Still others argue that the United States should pursue a pragmatic foreign policy based on traditional realism, an approach the U.S. government adopted during the Cold War but one that runs counter to America's traditional approach to foreign affairs. Given the lack of national consensus, the United States has pursued all three courses at various times since the Soviet Union's collapse in 1991.

We hope this fourteenth edition of *American Foreign Policy Since World War II* will inform this debate and promote understanding of the nation's conduct overseas. In our view, one cannot adequately grasp the current dilemmas facing the United States and consider possible solutions without reference to the historical patterns that have shaped its foreign policy for more than two hundred years. In the pages that follow, we examine these historical patterns, which are deeply rooted in the nation's political culture, and we identify similarities between U.S. foreign policy before and after the Cold War. Within this context, we explore how America's behavior during the Cold War diverged from its traditional style of foreign policy.

THE FOCUS OF THIS STUDY

A close look at America's conduct during the turbulent period since World War II reveals important lessons about the nation's style of foreign policy and how America's behavior has been influenced by long-standing cultural values, by the perceptions of its leaders and their definitions of friends and enemies, and by the inescapable demands posed by the volatile international system. In short, a careful examination of this period reveals how the United States behaves as a superpower.

This study further considers the extent to which today's international problems are legacies of the Cold War. American foreign policy continues to bear the Cold War's imprint in many important respects, including the structure and global deployment of U.S. armed forces, the composition of U.S. alliances, the regional tensions in many former theaters of superpower conflict, and the recurring disputes between the White House and Congress over war powers, intelligence gathering, human rights, and foreign aid. The United States often violated its own declared democratic principles in pursuing the Cold War, fueling dissension and cynicism both at home and abroad. Strong anti-American sentiment lingers in many parts of the world, finding expression in terrorist bombings, the spread of religious fundamentalism, and the proliferation of weapons.

This study focuses on the *conduct* of American foreign policy rather than its *formulation,* which is emphasized in many contemporary textbooks. While detailed knowledge of the sources and processes of foreign policy making is essential, students also must grasp how these causal factors are reflected in the practice of foreign policy. Establishing that linkage between form and function—and assessing its consequences for the United States and the international system—are the primary concerns of this book.

In informing students about American foreign policy, this book advances a distinctive point of view. As we will argue, the United States has approached the turbulent international system with a very peculiar national style, a byproduct of its geographic position, abundant natural resources, and revolutionary origins during the height of the Enlightenment. Any nation's foreign policy is in large measure an expression of its national style, which affects its relationship with private citizens and groups; its creation of political structures; and, most important for our purposes, its approach and response to the outside world.

In this respect we concur with critical theorists who emphasize the social construction of American society and government. Cultural values are intimately linked with political institutions and, in turn, with the domestic policies and outward behavior of states. But beyond this somewhat self-evident proposition, any comprehensive understanding of foreign policy demands recognition of a broader context: the global setting in which each state exists; the prevailing norms of interstate relations; and the national characters, historic inclinations, and practices of other states. The process of social construction does not occur in a vacuum; it evolves in a complex global environment inhabited by other states and societies that have very different cultural traditions and national styles—a vital dimension of world politics that creates its own pressures on foreign policy.

These systemic pressures weighed heavily on the United States just after World War II. When the Cold War began, the United States faced a formidable challenge from the Soviet Union and its leader, Joseph Stalin, whose prolonged assault on his own people in the 1930s had led to the deaths of more than ten million Soviet citizens even before another twenty million were killed in World War II. As the Soviet archives continue to be pried opened in the late 1990s, the horrific depths of Stalin's internal repression both before and during the Cold War are becoming better known. American leaders who knew and worked with Stalin during World War II faced a deeply troubling question in the postwar period: would the aging Soviet dictator, strengthened by nuclear weapons and the extension of his empire into central Europe, commit even more unspeakable acts against other nations, including the United States? Neither Stalin's internal policies prior to World War II nor his actions immediately following the war were reassuring.

The Western scholarly literature, so critical of U.S. behavior both at home and overseas, has paid comparably little attention to the patterns of social construction that occurred in the early years of both the Soviet Union and the People's Republic of China, America's primary Cold War adversaries. In these societies the writings of Karl Marx, Vladimir Lenin, Joseph Stalin, and Mao Zedong formed the basis of primary education and established a government line transmitted daily by a state-controlled press and immune from public debate or criticism. When political opponents or religious leaders challenged these regimes, they were imprisoned or executed en masse. Thus in the Soviet Union social engineering was imposed with little regard for the diversity and spiritual aspirations of its people; in China it reached ghastly proportions during the Great Leap Forward of 1958–1959 and the Cultural Revolution of the mid-1960s.

These events were not lost on the United States, explicitly identified as the primary adversary of both regimes and of many of the revolutionary movements in the Third World that emerged in the 1960s and 1970s after the process of decolonization. The American strategy of "containment" recognized this fundamental conflict and called for a sustained response on a global scale. To some critics of this strategy, the Soviet Union was a "satisfied" power that did not seek expansion. Its actions were explained in terms of a defense of vital areas to counter America's aggressive behavior. Thus the assertive American response was unjustified. But this was hardly the signal sent by Stalin as he broke his promises to withdraw from Iran, denied free elections in Poland, staged a coup in Czechoslovakia, blockaded West Berlin, and tacitly approved the North Korean invasion of South Korea. In any case, given its massive frontiers and its large numbers of hostile neighbors, the Soviet Union could never be considered truly secure, let alone "satisfied."

In describing America's national style of foreign policy, this study further challenges the assumptions of structural realism that have viewed world politics as a clash of interchangeable "billiard balls." Although the distribution of power is a crucial element of global stability, it does not render the national character of states irrelevant. To the contrary, aspects of political culture shape international objectives and the instruments of foreign policy, including the structuring of armed forces and the recruitment of allies. Models of world politics based narrowly on systemic structure generally have ignored these crucial factors. More serious, during the Cold War these mechanistic designs permitted the moral equation of the superpowers and thus overlooked the crucial normative dimensions of this conflict.

This edition of *American Foreign Policy Since World War II* devotes increased attention to the period prior to World War II, when the United States emerged as a continental and hemispheric power, and offers expanded coverage of the Cold War. Some material deleted from the previous edition, and missed by readers, has been restored. The final three chapters are devoted to the post–Cold War period, which finds the United States again searching for a coherent role in world politics.

We remain confident in our central arguments, which seem to have weathered the storm of historical experience. We hardly expect, nor do we desire, this most recent account to silence our critics. Indeed, we hope to contribute to the ongoing debate and, along with our students and colleagues, to seek a better grasp of American foreign policy since World War II.

ACKNOWLEDGMENTS

In preparing this edition we have benefited from thoughtful anonymous reviews and from the more informal critiques of our longtime readers. The authors wish to thank specifically Byung-Ok Kil, Peter J. Schraeder, Arthur Vanden Houten, William Watts, and Guang Zhong, whose comments on the last edition and our draft revisions were very helpful. Once again, we are grateful for the care and attention given to this manuscript by Brenda Carter, Nancy Lammers, and Talia Greenberg at CQ Press and by Sabra Bissette Ledent, who edited this and the last edition. We remain, of course, ultimately responsible for the substantive arguments put forth in these pages; readers are asked to point any slings and arrows squarely in our direction.

Madeleine Albright speaks outside the United Nations, where she had served as U.S. ambassador, in January 1997. The Senate had just voted unanimously to confirm her as America's first woman secretary of state.

CHAPTER ONE

The American Approach to Foreign Policy

The United States stands alone as the world's most powerful country in the final years of the twentieth century. Its military strength is unsurpassed; its economic production far exceeds that of any other country; and its democratic political system, which has endured for more than two centuries, serves as a role model for dozens of other governments.

Yet despite all this, and despite the resounding victory of the United States in the Cold War, many Americans feel uncertain about the country's future role in world politics. In the absence of any direct threats to American security, national attention has shifted to domestic problems such as corporate downsizing, crime, and faltering schools. During the presidential campaign of 1996, surveys showed that foreign policy had slipped to the bottom of the list of national concerns.

This sense of detachment from foreign policy was fueled by a series of regional crises abroad, demonstrating that the post–Cold War era

1

would be anything but the harmonious "new world order" anticipated by former President George Bush. Indeed, the Berlin Wall had barely come down before Iraq invaded neighboring Kuwait in August 1991 and threatened the other oil producers of the Persian Gulf. In response, the United States led a coalition of governments sponsored by the United Nations in forcing the Iraqis out of Kuwait. Soon afterward, Yugoslavia broke apart as the dominant Serbs unleashed a campaign of "ethnic cleansing" against Muslims that was reminiscent of Nazi Germany. In Russia, President Boris Yeltsin faced strong opposition to his political and economic reforms and unleashed a violent assault on his own province of Chechnya, whose citizens sought to be free of Moscow's control. And in eastern Africa, renewed fighting among ethnic groups and clans produced casualties on a gruesome scale.

One sign of the changing national attitudes toward foreign affairs: during the Cold War the foreign policy experience of presidential candidates had been essential to their election, but the 1992 defeat of Bush by Arkansas governor Bill Clinton, who admitted to having little experience in foreign affairs, sent a clear signal that times had changed. Clinton's winning strategy was to focus on the American economy "like a laser." Thus in his first term he devoted most of his efforts to reducing the federal deficit and making American companies more competitive in the global marketplace. He was largely successful in both areas.

The American people, however, were quickly learning that they could not escape the foreign entanglements of the post–Cold War era. In 1991 American troops had taken the lead ousting Saddam Hussein from Kuwait; in 1992 they were deployed again in large numbers to "restore hope" in Somalia; and in 1994 they intervened in Haiti to restore a democratically elected government. In 1995, after years of inaction by the European powers, the United States brought the Balkan rivals together in Dayton, Ohio, where they agreed to suspend their war and create a new government under the watchful eye of the North Atlantic Treaty Organization (NATO). All the while, the United States sought to expand the Middle East peace process, support the transition of many states to democratic rule, and promote "sustainable development" in the former Third World.

One critic, reflecting a widely held view of the foreign policy of the first Clinton administration, condemned it for being limited to "social work."[1] Previous administrations had been preoccupied with powerful and potentially dangerous powers—Germany, Japan, the Soviet Union, China. In contrast, the Clinton administration was largely consumed

---

1. Michael Mandelbaum, "Foreign Policy as Social Work," *Foreign Affairs* (January–February 1996): 16–32.

not with issues of national interest—defined as those issues that direct-ly affect American lives—but with ambiguous transnational problems such as the deterioration of the environment, human rights, and the res-cue of "failed states" such as Somalia and Haiti. Reflecting public skep-ticism about foreign aid, environmental reforms, and UN peacekeeping, the post-1994 Republican leadership of the U.S. Congress blocked many of Clinton's initiatives and sought a more modest American role in world politics—one based primarily on its self-interests rather than global concerns.

After his reelection in 1996, Clinton once again called for an assertive foreign policy. "Let us do what it takes to remain the indispensable nation, to keep America strong, secure, and prosperous," he told Con-gress in his January 1997 State of the Union address. It was striking that the leader of the world's most powerful country had to plead with his citizens to take the steps necessary to remain a world power. Also strik-ing was the lack of enthusiasm that met the president's appeal.

Thus the central questions remain: What is the role of the United States in the final years of the twentieth century? How much should it care about events in the Persian Gulf, Africa, Latin America, or even Rus-sia? Should it be concerned about global issues such as population growth, the spread of AIDS, narcotics trafficking, and the proliferation of weapons of mass destruction? How actively should it pursue open markets and investment opportunities, as opposed to protecting U.S. industries from foreign competition? To what extent could it be com-mitted to democracy and human rights, and be true to itself, when America's strategic allies engage in policical repression or economic exploitation? In sum, what *responsibility* would befall the United States to sustain a global order it had fought so hard to create?

LEARNING FROM EXPERIENCE

One way to address these and similar questions about the scope and character of America's role in the current international arena is to exam-ine how previous leaders defined American interests and how well they succeeded in achieving their goals. For all the changes taking place in world politics, its basic elements persist, and historical experience can usefully inform both the student and practitioner of American foreign policy.

The post–World War II era witnessed the longest and most active involvement of the United States in world affairs since the nation's founding. This book looks closely at how the United States defined its national interests during this turbulent period and how it pursued them in practice. The chapters that follow also consider how U.S. actions reflected the nation's proclaimed moral principles and to what extent U.S. actions frequently diverged from them. And they describe how the behavior of the United States in the Cold War's aftermath represents a return to historic patterns established long before the nation achieved its status as a global superpower.

This study begins at the end of World War II and the outbreak of the Cold War. But why? Of what possible relevance is the Cold War to the vastly different contemporary system? Simply put, a grasp on why the Cold War erupted and how it was conducted will illuminate the events that followed. If the Cold War were still on, there probably would not have been a war in the Persian Gulf in 1991, nor would there have been an exchange of recognition in 1993 between the Israeli government and the Palestine Liberation Organization, two bitter enemies who have long used violence against one another. The Middle East peace process, initiated by the United States after the defeat of Iraq, would in all likelihood have remained barren, instead of realizing the beginnings of a Palestinian state and the normalization of Israeli-Jordanian relations in 1994. And certainly it is dubious whether Czechoslovakia would have fragmented into two separate republics, or whether Yugoslavia would have dissolved into a vicious and bloody civil war. Nor is it likely that the United States would have had to intervene in Somalia to feed its people or in Haiti to restore its elected leader who had been overthrown by a military junta.

Beyond these events, without understanding American foreign policy since World War II one cannot fully grasp the dilemmas currently facing U.S. leaders. Nor is it possible to comprehend why the post–Cold War world, which had been expected to bring a new era of peace, has in fact been so troublesome, violent, and unstable, and has not afforded the United States and the American people the luxury of focusing on internal matters.

Coming to terms with the problems confronting the United States between World War II and the new millennium begins with the proposition that the American people, like those in other countries, have a distinctive perspective on world politics. How nation-states act in the international arena depends in large measure on their geography, resources, and historical backgrounds, as well as the environment in which they coexist with other states. These "national styles" vary considerably, but all states bring them to bear as they adapt to the rules of the game and do what they must to ensure their survival and achieve a measure of security.

Because for most of its existence the United States had insulated itself from the European state system, its national style has been molded far more than that of other Western powers by its domestic experiences and

cultural traditions. Not schooled by a continual immersion in international politics, Americans have approached foreign policy in a way that
is not only peculiarly theirs, but also significantly different from that of
other great powers. The contrast in approaches to foreign policy was
particularly strong between the United States and the Soviet Union,
which emerged after World War II as the chief adversary of the United
States. Perhaps one reason was that the United States felt secure in the
Western Hemisphere, but czarist Russia (later the Soviet Union) could
never feel secure because of its proximity to many other great powers
that, over the centuries, had their own territorial ambitions. Thus the
United States confronted a formidable rival—one that combined historic insecurity with strong, often repressive centralized control, abundant natural resources, potent military forces, and a revolutionary ideology based on the inevitable global expansion of its political and economic system.

This book, then, explores how America's political culture, or national style, has influenced the conduct of its foreign policy and how these
cultural factors led American leaders to perceive allies and adversaries a
certain way. More generally, it questions whether America's approach to
foreign affairs contributed to its victory over the Soviet Union, or
whether that style might instead have prolonged the struggle with the
Soviet Union. Indeed, in the post–Cold War period a few observers have
wondered aloud whether America's policy of "containment" really was a
necessary prerequisite for the Soviet defeat. We will search for answers to
those questions in the pages to follow, and seek lessons from them that
can guide policy makers today.

THE VOLATILE STATE SYSTEM

American foreign policy since World War II is largely the story of the
tension between the nation-state system, created long before the country's birth, and the American style of dealing with other countries. In the
nation-state system, each member—especially the great powers, its principal actors—is prone to a high degree of insecurity. In the absence of a
world government that could safeguard it, each state ultimately must
depend on itself for its preservation and safety. Understandably, then,
state leaders tend to regard their counterparts as potential adversaries,
threats to their own territorial integrity and political independence. The
very nature of the state system breeds such feelings of insecurity, distrust, suspicion, and fear.

It is not the alleged aggressive instinct of humans as "naked apes" or
their presumed desire for acquiring ever-greater power that accounts for
what is popularly called *power politics*. Rather, power politics stems from

each state's essential concern for its security, the essential prerequisite for enjoying its particular way of life. Because states perceive that the external environment is threatening their security, they react defensively, enhancing their power in many different ways. In such an environment it does not take much for one state to arouse another's suspicions and to stimulate reciprocal images of hostility that each finds easy to substantiate by its opponent's behavior. Indeed, in most instances this enmity is maintained despite evidence to the contrary and even avowedly friendly acts. Conciliatory behavior often is seen as a sign of weakness, and it may invite exploitation. Or it may be regarded as a trick to persuade foreign leaders to relax their guard.

In view of this "security dilemma" and in the absence of a world government, a balance of power among the strongest states is required to keep the volatile state system from breaking down. With a balance or equilibrium, victory in a war is less probable and more costly. By contrast, a state possessing *overwhelming* power might be tempted to undertake aggression. Unrestrained power in the system constitutes a threat to all states. As one observer of international politics noted long ago:

Under these conditions [of anarchy] the expectation of violence and even of annihilation is ever-present. To forget this and thus fail in the concern for enhanced power spells the doom of a state. This does not mean open constant warfare; expansion of power at the expense of others will not take place if there is enough counterpower to deter or to stop states from undertaking it. Although no state is interested in a mere balance of power, the efforts of all states to maximize power may lead to equilibrium. If and when that happens, there is "peace" or, more exactly, a condition of stalemate or truce. Under the conditions described here, this balancing of power process is the only available "peace" strategy.[2]

THE BALANCE OF POWER AND THE END OF U.S. ISOLATIONISM

What all this means is that the behavior of nation-states is profoundly shaped by the ever-changing distribution of power. As that distribution shifts at both the regional and global level, it alters the strategic environment, defines the options available to states, and informs their policy choices.

During the nineteenth century the United States was able to preserve its isolation from power politics and enjoy an unprecedented degree of security because a balance of power, created at the Congress of Vienna in 1815, existed on the European continent and was effectively maintained by Great Britain together with France, Austria, and Russia. The Concert of Europe imposed a degree of stability in Europe that was rare

---

2. Arnold Wolfers, *Discord and Collaboration* (Baltimore: Johns Hopkins University Press, 1965), 83.

in its history. But Germany's unification in 1870 and the rapid industrialization that followed eventually forced the United States to end its isolation.

Germany's growing strength coincided with and hastened the decline of British power. Indeed, the early years of World War I showed clearly that even when British power was thrown in on the side of France and Russia, the three allies could barely contain Germany. With the collapse of czarist Russia in 1915 and the transfer of almost two million German soldiers from the Russian to the western front, a German victory became a distinct possibility. The United States would then have faced a Germany astride an entire continent, dominating European Russia and, in alliance with Austria-Hungary and perhaps the Ottoman Empire, extending German influence into the Balkans and the Middle East. It was at that point that Germany's unrestricted submarine warfare, which included attacks on American shipping, led to a U.S. declaration of war. With America's entry into the war, the Allies were able to contain the German spring offensive of 1918, leading to Germany's defeat.

After its victory the United States retreated into its customary hemispheric isolation, but American bankers, with the tacit approval of the government, maintained ties with Europe, playing an important role in its economic recovery and stabilization during the 1920s. (Their primary motive, however, was to recover money loaned to the European allies during World War I.) Although the U.S. economy rivaled that of all of Europe and the United States exercised great economic influence, the government refused to define for itself a political and military role consistent with its economic power. U.S. military power had been decisive in Germany's defeat, but the United States wanted nothing to do with great-power politics. To the contrary, as Adolf Hitler consolidated his power in Germany and as Benito Mussolini, the Italian dictator, moved into Africa, the U.S. Congress passed two Neutrality Acts which prevented an assertive American response. President Franklin Roosevelt opposed these actions, warning that they would "drag us into war instead of keeping us out."[3] At the same time, a congressional committee held hearings to probe allegations that U.S. involvement in World War I had been inspired by international banks, arms manufacturers, and other "merchants of death."

The United States began to play a political role again only when the balance of European power was upset once more by the eruption of World War II in 1939 and the defeat of France in 1940. With America facing the possibility of Britain's defeat and the control of Eurasia by Ger-

3. Quoted in Howard Jones, *The Course of American Diplomacy*, 2d ed. (Chicago: Dorsey Press, 1988), 396.

many and its allies, Roosevelt undertook several measures to help Britain withstand any Nazi assault. He sent fifty old destroyers to defend the English Channel and set up the "lend-lease" program to provide munitions, food, and other material support. This commitment to Britain was necessary even though such actions increased the risk of war with Germany. In fact, by the time Japan bombed Pearl Harbor in December 1941, the United States was engaged in an undeclared naval war with Germany in the Atlantic. Full-scale war was merely a matter of time.

THE U.S. DEFINITION OF SECURITY

In any assessment of U.S. actions leading up to World War II, two points deserve emphasis. First, the defense of the United States always has involved more than physical security. The German threat during World War I was not the likelihood of an immediate invasion, nor was invasion the main threat even after the defeat of France early in World War II. Then why did the United States twice forsake its "splendid isolation?" Surely the width of the Atlantic and Pacific Oceans would protect the United States.

American security was threatened for one reason: any state—especially an antidemocratic state—that controlled all the resources of Eurasia, the Middle East, and Africa, and that transferred those resources into military power, might someday be able to attack North America. This would be particularly true if Great Britain were defeated and the British navy no longer guarded the sea highway to the Western Hemisphere. Even if Britain sank its navy rather than see it joined with the fleets of Germany and its allies, the German navy might come to dominate the Atlantic approaches to the Western Hemisphere. Such circumstances would require the United States to mobilize its resources fully and be on constant alert for attack by an opponent with superior resources. Most likely, to match this dominant Eurasian power the United States would have to transform itself into a "garrison state"—a disciplined, militarized society, which, in the name of security, would have to sacrifice democracy and individual liberty in the name of self-defense.

The broader rationale for U.S. intervention was that the security of a democratic America was inextricably interwoven with the survival of other democracies, especially France and Britain. After France collapsed in 1940, Roosevelt explained to the American public why the United States had to assist Britain: the United States could not survive as a lone democratic island surrounded by totalitarian seas. Democracy in America could not flourish unless democratic values prospered in other societies. There might be no physical threat to the nation, but the aim of American foreign policy had never been just the security of the United

States as a piece of real estate; the purpose had been to defend the security of a democratic America, which required that democratic values flourish internationally.

The other point to be emphasized: despite the U.S. concern with security in Europe, the timing of the interventions in 1917 and 1941 was not in each case a rational decision made by Washington. It was Berlin's decision in 1917 to launch unrestricted submarine warfare against all shipping to England that brought the United States into the war, and it was Tokyo's decision in December 1941 to attack the U.S. fleet at anchor in Hawaii that led to the American declaration of war against Japan. Without Hitler's reckless 1941 declaration of war against the United States—a country he held in great contempt—U.S. power would have been directed only against Japan, and Germany, the far stronger power, would have faced only Britain and Russia, both already reeling from German blows. Therefore, but for German and Japanese mistakes, the United States might *not* have entered the two world wars. The decisions to go to war were not made by the United States, even though the balances of power in Europe and Asia were imperiled and American security was at stake. The United States was saved from itself by its enemies.

Great powers usually do not leave decisions about their security to their adversaries. The strategy of the major states in the state system is—or should be—to oppose any state that seeks predominance because such predominance would constitute a grave threat to their own security. The failure of the United States twice to act according to the logic dictated by the balance of power largely stemmed from its particular national style.

THE AMERICAN NATIONAL STYLE

The style reflected in the American response to war in Europe and later to the Cold War was the product of domestic experience. By giving priority to internal political and economic tasks—a characteristic of the United States since its founding—the nation had successfully isolated itself from European power politics. With nonthreatening neighbors to the north and south and open seas to the east and west, the United States could take its security for granted. Free from external threats, it could focus on its own economic and political development.

THE AMERICAN SENSE OF DESTINY

The ability of the United States to maintain its detachment from great-power politics for such a long time cannot be attributed *only* to the nation's distance from Europe, or to Europe's preoccupation with industrialization and class conflict at home and colonialism abroad, or to the strength of the Royal Navy. The nature of democracy has to be considered as well. The United States saw itself as more than just the world's first "new nation"; it also was the world's first democracy and, as such, the first country in history with the desire to improve the lot of ordinary people, to grant them the opportunity to enrich and ennoble their lives. The "more perfect union" was to be an egalitarian society. European concepts of social hierarchy, nobility and titles, and bitter class struggles were not to be planted in America's democratic soil.

From the very beginning of their national life, Americans professed a strong belief in what they considered to be their destiny—to spread, *by example*, freedom and social justice and to lead humankind away from its wicked ways to the New Jerusalem on earth. Early settlers declared America to be "a city on a hill" and considered it their providential mission to inspire other societies to follow their lead. The massive immigration of the late nineteenth century served to reinforce this sense of destiny. "Repudiation of Europe," novelist John Dos Passos once said, "is, after all, America's main excuse for being." In the popular mind, Europe stood for war, poverty, and exploitation; America, for peace, opportunity, and democracy. But the United States was not merely to be a beacon of a superior democratic domestic way of life. It also was to be an exemplar of a morally superior pattern of international behavior. The United States, then, would voluntarily reject power politics as unfit for its foreign policy.

Democratic theory posits that people are potentially rational and moral, which means that their differences can be settled by rational deliberation and moral exhortation. Assuming this to be true, the only differences that could arise would simply be misunderstandings, and, since people are endowed with reason and a moral sense, what quarrels could not be settled given the necessary goodwill? Peace—the result of harmony among people—was considered the natural or normal state. Conversely, conflict was considered a deviation caused primarily by wicked leaders whose morality and reason had been corrupted by their exercise of uncontrolled authority. Power politics was an instrument of selfish and autocratic rulers—that is, leaders unrestrained by democratic public opinion—who enjoyed wielding it for personal advantage. To them, war was a grand game. They could remain in their palatial homes, continuing to eat well and to enjoy the luxuries of life, and suffer none of the hardships of war. These fell upon the ordinary people, who had to leave their families to fight, to endure the higher taxes to pay for the war, and possibly to see their homes and families destroyed. The conclusion was clear: undemocratic states were inherently warlike and evil; democratic nations, in which the people controlled and regularly changed their leaders, were peaceful and moral.

The American experience seemed to support this conclusion: the United States was a democracy, and it generally was at peace with foreign powers. Furthermore, peace seemed to be the normal state of affairs. It was logical, then, that democracy and peaceful behavior and intentions should be thought of as synonymous. Americans rarely asked themselves whether democracy was responsible for the peace they enjoyed, or whether peace was the product of other forces. The frequent wars of Europe appeared to provide the answer: European politics was power politics, reflecting the feudal origins of European regimes. Americans had cut themselves off from Europe and its class conflicts and power politics after the Revolutionary War; America had to protect its democratic principles and abstain from any involvement in the affairs of Europe lest it be soiled and corrupted. Hemispheric detachment, therefore, was the morally correct policy, for it allowed the United States to quarantine itself from Europe's hierarchical social structures and violent diplomatic traditions.

By confusing the results of geography and Europe's focus on Asia, the Middle East, and Africa with the virtues of American democracy, Americans could smugly enjoy their self-conferred moral superiority as the world's "first democracy." It was the Monroe Doctrine, proclaimed in 1823, that first stressed, officially and explicitly, this ideological difference between the New World and the Old World. It declared specifically that the American political system was "essentially different" from that of Europe, whose nations engaged frequently in warfare. The implication was very clear: democratic government equals peace, and aristocratic government—which was identified with despotism—means war. In this spirit President James Monroe warned, "We should consider any attempt on [Europe's] part to extend their system to any portion of this hemisphere as dangerous to our peace and safety."[4]

This view also allowed the U.S. to engage in a bit of hypocrisy by acting like other nations in its continental expansion but disguising its motives in the noblest of terms. In advocating U.S. military expansion into Mexico in 1845, for example, journalist John O'Sullivan argued that it was

the right of our manifest destiny to overspread and to possess the whole of the continent which Providence has given us for the development of the great experiment of Liberty and federated self-government entrusted to us. Its floor shall be a hemisphere—its roof the firmament of the star-studded heavens, and its congregation a Union of many Republics, compromising hundreds of happy millions . . . governed by God's natural and moral law of equality.[5]

4. Quoted in Armin Rappaport, ed., *Sources in American Diplomacy* (New York: Macmillan, 1966), 53. For a recent critique, see Gaddis Smith, *The Last Years of the Monroe Doctrine* (New York: Hill and Wang, 1994).
   5. Quoted in Jones, *Course of American Diplomacy,* 143.

By drawing the distinction between the New and Old Worlds, and by warning the Europeans to keep their "hands off" this hemisphere, Americans were in effect opening the way for the establishment of U.S. preeminence and dominance. It would not be the last time the United States would invoke such a double standard, proclaiming a moral position loftier than that of other great powers—and then behaving in much the same way.

THE DEPRECIATION OF POWER IN INTERNATIONAL POLITICS

But this association of peace with democracy was not the only reason for the American depreciation of power politics in the eighteenth and nineteenth centuries. Another was that the United States was largely a one-class society, in which most shared a belief in a common set of middle-class, capitalistic, and democratic values. America was unique among nations in this respect. The European countries were, by contrast, three-class societies. In addition to the middle class, they contained in their bodies politic an aristocratic class, whose energies were devoted either to keeping itself in power or to recapturing power and returning to the glorious days of a feudal past. Moreover, European urbanization and industrialization during the nineteenth century had given birth to a proletariat, which, because it felt it did not receive a fair share of the national income, became a revolutionary class. The nations of the Old World were a composite of these three elements: a reactionary aristocracy, a small but democratic middle class, and a revolutionary proletariat. These nations had, in an intellectual as well as a political sense, a right, a center, and a left.

The United States had only a center, both intellectually and politically. It had no feudal past and therefore possessed no large, powerful aristocratic class on the right. Because it was by and large an egalitarian society, it also lacked a genuine left-wing movement of protest, such as socialism and communism. America was, as French political observer Alexis de Tocqueville observed in 1835, "born free" as a middle-class, individualist, capitalistic, democratic society. "As a result one finds a vast multitude of people with roughly the same ideas about religion, history, science, political economy, legislation, and government."[6] The United States was not divided by the kinds of deep ideological conflicts that in France, for example, set one class of people against another. No one class was ever so afraid of another that it preferred national defeat to domestic revolution—as in France in the late 1930s when the *haute bourgeoisie* was so apprehensive of a proletarian upheaval that its slogan became "Better Hitler than Blum" (Leon Blum, the French socialist leader).

6. Alexis de Tocqueville, *Democracy in America* (New York: Harper and Row, 1966), 56.

This widespread agreement on the fundamental values of American society and Europe's intense class struggles reinforced the American misunderstanding of the nature and functions of power on the international scene. Dissatisfied groups never developed a revolutionary ideology because the growing prosperity spread to them before they could translate their grievances against the capitalist system into political action. African Americans were an important exception because they never shared this wealth or political power; the "peculiar institution" of slavery, in fact, so defied America's democratic principles that it thrust the country into a calamitous civil war. Otherwise, the United States was politically secure, socially cohesive, and economically prosperous. It was able to resolve most of its differences peacefully, and its people could believe in an evolutionary, democratic, economically prosperous historical process. Revolution and radicalism were condemned from this perspective. In sharp contrast, because of their internal class struggles and external conflicts among themselves, the nations of Europe fully appreciated that social conflict was natural and that power played a crucial role in resolving conflict.

In the past, in fact, Americans have been so in accord on basic values that whenever the nation has been threatened externally it also has become fearful of internal disloyalty. It is one of the great ironies of American society that, while Americans possess this unity of shared beliefs to a greater degree than most other people, their apprehension of external danger has repeatedly led them, first, to insist on a general and somewhat dogmatic reaffirmation of loyalty to the "American way of life," and then to hunt for internal groups that might betray this way of life. Disagreement often has become equated with disloyalty; people have been accused of "un-American" thinking and behavior and labeled "security risks." Perhaps only a society so committed to one set of values could be so sensitive to internal subversion and so fearful of internal betrayal. In contrast, perhaps only a society in which two or more ideologies have long since learned to live together can genuinely tolerate diverse opinions: who has ever heard of "un-British" or "un-French" activities? The United States often has been called a "melting pot" because of its many different nationality groups, but, before each generation of immigrants has been fully accepted into American society, it has had to be "Americanized." Indeed, few Americans have ever accepted diversity as a value. American society, in fact, has taken great pride in destroying diversity through assimilation.

Politics did not, in any event, seem very important to Americans during the nineteenth century, when, in an era of rapid economic growth, the basic assumption was that people were motivated by their own material welfare. Self-interest governed economic behavior. Individuals, seeking to maximize their profits, produced what consumers wanted. The laws of supply and demand and the free market therefore transformed each person's economic selfishness into socially beneficial results—"the greatest good for the greatest number." Politics mattered little in this utilitarian system based on entrepreneurs whose combined efforts improved the general welfare. The best government, as Thomas Jefferson declared, was the government that governed least. Arbitrary political interference with the economic laws of the market only upset the results these laws were intended to produce. Private property, profit, and the free market were the keys to ensuring the happiness of people by providing them with abundance. Capitalism, in short, reflected the materialism of the age of industrialization.

To state the issue even more bluntly: economics was good and politics was bad. This simple dichotomy came naturally to the capitalist middle class. For them, the benefits of economic freedom were as "self-evident" as the truths stated in the Declaration of Independence. Had this economic freedom, many asked, not been gained only through the long and bitter struggle of Europe's middle class to cut down the authority of the powerful monarchical state and, in France, to overthrow it by revolution? The middle class, as it had grown more prosperous and numerous, became increasingly resentful of paying taxes from which the aristocracy was usually exempt, of the restrictions placed on trade and industry, of the absence of institutions in which middle-class economic and political interests were represented, of the class barriers to the social status that came with careers in the army and in the bureaucracy, and of the general lack of freedom of thought and expression. Because the middle class identified the power of the state with its own lack of freedom, its aim was to restrict this power. Only by placing restraints on the authority of the state could it gain the individual liberty as well as the right to private enterprise it sought. Democratic philosophy stated these claims in terms of the individual's "natural rights." The exercise of political authority was equated with the abuse of that authority and the suppression of personal freedoms. The power of the state had to be restricted to the minimum to ensure the individual's maximum political and economic liberties.

It was with this purpose in mind that the drafters of the U.S. Constitution divided authority between the states and the federal government, and, within the latter, among the executive, legislative, and judicial branches. Federalism and the separation of powers were deliberately designed to keep all governments—and especially the national government—weak. Domestic conflicts would be resolved not by the state's political actions, but by the individual's own economic actions in society in peacetime.

The American experience reflected this philosophy; millions of people came to the United States from other lands to seek a better way of life. America's vast territory was the earthly paradise where everyone could earn a respectable living and pursue happiness in their own way. Abundant natural resources, modern technology, individual enterprise, and helpful governmental policies enabled the American people to become the "people of plenty." A good income was sought for two reasons: economically, to attain a comfortable standard of living and, psychologically, to gain social status and to earn the respect of one's fellow citizens.

It followed logically that if people in an egalitarian society were judged primarily by their economic achievements, they would concentrate on getting ahead. Economic wealth, not surprisingly, came closer to being the common standard of value in the United States than in any other country. Money was the symbol of power, prestige, and success, just as failure to earn enough money was a token of personal failure.

It was hardly surprising that in these circumstances the solution to international problems in America's first century was considered a matter of economics than of politics. Economics was identified with social harmony and the welfare of all peoples; politics was equated with conflict, war, and death. Just as the "good society" was to be the product of free competition, so the peaceful international society would be created by free trade. Trade depended on mutual prosperity; in contrast, war impoverished and destroyed and created ill will among nations. Commerce, which benefited all the participating states, created a vested interest in peace; war was economically unprofitable and therefore obsolete. Free trade and peace, in short, were one and the same cause.[7]

THE PENCHANT FOR CRUSADING

One result of this American depreciation of power politics was that the United States began to draw a clear-cut distinction between war and peace in its approach to foreign policy. Peace, on the one hand, was characterized by a state of harmony among nations; conflict, on the other hand, was considered abnormal and war a crime. In peacetime one needed to pay little or no attention to foreign problems; indeed, to do so would divert people from their individual material concerns and upset the whole scale of social values. The effect of this attitude was clear: Americans turned their attention toward the outside world with reluctance and usually only when provoked—that is, when a foreign menace

---

7. These ideas were most thoroughly developed at the time by Adam Smith in his 1776 book *The Wealth of Nations* (New York: Oxford University Press, 1976).

had become so forbidding that it could no longer be ignored. Or, to state it somewhat differently, the United States rarely initiated foreign policy; the stimulus that dictated America's response generally came from beyond its borders.

But once Americans were provoked and the United States had to resort to force, the employment of force was justified in terms of the moral principles with which the United States, as a democratic country, identified. War could be justified only by presuming noble purposes and completely destroying the immoral enemy who threatened the integrity, if not the existence, of these principles. American power, then, had to be "righteous" power; only its full exercise could ensure salvation or the absolution of sin. A second result of the depreciation of power politics, therefore, was that the national aversion to violence became transformed on occasion into a national glorification of violence, and wars became ideological crusades to destroy the enemy state and then send its people to democratic reform school. Making the world "safe for democracy"—the stated objective during World War I—was to be achieved by democratizing the populace of the offending nation, making its new rulers responsible to the people they governed, and thereby converting the formerly authoritarian or totalitarian state into a peaceful democratic state and banishing power politics for all time. Once that aim had been achieved, the United States could again withdraw into itself, secure in the knowledge that American works had again proved to be "good works."

This has been the historic pattern of American foreign policy: a pendulum-like swing "back and forth between the extremes of an indiscriminate isolationism and an equally indiscriminate internationalism or globalism."[8] According to Harvard professor Stanley Hoffmann, "both extremes have in common the intention to avoid the contamination of unhealthy foreign troubles."[9] As a self-proclaimed morally and politically superior country, the United States could remain pure only by abstaining from involvement in a corrupt world or, if the world would not leave it alone, by destroying the source of evil through the application of maximum force and total war. In short, both the isolationist and the crusading impulses sprang from the same source. These swings tended, moreover, to be accompanied by radical shifts of mood: from one of optimism, which sprang from the belief that America was going to reform the world, to one of disillusionment as the grandiose objectives the United States had set for itself proved beyond its capacity to

8. Hans J. Morgenthau, *A New Foreign Policy for the United States* (New York: Praeger, 1969), 15.
9. Stanley Hoffmann, *Gulliver's Troubles, or the Setting of American Foreign Policy* (New York: McGraw-Hill, 1968), 98.

reach. Feeling too good for this world, which clearly did not want to be reformed but preferred its old, corrupt habits, the nation retreated into isolationism to perfect and protect its way of life. Having expected too much from the use of its power, Americans then also tended to feel guilty and ashamed about having used their power at all.

The third result of the depreciation of power politics was that Americans divorced force from diplomacy. In peacetime, diplomacy unsupported by force was supposed to preserve the harmony among states. But in time of war, political considerations were subordinated to force. Once the diplomats had failed to keep the peace with appeals to morality and reason, military considerations became primary, and the soldier was placed in charge.

The United States, then, rejected the concept of war as a political instrument and Carl von Clausewitz's definition of war as the continuation of politics by other means.[10] Instead, it regarded war as a politically neutral operation that should be guided by its own professional rules and imperatives. Military officers conducted their campaigns in a strictly apolitical, technically efficient manner. And war was a purely military instrument whose sole aim was the destruction of the enemy's forces and despotic regime. Policy and strategy were unrelated; strategy began where policy ended. Thus after the Japanese attack on Pearl Harbor, the secretary of state turned to the secretary of war and said the situation was now out of his hands; it was all up to the War Department. As the war in Europe was coming to a close, the British asked Gen. George C. Marshall, architect of the Western allies' victory, to send U.S. forces to liberate Prague and as much of Czechoslovakia as possible before the Soviet army arrived. Marshall responded that he would not risk American lives for "purely political purposes"—a commendable sentiment, but what is war about if not the achievement of political purposes?

For Americans, then, war was a means employed to abolish power politics; war was conducted to end all wars. This same moralistic attitude also militated against the use of diplomacy in its classical sense: to compromise interests, to conciliate differences, and to moderate and isolate conflicts. Although Americans regarded diplomacy as a rational process for straightening out misunderstandings between nations, they also were extremely suspicious of it. For this reason, the U.S. government refused to create a large, permanent diplomatic corps until long after the nation's arrival as a great power.

10. This phrase sums up the essence of Clausewitz's famous book, *On War*. First published in 1832, it remains the most outstanding effort in Western history to understand war's internal dynamics and its relationship to political policy and goals. The best modern translation and editing are by Michael Howard and Peter Paret, *On War* (Princeton, N.J.: Princeton University Press, 1976).

If the United States was by definition moral, it obviously could not compromise, for a nation endowed with a moral mission could hardly violate its own principles. That constituted appeasement and national humiliation. The nation's principles would be transgressed, the nation's interests improperly defended, the national honor stained. Moreover, to reach a settlement with enemies rather than wiping them out in order to safeguard American principles would be to condone moral compromise. This attitude toward diplomacy, which, in effect, made its use as an instrument of compromise difficult, reinforced the American predilection for violence as a means of settling international problems. War allowed the nation to destroy its evil opponent but permitted it to keep its moral mission intact and unsullied by compromise.

AMERICAN FOREIGN POLICY ON THE EVE OF THE COLD WAR

On the eve of the Cold War, then, the American approach to foreign policy contrasted sharply in many ways with the conduct of states long immersed in international politics. Unlike most other states, the United States was highly secure; it needed no large army or navy to protect it. Moreover, the military and its values were widely distrusted because they were believed to be contrary to those of a democracy, and it was the building of democracy that the nation considered its first task. The result was the pattern just described: a swing from an isolationist position in which the country served as an example of social justice on earth to a posture of massive and violent intervention. Consistent, continual participation in the international system was not the norm.

Furthermore, the American perception of an international harmony of interests contrasted sharply with the state system's emphasis on the inevitability of conflict and differences of interests among states. Americans regarded conflict as an abnormal condition; the rest of the state system perceived harmony to be an illusion. The United States, long isolated from Europe and therefore not socialized by the state system, did not accept the reality and permanence of conflicts among its members. Indeed, differences between states were considered unnatural. But when they did occur, such differences should not be deep or long-lasting. Rather, they were attributed to wicked leaders (who could be eliminated), authoritarian political systems (which could be reformed), or misunderstandings (which could be straightened out if the adversaries approached each other with sincerity and empathy). Once these obstacles had been removed, peace, harmony, and goodwill would reign supreme.

Because the United States considered itself a morally and politically superior society, its attitude toward the use of power internationally was dominated by the belief that the struggle could be avoided by isolating the country from it or could be eliminated by crusading against those countries indulging in power politics. Moralism in foreign policy proscribed the use of power in peacetime; power could be employed only in confrontations with unambiguous aggression, transformed then into an obligation to fight in behalf of righteous causes. In short, power could be legitimated only by democratic purposes. Otherwise its exercise would be evil and would necessarily degrade liberty at home.

The great American compulsion to feel moral about the nation's behavior reinforced the cyclical swings from isolationism to crusading and back again. The perception of power as simply the raw material of international politics—its use as an instrument of compromise, conciliation, and moderation in interstate politics, its discriminating application toward achievement of specific and less-than-total objectives—was clearly antithetical to the American understanding of power. The term *power politics* was itself an anathema, a reminder of a way of doing things that the New World hoped it had left behind, and a potential threat to its virtue if the nation were to indulge in that kind of immoral Old World behavior.

One of the most telling characteristics of America's national style in conducting foreign policy has been that after every major war the reasons for the country's participation in struggle and bloodshed have been thoroughly scrutinized and openly criticized. Revisionist histories have had certain common themes: the conflicts in which the nation became entangled did not in fact threaten its security interests; it became involved because the politicians saw a menace where none existed, and this illusion was promoted by propagandists who aroused and manipulated public opinion, by soldiers with bureaucratic motives, and, above all else, by bankers and industrialists—the "merchants of death" of the 1930s, the "military-industrial complex" of the 1960s—whose economic interests benefited from the struggle. America's engagements in the two world wars of this century (as in the Cold War later) were mistakes; they were unnecessary or immoral, if not both. The enemy identified yesterday as the aggressor and *provocateur* actually did not represent a threat to American security at all; to the contrary, the threat came from within. But for certain domestic forces the United States could have continued to isolate itself from international politics. Note also that these domestic groups propelling the nation into war were said, in characteristic American fashion, to be motivated by profit.[11]

11. For examples of this revisionist literature during the Cold War, see Michael Parenti, *The Sword and the Dollar* (New York: St. Martin's Press, 1989); William Appleman Williams, *The Tragedy of American Diplomacy,* 3d ed. (New York: Norton, 1972); Gabriel Kolko, *The Roots of American Foreign Policy* (Boston: Beacon Press, 1969); and Walter LaFeber, *The New Empire* (Ithaca, N.Y.: Cornell University Press, 1963).

The fundamental revisionist assumption, then, was that America had a choice between employing or not employing power politics. Conversely, revisionism rejected the idea that the distribution of power in the state system left the United States—or any other country for that matter—with a choice only of whether or not it would help to maintain the balance of power. Power was equated in this instance with its abuse. Abstention from its use and the creation of a truly just society at home were considered wiser and more moral policies. Crusading, allegedly for the reform of the world, risked corrupting America's very soul because it diverted attention and resources from reform at home to military preparation and war. Revisionism, then, was essentially an argument for continued isolation from power politics.

But if one could not avoid power politics or abolish it, there was yet another solution: to flee the divisive world of power into the more united world of economics. The belief that political conflict among states could be transformed into cooperation among nations when they focused on what was truly important—the improvement of humanity's material and social life—was another major characteristic of American style. If power politics and concern for security led to conflict and war, economics with its concern for raising everyone's standard of living bound all people together, regardless of nationality or race. They had to cooperate for their common good.

Viewed in historical context, the revulsion American leaders felt for the concept of maintaining the balance of power, their emphasis on transnational interdependence after the Vietnam War, and the Clinton administration's more recent focus on "geoeconomics" are hardly novel. During the early days of the Republic, political boundaries were widely believed to be

artificial and ephemeral in comparison with the fine net by which the merchants tied the individuals of the different nations together like "threads of silk." . . . [T]he merchants—whether they are English, Dutch, Russian, or Chinese—do not serve a single nation; they serve everyone and are citizens of the whole world. Commerce was believed to bind the nations together and to create not only a community of interests but also a distribution of labor among them—a new comprehensive principle placing the isolated sovereign nations in a higher political unit. In the eighteenth century, writers were likely to say that the various nations belonged to "one society"; it was stated that all states together formed "a family of nations" and the whole globe a "general and unbreakable confederation."[12]

After World War II, therefore, the United States faced the world with attitudes and behavior patterns formed by its long period of detachment from the great powers of Europe. More specifically, in 1945 America con-

12. Felix Gilbert, *To the Farewell Address: Ideas of Early American Foreign Policy* (Princeton, N.J.: Princeton University Press, 1961), 57.

fronted the Soviet Union, formerly czarist Russia, a state with long experience in Old World diplomacy. The Soviet-American rivalry would dominate world politics for nearly half a century, with profound implications for the domestic and foreign policies of nearly every nation-state. And it would force the United States to apply its unique world view to the day-to-day challenges of great-power politics.

The experience of the United States in this struggle left a legacy that continues to be felt, both within the United States and abroad. The chapters that follow explore both the Cold War experience and its legacy in the context of America's enduring style of foreign policy. This exploration reveals that the country's ambivalence as a world power shaped its policies during the Cold War and remains evident in current debates about its international roles and obligations. "The United States retains sufficient international power to lead in a post–Cold War world," one analyst concluded. "Whether the United States also possesses the foreign policy purpose, however, is more uncertain."[13]

13 Michael Mastanduno, "The United States Political System and International Leadership: A 'Decidedly Inferior' Form of Government?" in *American Foreign Policy: Theoretical Essays,* 2d ed., ed. John Ikenberry (New York: HarperCollins, 1994), 343.

Franklin Roosevelt confers with Winston Churchill and Joseph Stalin in Tehran in November 1943. They would meet again in Yalta in February 1945 to discuss military strategy and the structure of the postwar world.

CHAPTER TWO

From World War to Cold War

The European land mass from France to Russia lay in ruin after World War II. In the East, Japan and its short-lived East Asian empire were devastated; China was immersed in civil war. The United States, however, remained strong after the war and emboldened by its victory over fascism in Europe and Asia. For the second time in three decades, the United States had been drawn into world war and had triumphed. It had attained a "preponderance of power" after seeing its influence expand steadily from continental to regional to global scale.[1] For those who were convinced that America was bound to achieve its "manifest destiny," the moment of truth seemed to have arrived.

But even before the embers of World War II had cooled, the sparks of a new conflict illuminated the future of American foreign policy, and the

---

1. See Melvyn Leffler, *A Preponderance of Power* (Stanford, Calif.: Stanford University Press, 1992), 203–206.

elation over military victory quickly was overtaken by new problems, responsibilities, and challenges to regional and global stability. Americans would face the equally daunting task of winning the peace.

Signs of the coming schism were largely ignored as the final battles of World War II were waged in central Europe and East Asia. Before one of the wartime conferences between Prime Minister Winston Churchill and President Franklin Roosevelt, a U.S. War Department memorandum forecasting the Soviet Union's postwar position concluded that it would be the dominant power in Eurasia for the foreseeable future:

With Germany crushed, there is no power in Europe to oppose her [the Soviet Union's] tremendous military forces. . . . The conclusions from the foregoing are obvious. Since Russia is the decisive factor in the war, she must be given every assistance, and every effort must be made to obtain her friendship. Likewise, since without question she will dominate Europe on the defeat of the Axis, it is even more essential to develop and maintain the most friendly relations with Russia.[2]

The importance of this assessment lies less in its prediction of the Soviet Union's postwar position, which was fairly obvious, than in its statement of American expectations about future Soviet-American relations. Military leaders apparently accepted without any major misgivings the prospect of the Soviet Union as the new dominant power in Europe; they did not imagine that it might replace Nazi Germany as a grave threat to the European and global balance of power. Although twice in the twentieth century the United States had been propelled into Europe's wars at exactly those moments when Germany became so powerful that it almost destroyed this balance, the lessons of history—specifically, the impact on American security of any nation's domination of Europe—had not yet been absorbed. Roosevelt and the American government did not attempt to reestablish a balance of power in Europe to safeguard the United States; they expected this security to stem from mutual Soviet-American goodwill, unsupported by considerations of power. This reliance on goodwill and mutual esteem was to prove foolish at best—and at worst potentially fatal.

AMERICAN WARTIME ILLUSIONS

Postwar expectations of an "era of good feelings" between the Soviet Union and the United States epitomized the quixotic style of American foreign policy, which perceived war as a disruption of the normal harmony among nations, military force as an instrument to be used only to punish the aggressors or war criminals, and those who cooperated in its

2. Quoted in Robert E. Sherwood, *Roosevelt and Hopkins*, vol. 2 (New York: Bantam Books, 1950), 363–364.

ideological crusade as equally moral and peace-loving. Once the war was finished, this thinking presumed, natural harmony would be restored and the struggle for power would end.

The implication was clear: the United States need take no precautionary steps against its wartime allies in anticipation of a possible disintegration of the alliance and potential hostility among its partners. Instead, it was hoped that the friendly relations and mutual respect that American leaders believed had matured during the war would preserve the common outlook and goals and guarantee an enduring peace. This rosy scenario pertained especially to the Soviet Union itself, despite its alien ideology and the tyrannical conduct of its leader, Joseph Stalin.

In Washington, government leaders generally reflected this idealism. They hailed the globalization of America's moral vision and its rejection of old-style power politics. As World War II wound down, Secretary of State Cordell Hull anticipated the day in which "there will no longer be need for spheres of influence, for alliances, for balance of power, or any other of the special arrangements through which, in the unhappy past, the nations strove to safeguard their security or to promote their interests."[3]

These optimistic expectations of future Soviet-American relations made it necessary to explain away continuing signs of Soviet distrust. This was particularly true during World War II when the West delayed opening up a second front against Germany. When the front was postponed from 1942 to 1943 to 1944, Stalin became bitter. He brusquely rejected Allied explanations that they were not yet properly equipped for such an enormous undertaking, and he especially denounced Churchill for declaring that there would be no invasion until the Germans were so weakened that Allied forces would not have to suffer forbiddingly high losses. To Stalin, this was a weak explanation because the Soviets accepted massive casualties as a matter of course. "When we come to a mine field," Marshal G. K. Zhukov explained to Gen. Dwight Eisenhower after the war, "our infantry attacks exactly as if it were not there. The losses we get from personnel mines we consider only equal to those we would have gotten from machine guns and artillery if the Germans had chosen to defend that particular area with strong bodies of troops instead of with mine fields."[4]

It was no wonder, then, that the Soviets dismissed Allied explanations and fastened instead on what was for them a more reasonable interpretation of American and British behavior. From the Marxist viewpoint

3. Quoted in Herbert Feis, *Churchill, Roosevelt, Stalin: The War They Waged and the Peace They Sought* (Princeton, N.J.: Princeton University Press, 1957), 238.
4. Quoted in Dwight Eisenhower, *Crusade in Europe* (New York: Doubleday, 1948), 514.

the Allies were doing exactly what they should be doing, postponing the second front until the Soviet Union and Germany, the two parties to the Molotov-Ribbentrop Pact, had exhausted each other. Then the United States and Britain could land in France, march into Germany without heavy losses, and dictate the peace to Germany and the Soviet Union. The Western delay was seen as a deliberate attempt by the world's leading capitalist powers to destroy their two major ideological opponents at one and the same time. Throughout the war the Russians displayed this fear of hostile Western intentions.

American leaders found a ready explanation for this perceived Soviet suspicion. They thought of Soviet foreign policy not in terms of the internal dynamics of the regime and its ideological enmity toward all noncommunist nations, but solely in terms of Soviet reactions to Western policies. New to great-power politics, they had little knowledge of Russian history and, therefore, of Russia's historical goals under czarist and Soviet rule. The few experts in the State Department were ignored; in fact, Roosevelt never took the secretary of state along to any of his wartime conferences with Churchill and Stalin.

Soviet distrust of the West was viewed by the president against the pattern of the West's previous anti-Sovietism: the Allied intervention in Russia at the end of World War I aimed at overthrowing the Soviet regime and, after the failure of that attempt, the establishment of a *cordon sanitaire* in Eastern Europe to keep Soviet influence from spreading; the West's rejection of Soviet offers in the mid- to late 1930s to build an alliance against Nazi leader Adolf Hitler; and, especially, the Munich agreement of 1938, when Britain and France stood by while the Nazi dictator destroyed Czechoslovakia, opening his gateway to the East. These Western efforts to weaken and ultimately destroy the Soviet Union, as well as its attempts to turn Hitler's threat away from the West and toward Russia, were considered the primary reasons for Soviet hostility.

To overcome this attitude, American leaders thought they had only to demonstrate good intentions. The question was not whether Soviet cooperation could be won for the postwar world, but how it would be gained. And if these efforts bore fruit and created goodwill, what conflicts of interest could not be settled peacefully in the future? Various Soviet policies and acts during the war—the disbanding of the Comintern (the vehicle for international communism), the toning down of communist ideology and the new emphasis on Soviet nationalism, the relaxation of restrictions on the church, and, above all, the statement of Soviet war aims in the same language of peace, democracy, and freedom used by the West—seemed to prove that if the Western powers demonstrated their *bona fides* (good faith) they could convert the Soviets into allies.

Roosevelt's efforts to gain this cooperation focused on Stalin. In that respect Roosevelt's instincts were correct: if he could gain Stalin's trust, postwar Soviet-American cooperation would be possible. But in another respect his instincts were poor. Roosevelt's political experience was in the domestic arena. He had dealt successfully with all sorts of politicians and had managed to resolve differences by finding compromise solutions. As a result, he had great confidence in his ability to win Stalin's favor. He would talk to Stalin as "one politician to another." In short, Roosevelt saw Stalin as a Russian version of himself, who, as a fellow politician, could be won over by a mixture of concessions and goodwill. It did not occur to Roosevelt that all of his considerable skills and charm might not suffice. At home these qualities were enough because he and his opponents agreed on ultimate goals; differences were largely over the means to achieve them. But between the United States and the Soviet Union the differences were over the ends, the kind of world each expected to see when the war was over.

In February 1945 at the Yalta Conference of the Big Three—Roosevelt, Stalin, and Churchill—Roosevelt and his advisers believed they had firmly established amicable and lasting relations with the Soviet Union. Stalin had made concessions on a number of vital issues and had promised cooperation in the future. He had accepted the establishment of the United Nations on the basis of the American formula that the veto in the Security Council would be applied only to enforcement action, not to peaceful attempts at the settlement of disputes. Moreover, in the Declaration of Liberated Europe he had promised to support self-government and allow free elections in Eastern Europe. He also had responded to the wishes of the American military and promised to enter the war against Japan after Hitler was finally subdued. And Stalin, to whom Roosevelt often referred in congenial terms, had repeatedly expressed his hope for fifty years of peace and great-power cooperation.

The new era of goodwill was to be embodied in the United Nations, where the peoples of the world would exercise vigilance over their national leaders. The United Nations was regarded as democracy working on an international scale. Just as citizens within democratic states were able to watch their representatives and prevent them from effecting compromises injurious to their interests, so the people of all countries would now be able to keep an eye on their national leaders, making it impossible for them to strike secret deals that would betray the people's interests and threaten the peace of the world. International public opinion, expressing its pacific ideals across national boundaries, would maintain vigilance over the diplomats and hold them accountable. Power politics would be replaced by reliance on sound universal principles and good faith. Upon his return from Yalta, Roosevelt told Congress and the

American people that his recent conference with Stalin and Churchill "ought to spell the end of the system of unilateral action, the exclusive alliances, the spheres of influence, the balances of power, and all the other expedients that have been tried for centuries—and have always failed." Instead: "We propose to substitute for all these, a universal organization in which all peace-loving nations will fully have a chance to join."[5]

The State Department had been even more emphatic about the subordination of power politics to universal moral principles. Its Subcommittee on Territorial Problems stated that "the vital interests of the United States lay in following a 'diplomacy of principle'—of moral disinterestedness instead of power politics." No comment could have summed up more aptly the American habit of viewing international politics in terms of abstract moral principles instead of clashes of interest and power. Moreover, no institution could have embodied more fully the immediate postwar hope for a return to "normalcy," the desire for minimal international involvement, and the expectation that the wartime cooperation with the Soviet Union would continue, than the United Nations, which was seen essentially as a *substitute* for a vigorous, self-reliant foreign policy.

THE RUSSO-SOVIET APPROACH TO FOREIGN POLICY

In Chapter 1 it was argued that before World War II American foreign policy was to a large degree driven by a cultural tradition that reflected the nation's detachment from Europe and its pursuit of a democratic way of life in the New World. Such cultural influences affect the foreign policies of every nation-state. It is thus useful to contrast the American tradition with that of its Cold War rival, the Soviet Union, whose leaders also inherited a distinct cultural style of foreign policy, the product of centuries of fractious coexistence with a diverse and often-menacing external environment. These leaders then integrated the lessons of Russian history with the maxims of Marxist-Leninist ideology to fashion an aggressive approach to postwar foreign affairs. But how were these historic Russian roots rendered compatible with communist ideology under the banner of the Soviet Union?

THE RUSSIAN BACKGROUND

As in the American case, understanding the source of the Russo-Soviet "style" of foreign policy begins simply by analyzing a globe. Unlike the

---

5. Quoted in James MacGregor Burns, *Roosevelt, The Soldier of Freedom* (New York: Harcourt, Brace, Jovanovich, 1970), 582.

United States and other maritime powers, Russia was not blessed by geography. Unprotected by natural barriers such as oceans or mountains, its people were vulnerable to invasions from several directions. And the enormous size of its territory rendered internal cohesion, communication, and transportation very difficult, especially given the diverse ethnic backgrounds of the Russian people.

During the thirteenth and fourteenth centuries, Russia was ruled by the Mongols from the East. By the 1460s Mongol domination had been repelled and Muscovy had emerged as the capital of a Russian superstate. In more modern times, Napoleon Bonaparte's armies invaded and captured Moscow in 1812; British and French armies landed in the Crimea in 1854–1856; and Japan attacked and claimed territories in eastern Russia in 1904–1905. Germany invaded Russia twice during the twentieth century, its first attack prompting the final collapse of the Russian monarchy, civil war, and the rise of the Bolsheviks to power.

Historically, then, Russia could not take its security for granted or give priority to domestic affairs. In these circumstances political power became centralized in the state, which, under both the czars and communist leaders, firmly held the far-flung regions together. Such efforts, however, required large standing military forces, and much of the Russian population was mobilized in their service. Indeed, the Russian armed forces were consistently larger than those of the other European great powers, a fact not lost on leaders in Warsaw, Budapest, Paris, and London.

This militarization of Russian society, purportedly for defensive purposes, also carried with it the potential for outward aggression. To the historian Richard Pipes, Russia no more became the world's largest territorial state by repelling repeated invasions than a man becomes rich by being robbed.[6] The same lack of natural frontiers that failed to protect Russia from invasion also allowed its power to extend outward from its frontiers. Indeed, sustained territorial expansion has been called the "Russian way." According to President Jimmy Carter's national security adviser, Zbigniew Brzezinski, any list of aggressions against Russia in the last two centuries would be dwarfed by Russian expansionist moves against its neighbors.[7]

Whether Russian motives were defensive or offensive, the result was a pattern of expansion. To the degree that Russian rulers feared attacks, they pushed outward to keep the enemy as far away as possible. Territo-

6. Richard Pipes, as quoted by Zbigniew Brzezinski, *Game Plan* (Boston: Atlantic Monthly Press, 1986), 19–20.
7. Zbigniew Brzezinski, "The Soviet Union: The Aims, Problems, and Challenges to the West," in *The Conduct of East-West Relations in the 1980s*, Adelphi Paper No. 189, Part I (London: International Institute for Strategic Studies, 1984).

rial extension became a partial substitute for the lack of wide rivers or mountains that might have afforded a degree of natural protection. Individual rulers' ambitions, such as Peter the Great's determination to have access to the sea, also resulted in territorial conquest and defeat of the power blocking that aim (in this case, Sweden). Even before the Bolsheviks seized power, authoritarianism, militarism, and expansionism characterized the Russian state; being a good neighbor was an alien concept. The basic "rules" of power politics—the emphasis on national interests, distrust of other states, expectation of conflict, self-reliance, and the possession of sufficient power, especially military power—were deeply ingrained in Russia's leaders.

THE SOVIET INGREDIENT

These attitudes were modified and strengthened by the outlook of the new regime after 1917. Russian political culture was fused with Marxist ideology, as adapted to Russian circumstances by Vladimir Lenin, to create an all-encompassing *weltanschauung* (world view). The new leaders' ideological outlook did not dictate action in specific situations, but it did provide them with a broad framework for perceiving and understanding the world.

To these new leaders, history centered around the class struggle between, on the one hand, the rich and privileged who owned the means of production, and, on the other hand, the greater numbers of propertyless citizens who worked for them. Why were most human beings poor, illiterate, and unhealthy? Why did states fight wars? The answer was that a small minority of capitalists, monopolizing the industrialized world's wealth and power, exploited the men and women who worked in their factories to maximize profits. To keep wages down, they kept food prices low so that agricultural labor also lived in destitution. Domestically as well as internationally, wars were one result of the ongoing search by these capitalists for profits.

Another result was the conflict waged over dividing up the non-European colonial world. For Lenin, global imperialism represented the "highest stage of capitalism." He viewed World War I as a climactic showdown among capitalist empires, a fight for the spoils of the developing world now that their own frontiers were closed. If human beings were ever to live in freedom and enjoy a decent standard of living in peace and fraternity with other countries, capitalism would have to be replaced by communism.

As Lenin was aware, the application of Marxism to Russia suffered from one glaring deficiency. In Karl Marx's dialectic view, communism stemmed directly from the failures of capitalism. Thus a communist society must first experience industrialization, urbanization, and the enlistment of its working classes into an organized "proletariat." This, of course, did not pertain to the largely agrarian Russia whose population was only then emerging from its feudal traditions. So Lenin attempted to resolve this problem by centralizing power in a "vanguard" of enlightened Marxists, who would bring communism to the Russian people without first exposing them to the contradictions and inequalities of capitalism. Once firmly in place within the Kremlin, this vanguard would then disseminate Lenin's ideological vision through a pervasive propaganda campaign.

Ideology was more than a way of viewing the world; it also gave the Soviet leaders a mission. For them, capitalism was the chief obstacle to humanity's liberation. Thus Soviet leaders considered the American and West European governments to be enemies because of what they were—capitalist. Moreover, unlike the traditional thinking of the great powers, who had no "permanent" friends or enemies and who shifted allegiances as the distribution of power changed, Soviet ideology clearly discriminated friend from foe on a permanent basis. Because the Soviet Union defined capitalist states as foes, and because the Soviet mission was to export its revolution and create a new postcapitalist international order, the relationship between it and the capitalist states would be marked by conflict until the victory of Soviet ideology. Its leaders, moreover, took it for granted that the capitalist states were equally hostile and determined to eliminate communism and the Soviet Union, if only to avoid their own demise.

The effect of this pattern was to perpetuate historic Russian suspicions of foreigners and feelings of insecurity. Soviet leaders believed the state system, increasingly composed of capitalist states with close economic ties, was a very hostile environment. They rejected the latter's professions of goodwill and peaceful intentions and committed their country to the "inevitable and irreconcilable struggle" against these states. They fostered a strong emphasis on self-reliance and an equally intense concern with Soviet power. Tactically, they were convinced that when an enemy made concessions in negotiations or became more accommodating, it was not because the enemy wanted a friendlier relationship but because it was *compelled* to do so by the Soviet Union's growing strength, a viewpoint that led to a self-sustaining rationale for ever more military power.

Russian history stood as a warning to Soviet leaders that peace was but a preparation for the next war. Their ideological perceptions strengthened the view that peace was but the continuation of the last war by other means. The Soviet world view, in short, reinforced the historically repetitious cycles that had previously and consistently resulted in a further expansion of Soviet power. Even if insecurity drove this expansion rather than any historical mission, the result for neighboring states remained the same—they were vulnerable. They were perceived as inherent threats to Soviet interests and they represented possible additions to the Soviet Union's own frontiers. Such a drive to achieve absolute security in a system in which no state could achieve that aim short of total domination left other states insecure and contributed to the volatility of the international system throughout the Cold War.

The contrast between American culture and national style, which emphasized peace as normal and conflict as abnormal, and that of the Soviet Union, which stressed the pervasiveness of war, could not have been more striking. Both societies felt a sense of historical mission, yet their principles, goals, and tactics were worlds apart. These clashing approaches to foreign policy were to confront one another as the Soviet and Western armies, led by the United States, advanced from the opposing ends of Europe.

SOVIET EXPANSION AFTER WORLD WAR II

The American dream of postwar peace and Big Three cooperation was shattered when the Red Army, having finally halted the Nazi armies and decisively defeated the Germans at Stalingrad in late 1942, slowly began to drive the enemy out of the Soviet Union and then pursue the retreating Germans to Berlin. The Soviet Union, which in 1940 had annexed the three Baltic states (Latvia, Lithuania, and Estonia) after signing the Nazi-Soviet pact, thus expanded into Eastern and central Europe and began to impose its control on Poland, Hungary, Bulgaria, Romania, and Albania even before the end of the war. (Yugoslavia was by then under the communist control of Marshal Josip Tito, the Yugoslav partisan leader who had fought bravely against the German occupation, and Czechoslovakia was under the threat of the Red Army.)

In each of the nations of Eastern Europe occupied by their troops, the Soviets unilaterally established pro-Soviet coalition governments. The key posts in these regimes—the ministry of the interior, which usually controlled the police, and the ministry of defense, which controlled the army—were in the hands of the communists. With these decisive levers of power in their grasp, the Soviets found it an easy matter to extend their domination and subvert the independence of these countries. As the war drew to a close, it became clear that the words of the Yalta Declaration, in which the Soviets had committed themselves to free elections and democratic governments in Eastern Europe, meant quite different things to the Soviets and to the Americans. For the Soviet Union, control of Eastern Europe, and especially Poland, was essential because this area was a vital link in its security belt. After suffering two German invasions in less than thirty years, it was perhaps inevitable that the Soviet Union would try to establish "friendly" governments throughout the area. To the Soviets, democratic governments meant communist regimes, and free elections meant elections from which parties not favorable to the communists were barred. The peace treaties with the former German satellite states (Hungary, Bulgaria, Romania), which were painfully negotiated by the victors in a series of foreign ministers' conferences during 1945 and 1946, could not loosen the tightening Soviet grip on what were by now Soviet satellite states.

In terms of the state system, the Soviet behavior was understandable. Each state had to act as its own guardian against potential adversaries in a system characterized by conflict among states and a sense of insecurity and fear on the part of its members. As the alliance against the common enemy came to an end, the Soviet Union predictably would strengthen itself against the power most likely to be its new opponent. As czarist Russia, with a long history of invasions from the East and West, it had learned the basic rules of the international game through bitter experience. As *Soviet* Russia, its sense of peril and mistrust had been intensified by an ideology that posited capitalist states as implacable enemies. In the war it had suffered over twenty million casualties, soldiers and civilians, and saw the establishment of noncommunist regimes in Eastern Europe as unacceptable. The American insistence on free elections was seen as an attempt to push the Soviet Union out of Europe. The assumption was that a noncommunist government would be an anticommunist one.

U.S.-SOVIET DIFFERENCES

No issue could have reflected more accurately the differences between the United States and Soviet Union. Roosevelt acted precisely on the assumption that noncommunist did not have to mean anti-Soviet. During the war, he had been all too aware of the consequences of a possible Soviet-American clash in the wake of Germany's defeat. He therefore single-mindedly pursued a policy of friendship toward the Soviet Union. Roosevelt, however, did not view free elections in Eastern Europe in terms of the creation of a new anti-Soviet belt. For him, free elections, noncommunist coalition governments in which communists might participate if they gained a sizable vote, and a friendly attitude between East and West were quite compatible.

The model he had in mind was Czechoslovakia. As the only democracy in that area, Czechoslovakia had maintained close ties with the West since its birth after World War I. But because France and Britain had failed to defend Czechoslovakia at Munich in 1938 and betrayed it by appeasing Hitler, it also had become friendly with the Soviet Union. After 1945 Czechoslovakia, like the other East European states, knew that it lay in the Soviet sphere of influence and that its security depended on getting along with, not irritating, its powerful neighbor. Thus Czech leaders expressed only amicable feelings for the Soviet Union and signed a security treaty with Moscow. And in one of the rare free elections the Soviets allowed in Eastern Europe, the Communist Party received the largest vote of any party and therefore the key posts in the government. To share power in a coalition government, however, was to share power with class enemies. A "friendly" state, to Soviet leaders, was one totally controlled by the Communist Party. Soviet security therefore required ideological homogeneity in Eastern Europe and Soviet domination. By contrast, a "friendly" state in Roosevelt's eyes was one sensitive to Soviet security interests but possessive of its domestic autonomy. A Communist Party monopoly of power was not a prerequisite for the states of Eastern Europe to adopt a pro-Soviet foreign policy. Great powers historically have created spheres of influence on their borders, and the neighboring states usually have accommodated this notion because they have recognized the wisdom of doing so.

During World War II the heroic Soviet war effort and sacrifices had created an enormous reservoir of goodwill in the West. Had the Soviets acted with greater restraint after the war and accepted states that, regardless of their governments' composition, would have adjusted to their Soviet neighbor, Stalin could have had the security he was seeking. But Stalin did not trust Roosevelt. No matter how personable the president was, no matter how sincere his statements of goodwill and postwar friendship, Stalin saw him as the leader of a capitalist nation. As a "tool of Wall Street," Roosevelt could not be sincere in his peaceful professions. To Stalin, Roosevelt was an American version of himself, a man who was fully aware of the impending postwar Soviet-American struggle and equally determined to weaken his adversary and gain the advantage for his nation. In Eastern Europe, Soviet bayonets enforced Stalin's will. The Soviet style ensured that the wartime alliance would break up and that eventually the Western allies would return Stalin's hostility, proving to him that he had been right all along about Western enmity!

Churchill, concerned about Stalin's behavior in Eastern Europe, urged the United States to send forces to capture the symbolically important German capital of Berlin (instead of rounding up the remnants of Germany's defeated army) and to advance the U.S. armies as far east as possible, including farther into Czechoslovakia. He also suggested that U.S. forces not pull back to their agreed-upon occupation zones in Germany until Stalin observed his agreements in Eastern Europe and that, until then, the United States not shift the bulk of its military power from Europe to the Far East for the final offensive against Japan. Roosevelt declined all these suggestions. He had assured Stalin that all American troops would be withdrawn within two years after the war. Why then should Stalin worry about American opposition to his efforts to control Eastern Europe? The Soviet leader exercised caution when he encountered opposition, but he ignored diplomatic notes of protest. Carefully waiting to see what the United States would do, Stalin allowed free elections in Czechoslovakia and Hungary, the two states closest to American power. But continued U.S. and British verbal warnings, unsupported by action, did not impress Stalin.

Consequently, Hungary's freedom was soon destroyed by the Soviets.[8] Then in 1948 even the Czech government, in which the Communist Party had the largest plurality, was overthrown by the Soviets in a coup d'état. Contrary to Roosevelt's expectations, not even a communist-controlled coalition government was acceptable to Stalin. Indeed, as the Soviet satellization of Eastern Europe was to show, the failure of the United States was not the failure of efforts to accommodate Soviet interests in Eastern Europe; it was the failure to resist Stalin earlier. Because Stalin apparently saw no limits to Soviet expansion and his conception of Soviet security left little, if any, security for his neighbors, those limits had to be defined by the two Western powers, of which the United States was by far the stronger at the end of the war.

THE SOVIET PUSH TO THE SOUTH

As in the two world wars, in which Britain had led the effort to contain Germany, it was London—not Washington—that took the first steps in opposing the Soviet Union after 1945. Indeed, the United States at first tried to play the role of mediator between the Soviet Union and Britain. Only when British power proved to be insufficient did the United States take over the task of balancing Soviet power. American initiative evolved gradually in the 1946–1947 period and was precipitated by Stalin's attempt to consolidate his power beyond Eastern Europe. The United States had accommodated itself to Soviet control of Eastern Europe, especially Poland, the corridor through which Germany had attacked Russia twice in a quarter century. Moscow's security interests in this region were understandable, and Washington, despite its disappointment over the Soviet failure to fulfill its Yalta obligations in Poland, quickly recognized the new Polish government as well as the other Soviet-installed regimes in Eastern Europe.

8. For an elaboration, see Charles Gati, *Hungary and the Soviet Bloc* (Durham, N.C.: Duke University Press, 1986).

As these events unfolded, however, the Soviets began moving toward the Mediterranean and the Persian Gulf. Turkey, Greece, and Iran were the first to feel pressure. If Soviet behavior in Eastern Europe could be explained in defensive terms, this was less true for the area south of the Soviet Union, the line that runs from Turkey to India. Long before Stalin, the czars had sought access to the Mediterranean via the Dardanelles Straits. Simultaneously they had tried to expand southward to establish a warm-water port and to bring Soviet power closer to the Middle East and the Persian Gulf.

The Soviet Union first sought to gain influence in Turkey. Indeed, the Soviets had begun to do this as early as June 1945 when they made several demands: the cession of several Turkish districts lying on the Turkish-Soviet frontier, the revision of the Montreux Convention governing the Dardanelles Straits in favor of a joint Soviet-Turkish administration, the severance of Turkey's ties with Britain and the conclusion of a treaty with the Soviet Union similar to those that the Soviet Union had concluded with its Balkan satellites, and finally, the leasing to the Soviet Union of bases for naval and land forces in the Dardanelles for "joint defense." The United States sent a naval task force into the Mediterranean immediately after the Soviets issued these demands. Twelve days later the United States formally replied to the Soviets by rejecting their demand to share responsibility for the defense of the straits with Turkey. Britain sent a similar reply.

In Greece, communist pressure was exerted on the government through widespread guerrilla warfare, which began in the fall of 1946. Civil war in Greece was nothing new. During World War II communist and anticommunist guerrillas had spent much of their energy battling each other instead of the Germans. When the British landed in Greece and the Germans withdrew, the communists attempted to take over Athens. Only after several weeks of bitter street fighting and the landing of British reinforcements was the communist control of Athens dislodged; a truce was signed in January 1945. Just over a year later the Greeks held a general election in which right-wing forces captured the majority of votes. In August 1946 the communist forces renewed the war in the north, where the Soviet satellites in Eastern Europe could keep the guerrillas well supplied.

Meanwhile, Soviet pressure on Iran intensified as the Soviets refused to withdraw their troops from that country. These troops had been there since late 1941, when the Soviet Union and Britain had invaded Iran to forestall increased Nazi influence and to use Iran as a corridor through which the West could ship military aid to the Soviet Union. The Soviets had occupied northern Iran, the British the central and southern sections. When the British withdrew, the Soviets sought to convert Iran into a Soviet satellite. The Iranian prime minister's offer of oil concessions to get the Soviets to withdraw was rebuffed. Moscow's goal was nothing less than detaching the northern area of Azerbaijan and then by various means pressuring Iran into servile status. The American government was once more confronted with the need to support Great Britain. After the United States and Britain delivered firm statements that they would use force to defend Iran, Stalin finally relented.

Although U.S. efforts in these areas were largely effective, actions taken by President Harry Truman, Roosevelt's successor, were merely swift reactions to immediate crises; they were not the product of an overall American strategy. Such a coherent strategy came only after a reassessment of Soviet foreign policy that placed the Soviet Union's actions in Eastern Europe and beyond in historic perspective.

TOWARD THE STRATEGY OF CONTAINMENT

Eighteen months passed before the United States undertook that review—from the surrender of Japan on September 2, 1945, until the announcement of the Truman Doctrine on March 12, 1947. Perhaps such a reevaluation could not have been made any more quickly. Public opinion in a democratic country does not normally shift drastically overnight. It would have been too much to expect Americans to suddenly relinquish their friendly attitude toward the Soviet Union, inspired largely by the images of Soviet wartime bravery and endurance and by hopes for peaceful postwar cooperation. Moreover, citizens of the United States wished to be left alone to occupy themselves once more with domestic affairs.

In May 1945, at the end of the war with Germany, the United States had an army of 3.5 million organized into 68 divisions in Europe, supported by 149 air groups. By March 1946 only 400,000 troops remained. Overall, the army had been reduced from 8 million to 1 million, the navy from 3.5 million to 1 million, and the air force from more than 200 to fewer than 50 combat groups. Thus the "most rapid demobilization in the history of the world" had largely been completed.[9]

This reduction in military strength, a symptom of America's psychological demobilization, no doubt encouraged the Soviet Union's intransigence in Europe and its attempts to extend its influence elsewhere. American diplomacy and force retained their traditional separation. America's large and powerful armed forces and its enormous industrial strength, which could have provided the basis for serious negotiations about Eastern Europe, were dismantled and converted back to the production of consumer goods. American policy, unsupported by sufficient

9. Stephen E. Ambrose, *Rise to Globalism*, 5th rev. ed. (New York: Penguin, 1988), 79.

SOVIET EXPANSION IN EUROPE, 1939–1948

Legend:

- Soviet gains in Western territory 1939–1947
- States under Soviet control by 1948
- Independent communist state
- — — — — Soviet border 1939
- ———— Soviet border 1947–1991

conventional military power, was impotent. And "atomic diplomacy," despite what revisionists have written, was not used extensively in the immediate postwar period. If it was used at all, it certainly did not frighten Stalin or deter him from strengthening his grip on Eastern Europe or trying to expand Soviet power into new areas.

When Soviet expansion finally led to a reevaluation of American policy, three strategic positions became clear. At one extreme stood that old realist Winston Churchill, who had long counseled against the withdrawal of American troops from Europe. He insisted that the presence of British and American troops would force the Soviet Union to live up to its Yalta obligations to allow free elections in Eastern Europe and to withdraw the Red Army from eastern Germany. After the United States had rejected his plea, Churchill took his case directly to the American public in a March 1946 speech at Fulton, Missouri:

From Stettin in the Baltic to Trieste in the Adriatic, an iron curtain has descended across the continent. Behind that line lie all the capitals of the ancient states of Central and Eastern Europe. Warsaw, Berlin, Prague, Vienna, Budapest, Belgrade, Bucharest, and Sofia, all the famous cities and populations around them lie in the Soviet sphere and all are subject in one form or another, not only to Soviet influence but to a very high and increasing measure of control from Moscow.[10]

Churchill did not believe that the Soviets wanted war: "What they desire is the fruits of war and the indefinite expansion of their power and doctrines." This could be prevented only by the opposing power of the British Commonwealth and the United States. Churchill, in short, said bluntly that the Cold War had begun, and that Americans must recognize this fact and give up their dreams of Big Three unity in the United Nations.

At the other extreme stood Secretary of Commerce Henry Wallace, who felt it was precisely the kind of aggressive attitude expressed by Churchill that was to blame for Soviet hostility. The United States and Britain, he said, had no more business in Eastern Europe than the Soviet Union had in Latin America; for each, the respective area was vital for national security. Western interference in nations bordering the Soviet Union was bound to arouse Soviet suspicion. "We may not like what Russia does in Eastern Europe," said Wallace. "Her type of land reform, industrial expropriation, and suspension of basic liberties offend the great majority of the people of the United States. But whether we like it or not, the Russians will try to socialize their sphere of influence just as we try to democratize our sphere of influence." The tough attitude demanded by Churchill and other "reactionaries" at home and abroad

10. The entire speech can be found in Thomas G. Paterson, ed., *The Origins of the Cold War,* 2d ed. (Lexington, Mass.: D.C. Heath, 1974), 11–17.

was precisely the wrong policy; it would only increase international tension. "The tougher we get, the tougher the Russians will get," Wallace
pointed out.[11] Only mutual trust would allow the United States and the
Soviet Union to live together peacefully, and such trust could not be created by an unfriendly American attitude and policy.

The American government and public wavered between these two
positions and tentatively adopted a third strategy. The administration
recognized that Big Three cooperation had ended. The U.S. government,
then, would make no further concessions to lend the appearance of
cooperation with the Soviet Union. It had tried to gain Soviet amity
through cooperation and unilateral defense cutbacks; now it was up to
Soviet leaders to demonstrate a constructive approach toward the United States as well. Paper agreements, written in such general terms that
they hid divergent purposes, were regarded as having little value. Something more was needed: Soviet words would have to be matched by
deeds. Thus the United States would seek neither to roll back communism nor to maintain cordial relations with Moscow.

The American secretary of state, James Byrnes, called this third strategy the "policy of firmness and patience." American steadfastness presumably would wear the Soviets down and moderate their conduct. But
there was no suggestion in this call for a tactical shift in how to negotiate with Moscow that the United States needed to organize international opposition to the Soviet Union. The new American position, as one
political analysis concluded, "meant to most of its exponents that the
Soviet Union had to be induced by firmness to play the game in the
American way. There was no consistent official suggestion that the United States should begin to play a different game."[12] The prerequisite for
such a suggestion was that American policy makers recognize that the
Soviet Union was no longer just a difficult ally but an enemy.

GEORGE KENNAN AND THE NEW
AMERICAN POLICY

George Kennan, the U.S. State Department's foremost expert on the
Soviet Union, presented in 1946 the basis of what was to be a new American policy that recognized the hostile character of the Soviet regime. In
a detailed telegram sent from the U.S. embassy in Moscow, Kennan analyzed the communist outlook on world affairs.[13] In the minds of the

11. Henry Wallace, "The Way to Peace," *Vital Speeches,* October 1, 1946, 738–741.
12. William Reitzel, Morton A. Kaplan, and Constance G. Coblenz, *United States Foreign
Policy, 1945–1955* (Washington, D.C.: Brookings, 1956), 89.
13. This "long telegram" was later reprinted in the famous "X article," entitled "The
Sources of Soviet Conduct," which appeared in the July 1947 issue of *Foreign Affairs.* Also
reproduced in George F. Kennan, *American Diplomacy, 1900–1950* (Chicago: University of
Chicago Press, 1951), 107–128.

Soviet leaders, he said, the Soviet Union had no community of interest with the capitalist states; to the contrary, they saw their relationship with the Western powers as one of an innate antagonism. Moreover, communist ideology had taught them that it was their duty to overthrow eventually the political forces in the outside hostile world, and in this feeling they were sustained by "the powerful hands of Russian history and tradition." After some time, observed Kennan, "their own aggressive intransigence with respect to the outside world began to find its own reaction. . . . It is an undeniable privilege for every man to prove himself right in the thesis that the world is his enemy; for if he reiterates it frequently enough and makes it the background for his conduct, he is bound to be right."[14]

According to Kennan, this Soviet hostility would continue until the capitalist world had been destroyed. From this antagonism flowed many of the elements the West found "disturbing in the Kremlin's conduct of foreign policy: the secretiveness, the lack of frankness, the duplicity, the war suspiciousness, and the basic unfriendliness of purpose." He explained that "these characteristics of the Soviet policy, like the postulates from which they flow, are basic to the *internal* nature of Soviet power, and will be with us . . . until the nature of Soviet power is changed."[15] Until that moment, he said, Soviet strategy and objectives would remain the same.

The American-Soviet struggle would thus be a long one, but Kennan stressed that Soviet hostility did not mean that the Soviets would embark on a do-or-die program to overthrow capitalism by a fixed date. Given their sense of historic inevitability, they had no timetable for conquest. In a brilliant passage, Kennan outlined the Soviet concept of the struggle:

The Kremlin is under no ideological compulsion to accomplish its purposes in a hurry. Like the Church, it is dealing in ideological concepts which are of a long-term validity, and it can afford to be patient. It has no right to risk the existing achievements of the revolution for the sake of vain baubles of the future. The very teachings of Lenin himself require great caution and flexibility in the pursuit of communist purposes. Again, these precepts are fortified by the lessons of Russian history: of centuries of obscure battles between nomadic forces over the stretches of a vast unfortified plain. Here caution, circumspection, flexibility, and deception are the valuable qualities; and their value finds natural appreciation in the Russian, or the Oriental mind. Thus the Kremlin has no compunction about retreating in the face of superior force. And being under the compulsion of no timetable, it does not get panicky under the necessity of such a retreat. Its political action is a fluid stream which moves constantly, wherever it is permitted to move, toward a given goal. . . . The main thing is that there should always be pressure, increasing

14. Kennan, *American Diplomacy,* 111–112.
15. Italics added. Ibid., 115.

constant pressure, toward the desired goal. There is no trace of any feeling in Soviet psychology that the goal must be reached at any given time.[16]

How could the United States counter such a policy? Kennan's answer was that American policy would have to be one of "long-term, patient, but firm and vigilant containment." He viewed containment as a test of American democracy to conduct an intelligent, long-range foreign policy *and* simultaneously contribute to changes within the Soviet Union that ultimately would bring about a moderation of its revolutionary aims. The United States, he emphasized in a passage that was to take on great meaning four decades later,

has it in its power to increase enormously the strains under which Soviet policy must operate, to force upon the Kremlin a far greater degree of moderation and circumspection than it has had to observe in recent years, and in this way to promote tendencies which must eventually find their outlet in either the breakup or the gradual mellowing of Soviet power. For no mystical, messianic movement—and particularly not that of the Kremlin—can face frustration indefinitely without eventually adjusting itself in one way or another to the logic of that state of affairs.[17]

And why was the United States so favorably positioned for a long-term struggle with the Soviet Union? The reason, Kennan argued, was that industry was the key ingredient of power and the United States controlled most of the centers of industry. There were five such centers in the world: the United States, Britain, West Germany, Japan, and the Soviet Union. The United States and its future allies constituted four of these centers, the Soviet Union just one. Containment meant confining the Soviet Union to that one. The question, Kennan said, was not whether the United States had sufficient power to contain the Soviet Union, but whether it had the patience and wisdom to do so.

ALTERNATIVES TO CONTAINMENT

Kennan's containment strategy was generally well received in Washington, whose leaders then embarked on the complex task of translating its generalities into specific initiatives. These would entail new strategies for the military services, a greater emphasis on economic statecraft and foreign assistance, and an ongoing effort to enlist foreign countries into bilateral and multilateral alliance networks (see Chapter 3). But in adopting containment, the Truman administration implicitly rejected two other courses of action that had substantial support.

The first was a retreat into the traditional pattern of U.S. isolation from European diplomacy. This alternative was rejected when, on the

16. Italics added. Ibid., 118.
17. Ibid., 127–128.

afternoon of February 21, 1947, the first secretary of the British embassy in Washington visited the State Department and handed American officials two notes from His Majesty's government. One concerned Greece, the other Turkey, but in effect they said the same thing: Britain could no longer meet its traditional responsibilities to those two countries. Because both countries were on the verge of collapse, the meaning of the British notes was clear: a Soviet breakthrough could be prevented only by an American commitment to stopping it.

February 21, then, was a turning point for the West. Great Britain, the only remaining power in Western Europe, was acknowledging its exhaustion. It had fought Philip II of Spain, Louis XIV and Napoleon Bonaparte of France, Kaiser Wilhelm II and Adolf Hitler of Germany. It had long preserved the balance of power that had protected the United States, but its ability to protect that balance had declined steadily in the twentieth century and twice it had needed American help. Each time, however, Britain had fought the longer battle; the United States had entered the wars only when it was clear that Germany and its allies were too strong for Great Britain and that America would have to help safeguard its own security.

The second course rejected in adopting the strategy of containment was a preventive war. The United States had an atomic monopoly until late 1949. In 1950 the United States had fifty bombs plus the means to deliver them, while the Soviet Union had only tested an atomic device. For a short time, then, the United States possessed the opportunity to establish a *Pax Americana,* or world empire. But exploitation of this atomic monopoly was never seriously considered. Quite apart from the relatively small size of the stockpile, the launch of an atomic Pearl Harbor on the Soviet Union was contrary to American tradition and universal standards of morality. Indeed, after Hiroshima the conviction grew that atomic weapons were too horrible to use and that in a future war there would be no winners. By the mid-1950s, after both superpowers had tested nuclear devices and had confronted one another in a number of crises, and after the range of destruction had taken a quantum leap from kilotons (thousands of tons of TNT) to megatons (millions of tons of TNT), this conviction grew to absolute certainty.

The bomb, then, signaled a significant change: historically the principal task of the military had been to win wars; from now on its main purpose would be to *deter* them. Atomic weapons could have no other rationale. Conflicts between great powers—between Athens and Sparta for the control of ancient Greece, between Rome and Carthage for control of the Mediterranean, or, in more modern times, between Germany and England for control of Europe—had been settled on the battlefield. Such a solution, however, was no longer feasible; the United States now had to conduct a *protracted conflict* alien to its style. The term frequently given to this conflict—Cold War—was apt indeed. *War* signified that the U.S.-Soviet rivalry was serious; *Cold* referred to the fact that nuclear weapons were so utterly destructive that war, even with conventional weapons, could not be waged.

While communist containment was adopted as the linchpin of U.S. strategy, it continued to attract widespread criticism. Some felt it did not go far enough, that it failed to exploit U.S. military and economic supremacy and provided the Soviets with the initiative to set the time and place of superpower confrontations. Others felt it went too far. By codifying the Soviet-American conflict, it cemented a pervasive U.S. role in Europe and beyond and ensured a prolonged and dangerous global competition. Located as it was between the two extremes, however, the containment alternative attracted support among moderates both in the United States and abroad. While subsequent leaders would modify the strategy, they adhered to its broader objectives with unusual consistency. It thus heralded an auspicious new era in U.S. foreign policy, perhaps best reflected in the title of Secretary of State Dean Acheson's memoir, *Present at the Creation*. To Acheson, the late 1940s

saw the entry of our nation, already one of the superpowers, into the near chaos of a war-torn and disintegrating world society. To the responsibilities and needs of that time the nation summoned an imaginative effort unique in history and even greater than that made in the preceding years of fighting. All who served in those years had an opportunity to give more than a sample of their best.[18]

The Cold War that followed was characterized by long-term hostility and by a mutual determination to avoid a cataclysmic military showdown. As it took over Britain's role as the keeper of the balance of power, the United States had to learn power politics. But in protecting itself, it also had to learn how to manage a protracted conflict in peacetime, a new experience and one at odds with its historic ways of dealing with foreign enemies and the international system.

THE CHANGING OF THE GUARD:
SEA POWER VERSUS LAND POWER

The United States was to play a role in the Cold War similar to that played traditionally by Britain: primarily a naval power, the United States was to contain the outward thrust of a land power from the Eurasian "heartland." After World War I a British geographer, Halford MacKinder, interested in the relationship of geographic position to international politics (referred to as *geopolitics*), stated the axiom "Who rules East Europe commands the Heartland [Eurasia]; Who rules the

18. Dean Acheson, *Present at the Creation* (New York: Norton, 1969), 725.

Heartland commands the World-Island [Eurasia and Africa, which, on the map, look like a centrally located island]; Who rules the World-Island commands the World."[19] A generation later an American geopolitician, Nicholas Spykman, coined a reply to MacKinder: "Who controls the Rimland [the peripheral areas around Eurasia] controls Eurasia; who rules Eurasia controls the destinies of the world."[20] Although these axioms may be considered too simplistic—and there is some danger in accepting geography as too deterministic a factor in explaining the behavior of states—they explain rather well the essence of the British-German and the U.S.-Soviet conflicts.

Indeed, before World War I, before the German threat received Britain's primary attention, *czarist* Russia—then incorporating Finland, the three Baltic states, and Poland—had been London's concern. Russian power was spreading east to the Pacific, southeast toward the frontier of British India, the area of today's Afghanistan and Pakistan, southeast from Siberia into Manchuria and into northern China, and southwest from the Caucasus to Turkey and Iran. British power along the rim running from Turkey to India guarded the perimeter around Russia. When Russia pushed into Korea toward Japan, Japan attacked and defeated Russia, thereby also limiting the spread of Russian influence in northern China. After that, Russia focused on the Balkans, where it came into conflict with Austria-Hungary, the ally of Germany, which had become the Continent's most powerful country. Germany became the great threat to British interests, and Britain twice went to war with Germany, which, in each conflict, invaded Russia. A victorious Germany would have controlled the heartland—indeed, in World War II victory would have conceivably given Germany control from the Atlantic to the Pacific—plus the Middle East, the area linking Europe, Asia, and Africa.

After Germany's second defeat in 1945 the Russian threat reemerged. Already the heartland power, Soviet Russia extended its arm into the center of Europe, reclaimed its dominant position in northern China, and sought to exploit weaknesses along its southern border from Turkey to Pakistan. Thus one reason for the postwar conflict was *geopolitical:* Russian land power expanded but was halted by the countervailing power exerted by a maritime nation, the United States. These clashes occurred along the perimeter from Turkey to Iran and then in Western Europe.

It is important to understand the location of the initial conflicts because revisionists argue that whatever the Soviet Union's intentions

---

19. Sir Halford J. MacKinder, *Democratic Ideals and Reality* (New York: Henry Holt, 1919), 150.
20. Nicholas Spykman, *The Geography of Peace* (New York: Harcourt, Brace, 1944).

were, its lack of a large fleet and intercontinental air power meant that it represented no threat to the United States. They point out, moreover, that the United States held an atomic monopoly. Thus the demobilization of U.S. conventional forces counted for little. In fact, the United States was a hegemon—that is, it was the dominant power in the system and there really was no serious Soviet threat.

Only one part of this argument is correct, however: the Soviet Union did not represent a direct threat to the security of the United States in the Western Hemisphere. But the Soviet army, even after substantial demobilization, remained a formidable force of 175 divisions and certainly one able to pressure Soviet neighbors to the south and in Europe and hold America's friends and potential allies hostage. That is why the governments of Iran, Turkey, Greece, and Western Europe feared a revival of American isolationism and sought U.S. countervailing support. To be sure, the small U.S. atomic arsenal could have wreaked great damage on Russian cities, but it could not have stopped the Soviet army from overrunning Western Europe.

In the balance that emerged after World War II, the United States greatly benefited from its productive economy, which had not been damaged by the war; from its atomic monopoly, although the number of bombs and bombers available to deliver them remained small in the first years after the war; and from the appeal of its democratic political system. The Soviet Union had the advantages of its powerful conventional forces; its geographical position at the center of Eurasia; and, at a time when democracy was still widely identified with the failed capitalism of the 1930s and the Soviet Union with its heroic resistance to the Nazis, its communist ideology. That ideology appealed to the working classes in nations such as France and Italy, as well as political movements that were seeking power in countries such as China. Thus American political leaders after 1945 did not conclude that the United States was a hegemonic power. To the contrary, they were anxious about a balance of power that to them appeared very precarious.

THE U.S. DECLARATION OF (COLD) WAR

On March 12, 1947, President Harry Truman went before a joint session of Congress to deliver one of the most important speeches in American history. After outlining the situation in Greece, he spelled out what was to become known as the Truman Doctrine. The United States, he said, could survive only in a world in which freedom flourished. And it would not realize this objective unless it was

willing to help free peoples to maintain their institutions and their national integrity against aggressive movements that seek to impose upon them totalitarian regimes. *This is no more than a frank recognition that totalitarian regimes imposed on free peoples, by direct or indirect aggression, undermine the foundations of international peace and hence the security of the United States. . . .*

At the present moment in world history nearly every nation must choose between alternative ways of life. The choice is often not a free one. . . .

I believe that we must assist free peoples to work out their own destinies in their own way.[21]

The president asked Congress to appropriate $400 million for economic aid and military supplies for Greece and Turkey and to authorize the dispatch of American personnel to assist with reconstruction and to provide their armies with appropriate instruction and training. And he implicitly offered U.S. assistance to other states with his open-ended appeal to "free peoples." One of his most critical tactical victories in winning approval for these measures was that over Michigan senator Arthur Vandenberg, a prominent Republican isolationist and chairman of the Senate Foreign Relations Committee. With Vandenberg's endorsement, the spirit and financial requirements of the Truman Doctrine were embraced by Congress.

The United States thus initiated the policy of containment. The emerging clash between the postwar superpowers, anticipated by the Truman administration in the late 1940s, was evident in the hostile actions being taken on both sides. To many, the defining moment occurred on July 2, 1947, when the Russian delegation walked out of a meeting in Paris of Americans and other Western leaders to discuss the distribution of Marshall Plan aid (see Chapter 3). From then on the two antagonists would not even put forward the appearance of great-power cooperation or *rapprochement*.

As for the Truman Doctrine itself, a closer look is required because of its universal nature and call for a new anticommunist crusade. In five respects the initiatives launched by President Truman served as the embodiment of America's acceptance of global responsibility.

First, Soviet expansion left the United States with little choice but to adopt a countervailing policy. With the war over, the United States would have much preferred to concentrate on domestic affairs, as the massive postwar demobilization clearly demonstrated. Americans were about to unleash their pent-up demands for consumer goods as U.S. industry converted from wartime to peacetime production. Not dependent on exports for economic growth, the United States did not need extensive foreign markets; the domestic market sufficed and the United States within a decade became the "affluent society." The change from isolationism to internationalism was the product of the postwar bipolar

21. Italics added. The drama of this period and Truman's speech to Congress are still best captured in Joseph M. Jones, *The Fifteen Weeks* (New York: Viking Press, 1955), 17–23.

distribution of power and the nature of the Soviet state. As in the past, the United States was reluctantly drawn into great-power conflict because of an impending imbalance in the nation-state system.

Second, the American response was propelled by Moscow's provocative moves in the late 1940s. During World War II the United States had sought to overcome the Kremlin's suspicions of the West, to be sensitive to Soviet security concerns in Eastern Europe, and to lay the foundation for postwar cooperation. At the end of the war, the principal concern of American policy makers was not to eliminate the self-proclaimed bastion of world revolution and enemy of Western capitalism, or to push the Soviet Union out of Eastern Europe; it was to prevent a complete return to the historic position of oceanic isolation. Containment was launched after repeated attempts to reconcile differences with Moscow failed and after continued Soviet pressure, denunciations, and vilification. Hostile Soviet behavior and words were the reasons for the gradual shift of American policy and public opinion from amity to enmity. American policy was not the product of a virulent and preexisting anticommunist ideology; rather, it was activated by the same concern for preventing a major nation from achieving dominance in Europe that had twice in the twentieth century led the United States into war. American policy after 1945 was consistent with U.S. behavior in 1917 and 1940–1941 when the nation had gone to war to prevent such an outcome. This was not fundamentally an ideological issue. In the two world wars the enemy was Germany. In the initial engagement Germany was led by a conservative monarchy, in the second by an extreme right-wing fascist regime. In the Cold War the adversary was Soviet Russia, a radical left-wing regime. American action, however, remained the same regardless of the ideological nature of the opponent.

Third, the role of anticommunism in American policy was essentially to mobilize congressional and public support for the policy once it had been decided on. A nation that historically had condemned power politics as immoral needed a moral basis for its new use of power. For a people who were weary after four years of war, who identified the termination of war with the end of power politics, who were used to isolation from Europe's internal affairs, anticommunism was like the cavalry's bugle call to charge. It fit neatly into the traditional American dichotomy of seeing the world as either good or evil, thereby arousing the nation for yet another foreign policy mission. President Truman was conscious of Americans' desire to retreat into isolationism after a war, and he was unsure they were ready to commit themselves to a potential conflict. The pressure for demobilization and a return to "normalcy"— isolationism—was strong in Congress. Thus Truman recognized the

47

need to "sell" the public on the United States's new role in foreign poli-cy by exaggerating the threat the nation faced.

The Truman Doctrine, with its dichotomy between the free world and communism and the United States' universal mission, served this purpose well. In 1950, following the first Soviet atomic test in 1949, years before it had been expected, the National Security Council, composed of the president's main foreign policy advisers, issued a famous report—NSC 68—depicting the all-encompassing character of the Soviet threat and the possibility of a Soviet atomic strike against the United States by 1954. The Soviet Union, it said, was "unlike previous aspirants to hege-mony . . . animated by a fanatical faith, antithetical to our own, and seeks to impose its absolutely authority over the rest of the world."[22] Because the United States stood in the way of realizing this goal, the Soviet Union had to destroy or subvert this country. The report was intended to arouse the foreign policy bureaucracy and alert it to the need for military rearmament to block Soviet designs. Until the Vietnam War undermined this anticommunist consensus, it served policy mak-ers' purposes; the policy of containment received widespread public and congressional support from both Democrats and Republicans. (Asian policy was to be the major exception to this rule—see Chapter 3.)

Fourth, despite the universalism of the Truman Doctrine its applica-tion was intended to be specific and limited, not global. American poli-cy makers were well aware that the United States, although a great power, was not omnipotent; national priorities had to be decided care-fully and power applied discriminately. American responses, then, would depend both on where the external challenges occurred and on how Washington defined the relation of such challenges to the nation's security. Containment was to be implemented only where the Soviet state appeared to be expanding its power. The priority given to balance-of-power considerations was evident from the very beginning. Despite the democratic purposes stated by the Truman Doctrine, its first appli-cation was to Greece and Turkey, neither of which was democratic. Their strategic locations were considered more important than the character of their governments.

In Western Europe, of course, America's strategic and power consid-erations were compatible with its democratic values. The containment of the Soviet Union could be equated with the defense of democracy. But outside of Western Europe, strategy and values often were incom-patible. The United States confronted a classic dilemma: protecting strategically located but undemocratic nations, such as Iran, Turkey, and

---

22. Quoted in Samuel F. Wells Jr., "Sounding the Tocsin: NSC 68 and the Soviet Threat," *International Security* (fall 1979): 116–158.

Greece, might make the containment of Soviet power possible, but it also risked America's reputation and weakened the credibility of its policy. Yet alignment only with democratic states, of which there were all too few, might make U.S. implementation of its containment policy impossible. The purity of the cause might be preserved, but the security of democracy would be weakened. This dilemma was to plague U.S. policy throughout the Cold War.

The fifth point, and perhaps the most important, is the contrasting nature of American and Soviet expansion. The Soviet Union, which already had annexed the Baltic states, imposed communist regimes on its neighbors and stationed Soviet forces there to ensure the loyalty of these states. None of these governments could have survived without the presence of Soviet troops. By contrast, Iran, Turkey, and Greece invited American assistance because they feared Soviet pressure and intimidation. Soviet expansion meant their loss of independence; America's expansion was designed to preserve it. If ever there were a defensively motivated expansion, it was the U.S. commitment in the eastern Mediterranean, which was followed by an even larger commitment to first revive and then defend the nations of Western Europe. All shared the U.S. perception of the Soviet Union as a threat to their political independence and territorial integrity and urged Washington to redress the post-1945 imbalance. Their concern was not U.S. expansion but a return to U.S. isolation.

In summary, the emerging bipolar state system and the character of the Soviet state were the fundamental factors precipitating the Cold War. What, if any, was America's contribution to the onset of the Cold War? Perhaps at the time the United States could not have done more than simply protest the Soviet satellization of Eastern Europe. It was true that the American people, like the British, admired the heroic efforts of the Red Army in stopping and driving back the Nazi forces. Moreover, the staggering Soviet losses, compared with the relatively light losses of the Allies, who until 1944 had fought the Germans only in North Africa and Italy, made Western leaders and publics feel guilty. In these circumstances, the hope for good postwar relations with the Soviet Union was understandable, and that this would feed the desire to believe the best of the Russians, to find explanations and excuses for their continued suspicions of and hostility toward their Western allies, and minimize the problems among the Big Three, was very natural.

But why didn't Roosevelt, whose optimistic assessments of the future were largely responsible for America's expectations, prepare the public better for what was to happen after the war? National self-determination was, after all, the fundamental Western principle underlying the war effort. On that basis, the president was quite willing to push a reluctant

Churchill to give national independence to British colonies; self-determination was not to be limited to the conquered nations of Europe. Yet,
why didn't Roosevelt rally the nation around this principle as Stalin's
conquest of Eastern Europe proceeded and try to deflate America's exaggerated wartime hopes for U.S.-Soviet harmony? World War II had
started over the independence of Poland; yet it ended with Poland under
Soviet domination. By proceeding with its hasty demobilization, the
United States, in fact, encouraged Stalin to expand Soviet power. Not
content with surrounding his country with subservient states, Stalin
appeared to have no limit to his ambitions. Where did Soviet security
interests end? Did they include all of Germany so that the states of Western Europe would then have to accommodate themselves to Soviet
supremacy? Could Soviet security interests be met without creating
insecurity problems for all states beyond the Soviet Union's new sphere
of influence? The answer clearly was no, and the threatened states took
the initiative in asking the United States to exert countervailing power.
The United States finally took the necessary measures to oppose Stalin
and draw the lines beyond which Soviet expansion would not be tolerated. Stalin, incapable of defining the limits of his ambitions, now found
that the United States would do it for him.

Harry Truman and Gen. Douglas MacArthur often clashed over military matters during the Korean War. MacArthur was dismissed before the war ended.

CHAPTER THREE

Containment: From Theory to Practice

Twenty-one years separated the two world wars of the early twentieth century, providing their combatants with time to recover from their losses, restore some semblance of domestic order, redefine their national interests, and prepare for future challenges. But that was not the case after World War II, which, by contrast, led directly to the Cold War. Even before the war was over, both the Soviet Union and the Western allies were posturing for spheres of influence in central Europe. And it was only six months after the Japanese surrender that Winston Churchill gloomily proclaimed that an "iron curtain" was descending across central Europe, drawing the battle lines of the next global confrontation. If there was an "interwar" period in this case, it was hardly perceptible.

Fortunately for the United States the late 1940s were among the most imaginative years in U.S. diplomatic history. President Harry Truman—with an unusually cohesive team that included George Marshall, Dean Acheson, and George Kennan—transformed U.S. foreign policy so the United States could compete indefinitely as a political, economic, and military superpower. Although they eventually would succumb to partisan attacks, these "wise men" were credited with establishing the basis of Western strategy, which ultimately prevailed in the Cold War.

As noted in Chapter 2, in the early postwar years American political leaders generally agreed that George Kennan's containment strategy constituted the most sensible response to Soviet expansionism. But beyond outlining his strategy, Kennan left it to others to put containment into practice. The broad nature of the challenge, which quickly was seen as a global one, assured that the effort to implement containment would be a monumental undertaking.

The obstacles were especially great given the traditional American penchant for withdrawal and isolation from great-power politics in peacetime, as well as the lack of an institutional basis for dealing with a worldwide threat not likely to disappear or be defeated militarily within a few years. The U.S. government had maintained a permanent foreign service only since the end of World War I, and a standing army always had been viewed with great apprehension. But as this chapter describes, American leaders quickly overcame these obstacles and created a web of national security structures, bilateral ties, and multilateral regimes that would frame the containment effort in the decades to come.

In Western Europe the Truman administration not only reestablished democratic political order; it also created a transatlantic security system and a viable West Germany. All of this was underwritten by a U.S.-created economic order, the Bretton Woods system, which was based on open markets and the coordination of global monetary, trade, and development policy. Bretton Woods provided the economic growth and prosperity that allowed members of the anti-Soviet coalition to carry out President Truman's containment strategy for nearly three decades.

As the United States undertook efforts to revive Western Europe, however, it became clear that containing communism would require U.S. involvement in other parts of the world. In the late 1940s and early 1950s the Asian perimeter of the Soviet Union and China became another focus of U.S. containment, attracting both U.S. economic resources and combat forces.

In contrast to Western Europe, many Asian states had only recently emerged from colonialism and their nationalistic and anti-Western feelings were very strong. Nationalist China's collapse and the establishment of a communist government on the mainland in late 1949 further weakened the U.S. position in Asia. Thus the United States no longer confronted only the Soviet Union; it faced the combined strength of two large, heavily populated, militarily powerful communist states. Whereas pressure on Europe united the Western powers, however, pressure on Asia divided them by producing a split over the character and nature of the new Chinese regime and the degree to which it threatened Western interests. In Washington, developments in Asia inspired a prolonged and heated debate between "Asia firsters" and those seeking to limit U.S. containment efforts to Western Europe. Events would quickly propel the United States into action on both fronts.

NEW NATIONAL SECURITY STRUCTURES

As the Cold War set in, President Truman received strong congressional support to reform what had been widely criticized as a chaotic and inadequate chain of command during World War II, when U.S. diplomacy and military strategy had been coordinated haphazardly. Under the National Security Act of 1947, the formerly separate Departments of the Army and Navy were brought together in the new Department of Defense (DOD), a successor to the Department of War. Now the United States would have a *permanent* military based on the general principle of national defense rather than war fighting. In another reorganization move, the air force, a third branch of the military formerly controlled by the army, became an independent service. It soon overshadowed the two older services because its principal task was to organize the growing U.S. nuclear arsenal, which was designed to deter or prevent a major war with the Soviet Union.

In addition, the act created the Central Intelligence Agency (CIA), an offspring of the Office of Strategic Services (OSS) which gathered foreign intelligence and conducted secret spy operations during World War II. The OSS was widely considered a "rogue" operation, conducting secret missions around the world with little oversight; it was disbanded immediately after the war. A larger intelligence operation than OSS, the CIA quickly became an essential, as well as controversial, part of America's containment effort—essential because it collected and analyzed information that presumably was to become the basis of policy; controversial because the agency, in the tradition of the OSS, often carried out "dirty tricks" overseas and sought to subvert governments believed hostile to the United States.

Finally, the act established the National Security Council (NSC) to help the president better coordinate foreign policy. Located in the White House, it was composed of the president (its chair), the vice president, and the secretaries of state and defense. The head of the Joint Chiefs of Staff and the CIA director also often attended NSC meetings, along with anyone else whose advice the president sought. A small NSC staff was created to provide information to these leaders, and the national security adviser, a newly created position, was to serve as a "gatekeeper" and close confidant of the president. Through the NSC, the president would presumably gain greater control over U.S. foreign policy, in part by coordinating departments such as State and Defense, whose leaders were widely suspected of being "captives" to their respective bureaucracies. Finally, the NSC would become the primary crisis management mechanism for the president, a function that took on increasing urgency in the nuclear age.[1]

Because the NSC was purely an advisory body, presidents used it and the other institutions of U.S. foreign policy very differently both during and after the Cold War in keeping with their own management styles and world views. Whereas Presidents Harry Truman and Dwight Eisenhower consistently took their lead from secretaries of state, John Kennedy and Lyndon Johnson tended to rely heavily on Defense Secretary Robert McNamara. And Richard Nixon, who greatly distrusted the diplomatic corps and resisted "interference" from the Pentagon, often acted as his own secretary of state and looked to National Security Adviser Henry Kissinger as his primary source of guidance and the country's chief manager of relations with the Soviet Union and China, as well as with Israel and its Arab neighbors.

The new arrangements did not eliminate the internal bickering that had plagued the old system; indeed, interservice rivalry and bureaucratic politics only became more intense, particularly between the secretary of state and national security adviser. But the president did gain greater control over U.S. foreign policy and a measure of flexibility. More generally, the new arrangements reflected the transformed status of the United States as a world power and the president's role as not only head of state but also chief diplomat and commander in chief. All this augmented the power of the presidency, which, of course, shared power over foreign policy with Congress, and strengthened the president's central foreign policy role. "Within months," one observer noted, "the United States was transformed from an officially neutral country with a tiny foreign policy bureaucracy to a participant in the [cold] war with a rapidly growing national security bureaucracy."[2]

1. See John Prados, *Keeper of the Keys: A History of the National Security Council from Truman to Bush* (New York: Morrow, 1991).

2. Jerel Rosati, *The Politics of United States Foreign Policy* (Fort Worth: Harcourt Brace Jovanovich, 1993), 82.

BRETTON WOODS AND THE LIBERAL
INTERNATIONAL ECONOMIC ORDER

Containment:
From
Theory to
Practice

Unlike the situation confronting other great powers, U.S. military strength was greater *after* World War II than before the conflict, accentuated by the country's undiminished industrial capacity, its monopoly on nuclear weapons, and its global deployment of troops. The U.S. economy also was strengthened by the war, both on an absolute basis and on a comparative basis; most of its competitors were physically devastated and faced years of reconstruction. Indeed, the United States accounted for nearly one-half of global output in the immediate postwar years, giving it unprecedented economic clout to match its military muscle.

Long before World War II ended, Western governments agreed that a new framework was needed for global economic relations. They recognized that trade restrictions, subsidies for national industries, and other forms of mercantilism contributed to the Great Depression of the 1930s, which in turn aroused nationalist passions and led to the birth of Nazi Germany. It was widely believed that a "liberal international economic order," based on open markets and economic cooperation and leading to the recuperation and economic growth of the European industrial states, could prevent a recurrence of this pattern. The new economic order also would minimize the appeal of communism by creating prosperous capitalist societies. American officials welcomed the opportunity to replicate the U.S. economic model on an international scale. Along with European leaders, they devised a plan for international economic, fiscal, and monetary cooperation to be underwritten by the vast economic resources of the United States. In 1944 representatives of forty-four countries met at Bretton Woods, New Hampshire, to approve this plan, which provided the essential blueprint for the industrialized world economy of the postwar era.

Among its specific provisions, the Bretton Woods accords established a system of fixed currency exchange rates based on the U.S. dollar, which itself was based on the value of its gold reserves at $35 an ounce.[3] The U.S. dollar thus became a "world currency" and would be considered "as good as gold." Other countries would base their currencies on the value of the dollar, thereby establishing stability in financial markets and a simple framework for trade and foreign investment.

The Bretton Woods accords created three institutions to manage these reforms. First, the International Bank for Reconstruction and Development (IBRD), or World Bank, would lend the funds needed by

---

3. The United States held about 75 percent of the world's gold reserves at the time, amounting to about $25 billion.

member states to rebuild their industries. The United States provided much of the World Bank's funding in the bank's early days, which it lent to member states on generous terms. As the recipients of World Bank funding recovered, which they did with surprising speed in the late 1940s and 1950s, they in turn contributed to World Bank programs designed to speed economic growth in developing countries, many of which were just becoming free of colonial rule. Second, the International Monetary Fund (IMF) would govern currency exchanges and provide credits for member states facing short-term currency crises. To receive these credits, recipients were required to enact IMF provisions for government taxing and spending and for adopting "responsible" monetary policies. Members were thus prevented from simply printing more money to cover their deficits, a practice that had led to rampant inflation and the collapse of central banks in many countries during the 1930s. Finally, the General Agreement on Tariffs and Trade (GATT) would establish rules to promote open markets and greater commerce across state borders.[4]

The Bretton Woods system laid the foundation for a more integrated world economy after World War II. Benefitting from Bretton Woods together with the Marshall Plan (described in the next section) and other assistance programs from Washington, American allies in Western Europe and Japan were able to rebound quickly from the war and enjoy unprecedented economic growth. Given its clashing political and economic system, however, the Soviet Union did not participate in the Bretton Woods system. Instead, it established its own program to provide the funds needed by its new satellites in Eastern Europe. Throughout the Cold War the two rival economic systems coexisted uneasily alongside their competing political and military alliances.

RECONSTRUCTION AND INTEGRATION IN WESTERN EUROPE

Europe's total collapse after World War II raised anew a fundamental question that had bedeviled U.S. leaders for years: Was this region vital to U.S. security? America's interventions in the two world wars suggested the answer was obvious. But both times the United States had been drawn into the conflicts only after prolonged periods of hesitation and by threats of German hegemony across the continent and beyond. The public had not understood the relationship between U.S. security and European affairs under other circumstances. At the end of each conflict the United States had tried to regain its detachment from Europe, the

4. See Richard N. Gardner, *Sterling-Dollar Diplomacy in Current Perspective: The Origins and Prospects of Our International Economic Order* (New York: Columbia University Press, 1980).

almost pathological instinct of Americans dating back more than two centuries. After the Second World War, however, the United States was forced, for the first time, to establish an *ongoing*, multifaceted relationship with Western Europe because, in the precarious postwar order, it alone had the resources to take the initiative.

Europe's vital importance became especially clear in the emerging bipolar world. It ranked second only to the United States in its collective economic power—in industry, productivity, and skilled workers, scientists, and engineers. Moreover, European-American trading and cultural ties were long-standing and strong. And, not least, as the Cold War intensified, Western Europe critically represented a "buffer zone" between the two superpowers. Given its enormous potential and its geographic position, its security was inseparable from U.S. security, and by the late 1940s this reality finally overcame national ambivalence toward the region.

The war in Europe devastated the economies of all the countries, winners and losers alike. Their economic distress produced social and political turmoil that threatened to undermine efforts to create a shield against Soviet influence in the region. Although the Soviet Union also was decimated by the war and faced a prolonged period of recovery, its growing hegemony over Eastern Europe provided Stalin and his successors opportunities to exploit instability across the iron curtain.

Britain's state of postwar exhaustion, largely economic in nature, was symptomatic of the situation throughout Europe. An island nation, it traditionally depended on international trade for its livelihood. But the war had crippled its merchant marine and destroyed many of its factories. With the means of financing its imports all but gone, Britain had to increase its exports; indeed, just to maintain the 1939 standard of living it had to raise its exports by 75 percent. By December 1946 Britain had reached only its prewar level of production. The future looked bleak and ominous: millions of Britons were unemployed, cold, and hungry—worn out by the long years of war and the determined postwar efforts to recover.

Postwar conditions in Germany also were dreadful. The war had been carried into its heart and few cities or towns had escaped Allied bombing, street fighting, or willful destruction by the Nazis as they retreated. Millions of people were without food or shelter. Three-quarters of the factories still standing in the American and British zones of occupation were closed. In January 1947 production fell to 31 percent of the 1936 level.

Allied policy initially was not designed to alleviate this situation. The Allies were primarily engaged in Germany's disarmament and demilitarization and with the elimination of all industries whose output could be used for military production. The United States and Britain were not particularly eager to rebuild Germany's industrial power; after all, it had taken the combined efforts of three world powers to bring the Nazi war machine to a halt. Nor were the Allies especially concerned with the lot of the German people during the immediate postwar days. After six years of brutal warfare, such concern hardly could have been expected. The revelations of Nazi atrocities and crimes, of wanton destruction, and of millions of innocent people slaughtered in concentration camps were too recent to be dismissed or forgiven.

The French, more than all others, were not in the mood to rebuild their huge, troublesome neighbor. Although the French economy had been badly damaged during the war, by late 1946 it had begun to recover. But iron and steel production had reached only half the prewar total. Coal was the key factor because the iron and steel industries were dependent on imported coal. European coal production was still well below the pre-1939 annual average, leaving the manufacturing industry in France unable to produce sufficient goods for its sizable population to buy. Meanwhile, the urban population was short of food, and the government had to spend scarce resources to buy food from abroad. The harsh winter of 1946–1947 only intensified these problems.

This situation was made to order for the large, well-organized French Communist Party. One-quarter of France's electorate—practically the entire working class—voted for the communists just after the war. In Italy the figure was one-third of the electorate. The reason was simple: French and Italian capitalism had alienated the voters. The workers were, in effect, internal émigrés who voted communist to protest a system they felt had long mistreated them; unlike workers in Britain and the United States, they had suffered all the hardships of capitalism while enjoying few of its benefits, such as good wages and social opportunities. As a result, the Communist Party in France enjoyed a powerful position in regional politics and trade unions.

These difficult conditions forced Western leaders to respond immediately. It was obvious that their actions could not be limited to a single area such as economic development, military defense, or political reform. Their response must be comprehensive, including all these areas, and, more important, take the form of an overriding dedication to preserving Europe as the front line of Cold War defense.

THE MARSHALL PLAN

With Western Europe on the verge of not only economic ruin but also political and social upheaval, everything seemed to force it into dependence on the United States. Most of the items needed for reconstruction—wheat, cotton, sulphur, sugar, machinery, trucks, and coal—

could be obtained in sufficient quantities only from the United States. But short of food and fuel, with its cities and factories destroyed, Europe could not earn the dollars to pay for the commodities required for its recovery. Moreover, the United States was so well supplied with everything that it did not have to buy much from abroad. The result was an ominous *dollar gap*, a term that frightened Europeans because it denoted Europe's dependence on the United States for recovery.

Because the United States could not permit the Soviet Union to extend its influence beyond the iron curtain, U.S. policy makers had to find a way to help Western Europe recover. The prescribed cure was a massive injection of dollars. Only a tremendous program of economic aid could restore Europe's economy, enabling it to surpass its prewar agricultural and industrial production.

President Truman's secretary of state, George Marshall, stressing the economic cooperation required by the United States, called on the European states to devise a plan for their *common* needs and *common* recovery. The United States would furnish the funds through the European Recovery Program (later known as the Marshall Plan), but the Europeans had to assume the initiative and do the planning. The result was the Organization for European Economic Cooperation (OEEC), which estimated the cost of Europe's recovery over a four-year period to be $33 billion. The president asked Congress for $17 billion, but lawmakers cut the sum to $13 billion. The amount actually spent between 1948 and the end of 1951, when the program ended, was just over $12 billion. Britain, France, and West Germany received more than half of this amount.

The original invitation by the United States to the nations of Europe to plan their joint recovery was deliberately extended to *all* European countries, including the Soviet Union and the nations of Eastern Europe. If the United States had invited only the nations of Western Europe, it would have placed itself in a politically disadvantageous position in which it would have been blamed for the division of Europe and the intensification of the Cold War. Actually, had the Soviets participated, Congress probably would not have supported the Marshall Plan for two reasons: first, the costs would have risen astronomically as a result of the very heavy damage suffered by the Soviet Union during the war, and, second, anti-Soviet feeling was growing. The risk had to be accepted, however; it had to be the Soviets, who, by their rejection of Marshall Plan aid, would be responsible for the division of Europe.[5]

Was the Marshall Plan a success? The results tell their own story. By 1950, when the Korean War broke out, Europe already was exceeding its

5. The Soviet Union created the Council for Mutual Economic Assistance (CMEA) to assist its client states in Eastern Europe.

prewar production by 25 percent; two years later this figure was 200 percent higher. British exports were doing well, French inflation was slowing, and German production had reached its 1936 peak. The dollar gap had been reduced from $12 billion to $2 billion. Europe's cities were being rebuilt and its factories were busy, its stores restocked, and its farmers productive. The Marshall Plan was a huge success, and at a cost that represented only a tiny fraction of the U.S. national income over the same four-year period. These were the State Department's best years as it took the lead in organizing a U.S. foreign policy that reflected the country's self-confidence and generosity, energy and imagination. And these were years of excitement as young men and women from government, business, finance, and academia flocked to Washington and Western Europe to ensure the success of the Marshall Plan, which Winston Churchill called "the most unsordid act in history."

ROOTS OF THE EUROPEAN UNION

In making American aid to Western Europe conditional on economic cooperation among the European states, the United States clearly was holding itself up as a model. The Economic Cooperation Act of 1948 called specifically for European economic integration. America, it stated, was "mindful of the advantage which the United States has enjoyed through the existence of a large-scale domestic market with no internal trade barriers and [believed] that similar advantages can accrue to the countries of Europe." In official American opinion, economic integration became the prerequisite for Europe's recovery and the necessary basis for long-range prosperity.

But it was renewed fear of Germany's rising strength that further stimulated efforts toward European integration. The specter of a fully revived Germany struck fear into most of its neighbors. The French, with their memories of the Franco-Prussian War (1870–1871) and both world wars, were particularly alarmed. Germany's recovery, stimulated by America's response to the Cold War, posed a serious problem for Germany's partners: How could they hold Germany in check when it was potentially the strongest nation in Europe outside of the Soviet Union?

After Germany's unification in 1871, France had dealt with the inherently greater strength of its aggressive and militaristic neighbor by forming alliances that could balance Germany's power. Because Britain usually preferred to retain a free hand, and because British interests were at times opposed to those of France, the French had relied primarily on Continental allies. Before World War I they had discovered such an ally in Russia, and between the two wars they had found partners in Poland, Czechoslovakia, Romania, and Yugoslavia. None of these alliances had saved France, however. In both world wars British and American power (aided by the Soviets in World War II) had been the decisive factor in defeating Germany. After the Second World War and despite the extension of Soviet power into the heart of Europe, France still saw Germany as the enemy, and in December 1944 the French signed a mutual assistance treaty with the Soviets, making an alliance they considered necessary for their security. But Soviet hostility soon disillusioned the French and deprived the treaty of any meaning. In fact, this hostility made it necessary to add Germany's power to that of the West.

The failure of this traditional balance-of-power technique, in which an inferior power seeks to balance a stronger one, led France to seek a new way to exert some control over Germany's growing power. French leaders found an imaginative means in European integration. Through the creation of a *supranational* community, to which Germany would transfer certain sovereign rights, German power could be controlled. Instead of serving national purposes, German power would serve Europe's collective purposes and its government could retain some measure of regional credibility.

France made its first move in the direction of a united Europe in May 1950, when Foreign Minister Robert Schuman proposed the formation of the European Coal and Steel Community (ECSC) composed of "Little Europe" (France, Germany, Italy, and the Benelux countries of Belgium, the Netherlands, and Luxembourg). The aim of the Schuman Plan, as it also was known, was to interweave German and French heavy industry to such an extent that it would be impossible to separate them. Germany never again would be able to use its coal and steel industries for nationalistic and militaristic purposes. War between Germany and France would become not only unthinkable but also impossible.[6]

The new French technique of restraining Germany was more than an incorporation of Germany's superior strength, thereby subjecting Germany to French hegemony. "Europeanization" also was a means for France to achieve a balance with Germany. The combination of the French and German coal industries would strengthen French heavy industry and create a Franco-German equilibrium within the ECSC. Economic integration would allow France to overcome its inferior industrial strength, caused primarily by its lack of energy sources such as the coal needed to heat furnaces; Europe's largest coal deposits lay in the German-controlled Ruhr and Saar regions.

The French plan, however, was not devised only to control Germany's resurgent power or to give France greater strength relative to Germany. The French had a third and more ambitious goal in mind: a united

---

6. See John R. Gillingham, *Coal, Steel, and the Rebirth of Europe, 1945–1955* (New York: Cambridge University Press, 1991).

Europe, independent of American pressure. France alone was too weak to pursue an active role in a world dominated by two superpowers. Even in the Western coalition, the most influential European nation was not France but Britain. With Germany's recovery, it was likely that Bonn's role in regional affairs would expand. By itself, France would remain dependent on its American protector, powerless to affect major Western policy decisions. A united Europe, with Franco-German unity at its core, was therefore France's alternative to remaining subservient to the United States.

These, then, were the benefits the French expected to gain from the Schuman Plan. They saw clearly that the nucleus of a united Europe would have to be a Franco-German union. But first the antagonism between these two states, born of their traditional enmity, would have to be healed. Moreover, French leaders recognized that a united Europe had to be built on a solid foundation—not simply on dreams or sentiment. They knew they would have to tie together the interests of politically powerful and economically important groups in the countries of Europe *across* national boundaries. The removal of trade barriers in the coal and steel sector would encourage the modernization of mines and plants. Once producers had adjusted to the wider market and witnessed its opportunities, they would want to remove national barriers in other areas.

The French showed great political astuteness in their selection of heavy industry as the first sector to be integrated because coal and steel formed the basis of the entire industrial structure and represented a sector that could not possibly be separated from the overall economy. The French expected that, as the benefits of the pooling of heavy industry became clear, other sectors of the economy would follow suit, possibly leading to political integration and the creation of a "United States of Europe." In brief, this "functionalist" approach stressed supranational cooperation and common institutions first within a limited sphere and then, after goodwill and a successful track record had been established, in other fields.[7]

MILITARY REARMAMENT AND THE NATO ALLIANCE

Soon after the Marshall Plan was launched it became clear that economic measures alone would not adequately counter Soviet expansion. In February 1948 the Soviets engineered a coup d'état in Prague, and—ten years after the Munich agreement and Adolf Hitler's subsequent seizure of that betrayed nation—Czechoslovakia disappeared behind

---

7. For an early articulation of this approach, see David Mitrany, *A Working Peace System* (Chicago: Quadrangle Books, 1966).

the iron curtain. A few months later, in June, the Soviets imposed a blockade on West Berlin in an effort to dislodge the occupying Allied powers. It is not surprising that the Western Europeans felt jittery at these overt signs of Soviet hostility and aggressive intent. It suddenly became clear that a prerequisite for Europe's continued economic recovery was military security.

The Europeans already had made some moves in this direction. In March 1947 France and Britain had signed the Treaty of Dunkirk to provide for their mutual defense against a threat to their security. A year later, Great Britain, France, the Netherlands, Belgium, and Luxembourg signed the Brussels Pact for their collective self-defense. Its members expected the system of collective defense, officially proclaimed the Western European Union, to attract American military support. They were not disappointed. In April 1949 these countries—along with the United States, Canada, Denmark, Iceland, Italy, Norway, and Portugal—created the North Atlantic Treaty Organization (NATO). The NATO treaty called for "continuous and effective self-help and mutual aid" among its signatories; an invasion of one "shall be considered an attack against them all." Former isolationist Arthur Vandenberg, chairman of the Senate Foreign Relations Committee, hailed the agreement as "the most important step in American foreign policy since the promulgation of the Monroe Doctrine."

For the United States, NATO set a precedent. For the first time in its history the country had committed itself to an alliance in peacetime. Instead of again allowing the balance of power to be upset and once more becoming drawn into a war after it had started, the United States now expected to prevent this by committing itself to the preservation of the European balance on a permanent basis. Collective security under NATO would be combined with economic development efforts to seal the long-term cooperation of the United States and its allies in Western Europe. Conversely, the formation of NATO would propel the integration of states in Eastern Europe under the Warsaw Pact and solidify the division of the continent.[8]

A central assumption underlying U.S. strategy was that Soviet fears of meeting NATO resistance and the promise of all-out war would *deter* aggression. The policy of deterrence relied almost exclusively on American nuclear power—that is, on the ability of the Strategic Air Command (SAC) to inflict such heavy damage that an enemy would, in effect, be committing suicide if it launched an attack. The United States would rely on this strategy of nuclear deterrence throughout the Cold

8. The Warsaw Treaty Organization (WTO), established in May 1955, comprised the Soviet Union and its seven satellite states in Eastern Europe. The WTO was modeled on NATO, although the Soviet satellites played a relatively minor role in managing the alliance.

War, continually expanding and modernizing its atomic arsenals so that its promise of apocalypse would be guaranteed.

But the explosion of the first Soviet atomic bomb in late 1949 foreshadowed a time when the Soviet Union, too, would possess a stockpile of nuclear weapons and the means to deliver them. Indeed, just as the NATO alliance was being organized, deterrence became a double-edged sword that would complicate the strategies and inhibit the actions of both sides. Under these conditions of emerging *mutual* deterrence, Western leaders pursued both strategic (nuclear) defense and conventional rearmament. The latter was aimed at shoring up NATO forces along the "tripwire" between East and West. The critical zone of collective security would, once again, be found in Germany at the intra-German border between East and West.

THE GERMAN PROBLEM AND THE 'FORWARD STRATEGY'

The need for ample military forces presented the European states with a painful dilemma. They were still in the midst of economic recovery and were not able to devote a large share of their national budgets to rearmament. The American answer was the rearmament of Germany. If France and Britain could not supply the troops needed along the iron curtain tripwire, Germany would have to. This "forward strategy" seemed eminently correct because it required NATO to hold onto West Germany, which bordered the Soviet bloc. In turn, of course, German rearmament reinforced the need for a forward strategy. The West Germans could hardly be persuaded to rearm if they could not be assured that West Germany would not be turned into a battlefield and that German troops would not be used merely for the defense of France and Britain. Thus the question of Germany arose once more. It was not a new question, but this time it received new answers.

Germany had held the key to the European balance of power since at least 1870 when Prussia defeated France, Europe's preeminent land power, and established a united Germany. This was true of Germany even after its defeat in 1945. Almost from the cessation of hostilities, the Soviet Union and the United States began their contest over Germany. East Germany was in Soviet hands; the Western powers occupied West Germany. Actually, the Allies were fortunate, for West Germany contained the great majority of Germany's population and the heart of its industrial power. East Germany possessed far fewer resources, and what little of value it retained after World War II was hauled away in boxcars to the Soviet Union.

During the war, Joseph Stalin, Winston Churchill, and Franklin Roosevelt had established a four-power Allied Control Commission (with

France as the fourth power) that would administer West Germany as a single economic unit. But in practice this task proved impossible. Shortly after the surrender of Nazi Germany, the Allied powers pursued separate goals in a divided Germany. The Soviet Union violated key aspects of the occupation plan, propelling Western distrust and ensuring the long-term division of Germany. Furthermore, as Europe's economic collapse became clearer and the Cold War began, it became necessary to lift Germany out of its economic stagnation and make its industry contribute to the general economic recovery of Europe. In July 1946 the United States offered to merge its zone in West Germany with those of Britain and France; West Germany was to be integrated to speed up its industrial recovery. The French, fearing Germany's reviving strength, at first refused to participate but later joined.

The Soviets reacted to this event by blockading West Berlin in 1948. Berlin, like Germany, was supposed to be administered by the four occupying powers, but the growing Cold War divided the city just as it did Germany. Lying deep in East German territory, surrounded by Soviet divisions, the western half of the city was an easy and vulnerable spot in which the Soviets could apply pressure on the Western powers. But the issue at stake was more than the Western presence in Berlin: it was Germany itself. Berlin, as the old capital of Germany, was the symbol of the ongoing conflict between the Soviet Union and Germany, two countries that had fought two cataclysmic wars in forty years. Germany had beaten Russia the first time and almost defeated it the second. The Soviets did not want to see West Germany become a partner of the West.

The Soviet Union's fear of Germany, however, was not completely responsible for its actions in Berlin. If Soviet fear of Germany had been so deep, the Soviets would have accepted an American proposal, offered by Secretary of State James Byrnes, of an alliance of twenty-five or even forty years to neutralize Germany. Moreover, although the Soviet Union had been much weaker than Germany before World War II, it emerged from that conflict far stronger—a superpower, in fact—while Germany, in spite of its potential strength, found itself only a second-class power. The Soviet-German balance of power had shifted decisively in the Soviet Union's favor, and another German attack on the Soviet Union was unlikely. In fact, in any war, whether it acted unilaterally or as an ally of the United States, Germany would be the battlefield and therefore the first country to be destroyed. Germany's fear of this consequence was a sufficient deterrent.

Playing it safe, however, the Soviets resorted to a test of strength to forestall West Germany's revival: a blockade of all ground access to West Berlin from West Germany. If the Allies could be forced out of Berlin, German confidence in the United States would be undermined. The

Germans would not attach themselves to a friend too weak or too fearful to protect them. Indeed, if American willpower crumbled under Soviet pressure, France and Britain also would lose confidence in the United States. Thus had it not been met, the Berlin crisis would have destroyed the evolving U.S. commitment in Europe (NATO was still in the future) and nullified U.S. efforts to rebuild Western Europe as a partner in the struggle against the Soviet Union. In short, the Soviet goal was to drive the United States out of Western Europe, leaving the United States with little choice but to defend its position in West Berlin because the consequences for failure were so enormous. To that end, on June 21, 1948, the United States launched a continuous airlift of supplies to Berlin instead of attempting to puncture the blockade on the ground, which might have sparked armed conflict between the superpowers.

The Soviets waited to see if the Western powers could take care of West Berlin's 2.5 million citizens indefinitely. It would take a minimum of 4,000 tons of food and fuel daily—an enormous amount of tonnage to ship in by air. But after 324 days the Soviets were convinced that the Americans and the British were more than equal to the task. Although the total supplies did not immediately reach the 4,000-ton target, Western planes eventually flew in as much as 13,000 tons daily. Planes landing at three-minute intervals flew in 60 percent more than the 8,000 tons that had previously been sent each day by ground transport. Faced with this colossal Allied achievement, the Soviets called off the blockade in May 1949.

The U.S. determination to hold Western Europe and not to allow further Soviet expansion had been demonstrated. The West Germans clearly saw that they could count on America to protect them. Just as NATO had been the prerequisite for Europe's economic recovery, the Berlin airlift was the final American act that led to Germany's resurgence. The United States had laid the basis for Germany's economic recovery through Marshall Plan funds; in NATO it would give Germany the sense of military security required for its economic reconstruction. For the time being, the Soviet efforts to "decouple" Western Europe from the United States ended.

To the French, the rearmament of Germany by the Western powers was distasteful and dangerous, but unavoidable because France could not supply NATO with more troops. The French remained determined, however, that the world would never see another *German* army, *German* general staff, *German* war ministry, or *German* ministry of armaments. Thus, even as the NATO alliance was taking shape, the French proposed the formation of a European Defense Community (EDC). A European army, composed of army corps in which no more than two divisions could be of one nationality, would be an instrument for checking Germany's rising military power while using it for Europe's defense. The EDC treaty was signed in May 1952. NATO, however, remained the supreme command and maintained a formal link to the EDC. Because all EDC members except Germany were members of NATO, this link ensured that Germany would be obligated to come to NATO's defense and vice versa. It also made clear that NATO had a double purpose: contain Soviet power and control German power.

For West Germany, entry into the EDC was another step toward regaining full equality with the other Western powers and asserting its political prestige. Most important, in return for providing the EDC with 500,000 troops organized into twelve divisions, Germany recovered its sovereignty, as the Federal Republic of Germany (FRG), with certain limitations. The Allies reserved their authority to protect the security of their forces in the FRG (not only against external aggression but also against possible attempts by the extreme left or right to subvert West Germany from within), to govern Berlin, and to preserve their exclusive right to negotiate with the Soviet Union on the question of German reunification.

The likelihood of German reunification, however, was small because Western proposals to unite Germany always included terms that the Soviet Union could not possibly accept, such as reunification via free elections in both halves of Germany and the freedom for a reunified Germany to conduct its own foreign policy. Thus the Allied terms effectively ensured the continuation of a divided Germany, which was precisely what the Western Europeans, especially France, wanted. The division of Germany solved the German problem for Moscow as well because it brought Soviet power to West Germany's doorstep, reminding it of the dangers of any further military adventures, and legitimated the presence of the Soviet army in Eastern Europe.

In short, the division of Germany served both adversaries' purposes and—except for a short but dangerous period in the late 1950s and early 1960s when the Soviets again tested the status quo—served as the basis for the longest peace Europe has known in the twentieth century. A divided Germany might not have fulfilled the principle of national self-determination, but it was part of a clearly split Europe in which both Moscow and Washington knew where the lines were between their respective spheres of influence and the dangers of crossing the lines at any point.

Thus American foreign policy in Western Europe in the immediate aftermath of World War II had been a success. The Truman Doctrine had inhibited Soviet opportunism in the Mediterranean and the Middle East. The Marshall Plan and Bretton Woods accords had set Western Europe on the path to economic recovery, democracy, and social stability. And the United States had transformed a position of great weakness and vulnerability into one of relative strength. It had drawn a clear line between the American and Soviet spheres of influence and demonstrated, in Turkey, Greece, and Berlin, that it was in Europe to stay.

CONFRONTING REVOLUTION IN ASIA

In the American defense strategy of the early Cold War years, Europe held strategic priority; Asia was of secondary interest, as it always had been. Western Europe, in fact, was seen as so vital to American security that any Soviet move into the region would be met with an all-out clash with the United States and NATO (a promise delivered explicitly to Soviet leaders throughout this period). In contrast, no single area in Asia was thought to be worth the cost of total war. The region was too distant, its economies too peripheral to Western interests, its political and social systems too distinct from those in the West. But as the United States undertook efforts to revive Western Europe, it became clear that containing communism would require U.S. involvement in other parts of the world. Thus in the late 1940s and early 1950s the Asian perimeter of the Soviet Union and China became another focus of U.S. containment, attracting both U.S. economic resources and combat forces.

The collapse in 1949 of Nationalist China, on whom the United States was counting in the emerging Cold War, led to the establishment of the People's Republic of China (PRC) under the leadership of communist Mao Zedong. The communists' victory was quickly followed by the PRC's annexation of neighboring Tibet, a ten-year treaty of friendship between China and the Soviet Union, and the invasion of South Korea by communist North Korea. The Chinese civil war thus ended as a major victory for communism and a new threat to global stability in the aftermath of World War II. The logic of Kennan's containment strategy would be put to the test far from the Iron Curtain, as would the leadership of the United States in the emerging anticommunist coalition. American resolve would require more than words; concrete action would be essential to sustain containment.

The invasion of South Korea in June 1950 provoked a military response by the United States, under the aegis of the United Nations and represented the first test of Kennan's containment policy. The invasion followed by two months the release of NSC-68, a dire warning by the National Security Council about communist expansion beyond Europe. Its release just before the Korean War produced a stronger sense of alarm in Washington.

As the Korean War dragged on without resolution, President Truman and his administration lost popularity. Charges of conspiracy and betrayal and of "losing" China and being "soft" on communists at home and abroad were made by Truman's political opponents and became a central issue in the 1952 presidential campaign. However distorted the charges were, they limited the Truman administration's diplomatic freedom and pressured it into a policy of global anticommunism.

The U.S. failure to establish normal relations with China after the communist revolution was a strategic error of the first order. It helped to provoke Chinese intervention in the Korean War, prevented Washington from exploiting Sino-Soviet differences when they first surfaced, and was a major cause of the tragic U.S. intervention in Indochina. Indeed, the events in Asia in the late 1940s and early 1950s were to have a profound impact on American foreign policy throughout the Cold War.[9]

THE CHINESE REVOLUTION AND U.S. RESPONSE

During World War II the United States had a twofold purpose in the Pacific: to defeat Japan and to help to create a powerful and friendly China that could play a leading role in protecting the postwar peace in the Far East.[10] At the Cairo meeting of Roosevelt and Churchill in 1943 the United States and Great Britain had promised to return "all the territories Japan had stolen from the Chinese, such as Manchuria, Formosa, and the Pescadores." They also awarded China one of the five permanent seats on the United Nations Security Council. Thus China was granted equal status with the Soviet Union, Great Britain, France, and the United States.

In typically American fashion, President Franklin Roosevelt and his advisers thought that the mere pronouncement that China was a great power could actually convert it into one: one need only believe strongly enough in the desirability of an event for it to happen. Perhaps American policy makers also hoped that if China were considered a great power, it would behave like one. But American faith without a viable Chinese government was not enough to accomplish the task. In their quixotic desire to create stability in East Asia based on such a Sino-

9. See Robert M. Blum, *Drawing the Line: The Origin of American Containment Policy in East Asia* (New York: Norton, 1982); and William W. Stueck Jr., *The Road to Confrontation: American Policy toward China and Korea, 1947–1950* (Chapel Hill: University of North Carolina Press, 1981).

10. See Herbert Feis, *The China Tangle: The American Effort in China from Pearl Harbor to the Marshall Mission* (New York: Atheneum, 1967).

American alliance, the Roosevelt and Truman administrations ignored the depth of hostilities between the Chinese nationalists and communists in China and the unlikelihood of a negotiated settlement on terms favorable to the United States.

The primary obstacle to establishing an ally in China was resolving the ongoing civil war. Quite apart from the Japanese occupation of large areas of the country during World War II, there were two Chinas: a Nationalist China and a communist China. The communists were not scattered throughout the whole population, as they were in Europe. Already in control of large segments of northwest China before World War II, the communists had extended their sphere during the war by expanding into north-central China. As this protracted struggle continued, it became clear that a negotiated settlement was impossible. Both sides sought a monopoly of power, and each believed that it could defeat its opponent; compromise was thought to be unnecessary.

China's pro-American Nationalist government, however, was losing popular support and disintegrating. Perhaps the Nationalists were the victims of fate. Except for the two years from 1929 to 1931, the government had to fight for its very survival—against the Japanese, who attacked Manchuria in 1931 and China in 1932 (Shanghai) and 1937, as well as the communists. Faced with both external and internal dangers, Nationalist leader Chiang Kai-shek had neither the time nor the resources to formulate and implement the political, social, and economic reforms China needed. His principal concerns were military: to stem the Japanese advance and maintain himself in power. The modernization of China—above all, the problem of meeting peasant aspirations—was strictly secondary.

Indeed, Chiang's failure to appease the peasants, the vast majority of China's population, as well as unchecked inflation and rampant corruption among government officials, would prove fatal to his efforts to gain control of the country. A government whose principal social and economic support came from the landlords was unlikely to carry out reforms the peasants sought. These same peasants provided most of the conscripts for the army, whereas the eligible sons of the rich were likely to avoid military service because their families were able to bribe corrupt officials. In the same way, the rich tended to avoid paying taxes. Thus Chiang's government, far from attracting the peasants, seemed to be doing its best to alienate them. Indeed, as the government continued to lose popularity, it turned to repressive measures to hold its position. The resulting police and military crackdowns further alienated the people, ensuring a communist victory in the civil war.

The blame for these events often has been attributed to President Franklin Roosevelt and the Yalta "betrayal." It was charged that concessions made to Stalin—designed to expedite the end of World War II against Japan by having the Soviet army attack Japanese troops in Manchuria—undermined America's major ally, Nationalist China. But that was not true. The facts were: the American military was unsure the atomic bomb would be a success; it believed an invasion of Japan would be necessary to bring about Japan's surrender; it expected to suffer large numbers of casualties and feared even more if the Japanese reinforced the home-island garrison with troops from Manchuria and northern China; and, therefore, it wanted the Red Army to tackle these mainland forces before the U.S. invasion. The American government was willing to reward the Soviets if this would help save the lives of American soldiers.

Ultimately, it was the military struggle in China that played the key role in determining the outcome of the civil war there and the communist victory. Gen. David Barr, head of the American military mission in China, summed up the situation succinctly: "No battle has been lost since my arrival due to lack of ammunition or equipment. Their [the Nationalists'] military debacle, in my opinion, can all be attributed to the world's worst leadership and many other morale-destroying factors that led to a complete loss of the will to fight."[11] Nowhere was this more clearly demonstrated than in Chiang's failure, after his loss of northern China, even to attempt a defense of south China by making a stand along the Yangtze River. Chiang withdrew to Taiwan (in those days also called Formosa), an island lying one hundred miles off China's coast. In the fall of 1949 Mao proclaimed the communist victory and establishment of the People's Republic of China.

One question about Nationalist China's defeat remains: Could the United States have prevented it? The answer is "perhaps"—*if* American officers had taken over the command of the Nationalist armies, *if* the United States had been willing to commit large-scale land, air, and sea forces, and *if* the United States had been willing to commit even greater financial aid than the approximately $2 billion it already had given since V-J Day. But these conditions could not have been met. America's rapid demobilization left it with too few forces either to supply the officers needed to direct the Nationalist forces or to intervene in China; the United States had only a small standing army at home. Nor were the American people in any mood to rearm and remobilize in 1947–1948. There was little enough sentiment in favor of "rescuing" Eastern Europe from Soviet hegemony—and far less for fighting a war in China.

Nor could more economic aid have saved Chiang. His corrupt, inefficient, and reactionary government did not provide a politically effec-

11. U.S. Department of State, *United States Relations with China* (Washington, D.C.: Government Printing Office, 1949), 358.

tive instrument through which to carry out the social and economic reforms China needed. In contrast, U.S. economic aid to Europe, the area considered most vital to American security, had a good chance of achieving its objective of the political and economic recovery of Britain and the continent. It would have been unwise under these circumstances to divert a large slice of the government's limited funds to attempt to restore a government that had lost the confidence of its own people. The power and wealth of the United States were, after all, not infinite; they had to be applied selectively. Areas of vital interest were to be the prime focus. Thus in Europe aid helped to build a wall of containment, but Nationalist China was a sieve. As Secretary of State Dean Acheson observed:

Nothing that this country did or could have done within the reasonable limits of its capabilities could have changed that result; nothing that was left undone by this country has contributed to it. It was the product of internal Chinese forces, forces which this country tried to influence but could not. A decision was arrived at within China, if only a decision by default.[12]

Despite Chiang Kai-shek's debacle and the disintegration of his Nationalist government, the U.S. government took an optimistic view of developments. Shortly after the Nationalist collapse Acheson expressed his belief that, despite the common ideological points of view of the Chinese and Soviet regimes, they eventually would clash. Acheson predicted that Russia's appetite for a sphere of influence in Manchuria and northern China would arouse Chinese nationalism. The implications of this point of view were clear. If the Chinese communists were genuinely concerned with the preservation of China's national interest, they would resist Soviet penetration. Mao might be an independent communist leader like Yugoslavia's Marshal Tito. If Mao proved subservient to the Soviet Union, however, he would lose the support of the Chinese people. His regime would be identified with foreign rule because he would appear to serve the interests of another power, not of China. Whichever of these two developments occurred, the United States could only gain from the contradictions between communism and Chinese nationalism.

This analysis of Sino-Soviet relations indicated that the United States first had to disentangle itself from Chiang. Without this disassociation, the Chinese would link the United States with the government they had rejected. Moreover, a continued connection would foster the growth of anti-American sentiment in China, which was just what the administration hoped to prevent. The attention of the Chinese people must remain on the Soviet Union's actions. Under no circumstances, Acheson

12. Ibid., xvi.

emphasized, must America "seize the unenviable position which the Russians have carved out for themselves. We must not undertake to deflect from the Russians to ourselves the righteous anger, and the wrath, and the hatred of the Chinese population which must develop."[13] Only by disengaging itself from Chiang Kai-shek could the United States exploit the anticipated clash of interests between China and the Soviet Union.

In short, the Truman administration wanted to do in 1950 what Richard Nixon finally did in 1972—reconcile its ideological differences with communist China and drive a wedge between it and the Soviet Union. But before this could happen, war broke out in another area in the region, Korea, with the unfortunate result of a bitter gulf, lasting twenty-two years, between the United States and the new China.

HOT WAR IN KOREA

Korea had been a divided country since the end of World War II. Under the terms of the postwar settlement, the Soviets would disarm the Japanese above the thirty-eighth parallel and the United States below, thereby dividing the country until a new government could be established. With the beginning of the Cold War, however, this division became permanent. All American attempts to negotiate an end to the division and establish a democratic and united Korea failed.[14]

The United States had taken the problem to the United Nations in 1947, calling on that organization to sponsor free elections throughout the Korean peninsula. The Soviets, however, refused to allow the elections in North Korea, which had been transformed into a dictatorship, and the election was thus limited to South Korea. After the election the United States recognized South Korea as the official republic and the government of Syngman Rhee as its legitimate representative. It also extended economic, technical, and military aid to bolster his government. Although South Korea was not formally an ally of the United States, there could be little doubt that it was America's protégé.

Both the South and North Korean governments regarded themselves as the legitimate representatives of Korean nationalism, and each was dedicated to the reunification of the peninsula under its control. In that sense, the war that broke out when North Korea attacked South Korea on June 25, 1950—after protracted border fighting—was a civil war between two regimes determined to eliminate each other. But it also was an international war because events in Korea after 1945 had largely

13. "Crisis in Asia—An Examination of United States Policy," *Department of State Bulletin,* January 23, 1950, 115.
14. See William W. Stueck, *The Korean War: An International History* (Princeton, N.J.: Princeton University Press, 1995).

6. China enters war, November 1950

5. Farthest UN advance, October–November 1950

8. Armistice line, July 1953

1. Original partition line, 38th parallel

2. War begins, June 25, 1950

7. UN armies forced back by Chinese–North Korean armies, January 1951

3. Farthest North Korean advance, September 1950

4. MacArthur's UN forces land, September 1950

CHINA

MANCHURIA

U.S.S.R.

NORTH KOREA

SEA OF JAPAN

Chosan

Pyongyang

Panmunjom

Seoul

Inchon

YELLOW SEA

SOUTH KOREA

Pusan

JAPAN

Tumen R.

Yalu R.

·········· Communist offensive
━━━━━━ UN offensive

THE KOREAN WAR, 1950–1953

reflected the Cold War rivalry and conflict between the Soviet Union and the United States. North Korea's invasion could not have occurred without Stalin's acquiescence, if not approval (which, according to recently disclosed evidence, was given in March 1949), and considerable Soviet military aid. In contrast, the United States, worried that Rhee might go north, withheld heavy tanks and other military equipment needed for such a thrust, leaving the South Korean army insufficiently armed to resist a large-scale invasion.

Americans, in any event, were taken by surprise by the North Korean attack. U.S. policy makers had been preoccupied with total war. In that context Korea had been left outside the American Pacific defense perimeter, which, Acheson explained in congressional testimony, ran from the Aleutians to Japan, through the Ryukyus (Okinawa) to the Philippines. Indeed, in an all-out war the Korean peninsula itself would be neutralized by American air and sea power. American troops, in fact, had been withdrawn from Korea because in a major war they would probably be trapped by Soviet land forces. Thus the absence of a clear American commitment, as NATO served in Europe, had turned South Korea into a vacuum for communist expansion. Not expecting the United States to intervene in these circumstances, Stalin assented to the North Korean invasion.

Nevertheless, the survival of South Korea became immediately identified with the security interests of the United States. North Korea's aggression, which in Washington's opinion could not have been launched without Soviet encouragement and support, altered the basis on which Korea's strategic significance had been calculated. The Cold War focused attention on the wider political and military implications for the containment policy of a North Korean military victory. For example, if the principal purpose of containment was to prevent further Soviet expansion, American inaction in the face of Soviet aggression would only encourage future aggressive acts. And if containment was possible only through an alignment of U.S. power with that of its allies, then failure to respond to South Korea's pleas for help would ensure the isolation of the United States. And, finally, if the United States stood by while South Korea fell, it would demonstrate to the world that the United States was either afraid of Soviet power or unconcerned with the safety of its friends or allies. American guarantees to help to preserve other nations' political independence would be regarded as valueless, leaving them with no alternative but to turn to neutralism for protection and to seek some form of accommodation with the Soviet Union.

In Asia this reasoning applied especially to Japan, a potential ally after Nationalist China's collapse and a nation that had long regarded South Korea as critical to its security. In Europe, NATO members recalled the

U.S. retreat to isolationism after World War I. If the United States failed to come to the defense of South Korea, they would believe that, despite its recent NATO pledge of protection, the United States could not be counted on to keep its word. The stakes in Korea were therefore enormous: Japan would remain nonaligned and Western Europe would be neutralized. Inaction would shift the Eurasian balance toward the Soviet Union and the PRC, leaving the United States strategically isolated. Washington, then, believed it had no choice but to respond with force.

At first the United States tried to stem the North Korean advance using air and sea forces alone. But after a few days Gen. Douglas MacArthur, the commander in chief in the Far East, reported that Korea would be lost unless ground forces were employed to halt the advancing enemy army. In response, Washington ordered its occupation troops from Japan to Korea to participate officially in a multinational United Nations peace-keeping force. UN involvement in the conflict suited the United States because one of the aims of American foreign policy was to associate its Cold War policies with the symbolic, humanitarian values of the United Nations. Although nations traditionally had justified their policies in moral terms, the United States had shown a marked propensity for doing so. American power had to be "righteous" power used not for purposes of power politics and selfish national advantage, but for the peace and welfare of all people. All this being said, however, the war was an American effort, not one controlled by the United Nations.

After initial setbacks the war went well for a while. In a daring operation on September 15, MacArthur, now UN supreme commander, landed an army at the west coast port of Inchon, 150 miles behind the North Korean lines. These forces then drove northward, trapping more than half the enemy army. The rest of the shattered communist army was in flight. On September 30 the UN forces reached the thirty-eighth parallel. The question confronting the United States was whether to cross it. The political aims of the war were compatible with the restoration of South Korea; they did not require a total war and the elimination of the North Korean government or the unconditional surrender of its troops. But the military situation favored the fulfillment of an American goal of several years' standing: the unification of the Korean peninsula. Thus the U.S. government shifted its emphasis from containing the expansion of Soviet power to the forceful elimination of a communist state. The result—North Korean retrenchment and ultimate stalemate—was to teach the United States the foolishness of changing limited political goals in the middle of a war in response to battlefield successes.

What was astounding was that the U.S. government believed it was politically safe to cross the thirty-eighth parallel and unify Korea. The administration did not think the Chinese communist leaders would consider the UN advance a threat to their security; after all, they were Chinese first and communists second. Mao and his colleagues were thought to be so involved in their struggle with the Soviet Union over the detachment of northern China, Manchuria, and Sinkiang that their eyes would be fixed on their own northern provinces rather than on North Korea. There was therefore nothing to fear. The new objective of a militarily united Korea was sanctioned by a UN resolution on October 7.

But American policy makers miscalculated. The Chinese indeed viewed the American march to their border as threatening, just as Washington had perceived the North Korean march southward toward Japan as threatening. So Beijing sent its armies into North Korea under the guise of "volunteers," and in late November it launched a major offensive that drove the UN forces back below the thirty-eighth parallel. Throughout December 1950 and early January 1951 there was no certainty that UN troops could hold the peninsula, but they rallied and turned back the Chinese offensives. By March they had once more advanced to the thirty-eighth parallel. The administration was again faced with the decision of whether to seek a militarily unified Korea or accept the status quo, a divided Korea.[15]

There was no doubt about what MacArthur, articulating the traditional American approach to war, wanted to do. War, he said, indicated that "you have exhausted all other potentialities of bringing the disagreements to an end," and, once engaged, "there is no alternative than to apply every available means to bring it to a swift end. War's very objective is victory—not prolonged indecision. In war there is no substitute for victory." One cannot fight a half war, he contended, although the administration's policy was based on that assumption.[16] MacArthur recommended a naval blockade of the Chinese coast; air bombardment of China's industrial complex, communications network, supply depots, and troop assembly points; reinforcement of his forces with Chinese Nationalist troops; and "diversionary action possibly leading to counter-invasion" by Chiang against the mainland.

The Truman administration rejected MacArthur's proposals as too risky. It feared that bombing China and defeating the Soviet Union's principal ally would lead to another global war. The Sino-Soviet treaty of February 1950 bound the Soviet Union to come to the aid of China if it were attacked by Japan "or any other state which should unite with Japan" (an obvious reference to the United States). Soviet self-interest in the Far East and the need to maintain Soviet prestige in the communist

15. See Rosemary Foot, *A Substitute for Victory: The Politics of Peacemaking at the Korean Armistice Talks* (Ithaca, N.Y.: Cornell University Press, 1990).

16. Quoted in John Spanier, *The Truman-MacArthur Controversy and the Korean War* (Cambridge, Mass.: Belknap, 1959), 222.

sphere would make it difficult for the Soviet Union to ignore a direct attack on the Chinese mainland.

Inherent in the administration's rejection of MacArthur's recommendations—and his dismissal from his post when he continued to push them—was the abandonment of the total-war objective of a unified Korea and the elimination of its government. Instead, the original limited aim of the war, the defense of South Korea, was reasserted. This goal also was compatible with the other principal political reasons for which the United States had gone to war: the defense of Japan and the preservation of the NATO alliance. Indeed, by the time the war ended in 1953, Japan had become a U.S. ally, and NATO had been not only preserved but also strengthened by its own rearmament and the stationing of four American divisions in Europe. The wisest course therefore was to end the war where it had begun.

FROM ANTI-SOVIETISM TO ANTICOMMUNISM

The Chinese revolution and Korean War transformed U.S. foreign policy less than a decade after it was formulated in the wake of World War II. Whereas the earlier focus of U.S. policy had been limited to containing Soviet power in Western Europe and the eastern Mediterranean, it now spilled over into a broader anticommunist crusade.

The alleged "loss" of China initiated this change. Americans had regarded China as their special ward since just before the turn of the century. The original interest in China had been not political but commercial—China was seen as a potentially huge market for American products. To that end, the United States had long regarded itself as the protector of China from foreign exploitation and invasion. Through the 1899 Open Door policy—aimed at preventing Great Britain, France, Russia, Germany, and Japan from shutting American commerce out of China and at obtaining an equal opportunity to sell on the Chinese market—the United States had become politically committed to preserving the territorial integrity and political independence of China.

Because the American people had never been prepared to fight for this objective, however, the United States had failed to protect China from external pressures and invasions. The Russians had established a sphere of influence in Manchuria by 1900, and the Japanese had replaced them after the Russo-Japanese War. During and after World War I, Japan had expanded its influence and control over China and in 1931 had begun another war to further its ambitions. The Open Door policy was, therefore, empty in practice. Indeed, the United States had never been prepared to support this policy militarily; it was one in which diplomacy was divorced from force. The result was the illusion that the United

States had long been China's friend, extending to the Chinese people the bountiful benefits of Western civilization and coming to their rescue during World War II.

Americans were therefore shocked by the collapse in 1949 of Chiang Kai-shek, who during World War II had been lauded as a Chinese George Washington, and the establishment of communist control of the Chinese mainland. Certainly, they were totally unprepared for, and deeply resentful of, the propaganda emanating from Beijing accusing the United States of being "the Chinese people's implacable enemy . . . a corrupt imperialistic nation, the world center of reaction and decadence . . . a paper tiger and entirely vulnerable to defeat." They had expected that a "loyal" and fundamentally democratic China, grateful to America for protection and help, would emerge from World War II as a strong friend and powerful and reliable ally. The failure of these expectations in late 1949 came as a blow. Suddenly the relative security achieved by the containment policies in Europe—the Truman Doctrine, the Marshall Plan, the Berlin airlift, and NATO—seemed to have disintegrated. It appeared that the United States had stemmed the communist menace in Europe only to allow it to achieve a breakthrough in Asia.

The resulting insecurity and anxiety were further heightened by two other events. The first was the explosion in 1949 of the Soviet Union's first atomic bomb, which shattered the American monopoly on the weapon widely regarded as the principal deterrent against a Soviet attack. The second was the successful prosecution in early 1950 of Alger Hiss, a high-ranking U.S. government official during World War II, for perjury in connection with charges he had delivered classified U.S. documents to the Soviet government in the 1930s. The Hiss case was followed shortly by the confession of British scientist Klaus Fuchs that he had passed atomic secrets to the Soviets, apparently pointing to Soviet espionage in high places. The outbreak of the Korean War and communist China's subsequent intervention compounded America's sense of betrayal and anxiety.

PARTISANSHIP IN ASIAN POLICY

At the time all this was occurring, bipartisan support for U.S. policy in Asia was ending. The congressionally dominant conservative wing of the Republican Party had long been restless. The party, led by liberal Republicans, had lost the presidential elections of 1940, 1944, and 1948. They wanted to win with a conservative leader in 1952, but they could not win the presidency on the Republican record on domestic issues. The Republicans were the party of President Herbert Hoover and the Great Depression. The Democrats, who had won every presidential election since 1932, were the party of Roosevelt and the New Deal. Conservative Republicans therefore needed a foreign policy issue with which to beat the Democrats, even though liberal and moderate Republicans, led by Sen. Arthur Vandenberg, a former isolationist, had supported the internationalist policy of the Truman administration. But Vandenberg was dying, and, after China fell to the communists, bipartisanship on the Far East had begun to erode. Foreign policy became a partisan issue as the Republicans decided to exploit the public's frustrations with the perceived failures under Democratic administrations.

In the past, the Republicans recognized, whenever the United States had been drawn into the international arena its actions had met with quick success. It had beaten the British, the Mexicans, the Spanish, the Germans, and the Japanese. America had never been invaded, defeated, or occupied, as most other nations had been; it had, to be sure, made mistakes, but with its great power it always had been able to rectify them. America's history had witnessed only victories; its unbroken string of successes seemed evidence of national omnipotence.

This unquestioned assumption suggested to the Republicans the reason for America's failures: treason within its own government. If America was all-powerful, its setbacks must have been the result of its own policies. Ostensibly the reason China fell was that the "pro-communist" administrations of Franklin Roosevelt and Harry Truman either deliberately or unwittingly had "sold China down the river." This conspiracy charge, articulated by Republican senator Joseph McCarthy and supported by fellow Republican senators Robert Taft and Richard Nixon, was simplicity itself: America's China policy had ended in communist control of the mainland; the administration leaders and the State Department were responsible for the formulation and execution of foreign policy; therefore, the government must be filled with communists and communist sympathizers who "tailored" American policy to advance the global aims of the Soviet Union. Low morale among the Chinese Nationalists, administrative and military ineptness, and repressive policies that had alienated mass support had nothing to do with it, nor did the superior communist organization, direction, morale, and ability to identify with popular aspirations.

The State Department bore the brunt of this rhetorical onslaught, with incessant attacks on its Foreign Service officers and regional directors and on Secretary of State Acheson himself. But the accusations, usually carried in the press, were not directed only toward the State Department or government officials. Academics and others also were charged as being security risks or were accused of being "un-American." Many such individuals were fired, and others—especially stage actors and Hollywood figures—were blacklisted. The political atmosphere during the 1950s, in short, often bordered on national hysteria.

The most significant result was a shift in U.S. foreign policy from a limited anti-Soviet orientation to a broader anticommunist crusade. To be sure, actions by the United States in the eastern Mediterranean and in Western Europe had been carried out in the name of anticommunism, but operationally these actions had been limited to countering Soviet moves. Washington had not hesitated to support communist Yugoslavia after its break with Moscow, and for a brief moment it had even predicted the likelihood of conflict between communist China and the Soviet Union. But the Republican attacks on the Democrats and the charges of appeasement, of being soft on communism, of losing China, and of treason placed the Democrats in a vulnerable position.

The aim of U.S. policy now became the prevention of any expansion by any member of the Sino-Soviet bloc. All communist states were considered enemies, regardless of whether they were large or small, strategically located or not, tied to Moscow as satellites or nationalist communist states, which, like Yugoslavia and communist China, were likely to pursue their own interests, even in conflict with the Soviet Union. Distinctions between America's vital and secondary interests, the importance of concentrating on the main adversary and not getting bogged down and wasting resources on conflicts with secondary enemies, and the ability to distinguish communist regimes that represented a threat to American interests and those that did not—all were lost in the crusading spirit. And how did all this affect the presidential election of 1952? The Republican charges hurt the Democrats so much that they lost that presidential election and were kept out of power for eight years. Moreover, future Democratic administrations, trying to avoid Republican accusations of being soft on communism, were particularly disposed to anticommunist interventions.

SINO-AMERICAN ENMITY

Anticommunism also intensified the deep rift between the United States and China. In 1950 Beijing observed that the United States not only did not recognize the communist government but also continued its support for the rival Nationalist regime in Taiwan. Moreover, the United States was increasingly assisting the French fighting in Indochina; it was strengthening its alliance with Japan, China's enemy; and U.S. troops were marching to China's border with North Korea, despite Chinese warnings not to do so. Fearing that U.S. forces might cross the border, the Chinese government intervened in Korea, thereby turning the friendly relationship the United States once thought it had with China into armed conflict. That the United States had once been China's protector and benefactor may have been an illusion, but it was widely held, and the betrayal of friendship, alleged or real, always leaves a sense of frustration and anger. The Sino-American relationship had an emotional intensity that did not characterize the relationship between the United States and the Soviet Union.

One can only speculate how events might have turned out during the Korean War if the United States had recognized the new Chinese government and had diplomatic representatives in Beijing. Diplomats might have alerted Washington that the Chinese were alarmed at the U.S. advance in North Korea and that the repeated warnings to the United States to halt its forces short of China's frontier ought to be taken seriously. The American government received similar warnings from the Indian ambassador but, believing the ambassador to be pro-Chinese, the United States rejected the warnings. It would have had less reason to be suspicious of its own representatives and therefore might not have later blundered up to China's border.

The United States paid a heavy price for the breakdown of bipartisanship, for McCarthy's charges of treason, and for the crusading style that Nationalist China's collapse unleashed. But the even greater folly may have been that U.S. policy makers, now applying containment to the Sino-Soviet bloc, no longer seriously considered the possibility that Mao Zedong might become a second Tito because Mao, like Tito, drew his power from control of his party and military, not from Soviet troops in his country. Nor, therefore, did Washington any longer entertain the possibility that communist China might be used to contain Soviet power. Instead, for more than two decades the United States and China were bitter enemies as the United States felt compelled to contain both Soviet and Chinese power.

Secretary of State John Foster Dulles reports to Dwight Eisenhower on his mission to initiate a Korean political conference.

CHAPTER FOUR

Defining Spheres of Influence

When the Republicans won the presidential election of 1952, it was their first in twenty-four years. They won because they exploited public weariness with a containment policy that they charged had no end in sight. Whatever its successes in Europe, the policy had ended in the collapse of Nationalist China and the Korean War, a limited war contrary to the American tradition of all-out war and a clear victory on the battlefield. That war too appeared to have no end in sight, and after communist China's intervention it became—until Vietnam—the most unpopular war in American history. Led by World War II hero Dwight Eisenhower, the architect of the victory in Europe, the Republicans promised that they would be better stewards of the American national interest.

In preparing the nation for the long-term competition with the Sino-Soviet bloc, as it was then perceived, the Republicans promised a strategy that would avoid bankrupting the nation and placing too heavy a tax burden on the American people, as well as fighting more limited wars. To this end, they proposed three measures. The first was to halt the Korean War, which would allow the administration to cut the size of the army and eliminate the cost of maintaining large standing ground forces. The second was to draw a clear line of containment, or "frontier," around the entire Sino-Soviet bloc. The Democrats already had drawn such a frontier from Norway to Turkey; the Republicans expected to strengthen and extend this frontier to the Middle East and the Far East. The third measure was to preserve this global boundary around the communist world with the deterrent power of the Strategic Air Command (SAC). The fear of total war with the United States was expected to deter the Soviets and Chinese from crossing the line. Moscow had only a minimum capability to reach the United States; Beijing had none. By contrast, SAC's bomber force was to reach two thousand in the 1950s.

The reliance on strategic air power also was expected to appeal to the American public. "Massive retaliation" sounded more dynamic than containment and made possible a reduction in overall military expenditures. But, above all, massive retaliation was consistent with America's style in foreign policy, a style that traditionally has been based on a world view of mutually exclusive conditions: war or peace, force or diplomacy, aggressors or peace-loving states. Peace was normal; war was abnormal. Force was not necessary in the absence of conflict and hostilities; it was to be used only in wartime to destroy the source of war itself. Massive retaliation, then, fit this American approach completely. It was an all-or-nothing strategy that could not be used short of a Soviet attack on the United States or Western Europe. At the same time, American presidents consistently rejected preventive war, both at the time of the nation's atomic monopoly and later, during the 1950s and 1960s, the period of gradually declining strategic superiority. Deterrence was the American goal; nuclear weapons would be used only after the opponent had struck first. If the United States were attacked, however, it would use massive retaliation to punish and destroy the enemy in ways not conceivable until 1945.[1]

Massive retaliation, by reducing the enemy's population centers and industries to rubble and radioactive dust, carried the American approach to war to its ultimate conclusion. Although some bombs were targeted on the small Soviet air force, the rapidly growing U.S. stockpile was to be used against all targets, both military and civilian, in one huge war-winning blow. The hydrogen bomb's megaton explosive power, as

---

1. For an elaboration, see Lawrence Freedman, *The Evolution of Nuclear Strategy*, 2d ed. (New York: St. Martin's Press, 1989).

opposed to that of the atomic bomb's kiloton power, made that possible. In the words of a navy captain attending an air force briefing on SAC's strategy at the time, the Soviet Union was to be left "a smoking, radiating ruin at the end of two hours."

In one sense, then, atomic weapons and the more destructive hydrogen weapons enabled the United States to pursue an old American dream in a new and gruesome way. By making nuclear war too destructive to fight, by making the distinction between victor and loser in such a conflict increasingly meaningless, the deterrent strategy aimed at eliminating war itself. This old goal had been sought through the "war to end all wars" crusade, or through international organization and cooperation, or through free trade and economic interdependence among nations. The goal could now be realized because war had become "unthinkable."

But however traditional the philosophical basis of massive retaliation and whatever the benefits of economic and military retrenchment, Dwight Eisenhower's policy was not really that different from Harry Truman's it sought to contain communism but to extend containment beyond Europe by drawing a frontier around the Sino-Soviet periphery and supporting that frontier with nuclear air power. Only in one essential aspect was the new administration's policy quite different—and this difference was critical. Truman and his secretary of state Dean Acheson had relied on atomic striking power to deter an attack on either the United States or America's "first line of defense" in Europe. But in Asia, when the communists had faced them with a limited aggression, the Truman administration had met the challenge with ground troops. The Eisenhower administration also expected to deter an all-out war with the threat of massive retaliation but declared that it would not fight local ground wars. Presumably this meant that it planned to deter any future limited attacks by threatening to retaliate against the Soviet Union or China.

This basic policy decision reflected Secretary of State John Foster Dulles's strong conviction that the only effective means of stopping an invasion was to give fair warning of what constituted aggression and to make clear that the punishment for an attack would far outweigh any possible military gains. Dulles believed that South Korea never would have been invaded had the communists known that their attack would be met with retaliatory air strikes on Moscow. It was the absence of such a warning that had led North Korea to act. The Eisenhower administration did not intend to repeat this mistake. It meant to draw the line so clearly that the enemy would have no doubt about the consequences of crossing the line. The expectation was that by going to the "brink of war," the United States would be able to deter future Koreas. This policy, which later became known as "brinkman-ship," was to be applied first in an attempt to bring about a cease-fire in Korea.[2]

SUPERPOWER TENSIONS AT THE BRINK

The idea of deterrence was to use the threat of a nuclear war to avoid having to fight one. At the same time the West also used this threat to preserve its wall of containment around the Sino-Soviet bloc. But how credible was this threat? Indeed, might it provoke the very war it sought to avoid? In the years to follow, these questions would be answered as the superpowers postured for advantage in several regional conflicts, testing the Eisenhower-Dulles formula and the more general strategy of communist containment.

ENDING THE KOREAN WAR

The truce talks that had begun in Korea in the summer of 1951 dragged on fruitlessly until they reached a deadlock. The war was a drain on the United States; it had to be ended. When the Eisenhower administration took office in January 1953, it decided that if its efforts to gain an armistice failed, it would bomb Chinese bases and supply sources in Manchuria and China, blockade the mainland coast, and possibly use atomic weapons. Later it claimed that its willingness to use force and not confine hostilities to the Korean peninsula were conveyed to the Chinese via the government of India.

In early June 1953 the deadlocked negotiations resumed, and in late July the armistice was signed. It is doubtful that the administration's threats were primarily responsible for the Chinese government's willingness to conclude the war; there is no evidence that threats were made publicly or privately, or passed on to the Chinese directly or indirectly. Other factors appeared more critical. Chief among these was Joseph Stalin's death in March 1953. His successors proclaimed their belief in "peaceful coexistence" and tried hard to convince the noncommunist world that they wanted to relax international tensions. Agreement on an armistice and an end to the war would provide evidence of their earnestness. More important, they could not afford to risk increased international tensions and an enlarged war—which the Americans might launch if diplomacy failed to end this conflict—at a time when they were engaged in a struggle among themselves to succeed the late dictator.

2. Richard H. Immerman, *John Foster Dulles and the Diplomacy of the Cold War* (Princeton, N.J.: Princeton University Press, 1990).

The Korean War ended just where it had begun—at the thirty-eighth parallel—and on basically the same terms the Truman administration had been unable to reach. The Korean dividing line then became part of the global dividing line between the communist bloc and the noncommunist bloc. In August 1953 the United States signed a mutual security pact with South Korea designed to deter another attack from the north.

CONFLICT IN THE TAIWAN STRAITS

The line of containment also was drawn in the Taiwan Straits, where Sino-American relations had turned increasingly bitter and confrontational after the United States intervened in the Chinese civil war and China intervened in Korea. Soon after the Korean War ended, the People's Republic of China (PRC) sought to eliminate its rival on Taiwan. During the summer of 1954 the PRC began shelling the Nationalist-held offshore islands.

The United States and the Nationalists had signed a treaty of mutual defense in 1953 under which the United States guaranteed the security of Taiwan. In turn, the Nationalists pledged not to attack the mainland or to reinforce their offshore garrisons without the consent of the United States. While the offshore islands were not specifically included under the terms of the treaty, the president requested and received from Congress the authority to employ American armed forces to protect Taiwan and "such related positions and territories" as the president judged necessary. Although this did not specifically clarify whether the United States would defend Quemoy and Matsu, the communists certainly thought that it might, and they abstained from any invasion attempts of these islands, which were within artillery range of the mainland. When in August 1958 the communists resumed shelling the offshore islands, the United States again supported the Nationalists.

Thus the line remained where it had been before the two Taiwan crises—a few miles off the PRC's coast. Some months later Dulles reaffirmed this line when he firmly rejected Nationalist leader Chiang Kaishek's calls to take back the mainland. American policy in the straits was committed to the preservation of the status quo. Each side should keep what it had and refrain from attacking the other. The Eisenhower administration thereby recognized what neither it nor its predecessor had been willing to admit publicly before: that the Nationalist expectation of recapturing the mainland was a myth. At the same time it tacitly acknowledged the Chinese communist government as continental China's de facto government. It had reconciled itself to the communist conquest of the mainland.

In the straits the administration was able to support its position with air and sea power; yet the possible use of nuclear weapons had been mentioned—if it became necessary to defend the status quo. But during this period the nuclear threat, which had not been invoked to end the Korean war, was shown to be a bluff. For all of his talk of American readiness to use nuclear weapons in defense, Eisenhower had no intention of using them in China. As a military man he knew that there were no appropriate targets, and as president he knew that the use of nuclear weapons was not politically feasible. To drop a bomb once again on Asians would lead to outrage and condemnation from the whole world, including America's allies in the North Atlantic Treaty Organization (NATO). America's declared policy of massive retaliation was in fact one of self-deterrence.

THE FIRST INDOCHINA WAR

After World War II, colonies that had long been ruled by European powers renewed their demands for independence. The British complied in India, Burma, and Ceylon, but the French in Indochina did not. Returning to Vietnam after its years of Japanese occupation, the French refused to grant any meaningful concessions to the government, which, under Ho Chi Minh, had proclaimed Vietnam's independence. Determined to reestablish sovereignty over their colony, the French recognized Ho's "Democratic Republic of Vietnam" as a free state within the French Union. As a part of the agreement the French would be allowed to maintain garrisons in Vietnam for five years. But in less than a year the Vietminh (as the Revolutionary League for the Independence of Vietnam was known) accused the French of violating the agreement. The Vietminh had been organized by Ho during World War II to convert Vietnam from a feudal society to a classless communist society. After the war it emphasized nationalism rather than communism to win independence for Vietnam. As a result, open conflict developed in 1946 between France and the communists and nationalists and soon escalated into the first Indochina war, which lasted eight years.

When France established an "independent" state of Vietnam in 1949 under Emperor Bao Dai, the Vietminh became, in effect, "rebels," but with the important difference that they were rebels identified as fighting for the independence of Vietnam. By contrast, Bao Dai, who spent much of his time on the French Riviera, was seen as a French puppet; in fact, he could not have survived one day in office without the support of French arms. Like Mao Zedong in China, Ho conducted guerrilla warfare and met with considerable success. The French, who generally held the cities, were at a disadvantage from the beginning, for, in the absence of genuine independence, the Vietnamese identified themselves with the Vietminh and saw the French as colonial rulers. In the long run France paid a high price for the war in lost lives, matériel, and prestige.

During the first years of the war, American public opinion was unsympathetic to France's attempt to reestablish its colonial control over Indochina. But three events led to U.S. involvement in this conflict. The first, in China, was the defeat of Chiang Kai-shek in 1949. This was seen as a blow to France because it meant that the new People's Republic of China could now provide assistance to the Vietminh. The second event was the outbreak of the Korean War, with the resulting shift of containment to Asia. And the third was the change in the political climate in the United States to anticommunism. The French, who earlier were seen as trying to hold onto the vestiges of their colonial empire, now were regarded as fighters in the common struggle against communism.

In 1950 the United States began to provide France with economic and military aid, and by 1954 the United States was paying about 75 percent of the costs of the war. The French position continued to deteriorate, however, especially once the Korean armistice was signed. Despite American warnings, communist China shifted its pressure from Korea to Indochina and increased its assistance to the Vietminh. On March 13, 1954, Vietminh forces launched an assault on the French fortress at Dienbienphu. The French position in northern Vietnam seemed close to collapse. It became painfully clear that the French could not hold on without American intervention. What was the United States to do?

Dienbienphu was the moment of decision for the administration. Eisenhower and Dulles had declared Indochina to be of strategic importance to American security and had cautioned China against direct or indirect intervention. But the Chinese had ignored these warnings, and the U.S. government had to "put up or shut up." It shut up; its threats turned out to be only bluffs.[3]

THE REFUSAL TO INTERVENE

The reason for U.S. inaction was fairly clear: American public opinion might have been strongly anticommunist, but it also indicated that the nation was tired of war. For that reason Eisenhower had withdrawn from Korea, and now he was unwilling to involve the United States in another such war. Furthermore, the administration already was cutting the size of the army in order to build U.S. nuclear forces for a policy of massive retaliation, and the army chief of staff counseled against intervention because of a lack of available troops. The administration, then, considered two courses of action. The first was to rescue the French by attacking the communist positions around Dienbienphu with air power alone, but this was rejected because air strikes by themselves could not

---

3. See Stanley Karnow, *Vietnam: A History* (New York: Penguin, 1984), 189–194.

halt the communist ground advance. Air power had failed to stop the North Korean army during the opening days of that war, forcing the commitment of U.S. troops.

The alternative course of action was to attack China with nuclear weapons. That would have been consistent with the administration's announced policy of massive retaliation. But the administration did not follow its policy. The reason was simple: it is one thing to deliver a threat of massive retaliation to an opponent and quite another to have the opponent believe it. The Soviets had not believed it before Korea, nor did the Chinese in Indochina. Thus the possible use of nuclear weapons was discussed—and rejected—by the president and his advisers. Both communist powers correctly guessed that the United States would not risk a total war for anything less than an attack on the United States or Europe. In any event, Eisenhower, as well as Truman before him, believed that an attack on China would risk Soviet intervention and a Soviet-American war.

Truman's experience with Korea had shown clearly that containment could not be successful without the willingness and capability to fight a limited war. Reliance on strategic air power was not a credible strategy for deterring or winning "Koreas." Ground forces were absolutely necessary if the United States was to escape either defeat or involvement in a total conflict. In their absence, U.S. nuclear threats were not really credible.

The result was the French government's decision to make the best of the situation by negotiating in Geneva, Switzerland, for an end to the war. The French people, who were thrust into a second war in Algeria during this period, were as weary of Indochina as the American public had been of Korea. When the negotiations were over, the first Indochina war ended with the division of Vietnam at the seventeenth parallel. The communists retained control of northern Indochina, but it seemed only a matter of time until they took the rest of the country because the collapse of the southern rump state seemed imminent. The United States, however, prevented such a takeover by supporting the new government of Ngo Dinh Diem, a staunch anticommunist nationalist appointed by Bao Dai after Dienbienphu. The Eisenhower administration gave Diem economic and military aid to stabilize the situation in Vietnam, and the danger of collapse receded, if only temporarily.

SEATO'S FOUNDING

The seventeenth parallel, like the thirty-eighth parallel in Korea, became part of the international frontier separating the communist and noncommunist worlds. In September 1954, to protect this frontier, the

United States, Britain, France, Australia, New Zealand, the Philippines, Pakistan, and Thailand signed a treaty forming the Southeast Asia Treaty Organization (SEATO). The organization's protective reach extended over the South Pacific, with the exception of Hong Kong and Taiwan. A protocol to the treaty extended SEATO's protection to Vietnam, Laos, and Cambodia. It also provided for joint action to meet aggression; an attack on any SEATO member would be considered a threat to all, and each would act to meet the common danger in accordance with its constitutional processes. In case of subversion, the parties agreed to consult one another immediately and to agree on common measures to meet this threat.

SEATO, unlike the NATO alliance, had no unified command or joint forces. Its principal force was American sea and air power. The crucial element—land power—would have to be supplied by the member nations if the occasion arose. Moreover—and again unlike NATO— SEATO did not include most of the nations in the areas it planned to protect. Having just emerged from Western colonialism, India, Burma, Sri Lanka, and Indonesia were unwilling to be tied again to the West through a military alliance. They preferred to remain neutral in the struggle between the Western powers and the Sino-Soviet bloc. The Philippines was willing to join only because of its colonial ties to the United States, and Pakistan because it wished to acquire a source for arms against India. Only Thailand was genuinely concerned about the PRC's expansion. Australia and New Zealand were not really Asian powers, located as they were in the South Pacific.[4]

SEATO, therefore, was mainly a non-Asian alliance formed for the defense of an Asian area, a weakness that was to plague the group. The absence of regional concern about China's expansion ensured SEATO's eventual failure, and French and British membership did not prevent that result. France was unlikely to defend an area from which it had been forced to withdraw in humiliation. Britain, which had opposed U.S. intervention in Indochina, saw the alliance as a means of restraining the United States in the future. SEATO was, in reality, a U.S. guarantee for the defense of South Vietnam; it would provide a legal basis for a unilateral intervention to preserve the dividing line between the two Vietnams. Like West Germany and South Korea, South Vietnam had become part of the "free world"—that is, the American sphere of influence.

Presumably this ended the Vietnam problem since the Soviet Union and China appeared to accept the division of Vietnam. But Ho Chi Minh did not, as the United States was to discover. As for President Eisenhow-

4. These two countries joined with the United States in the 1951 Australia–New Zealand–United States Tripartite Treaty, commonly known as the ANZUS alliance.

er, he had kept the country out of war, but he also had, because of the strength of anticommunism in the country, especially in his own party, kept America in Vietnam. He, in fact, substituted an American presence for a French presence—a situation for which the country was to pay dearly later.

But for the moment, at least, the situation in the Far East had been partially stabilized. The frontier between the American and Soviet-Chinese spheres had been drawn at the thirty-eighth parallel in Korea, in the Taiwan Straits, and at the seventeenth parallel in Indochina. And although it would not be clear until years later, the United States had, by standing fast in the Taiwan Straits, also helped to bring Sino-Soviet differences close to the breaking point. For China, unification with Taiwan was a priority; for the Soviet Union, Taiwan was not worth the risk of a war with the United States. Consequently the tiny islands of Quemoy and Matsu were to play a profound long-term role in accentuating Sino-Soviet differences and in eventually splitting the alliance between the two largest communist powers.

THE SOVIET SHIFT BACK TO EUROPE

In Europe NATO already had drawn the defense line. The strength of this line on the ground, however, depended on supplementing NATO forces with West German troops, and the NATO allies had chosen the European Defense Community (EDC) to achieve this goal (see Chapter 2). But in August 1954 the French National Assembly rejected that role for the EDC by a decisive majority; fear of Germany remained too great, and French nationalists wished to maintain France's autonomy. This decision was a real blow to the efforts toward creating a situation of strength in Europe. The whole basis of NATO strategy and European integration was suddenly imperiled. The British found a new solution, however, in the forgotten Brussels Treaty, which was revised to include Germany and Italy within a Western European Union (WEU). With the British commitment of four divisions to the continent, France dropped its reservations to a German military presence.

The Paris Pact, which established the WEU, came into force in May 1955. Thus ten years after Germany's defeat, its occupation came to an end, and the Federal Republic regained its sovereignty and entered NATO via the WEU. West Germany's military power could now be added to Western strength. Two important declarations were appended to these Paris agreements. In the first, the West German government subscribed to the principles of the United Nations and vowed never to use force to achieve the reunification of Germany or to modify its boundaries. In the second, the United States, Britain, and France declared that they recog-

U.S. COLD WAR ALLIANCES

Rio Treaty (Organization of American States)		
UNITED STATES	HAITI	PERU
CUBA	DOMINICAN REP.	BOLIVIA
HONDURAS	COSTA RICA	PARAGUAY
MEXICO	PANAMA	BRAZIL
GUATEMALA	VENEZUELA	CHILE
EL SALVADOR	ECUADOR	ARGENTINA
NICARAGUA	COLOMBIA	URUGUAY

North Atlantic Treaty Organization (NATO)	
UNITED STATES	BELGIUM
CANADA	LUXEMBOURG
ICELAND	ITALY
NORWAY	PORTUGAL
UNITED KINGDOM	FRANCE
NETHERLANDS	GREECE
DENMARK	TURKEY
W. GERMANY	

Central Treaty Organization (CENTO)	
UNITED STATES	PAKISTAN
UNITED KINGDOM	IRAN
TURKEY	

Southeast Asia Treaty Organization (SEATO)	
UNITED STATES	AUSTRALIA
UNITED KINGDOM	THAILAND
FRANCE	PAKISTAN
NEW ZEALAND	PHILIPPINES

Australia, New Zealand, and the United States (ANZUS) Treaty		
AUSTRALIA	NEW ZEALAND	UNITED STATES

nized the Federal Republic as the only freely and legitimately constituted government entitled to speak for all of Germany, thereby indicating a policy of nonrecognition of the East German government. In addition, the allies would pursue German reunification by peaceful means, which in effect meant the preservation of a divided Germany. Finally, the Western powers stated that until "the conclusion of a peace settlement" they would continue to exercise their responsibilities with regard to the security of West Germany and West Berlin. NATO, like the European Coal and Steel Community (ECSC), was thus an instrument for uniting Western Europe and harnessing German power for its collective defense, as well as for controlling and restraining that power.

THE BIRTH OF THE COMMON MARKET

With Germany safely enrolled as a member of NATO, the continental European allies took a momentous step toward further economic and political integration. On June 1, 1957, France, West Germany, Italy, Belgium, the Netherlands, and Luxembourg established the European Economic Community (EEC), more commonly known as the Common Market, whose objective was to join them together into an economic union. Their plan was to achieve this in a twelve- to fifteen-year period, during which all six states would completely eliminate the tariffs and quota systems that hampered trade among them. They also would abolish restrictions on the intercountry movement of labor, capital, and services, with the exception of agriculture.

What were believed to be the chances for the development of this Common Market as it was being launched? The economic benefits were thought to guarantee it. As trade barriers were lowered and then eliminated, the increasing competition would result in the growth of efficient companies and the demise of the less efficient ones, unless they modernized or converted to new lines of production. All members were expected to gain. At its heart the Common Market was a bargain between French agriculture and West German industry. Both stood to benefit enormously from a continent-size market. Yet another factor was that the community would collectively receive advantages against third parties; it was strong enough to demand reciprocal lowering of tariffs. All these advantages outweighed the burdens each nation would suffer as a result of economic dislocation and hardships, which in fact would be minimized by being extended over a period of years and by being shared among all members.

The principal advantage of the Common Market, however, was seen to be political, not economic. A common market needs common policies; only one set of rules—not six—can govern its competitive behavior. In the long run the Common Market's success would lead to the adoption of common fiscal policies to control the ups and downs of the business cycle, a common currency, and a central bank. The economic "spillover"—from the original common market in coal and steel into a common market for all sectors of the economy—was expected to stimulate political unification. Indeed, it was precisely the formation of a political union that had inspired the ECSC.[5]

Initiated by France and strongly supported by West German chancellor Konrad Adenauer, the EEC was the culminating act of the movement to tie Germany so closely to a European community that it would never again be able to use its power for purely national ends. The formation of what came to be called the Inner Six was nothing less than the last link subjecting Germany to European restraints and responsibilities. Its success would make it impossible for Germany ever again to pursue a unilateral and aggressive course.

5. See Ernst Haas, *The Uniting of Europe* (Stanford, Calif.: Stanford University Press, 1958), 29–31.

Not surprisingly, the Soviet Union reacted quickly against the Common Market and attempted to break it up. A strong Europe, economically prosperous and politically stable, not only would prove a powerful barrier to Soviet expansionist ambitions, but also might threaten the Soviet status quo in Eastern Europe. The West European societies exercised a magnetic attraction for the satellite countries. West Berlin, alongside communist East Berlin, hampered Soviet control of East Germany. Hundreds of thousands of young, skilled and professional men and women left East Germany through West Berlin; it was an escape hatch that was depopulating the German Democratic Republic (GDR), as it called itself, of the very people it needed to run its society. Indeed, the real issue was the very survival of the GDR. Because it was an artificial creation, not recognized by most states that recognized West Germany as the true representative of German interests, the loss of the younger generation for whose welfare the GDR supposedly existed deprived it of a rationale for existence. And if East Germany were to collapse, would Poland and other East European states not follow? Thus if the existence of West Berlin and West Germany made the Soviet Union feel insecure about the status quo, the notion of a united Europe made Soviet apprehensions even greater.

THE SECOND BERLIN CRISIS

From Moscow's vantage point the stability of the Soviet position in central and Eastern Europe depended basically on destroying the freedom of West Berlin. To achieve this objective the Soviet Union announced in November 1958 that at the end of six months it intended to end the four-power occupation of the city. This ultimatum—the first Moscow had ever given the West—was clearly aimed at forcing the Allies to withdraw from West Berlin, thereby turning it into a "free city," but, in effect, incorporating West Berlin into East Germany. Once Western troops had left the city, West Berliners would feel isolated and unprotected, abandoned and completely helpless. The Soviet army and the East German army and police would surround them. In these circumstances what could the defenseless West Berliners do?

One way or another, then, the Soviets planned to remove a troublesome thorn from their side so that they would be in a better position to stabilize the status quo. Indeed, the destruction of West Berlin would have accomplished not only the Soviet Union's defensive aims but also its long-standing offensive purpose of weakening its opponents, perhaps fatally. If the Soviets could drive the Western powers out of Berlin, they also would be able to cut off the development of the Common Market before it gathered too much momentum and to shatter the NATO alliance. It was, above all, American power that guaranteed the freedom of the two million Germans living in West Berlin. If the United States were forced to abandon them, the Europeans would lose faith in America's ability to protect them. The Germans would be the first to read the lesson: because America could not guarantee their security, they would have to approach the Soviets independently.

Once approached, the Soviets would certainly demand that Germany abandon all its political, economic, or military ties to the West. But without Germany, there could be no Common Market because Germany provided much of the capital its partners needed for their economic development. And if Germany pulled out of the NATO alliance, the United States would have to send its troops home because it would be politically and strategically impossible to station them in France. Yet these troops were a symbol of the American commitment to defend Europe; they were psychologically and politically indispensable. No written guarantees could be substituted for this living embodiment of America's stake in Europe. Thus the central stake was the future of NATO and whether the Soviet Union could achieve a dominant position in Europe by neutralizing West Germany and driving the Americans back across the Atlantic Ocean.

THE SHIFTING BALANCE OF NUCLEAR FORCES

Berlin was the major test of postwar American policy, but it was not a repeat of the 1948 situation. At that time Stalin had acted on two assumptions: first, that the far larger Red Army contingents could deter an Allied attempt to break through to West Berlin on the ground, and, second, that the United States and Britain could not keep West Berlin alive. The first assumption proved to be correct, but the second was wrong. When Stalin realized this, he had to either call off the blockade or shoot down Allied planes and risk a war. America's atomic monopoly favored the first solution. But by 1957, a year before the Berlin ultimatum, the tide had turned technically for the Soviet Union. That year the Soviets tested the world's first intercontinental ballistic missile (ICBM), making America's determination to defend Berlin the next year riskier and costlier. Moreover, the ICBM test had followed a series of spectacular Soviet accomplishments in space. Soviet *Sputnik* satellites, which orbited the Earth every ninety minutes, and the ICBM test were at the time considered impressive symbols of Soviet technological progress.

In turn, they raised serious questions in the United States about its historic technological leadership and the future of the balance of power. Soviet premier Nikita Khrushchev, in fact, immediately talked of mass-producing ICBMs and asserted that the balance of nuclear or strategic power was shifting toward the Soviet Union. In the United States widespread public concern and anxiety spread about a future "missile gap," which, because ICBMs were faster than bombers, meant that U.S. strategic forces would become more vulnerable to a surprise attack and might no longer be as effective as deterrent forces.

The Berlin crisis, in brief, was the most serious confrontation Washington had faced since 1948–1949. The Truman Doctrine, Marshall Plan, Berlin airlift, and NATO had made it very plain to Moscow that Western Europe was an area of vital American interest. Soviet domination over the western edge of the Eurasian continent was no more tolerable to the United States than German control. Presumably this knowledge had deterred the Soviets in the late 1940s, and it was the fear of war that had led them to direct their challenges to areas outside of Europe.

Now, however, ten years after the first Berlin crisis, the Soviets were once more challenging the West in Europe. Indeed, in reopening the Berlin issue the Soviets were seeking to convey a new sense of confidence in their ability to deal with the West. That confidence seemed to reflect the Soviet claim that the strategic balance was changing in their favor. Clearly Khrushchev was attempting to cash in on this claim, to undermine European confidence in the United States, and to drive a wedge between the European members of NATO, especially West Germany, and their transatlantic protector. This had been a Soviet goal since the early Cold War.

Given the limited nature of the Soviet challenge and the all-or-nothing nature of massive retaliation, what strategy could the United States devise to prevent the Soviet Union from slowly choking West Berlin to death? How could massive retaliation, a policy intended to deter an attack on the United States or invasion of Western Europe, be used to prevent the strangulation of West Berlin? Would Moscow be restrained by U.S. threats of massive retaliation in Berlin's defense when the United States had been self-deterred in Asia against far lesser threats to its interests?

EISENHOWER'S LEGACY TO KENNEDY

In the months of tension as the superpowers tested one another, it became increasingly clear that the United States was determined to stay in West Berlin, and that the Soviets were equally determined to push their adversary out of Berlin. In an effort to defuse the crisis, Eisenhower invited Khrushchev to visit the United States in September 1959. His acceptance represented a tactical victory for the Soviets because Khrushchev knew that this summit conference could heighten the fears of the NATO allies that the United States and Soviet Union would negotiate a separate agreement at their expense.

This being said, Khrushchev's visit to the United States did have one positive result: the Soviets withdrew their threat to take unilateral action in Berlin in return for American willingness to negotiate on the problems of Berlin and Germany at a four-power summit meeting, which was scheduled for May 1960 in Paris. For American policy makers, this meant a postponement of the painful decision on whether Berlin was worth the cost of war. But if the administration believed that the crisis had ended, that from then on it could negotiate leisurely on Berlin and, if the Soviets did not accept its terms, preserve the status quo, it was quickly disabused of this notion. Khrushchev soon resumed his threats.

Shortly before the Paris summit, however, an event took place that shattered the conference after only one session and further postponed negotiations on Berlin. On May Day, 1,300 miles into Soviet territory, the Soviets downed an American spy plane loaded with photographic equipment for gathering intelligence data. The Eisenhower administration reacted to this unexpected and unhappy turn of events with considerable diplomatic ineptitude—first by lying about the U-2's mission and then, when the Soviets exposed the lie, by admitting, in a move unprecedented in diplomatic history, that the American pilot had been taking aerial photographs of the Soviet Union and that the White House had lied in its previous announcement. The administration justified its actions by saying that Soviet secrecy necessitated this means of information-gathering to prevent a surprise attack; moreover, it asserted that it would continue this behavior.

For the Soviet premier to let this pass would be like acknowledging to the world, to his people, to his domestic enemies, and to his allies that he had surrendered to the United States the right to violate Soviet territory. Khrushchev could not survive such an admission. He therefore struck a belligerent pose in Paris, launched a blistering personal attack on Eisenhower, and demanded his apology for past U-2 flights and a promise that the flights would cease. These demands were rejected. Khrushchev thereupon suggested that the summit conference be postponed for six to eight months, and he bluntly told Eisenhower that he would not be welcome to visit the Soviet Union in June, as they already had planned. In short, Khrushchev said that he wanted nothing more to do with Eisenhower and that he would wait to negotiate the Berlin problem with the next administration. A new crisis had been put off for a little while longer.

THE BERLIN WALL AND KENNEDY'S RESPONSE

It was inevitable, therefore, that the Soviets would raise the Berlin problem again once the new administration had taken over in January 1961. Khrushchev was still convinced that the global balance was shifting in his favor, and he remained confident that he was strong enough to acquire West Berlin. The new president, John Kennedy, fearing that Khrushchev might miscalculate, met the Soviet premier in Vienna to convey to him America's determination to defend West Berlin. Khrushchev discounted these warnings. His response was characteristic: a test of the president's resolution by reviving the original threat that the Berlin situation would have to be resolved within six months—that is, before the end of 1961. Thus the Vienna summit produced a result quite opposite of that sought: the very type of Soviet brinkmanship against which Kennedy had sought to caution the Soviet leader.

Kennedy, then, was quickly confronted with his own Berlin crisis. Declaring his willingness to negotiate, he also stated that the United States was not willing to discuss how the West would withdraw from the beleaguered city, thereby leaving it for the communists to swallow. The West's right to be in the city stemmed from its victory over Nazi Germany. The Western presence in and access to the city and the freedom of West Berlin were not negotiable. Kennedy said, "We cannot negotiate with those who say: 'What's mine is mine, and what's yours is negotiable.'" More specifically, he asked, if the West refused to meet its clear-cut commitments in Berlin, where would it meet them?

On August 13, 1961, the communists built a wall that divided the city, thereby eliminating the escape hatch for East Germans. More than 200,000 East Germans already had escaped to the West in 1961 alone. They were to be added to the 2.5 million who had migrated westward from 1948 to 1960—20 percent of East Germany's entire population! The wall ended West Berlin's usefulness as a "showplace for Western capitalism" and violated the quadripartite status of Berlin. The West did not knock the wall down with bulldozers for fear of military conflict with communist—especially Soviet—forces. This passivity intensified Khrushchev's conviction that the United States would not fight and that he could, slowly but surely, increase the pressure on NATO and drive the West out of Berlin.

This possibility, and the American fear that the Soviet leader might miscalculate Western resolve and accidentally trigger a war, accounted for the difference between Kennedy's and his predecessor's reactions to the Berlin crisis. Unlike Eisenhower, Kennedy used the tensions over Berlin to build up American military power; the new president was determined to show Khrushchev that the United States was not bluffing when it declared its intentions to defend West Berlin. Kennedy moved in two directions; indeed, he had begun to do so almost immediately after assuming office. One aim was a "flexible response"; the United States needed more options than massive retaliation's suicide-or-surrender alternatives. This increased flexibility was to be achieved by building larger conventional forces. In Europe a conventional buildup would give NATO a more credible defense. Outside of Europe the United States also would have a capability to respond to limited challenges.

The other critical aim was to reduce SAC's vulnerability during the changeover from bombers to missiles. Bombers located at known sites were highly vulnerable to surprise attack. Even in a situation of mutual deterrence, the possibility that many of the enemy's bombers might be destroyed on the ground remained an incentive to attack. If they could be destroyed, the retaliatory attack by a crippled remnant force might not be fatal to the attacking nation. In a crisis situation this possibility could tempt either side to launch a preemptive strike—even if the other side had no intention of striking. But long-range missiles, like the air force's Minuteman, could be widely dispersed and protected, or "hardened," in underground silos instead of being concentrated on a few above-ground bases; Soviet missiles were not yet accurate enough to hit such silos. And the navy's Polaris missiles would be mobile underwater so that the enemy would at no time know where to strike them.

These concealment tactics deprived a surprise attack of its rationale. Obliterating the enemy's cities would benefit the aggressor very little if the enemy still retained its retaliatory capacity. Surprise, therefore, no longer conferred any significant advantage to the side that struck first. Indeed, there was no longer any need to hit preemptively because enough missiles would survive the first strike to retaliate fully against the aggressor in a second strike. A first strike in these circumstances—which American policy makers effectively conceded to the Soviets—would be completely irrational.

Invulnerable second-strike forces were believed to be the basis of stable *mutual* deterrence. Mutual deterrence, according to the arms control philosophy the Kennedy administration adopted, would not guarantee that war could be avoided, however. If the means of delivering nuclear bombs or warheads were vulnerable to attack, such a situation might, particularly in crisis, tempt one side or the other to launch a first strike. Mutual deterrence in these conditions was unstable. Stabilizing the deterrent balance was therefore a priority for the new administration, which, over the next few years, deemphasized bombers and replaced them with hardened land-based and mobile sea-based missiles.

In the meantime, Kennedy, as cautious as Eisenhower, vacillated between his determination to stay in West Berlin and his equally strong determination to avoid conflict. Like Eisenhower, he was willing to negotiate with the Soviets. The meager results of all bilateral American-Soviet negotiations, however, stemmed primarily from Soviet unwillingness to concede the right to any Western presence in Berlin. Khrushchev was convinced that he had only to maintain Soviet pressure to evict the Western powers from the communist-surrounded and divided city. If, during this early period of the Kennedy administration, as during the late years of the Eisenhower era, the Soviets were unwilling to risk the final test, they had shown they would not hesitate to push the issue to a point of high tension by implying that they were willing to risk war and thereby exploit the West's fear of nuclear hostilities. This augured ill for the future if, first, the Soviet leaders could keep their challenges below the level of provocation that might arouse an American nuclear response, and, second, the Soviets could confine their challenges to the periphery of Western power, especially an isolated outpost such as West Berlin. As long as they followed these two fundamental precepts, they could continue to try to exploit the dilemmas of American strategy.

But it was the second rule that the Soviets failed to follow when they shifted the challenge to ninety miles from the American mainland—to Cuba—where the United States had little choice but to defend what it conceived to be its vital interests. Ironically, the Soviets placed missiles in Cuba because the Kennedy administration had concluded that no missile gap favoring Moscow existed, thus undermining the latter's claim of a changing strategic balance that should be reflected geographically in Europe. Cuba, then, was an effort to weaken U.S. strategic superiority and regain enough Soviet leverage to bring the Berlin crisis to a satisfactory conclusion.

SUPERPOWER CONFRONTATION IN CUBA

Cuba's revolutionary government dated from January 1, 1959, when its leaders overthrew the tyrannical dictatorship of Fulgencio Batista. During his struggle against Batista, Fidel Castro had identified himself with democratic government and social and economic justice and had gained widespread popularity among the Cuban people. This public support ensured the victory of his guerrilla army against the larger government forces. The Castro revolution was essentially a social revolution. Thus in the opening months of its rule, the new government moved to remedy the conditions of the people by instituting land reform and by building low-cost housing, schools, and clinics. But some features of this social revolution were bound to clash with the interests of the United States.

Although the United States had been instrumental in freeing Cuba from Spain in the Spanish-American War at the turn of the century, it had subsequently passed the Platt Amendment, which granted Americans the right to intervene at any time in Cuba for the preservation of Cuban independence, for the protection of life, property, and individual liberty, and for the discharge of Cuba's treaty obligations. By 1934, when the amendment was repealed, the United States had intervened militarily once in Cuba (1906–1909); it also had established a naval base at Guantánamo Bay. American capital controlled 80 percent of Cuba's utilities, 90 percent of its mines and cattle ranches, nearly all of its oil, and 40 percent of its sugar; approximately 25 percent of the American market was reserved for Cuban sugar. Despite this special commercial link, it was not surprising that the Cuban revolution directed its long pent-up nationalism and social resentment against the "Yankee imperialism" that dominated Cuba's economy. America's support of the Batista dictatorship until the moment of its collapse intensified anti-American sentiment. "Cuba, si! Yanqui, no!" became the Castro regime's rallying cry, the ceremonial burning of the American flag its ritual, and the confiscation of American property its reward. Yet Cuba in 1959 ranked fourth among Latin American nations in economic development, based primarily in agriculture and tourism.

This anti-American nationalistic feeling, deliberately fostered by Castro to increase the popularity of his regime, led his government to become increasingly identified with communism. If he were going to break with the United States, which, Castro assumed, would oppose his reforms, then he had to look to Moscow, its rival. By doing so, Castro betrayed the revolution's original democratic promises, and Cuba became a dictatorship. All parties were abolished except for one—the Communist Party—upon whose organizational strength Castro had become increasingly dependent. Castro also linked Cuba closely to the communist bloc. The Soviet Union supplied Cuba with vast amounts of arms and accompanying military advisers. Cuban airmen were sent to Czechoslovakia to learn how to fly Soviet fighters, and a large number of Cuban technicians were trained in communist countries. Cuba's armed services soon ranked second only to America's as the largest in the Western Hemisphere. Diplomatic relations were established with all communist countries except East Germany, and economic agreements were signed with many of the same countries, including East Germany. Indeed, Cuba's economy became integrated into that of the communist bloc; 75 percent of the island's trade was with countries behind the iron curtain.

In January 1961 the United States cut off diplomatic relations with Cuba after a series of alleged provocations. If Castro at that point had attempted to seize the Guantánamo base, there would have been an excuse for open American intervention. Castro, though, was too shrewd to risk a seizure, but he also ruled out an accommodation with the United States. This dictator wanted to play a major role on the world stage—a role he could not achieve as the leader of either a pro-American or a neutral country of ten million people on a small Caribbean island. He could do so only as a revolutionary leader who took on his giant neighbor as an enemy. But to stand up against the United States he would need the support of the other giant, the Soviet Union. Thus Castro turned down all friendly overtures from the United States after he took power: a new, sympathetic American ambassador was kept waiting for weeks before being allowed to present his credentials and offers of foreign aid were rejected.[6]

THE BAY OF PIGS

As Cuban-Soviet relations consolidated, the Eisenhower administration began to plan for Castro's overthrow. To this end, in April 1961 the new Kennedy administration launched an attempt by a small force of Cuban exiles—many of them former Castro associates who had become disillusioned by the premier's increasingly tyrannical rule, communist sympathies, and alignment with the Soviet Union—to land in Cuba and attempt to overthrow Castro. The U.S. Central Intelligence Agency (CIA), which had developed the plans for this operation and supervised their execution, assumed that, once the exiles had gained a beachhead in the Bay of Pigs, some units of Castro's army and much of Cuba's population would welcome the invaders as liberators. But the operation was a dramatic and appalling failure. The United States bungled it by basing a major foreign policy move involving American prestige on the glib assumption that a feeble beachhead operation would result in a mass uprising of Cubans against their government. The rumors and press reports, which conveyed the impression of a major invasion, made the failure appear even greater.

American prestige, already lowered by the Soviet Union's man-in-space achievement, sank to a new low. In his pointed comment in the *New York Times,* columnist Cyrus Sulzberger observed, "We looked like fools to our friends, rascals to our enemies, and incompetents to the rest." The administration had fallen victim to its own half-heartedness. The results of an unsuccessful invasion could have been predicted: an increase in Castro's domestic support, a revival of Latin American fears of "Yankee imperialism," a blunting of Kennedy's initially successful attempts to identify the United States with anticolonialism, and a loss of confidence in America's leadership by its allies.

Moreover, Kennedy was to set an unfortunate precedent for what was to become a pattern: to proclaim that a communist regime in the Caribbean–Central America area was a security threat to the United States, then to use proxies in an effort to eliminate it, and finally to abandon those proxies when the going got tough because of fear of escalation and war or congressional and public opposition or alienation of Latin

6. The changing U.S. views of Castro and his policies over his first two years in power are chronicled in *Emperor Dead and Other Historic American Diplomatic Dispatches,* ed. Peter D. Eicher (Washington, D.C.: Congressional Quarterly, 1997), 442–448.

America's rising middle class. If vital interests really were at stake, this course was unworthy of a great power. In short, the United States attempted to counter the Soviet exploitation of the new nationalist and social revolution to its south by "partial measures and through proxies. It . . . sought solutions on the cheap."[7]

THE CUBAN MISSILE CRISIS

Thus Cuba survived as a communist base from which the Soviet Union could threaten the United States and subvert the security of other nations in the Western Hemisphere. The importance of this development must not be underestimated. The American position in the Western Hemisphere had been preeminent. In 1823 the Monroe Doctrine had announced to the world that Latin America fell within the American sphere of influence and that Europe's colonial powers were to keep their hands off. In the decades that followed, the United States had intervened repeatedly, especially in the Caribbean and Central America. Although the motives for intervention varied, principal among them was the fear that a European power might establish its influence in an area that could be called America's "strategic rear," or, to use a Churchillian phrase, its "soft underbelly." During the early 1940s the concern had been with German power; after that, with Soviet power. A Marxist government had come to power in Guatemala in 1954. When it received arms from Czechoslovakia, the Eisenhower administration had intervened covertly to overthrow it, thereby setting a precedent for the Bay of Pigs. In short, the United States had never tolerated Latin American governments that leaned toward Germany or the Soviet Union—at least not in the smaller countries close to the Rio Grande and Florida.

With Fidel Castro's survival after the Bay of Pigs invasion, the United States no longer held a monopoly of power in the Caribbean and Central America. The Bay of Pigs disaster also incited Soviet intervention. In Moscow, where unfriendly regimes were not tolerated but crushed, Kennedy's prestige plummeted. According to the Soviet way of thinking, if it had been in the interest of the United States to eliminate Castro, then U.S. military intervention should have followed the bungled attempt by the CIA. A "serious" power does not tolerate its enemies so near and does not act squeamishly. It does what it has to do, regardless of international opinion. Moreover, if Castro's elimination had not been important enough for the United States to risk criticism, then the intervention should not have been launched in the first place. But to do so and fail suggested weak nerves and a lack of foresight. Worse, it suggest-

---

7. Zbigniew Brzezinski, "America's New Geostrategy," *Foreign Affairs* 66 (spring 1988): 691.

ed fear of the Soviet Union. Why else would the United States not intervene with its own military forces in an area so close to it, as it had done many times in the past? Perhaps the Soviet Union should push a little further and see if Kennedy would tolerate a further extension of Soviet power.

And that is just what it did. Once the Soviets saw that the communist regime in Cuba was tolerated, they began to establish a missile base there. Washington had believed that the Soviet Union would not dare to do this in America's sphere of influence. In October 1962, however, a U-2 spy plane suddenly discovered, to the great surprise and consternation of American policy makers, that the Soviets were building launching sites for approximately seventy medium- and intermediate-range ballistic missiles (a number that could be increased later). That Khrushchev had dared to move his missiles so close to the United States and that he apparently expected no counteraction beyond ineffective diplomatic protests was a dangerous sign. He knew that war by miscalculation was the great danger; to prevent miscalculation was therefore an absolute necessity. But American vacillation at the Bay of Pigs and afterward had convinced the Soviet premier that the United States would not fight to protect its vital interests. Besides, Khrushchev thought Kennedy too young and inexperienced; Kennedy, Khrushchev told an American visitor, was "too liberal to fight."

Khrushchev had a great deal to gain. A failure to respond to his move would prove to America's NATO allies what they already feared: the United States had become vulnerable to attack and could no longer be relied on to protect Europe. Moreover, inaction in the face of Soviet missiles so close to the American coast would have validated Khrushchev's claim of a shift in the nuclear balance. The promised renewal of Soviet pressure on Berlin after the midterm U.S. congressional elections, together with the likelihood of an even more cautious American reaction than before, would have reinforced this impression. Only this time the Soviets could deliver an ultimatum to get out of Berlin or else, and they were in an increasingly favorable position to exert their will.

The threat in Cuba therefore had broad consequences. For the first time ever a large part of the North American continent would be vulnerable to Soviet missiles. The early warning systems against bombers and missiles were in the north because a Soviet attack always had been expected to come in over the Arctic. Moreover, American prestige was on the line, and not only in Europe. The sudden and unchallenged appearance of the opposing superpower in an area where the United States had long been paramount would have eroded America's authority and status and encouraged the spread of Castroism throughout Latin America. All anti-Castro forces, including the indispensable and all too few genuinely democratic reformers, would have been demoralized and perhaps paralyzed by Washington's inaction.

But for once Khrushchev overplayed his hand. He pressured the United States in the wrong place, and Washington could not avoid the test. If the stakes were high for the Soviet Union, they were even higher for the United States, and Kennedy felt that under no circumstances could he afford to lose. Indeed, because he had warned the Soviet leader against placing offensive missiles in Cuba, Kennedy had to compel their withdrawal to preserve his credibility and America's. From the outset, however, the young president realized that the central issue was Soviet and allied perceptions of the balance of power.

Khrushchev's confidence, Kennedy realized, stemmed from a conviction that the United States no longer possessed the will to defend its interests. But such a notion was dangerous because, if left uncorrected, it would lead to a renewed and more determined challenge in Berlin— as Khrushchev already had announced. If the United States declared it would stand firm in Berlin but the Soviet leader did not believe it, a violent clash, possibly a nuclear war, might result. Characteristically, the Soviets had not committed themselves irrevocably in Cuba. They were willing to gamble for a big payoff, but they also were willing to suffer a serious setback to avoid a catastrophic clash. The Soviets were still seeking the limits of American tolerance in the Western Hemisphere.

To meet this crisis Kennedy placed a blockade around Cuba to prevent any further missile shipments, and he demanded the removal of the missiles already in place. American firmness and determination left Moscow little choice. For once the Soviets had to decide whether to fire the first shot—to break the American blockade of their missile-carrying ships— and risk a possible escalation of the conflict. Much to everyone's relief, the Kremlin backed down. It recognized that the United States had enormous conventional, especially naval, superiority in the Caribbean, and that it also could have mounted an invasion if it had been necessary. In the absence of sufficient conventional forces to support his ally so far away, Khrushchev was left with only one choice—risk nuclear war, which he was unwilling to do because he respected U.S. strategic superiority. America still had a huge bomber force, and Kennedy already had built up two hundred ICBMs (of what a few years later was to be an ICBM force of a thousand). Khrushchev knew that his country had fewer than fifty first-generation missiles, exposed above the ground, and that it possessed no missile force to speak of despite its claims to the contrary. In fact, in 1961 U.S. satellites had learned the truth: there was indeed a missile gap, and it favored the United States. The shipment of Soviet missiles to Cuba was part of an attempt to reduce the nuclear imbalance that had resulted from Kennedy's rapid buildup, which had been stimulated by the years of

Khrushchev's missile threats over Berlin and claims that he was mass-producing the new Soviet ICBMs. In any case, the resulting U.S. strategic strength set a clear upper limit to the pressure the Soviets could exercise on the United States. And the level of tension therefore rapidly declined as America's determination and willingness to use its power became clear. As Secretary of State Dean Rusk vividly described it, "We were eyeball to eyeball, and the other fellow just blinked."[8]

Kennedy's critics had predicted that a Soviet humiliation in Cuba would compel Khrushchev to recoup his lost prestige by forcing the West out of Berlin. Khrushchev, however, called off both challenges, apparently believing that America's superior nuclear strength, as demonstrated in the Caribbean, also could be marshaled in Berlin. Local conventional superiority, which the Soviet Union possessed around Berlin, was not the decisive factor.

The missile crisis was therefore followed by years of détente (a relaxation of tensions). But there were two other outcomes as well. First, the United States declared publicly that it would not invade Cuba. Thus although America had won a brilliant tactical victory, the Soviet Union had not suffered a strategic reversal; its base in the Caribbean remained intact. Second, Moscow decided it would never be humiliated again; it would build up its strategic nuclear power to U.S. levels, if not surpass them. The missile crisis had therefore been instructive to the Soviets—nuclear strength was politically usable.

AMERICAN STRATEGY AND FRONTIER DEFENSES

In the recurring crises over West Berlin from 1958 to 1962, as well as the Cuban missile crisis, the United States learned several lessons helpful to preserving the line around what was then still viewed as a cohesive Sino-Soviet bloc. The first lesson was that the threat of nuclear weapons could be used to deter the possibility of an all-out attack and contain limited challenges, but it could not prevent them. The advent of nuclear weapons, noted President Eisenhower, left no alternative to peace. However destructive, a conventional war (like World War II) distinguished winners from losers and, with time, both recovered from the human losses and the destruction of their cities and industries. But a nuclear war was likely to be suicidal; all participants would lose. The destruction would be on such a scale that no recovery would be possible. Total war, in short, had become irrational because the cost of war was completely disproportionate to any conceivable gains.

8. For a more detailed assessment, see Raymond Garthoff, *Reflections on the Cuban Missile Crisis,* rev. ed. (Washington, D.C.: Brookings, 1989).

The United States, the Soviet Union, and the People's Republic of China were all very aware of this historic change in the nature of warfare. World Wars I and II had been extremely costly; warfare now had become prohibitive. Thus policy makers in all major capitals, while on occasion talking tough and even threatening to go to war and use nuclear weapons, were in reality extremely careful in the conduct of policy to ensure that confrontations were resolved diplomatically, even if they involved public retreat and humiliation. This was better than escalation to armed clashes that might lead to a nuclear holocaust.

Thus despite massive retaliation and the talk of brinkmanship, the United States did not invoke the threat either in Korea in 1953 or in Indochina in 1954. And while nuclear war was certainly lurking in the background of the Berlin crises, the possibility of its use came to the fore only during the Cuban missile crisis because of the likelihood of a U.S.-Soviet clash if the Soviet missiles were not withdrawn. The Soviet Union, while invoking the threat of war more menacingly and frequently to exploit Western fears of nuclear war, especially in Berlin, also remained extremely cautious even while its words were reckless. In the Taiwan Straits, in particular, this was dramatically demonstrated when it refused to back the PRC's efforts to reunify China, laying the Sino-Soviet schism open to public view while deepening it. And in Cuba it tried to install its missiles secretly before the United States could become aware of its move.

Nor was the PRC so eager to reunite with Taiwan or face the United States in Korea or Indochina that it would risk a confrontation, nuclear threat or not. Nuclear arms did not have to be invoked; they were just "there" and all the great powers knew it. Thus the nuclear powers were self-deterred from pushing any clash too far.

The second lesson was that mutual deterrence was not automatic. Indeed, advancing technology might upset the stability of the deterrent balance. And simply possessing the bomb was insufficient; the key to a *stable* deterrent balance was an invulnerable retaliatory force. If country A's forces were vulnerable to attack by country B, A might be tempted to strike B preemptively rather than have its forces caught on the ground. Or A might lead B to strike first because B also feared a preemptive strike. In the late 1950s and early 1960s the Soviets claimed that they were mass-producing missiles that made American bombers vulnerable. If true this would have meant that the U.S. deterrent capacity would have declined as the Soviet first-strike capability grew. It affected, in any case, the psychology of the policy makers in Moscow and Washington, emboldening Khrushchev and making Eisenhower and Kennedy more cautious—until the latter was forced to the wall.

The Soviet Union's willingness to challenge the United States in Europe ten years after the first Berlin crisis was symptomatic of the effects of this perceived change in the balance. A Soviet claim of a shift in the nuclear balance led the Soviet Union to try to use "nuclear blackmail" or coercion to undermine the status quo. If Moscow could compel the United States to withdraw from West Berlin, NATO would collapse and the Soviet Union would become the hegemonic power in Europe. Only in Cuba in 1962, after it had become clear that Khrushchev had been bluffing and that he was not mass-producing ICBMs, did Washington regain its self-confidence and react vigorously.

Preserving deterrence, then, was a continuing, never-ending task, not because some change in the balance might have precipitated war, but because it might have affected the risks each side was willing to take as one side challenged the other. Neither side ultimately was willing to push too far diplomatically, lest it provoke nuclear war, but there was no question that the perception of the strategic balance did affect the degree of risks policy makers were willing to accept in a specific situation: how far they calculated they could push their opponent and how far they expected the latter to retreat and comply with their demands. If Washington had still believed that U.S. strategic forces might have been vulnerable, would it have been willing to demand that the Soviets withdraw their missiles from Cuba? If Moscow had really believed that the balance was changing in its favor, would it have complied or continued to seek the West's exit from Berlin?

The third lesson was that unregulated arms competition was potentially dangerous. In the rivalry between a democratic state and a totalitarian one, the totalitarian state had a distinct advantage in the presatellite era. The Soviet Union could easily gather information on U.S. arms, but because the Soviet Union was a closed society, the United States could not accumulate information on the number and types of Soviet nuclear arms. After 1956, high-altitude U-2 aircraft were the principal American means of collecting information. But because these aircraft could not survey Soviet territory daily, Khrushchev could use his strategy of deception and claim that the Soviets had weapons that they did not, in fact, possess and assert a capability to destroy the U.S. deterrent bomber force—a capability the Soviets also did not have. The United States could not be sure what was true. Earlier, in the 1950s, the Soviets had flown the same few bombers around Moscow repeatedly to deceive Western military observers. Only from 1961 on did Washington gain more reliable information from satellite observations and, for example, expose the falsity of Soviet missile claims and the changing strategic balance.

But without the types of arms control arrangements that were to become familiar after the 1950s, U.S. worst-case assumptions about Soviet strength were understandable. When hard information on Soviet nuclear strength was lacking, the American reaction to Soviet claims was fear that bomber and missile "gaps" existed and that they favored the Soviet Union. The United States overreacted—for example, by increasing the number of missiles beyond that originally planned. Meanwhile, once Moscow knew that Washington knew that it had lied, the Soviets felt compelled to compensate for its ICBM inferiority by placing in Cuba medium- and intermediate-range missiles, of which it had plenty. The subsequent missile crisis made leaders on both sides more aware of the need for arms control to complement the unilateral acquisition of arms and the resulting action-reaction arms competition.

Finally, as Berlin and Cuba demonstrated, the chief function of military power was to draw and protect "frontiers." These frontiers were clear: along the inter-German border and through the middle of Berlin; at the thirty-eighth parallel in Korea and the seventeenth parallel in Vietnam; along the coast of China at Quemoy and Matsu; and along the "southern tier" of Asian states from Turkey to Iran and Pakistan. Any attempt by communist forces to cross these frontiers, either openly by direct attack or covertly by guerrilla warfare, risked hostilities. Admittedly, the lines drawn outside of Europe were extremely tenuous. The Central Treaty Organization (CENTO)—established in 1959 by the United States, Britain, Iran, Pakistan, and Turkey—and the Southeast Asia Treaty Organization (SEATO) were alliances in areas where nationalist forces opposed them. As a result, the alliances had little popular support in those regions, even in those states that were members, and the governments seeking to maintain the lines were often unable, despite American help, to mobilize indigenous support, as was to become evident in Vietnam during the 1960s.[9]

Indeed, the United States may have been better off had it not created what turned out to be poor replicas of NATO, which existed in a region where its people supported containment against clearly perceived potential external aggression. The less-successful alliances were organized in non-Western areas where containment was widely perceived as an attempt to preserve Western influence and reactionary regimes. America's containment strategy thus encountered greater difficulties as its geographic scope widened, a pattern that would become painfully evident in the developing world in the 1960s and 1970s.

9. This lesson should be clear to American leaders in the late 1990s who have suggested returning to some of these alliances to counter Chinese military expansion. See Thomas Friedman, "Dust Off the SEATO Charter," *New York Times*, June 18, 1995, A19.

In many developing countries economic growth has not kept pace with increasing population, political upheaval, and natural disasters.

CHAPTER FIVE

The Third World in the Crossfire

The expansion of the Cold War in the early 1950s beyond its European roots to Asia elevated four areas of the world to major power centers: the United States, the Soviet Union, Western Europe, and the People's Republic of China. "In all four," one scholar observed at the time,

productivity is on the increase, and the political system performs relatively well its integrating and decision-making functions. Despite major differences among them . . . these four areas are likely to be in a position to play major roles in political, economic, and cultural international affairs in the coming decade. In contrast, the Middle East, Southeast Asia, tropical Africa, and Latin America are apt to remain power vacuums during this period, owing to their lack of unity, political instability, economic stagnation, and cultural heterogeneity. It seems highly improbable that ten years from now any of the areas mentioned above will cease to be, respectively, a power center or a power vacuum.[1]

During the 1950s and 1960s, which witnessed the liberation of many European colonies in Africa and southern Asia, U.S. leaders became

1. Guy J. Pauker, "Southeast Asia as a Problem Area in the Next Decade," *World Politics* (April 1959): 325.

increasingly anxious about the unstable political and economic conditions that accompanied the birth of the new nation-states in the emerging "Third World."[2] The evolving membership of the United Nations over a fifty-year period has confirmed the importance of the developing regions. In 1946 the United Nations had 55 members. By 1955 there were 76 members; by 1970, 127; by 1980, 160; and in the mid-1990s the figure stood at 185. The vast majority of these member states (and most of the world's population) were in developing regions. And in the UN General Assembly, with its principle of one country-one vote, these member-states could—and would—dominate the agenda.

In the bipolar context of the Cold War, the Third World did not represent an independent center of power but rather an object of competition for the two superpowers, each seeking the support (and UN votes), if not the allegiance, of the former colonial states. During their early years of independence, however, most developing countries refused to align themselves politically and militarily with either superpower. Among their first collective efforts, in fact, was the establishment of a "nonaligned movement" and the assertion of their independence from Washington and Moscow.

Communist leaders perceived the decolonization process as proof that the international capitalist order was disintegrating. The colonial powers such as Great Britain and France had maintained capitalist economies which, according to Marxist-Leninist theory, depended on captive overseas territories for raw materials and export markets. It was equally significant, to this theory, that the First World War and the Great Depression occurred only after capitalist states had exhausted their opportunities for colonial expansion.[3] Given this perception of history and the understandable resentment within many developing countries toward their former colonial rulers, both Soviet and Chinese leaders saw an opportunity to embrace and support the new states.

From Washington's very different perspective, the challenge of Soviet and Chinese communism in the Third World stemmed not from conspiracy or military takeover but from the repressive model of development that communism offered the developing countries. The Soviet Union, discounting its rapid industrialization under Czar Nicholas II at the turn of the century, held itself up as a model of an underdeveloped country that had transformed itself into a modern industrial society in

2. Although the term *Third World* clearly obscures the regional diversity among developing countries, for political leaders and most scholars of the period the term served to differentiate these largely impoverished states from Northern capitalist countries—the *First World*—and communist countries—the *Second World*.

3. Vladimir Lenin, *Imperialism: The Highest Stage of Capitalism* (New York: International Publishers, 1939).

one generation. Overlooked, however, were the force, massive terror, and staggering human cost associated with that accomplishment. Joseph Stalin's forced collectivization of Soviet agriculture resulted in the death of more than ten million peasants (*kulaks*), either through the purges and mass murders of Stalin's opponents or through the crushing famine of the early 1930s.[4] An even greater number of Chinese peasants died under Mao Zedong's reform efforts, particularly the "Great Leap Forward" that ended in chaos in 1959. U.S. leaders worried, nevertheless, that the leaders of poor countries that had not known democracy might decide that the appeal of rapid economic growth outweighed its social costs.

In this context, the choice of which path to economic development the developing countries would choose was seen as critical to U.S. security and, more broadly, to an international environment safe for open societies and democratic values. Thus for American policy makers, offers to help the new countries establish a base for economic growth stemmed not just from a humanitarian concern for the countries' long-suffering populations but, more fundamentally, from recognition that their progress toward prosperity and political stability would lessen the appeal of communism, thereby serving U.S. self-interests by creating a more amicable international order.

THE REVOLUTION OF RISING EXPECTATIONS

Paradoxically, the disintegration of Western colonialism after World War II provided the most eloquent testimony to its success. The Western powers, including the United States in the Philippines, had justified their imperial domination in terms of bringing the "backward" peoples of the earth the benefits of Western democracy, medical science, and technology. It was the "white man's burden," or duty, to educate the people so that one day they could govern themselves.

The colonial powers apparently had taught their lesson well; they had ruled their colonies autocratically while proclaiming the virtues of democracy. Ironically, the nationalist movements later used the same democratic ideals to challenge their rulers and ask them to practice what they preached. Indeed, many leaders of these movements, who often were educated in Europe or the United States, fought the colonial rulers by using the principles of democracy and national freedom they had learned. For them, these principles were incompatible with imperialism and a rationale for wars of "national liberation."

4. See Robert Conquest, *The Great Terror: A Reassessment* (New York: Oxford University Press, 1990).

Once these countries became independent, however, they confronted a legacy of poverty, illiteracy, and disease. For example, in the 1950s the annual per capita income in these states rarely reached $100, and life expectancies seldom exceeded fifty years. To remedy their underdevelopment and to narrow the enormous gap between poor and rich nations, many new countries sought to transform their traditional agrarian societies into modern industrial states. This transformation also had great political significance, for it demanded that the citizens of developing countries transfer the allegiance from their local communities and the ethnic and religious groups that had held their loyalty to their new nations. The fact that the concept of national loyalty was largely unfamiliar to the citizens of the newly independent countries intensified the need to satisfy the popular "revolution of rising expectations." The fledgling nations had to prove they could offer their people something not otherwise attainable. By achieving improved standards of living, these nations would demonstrate that they deserved the popular support and allegiance they needed to survive and grow.

THE CONSEQUENCES OF POPULATION GROWTH

In considering their prospects for economic development, leaders of the new countries realized their success depended to a large extent on whether their economic progress would occur faster than their population growth—that is, whether their "population explosions" would eat up any increase in national income. In 1830 the world population was 1 billion; by 1930 it had doubled to 2 billion, and by 1975—just forty-five years later—it had doubled again to 4 billion. According to the best estimates, the world's population will grow to almost 6 billion people by the year 2000, to 7 billion by 2010, and to more than 8 billion by 2020. Just as the developing countries represented a majority of nation-states by 1970, their share of the world's population also grew dramatically so that in 1995 nearly 80 percent of the 5.7 billion inhabitants of the world lived in developing countries.[5]

The concern among leaders of rich and poor countries alike was that, despite the expected slowing of the population growth rate sometime in the twenty-first century, the developing countries might continue to face the problem described by the Rev. Thomas Malthus more than 150 years ago: hunger and poverty result when population growth exceeds the means of subsistence. Malthus, who also was an economist, predicted this fate unless population growth was limited either by "positive checks" such as wars or epidemics, which result in high death rates, or

5. Population Reference Bureau, *1995 World Population Data Sheet* (Washington, D.C.: Population Reference Bureau, 1995).

by "preventive checks" such as family planning, which produce low birth rates.

In contrast to the developing countries, the West had made impressive economic progress after the Industrial Revolution of the late eighteenth century, despite a population increase. Improved harvesting techniques provided plentiful food, and industrial advances raised living standards to heights never before attained, thereby refuting Malthus's gloomy prediction. The conditions facing the developing countries, however, were quite unlike those found in Western countries. One chief difference was that the Western countries had far smaller populations when they began industrializing, and their population growth did not outpace economic growth. But India, for example, began its modernization with a population of 350 million, a number that grew to nearly 1 billion by the late 1990s. China, with a population of 547 million in 1950, was home to 1.3 billion people by the end of the century. Incredibly, if upon its independence the United States had possessed a population density equivalent to that of Egypt, today it would have more than a billion people instead of less than 300 million. Under these circumstances perhaps the United States would not have become a "developed" nation.

The European states also enjoyed an enormous benefit in the New World and in their colonial empires, which provided them with outlets to relieve their population pressures. Indeed, about 60 million Europeans emigrated during the nineteenth and early twentieth centuries. By the 1950s about 400 million people of European descent were living outside Europe. The United States and Canada, rich in resources and fertile land, easily absorbed millions of immigrants and still increased their living standards. Australia, New Zealand, and South Africa also expanded their populations and economies, although on a smaller scale. By absorbing a population that might otherwise have led to overcrowding in Europe, the colonies added materially to the European nations' wealth. Upon their independence, however, the developing countries were not able to find such empty and rich spaces to absorb their burgeoning populations.

Also unlike in Europe, new agricultural technologies increased food supplies and temperate climates were more favorable to food production than the harsh climates prevalent in many developing countries. The former colonies often had few resources with which to adopt modern means of agricultural production. Even so, some developing countries experimented with intensive farming techniques. Using high-yielding crop varieties, improved but costly chemical fertilizers, and more effective pesticides, the so-called Green Revolution increased food production enough in these countries to keep up with their population growth. By the 1990s a handful even exported food. Still, many could not feed themselves.

In the West, birth rates declined after 1850; with industrialization and the growth of cities came the spread of literacy and artificial birth-control techniques. Indeed, the fate Malthus anticipated for the West did not materialize because preventive checks were adopted, with many industrialized states achieving zero population growth by the late twentieth century and some facing the prospect of declining populations. But the Third World, where advances in health care reduced infant mortality and raised life expectancy, had not yet reached a similar level of economic development, and knowledge of birth-control methods and the willingness to use them spread more slowly than had been expected. The poorer the populations were in developing countries, the higher were their rates of population growth.[6]

FINANCIAL, CULTURAL, AND POLITICAL OBSTACLES TO DEVELOPMENT

With the exception of a few newly industrialized countries such as Taiwan and South Korea, most developing countries during the Cold War decades of the 1950s and 1960s failed to match their economic development to their fast-rising rates of population growth, much less surpass them. Many of these countries were burdened with not only too many people but also not enough capital. Sufficient internal savings could not be squeezed out of people living at a subsistence level—at least, not without authoritarian controls. As for earning capital through trade—particularly exports of primary products or raw materials such as coffee, tea, rubber, and tin—the developing countries had discovered in the past that such exports limited their earning capacity. Because upon independence their economies remained tied to those of their former colonial masters, their exports rose or declined with every fluctuation in Western prosperity. If a major Western recession reduced the demand for and price levels of natural resources (even oil until 1973), the resulting losses of income often exceeded the large volumes of Western aid extended during the same period. Furthermore, markets would become glutted with certain items because of overproduction or substitution. A state trying to raise its income by increasing production found its competitors doing the same, which lowered world prices further.

---

6. Whereas the population growth rates of industrialized countries averaged 0.2 percent in 1995, the growth rates of developing countries averaged nearly 2 percent, with many of the world's poorest countries in sub-Saharan Africa recording growth rates well over 3 percent. For an elaboration of this trend, see Richard J. Tobin, "Environment, Population, and the Development World," in *Environmental Policy in the 1990s*, ed. Norman J. Vig and Michael E. Kraft (Washington, D.C.: CQ Press, 1997), 321–344.

Another problem was that the Western industrial states, whose ever-increasing demand for raw materials was supposed to furnish the capital for economic development, no longer needed the developing countries to the degree anticipated because of the emergence of synthetic substitutes or changing consumer habits. Thus the lack of stable international commodity prices, similar to the parity prices paid to American farmers, as well as the inventiveness of modern technology, limited the prospects of financing industrialization via earnings from raw materials.

Foreign investment was another source of capital for economic development. In the first years after independence, however, private capital was in short supply for the kind of long-range investment needed by the developing countries. Private American investments outside the United States were largely being made by a small group of oil companies to build refineries and to discover and pump out oil fields in Latin America and the Middle East, but most investment capital stayed home because of the boom the American economy experienced for most of the Cold War period. This was true for Europe as well. European capital was concentrated on rebuilding, modernizing, and expanding Europe's industrial base. American capital that did go abroad often went to the Common Market, where it would return sizable and relatively speedy profits. In addition, because many leaders of developing countries often associated capitalism with colonialism, they resisted private investment and greater involvement in global trade and capital markets.

Economic growth, then, was the principal task of the developing countries, but their leaders soon realized that it was not just an economic undertaking; it was a political, social, and intellectual undertaking as well. Indeed, economic development was a revolutionary process frequently marked by political instability and violence rather than evolutionary, peaceful change.

One reason for this instability was that, as noted earlier, most of the new states lacked administrative and political cohesion. Generally their populations had no single common culture or language; in fact, tribal and regional conflicts abounded. Citizens had no natural loyalty to their states, whose boundaries were drawn crudely along colonial frontiers, and no tradition of cooperation was in place except on the one overriding issue of eliminating the colonial ruler. Once the struggle for independence ended, power tended to fragment. India, for example, split violently into Hindu India and Muslim Pakistan after independence, and the latter dissolved further into Pakistan and Bangladesh. The Belgian Congo fell apart when the Belgians withdrew. Cyprus divided into Turkish and Greek factions. And Biafra broke away from Nigeria, only to lose the subsequent civil war.

AFRICA IN 1945

Legend:
- Spanish
- Belgian
- Portuguese
- Former Italian Territory under British or French occupation
- French
- British
- Union of South Africa

Even where actual disintegration did not occur, religious, linguistic, and racial differences tended to tear apart the fabric of those states that lacked any history of nationhood. In 1972, for example, the Tutsi in Burundi reportedly slaughtered 120,000 Hutus; this violence recurred on an even more ghastly scale in the 1990s. In the late 1980s Sri Lanka, formerly Ceylon, a large island lying just off the southeastern coast of India, was immersed in fighting between Hindu Tamils and Buddhist Sinhalese. The lesson appeared obvious: before the formal process of "state building" could occur, stable *nations* in which the needs of disparate peoples were respected had to be created.

The absence of a strong sense of national consciousness was soon reflected in the way many of the leaders of the new countries built themselves up as symbols of nationhood. They did not find this essential task difficult because, as leaders of the movements for indepen-

AFRICA TODAY

dence, their prestige was usually high. Indeed, just as Louis XIV had proclaimed, *"L'état, c'est moi,"* they too *were* the state. Without their presence as its symbol the nation would not hold together as a unit. One-party rule or military governments existed almost everywhere in the Third World. In Africa, for example, the world's last continent to be freed from colonialism, three-fourths of its 345 million people lived under single-party or military rule by the late 1960s, ten years after independence.

Such policies might have seemed undemocratic, but they were widely justified by political leaders and believed to be necessary. Most people in the new states felt less loyalty to the government than to ancestors, family, village, or tribe. Wherever the opposition represented these centrifugal forces, an American-style democracy would have led not just to a change of government but to the disintegration of the state. The alternatives facing the leaders of these countries often were not democracy or dictatorship but statehood or disintegration.

The political and revolutionary context of development also was revealed in the nature of nationalist revolutions, which directed their opposition not only against colonial rulers but also against traditional governing elites if they remained in power after independence. Many developing countries were split into three main groups when they gained independence. The first was the ruling minority, usually composed of landowners or merchants, whose vested interest lay in preservation of the status quo. Their wealth and power derived from continuing, as in the old colonial days, to send their nations' natural resources to the West rather than striving to become economically independent. The second group was peasants, villagers, small artisans, and shopkeepers—the vast majority of inhabitants, whose energies were spent largely on the day-to-day struggle for survival. This group, which had for centuries borne its hardships silently, arose and demanded a better life. The third group, the urban intelligentsia, educated in Western ideas and committed to nationalism and development, voiced its resentments against the old way of life and articulated the new aspirations while it sought power to affect the political, social, and economic transformation of the country's societies. Without such social change—that is, the overthrow of the old ruling elites—development was inhibited. This was not a matter of "reform" but of revolution because the crucial issue was power. Who controlled the nation? The old ruling elite committed to the preservation of the traditional, preindustrial society or those who sought to democratize, modernize, and industrialize the nation? Only one thing was certain: few who rule yield their dominant political, social, and economic position without a struggle.

OTHER SOURCES OF DISCONTENT

Instability was able to take root even where economic development occurred, where national bonds did not disintegrate, and where a reform-minded elite was in control. Such instability stemmed from a standard of living that, while improving, did not improve rapidly enough to create a satisfied population. Capital for investment historically has been accumulated by keeping wages low, which, in turn, has allowed the reinvestment of the capital saved into further economic expansion. In the newly independent countries higher wages and mass consumption were postponed in favor of "capital formation" and economic expansion. Thus although living conditions may have improved slowly over time, they could not overcome rising expectations.

Once the populations of developing countries realized they no longer had to live in the poverty of the past, that change was possible, and that people could create a better life through their own efforts, their dissatisfaction grew. This gap between their expectations and achievements was particularly aggravating when the rulers lived well, even ostentatiously. Those living less well became frustrated, and their frustration in turn spawned social discontent and an increasingly sullen, hostile, and more radical mood. In the 1960s and 1970s this pattern led the governments and peoples of many developing countries to become more hostile toward the United States and other industrialized countries, their former rulers, further aggravating relations between the industrialized North and the developing regions of the Southern Hemisphere.

Social instability and turmoil were further promoted by the intellectual and cultural changes that accompanied the transformation of a traditional, static, rural society into a modern, dynamic, urban-industrial state. Many of the old customary and religious values that had provided for some measure of social stability simply collapsed. People became disoriented, torn from their age-old moorings for which they had not yet found a substitute. Their precolonial traditions had provided cultural meaning for their lives; robbed of this, they became isolated and insecure in a rapidly changing environment that they neither made nor comprehended. Secular values, emphasizing materialism and progress, often replaced religious values that denied the importance of earthly existence and material possessions. A society in which individual effort was rewarded and people could rise socially according to merit replaced a society with a rigid social structure in which birth determined people's place and religion often governed their mode of conduct.

Nationalism thus replaced local loyalty, and modern transportation and communication led individuals to become aware of the larger societies in which they lived and worked. Impersonal ties to people far away in their country replaced former face-to-face relations with neighbors, and new skills and ways of thought had to be learned. In short, people had to forget many of their old ways and adapt to new conditions. In the best of circumstances these changes were difficult and agonizing. In other cases they produced social revolutions that often brought new regimes to power—and turned back development efforts. The Iranian people, for example, experienced this kind of upheaval in late 1978 and early 1979: their religious leaders opposed the American-backed shah, leading to his overthrow and the establishment of an Islamic theocracy. Precisely because economic development was associated with secular values, few in the West had taken seriously the possibility of the Ayatollah Ruhollah Khomeini's succession. The idea of an old man, a religious icon, coming to power was so at odds with contemporary ideas of modernization that the likelihood of its occurrence was dismissed as preposterous. Yet for the poor and the powerless in a rapidly changing society where tradition and customs were being eroded, often by forces alien to the indigenous population, religion retained a strong attraction and comfort.

CLASHING MODELS OF ECONOMIC DEVELOPMENT

Confronting an amalgam of political, social, and cultural changes (not just economic development) and experiencing revolutionary transformations (not just evolutionary progress), developing countries in the 1960s had no guarantee that they would climb what the economist Robert Heilbroner termed the "Great Ascent."[7] In this context, the Soviet Union and China were willing to present themselves as models of development. To people suffering from chronic hunger and poverty, it may not have mattered that the Soviet Union had achieved industrialization by setting up totalitarian governments that brutally squeezed the necessary sacrifices out of the people, or that Maoist China had modernized its system of agriculture at the cost of tens of millions of lives. "Command" economics would at least provide the organization and efficiency to extract the sacrifices from the masses and the discipline to hold the nations together, to speed up the pace of their cultural revolutions while controlling social tensions produced by the early stages of development, and to depose ruthlessly the traditional ruling classes blocking progress.

As for communism itself, it offered a disciplined means of bringing about fairly rapid political, social, economic, and cultural changes. The beneficiaries of this system supposedly were not the rulers, to whom communism offered a means of seizing power and legitimizing dictatorial rule, but the mass populations who had labored for centuries without receiving a significant share of the wealth they produced. Communism, either in the Soviet (Leninist) or Chinese (Maoist) forms, thus promised an egalitarian form of economic growth with the benefits of development redistributed fairly among all segments of the population. The emphasis was to be on internal development and the detachment of the developing countries from a global market that, according to neo-Marxist thought, benefited the "core" Western capitalist states and perpetuated the dependency of "peripheral" developing countries.[8]

Western economists and political leaders argued, conversely, that for the developing countries the best route to economic development lay in

7. Robert L. Heilbroner, *The Great Ascent* (New York: Harper Torchbook, 1963).
8. See Immanuel Wallerstein, *The Modern World System* (New York: Academic Press, 1974); Gunner Myrdal, *Economic Theory and Underdeveloped Regions* (New York: Harper and Row, 1971); and Andre Gunder Frank, *Capitalism and Underdevelopment in Latin America* (New York: Monthly Review Press, 1969).

integration in, rather than isolation from, the "liberal international economic order" established by the United States after World War II (see Chapter 3). They viewed the global market, which presumably drew from the "comparative advantages" of all regions of the world, as the catalyst for economic growth, and they disputed the claims of Marxist critics that the governments of capitalist states were merely puppets of business interests. To the contrary, they optimistically predicted that with the *assistance* of industrialized states, the developing countries would evolve through predictable "stages of growth" into modern, industrial, democratic societies.[9]

It was in this polarized environment that the United States, other Western states, and multilateral agencies such as the World Bank, International Monetary Fund, and Organization for Economic Cooperation and Development (OECD) first offered the developing countries economic aid and technical assistance. Western aid was intended to close the gap between rich and poor states, to modernize the new nations without compelling them to use totalitarian methods, to satisfy their "revolutions of rising expectations," and thereby to create politically and socially stable societies. This process, in turn, was expected to create democratic governments and a more peaceful world by giving developing countries a vested interest in the international order and Western values.

Although the nature of the problem seemed clear to many Western policy makers, the rationale for economic aid to assist the new nations' development never attracted the degree of public support that the more easily understood military preparations against the Soviets did. What probably was required, as many suggested, was a progressive international income tax by which all the advanced Western nations would contribute 1–2 percent of their annual national income for development. In 1969 the World Bank's Pearson Commission endorsed the 1 percent figure, but no Western country was giving that much. Despite the rapid economic growth of the industrial states during the 1960s, their foreign aid spending had declined. This was particularly true for American aid to Europe, which, at the time of the Marshall Plan, had been 2.75 percent of the gross national product (GNP). Aid to developing countries was always less than 1 percent of GNP. In short, at a time when the American GNP had risen by hundreds of millions of dollars, the national effort to aid the developing world was out of proportion with America's increasing capacity to pay and with the growing gap between the rich and poor nations.

9. See W. W. Rostow, *Politics and the Stages of Growth* (New York: Cambridge University Press, 1971).

Indeed, the term *economic aid* was something of a misnomer. After 1950 and the eruption of the Korean War, most economic aid was, in fact, military aid. Moreover, after Western Europe's recovery most of this aid was channeled to allied countries that were not among the world's poorest: Turkey, Pakistan, South Vietnam, South Korea, and, in the 1980s and 1990s, Israel and Egypt. The final sum actually allocated to economic development also was concentrated in relatively few countries. Most developing countries got next to nothing.

Apart from the lack of public support for foreign aid, U.S. policy toward the developing countries suffered from three other liabilities. The first was that American dollars were all too often offered with the explicit or implicit assumption that the recipients would associate themselves with U.S. Cold War policies. Even if they did not formally ally themselves with the United States, they should often thank it for its generosity, praise it for the morality of its anticommunist stand, and certainly refrain from criticizing it. The United States was reluctant to give dollars to nations that would not join its side. But in these countries the basic aspiration was to concentrate on internal matters, to raise the standard of living and strengthen their independence, and to minimize involvement in the Cold War. Most, therefore, sought to remain nonaligned in the struggle between the United States and Soviet Union.

In preferring a generally nonaligned position, the leaders of many developing countries believed they were following America's example. After all, after the United States had gained its independence, it too had avoided "entangling alliances" and occupied itself with internal developments. As a developing country, the United States had been aware that its newly realized independence meant little without economic and political strength. Moreover, the United States had just thrown off the shackles of colonialism; its citizens had no desire to be once more tied to European powers. But American policy makers, especially during the 1950s, forgot that it was the United States that had set this example.[10]

The second liability that hampered U.S. policy toward the developing countries during the early Cold War was racial discrimination within the United States itself. The persistent segregationist practices and exploitation of blacks in both the South and the North were flagrant violations of the democratic principles of freedom and human dignity so often proclaimed by the United States. The peoples of developing countries not only claimed equal status for their nations but also sought equality as human beings. Segregation in America reminded them of their colonial days when white rulers had treated them as inferiors

---

10. European governments, meanwhile, concentrated their aid on their former colonies, prompting charges of "neocolonialism" from many Third World populations. See Steven W. Hook, *National Interest and Foreign Aid* (Boulder, Colo.: Lynne Rienner, 1995).

because of the color of their skin. Conditions in the United States to change, however, during the Kennedy and Johnson administration. As African Americans heard the Rev. Martin Luther King Jr. articulate their aspirations for a life of greater dignity and fuller participation in American society—and as the ghettos exploded after King's assassination—the government began to outlaw certain discriminatory practices against blacks and to provide greater opportunities in jobs and housing. But racial problems continued to haunt the United States on the foreign front. In Rhodesia (now Zimbabwe) and South Africa, minority white-controlled governments, determined to stay in power, used abhorrent methods to control the majority native populations such as apartheid and strict police surveillance. The United States, despite its oft-expressed disapproval of these policies, did not follow through with action. It imported Rhodesian chrome for years despite a UN embargo. And American companies in South Africa, although they provided their black workers with better working conditions and pay than local companies, lent support to South Africa through investment. America, the world's first state to articulate that all men were created equal, seemed all too often to say to the world that there was a qualifying phrase: "except blacks."

Third and more fundamental, U.S. relations with many developing countries were hampered by the American lack of understanding of class struggle and social politics. America, "born free" as a bourgeois democratic society, had managed to avoid the kinds of domestic conflicts over basic values that the countries of Europe had experienced and that plagued many developing countries. The United States had not experienced a genuine social revolution at its birth, for a revolution is characterized by violence; it seeks to destroy the institutions and social fabric of the old society and create a new society with new institutional and social class arrangements. Despite its self-proclaimed revolutionary character, the United States has been, according to former senator William Fulbright, a nonrevolutionary, conservative country.[11] It was not surprising, therefore, that America was not particularly sympathetic to revolutions and tended to equate revolution, per se, with communism. Deviations from middle-class American values were likely to be condemned as "un-American" and sinful, to be rooted out so that the "American way of life" would remain pure and unadulterated.

Indeed, the principal challenges to these values had come not from within the system but from outside the U.S. borders, and the United States had reacted to foreign threats—German, Japanese, Soviet—in two ways. Internally the government had hunted subversives, a procedure

11. J. William Fulbright, *The Arrogance of Power* (New York: Vintage Books, 1967), 72–73.

ɔn civil liberties and endangered the security of tradi-
ɔ. Externally, government policy, before the atomic bomb,
ʌestruction of the hostile regime so that American princi-
ɾvive untainted. Thus, as already noted, the real or imag-
ɪnist threat in the early 1950s led to McCarthyism, a search
ɑ which the goal of eliminating alleged un-American atti-
behavior justified any means, including disregard for due
law, the basic guarantee of all civil liberties. In foreign policy
ɔn to the communist threat was to support almost any regime,
no matter how repressive, if it claimed to be anticommunist. As a result,
the United States often allied itself with governments whose days were
numbered; Chiang Kai-shek in China, Bao Dai in Indochina, and Ferdinand Marcos in the Philippines are but three of many examples.

This attitude was typical of American absolutism and its inability to
understand the deeper social struggles of the Third World. In its attempt
to contain communism—that is, to preserve the global status quo—the
United States became committed to the domestic, social, and political
status quo in these regions. In trying to preserve freedom, the United
States was paradoxically supporting ramshackle anticommunist autoc-
racies that were unrepresentative of their peoples' aspirations. But this
internal contradiction within the U.S. alliance system eventually had to
resolve itself. American support for traditional regimes only bottled up
the social and political resentment and ferment even more, thereby
adding to the explosive forces that would burst forth either during the
Cold War or in its aftermath.

REGIONAL CONFLICTS IN AFRICA
AND THE MIDDLE EAST

During the 1960s and 1970s, to almost no one's surprise, the domestic transformation of the developing countries had repercussions
beyond their borders. The upheavals tended to disturb an international
system largely defined by the frontiers drawn between the two superpowers' spheres of influence and by the Cold War rivalries. When the
internal difficulties of the countries of the Third World spilled over into
the external arena of international politics, or when they resulted in civil
war or regional rivalries, they attracted the Soviet Union or the United
States, leading to confrontation and often military conflict.

The two superpowers were attracted to Third World conflicts because
such friction could either bring to power a group one superpower liked
and the other disliked, or result in regional expansion and influence that
could be perceived as benefiting one and hurting the other. If one superpower were unwilling to tolerate what it considered to be, in terms of the

overall balance of power, a local or regional setback, it would intervene. Or, if it feared that if it did not intervene then its opponent might, the result might be preventive intervention. In both cases it risked a similar move by its opponent. Looking to the future, Pauker in 1959 observed, "Power vacuums are likely to disturb international relations increasingly. They are the natural targets for power centers wishing to extend their hegemony. They should be the object of anxious attention for those powers which want to strengthen the international balance." [12]

NATIONAL DISINTEGRATION AND CIVIL WAR: THE CASE OF ZAIRE

If a new nation-state disintegrates into two or more parts, those who seek to reunify their land or establish new splinter states may appeal for help to sympathetic states that, for reasons of their own, may wish to see either a nation preserve its unity or a splinter state its independence. Such appeals were addressed especially to the Soviet Union or the United States in the early years of the Cold War.

One of the more dramatic examples of the way the survival of a new state involved the superpowers occurred in 1960 when the Belgian Congo became independent. Almost immediately the Congo fell into disorder. First, the rich mining province of Katanga, on whose copper and cobalt exports the Congo was largely dependent as a major source of revenue, split off into a separate state. Katanga's president had the support of the powerful Belgian mining interests, eager to protect their investments. Then the army began to revolt because it resented the continued presence of its Belgian officers and wanted them replaced with native leadership. In a wild spree, Congolese soldiers began to attack white women (including nuns) and children, causing the Belgian settlers to flee, as well as the experts the Belgians had expected to leave behind to help the Congolese in their early period of self-government. All public services then collapsed because the Congo lacked an educated native elite. The Belgians had never trained one.

When the Belgians flew in paratroopers to protect their nationals, Congolese premier Patrice Lumumba saw the move as a Belgian attempt to restore colonial rule, and he appealed to the United Nations to send forces to help him. It was at this point that the Cold War was injected into the Congo. The UN troops, with no forces from the great powers, did not compel the Belgians to evacuate their paratroopers. UN Secretary-General Dag Hammarskjöld had ordered UN forces not to become involved in internal conflicts or in the contending political factions seeking to gain power over their rivals. This, however, had the effect of

12. Pauker, "Southeast Asia," 325.

underwriting the divisions of the Congo. Lumumba turned against the United Nations, bitterly attacked the secretary-general, and accused Belgium and the Western powers, especially the United States, of conspiring against him. Lumumba's attacks grew increasingly racist. Finally, he asked the Soviet Union for help and received Soviet diplomatic backing, military supplies, and offers of troops, or "volunteers."

In early 1962, after all efforts to unify the Congo had failed, the United Nations reversed its original stand in order to preempt possible Soviet intervention. It finally adopted the policy of forcefully squashing the opposition. Although UN efforts took many months and cost lives, the country was "unified." Mobutu Sese Seko, who emerged as Zaire's leader for several decades, was supported by the United States for his anticommunist policies. Mobutu received vast amounts of American foreign aid, much of which he used to solidify his rule. Along the way he managed to expropriate much of the aid and the country's commercial wealth for his own purposes, to the point that by the time he was ousted in 1997 he had become one of the world's richest men, while his country slipped further into poverty and internal turmoil. His actions, and the case of Zaire in general, symbolized the disarray that resulted from the collision of Cold War politics and Third World development. And the revolt against Mobutu in 1997 demonstrated how vulnerable such rulers were to popular backlash once deprived of their Cold War patrons.

REGIONAL RIVALRIES: THE 1956 AND 1967 ARAB-ISRAELI WARS

Beyond the impoverished states of Africa, no area better exemplified how regional disputes became intertwined with the Cold War than the Middle East. Specifically, three sets of rivalries intersected: the Arab-Israeli enmity, intra-Arab rivalry, and the superpower competition. Each tended to reinforce the other. The Arabs, especially Egypt and Syria, received weapons and political support from the Soviet Union; Israel received similar support from the United States. With all this help, then, the Arabs and Israelis were able to fight repeated wars.

While the victor, Israel, could never impose a settlement on its enemies because the Soviets would not allow their clients to be totally defeated, the Arabs never paid the penalty for losing and could always rearm and try to destroy Israel the next time. To expand their influence and weaken that of their Cold War adversary, the superpowers supported their respective client states; simultaneously, they restrained their respective clients lest they be drawn into a direct confrontation. The larger Arab states tended to compete among themselves for leadership of the Arab world in terms of who would best defend Arab interests by the militancy of its anti-Israeli stance; even moderate and pro-Western Arab states (largely the oil producers) had to be anti-Israel.

It was the Eisenhower administration's effort to complete its wall of containment around the Sino-Soviet world that introduced the Cold War into the Middle East. In 1955 Britain, historically the preeminent Western power in the area, with American support established the Middle East Treaty Organization (METO), which included Turkey, Iraq, Iran, and Pakistan. Also known as the Baghdad Pact, METO extended the NATO line from Turkey to India. With the exception of Iraq, this "northern tier" was drawn along three thousand miles of the Soviet Union's southern frontier and therefore drew a sharp reaction from that country. Although they had been rebuffed in Iran and Turkey, the Soviets had not surrendered their ambitions in the region. The Middle East linked Europe, Africa, and Asia. For Britain, the area—and especially the Suez Canal—had long been the lifeline to India, the "Jewel in the Crown" of the old empire, and to its present Commonwealth. Of greater importance, Europe's economy was becoming increasingly dependent on the Middle East for oil (America was still self-sufficient). The power that could deny Europe oil would be able to dictate its future. In short, for the Soviet Union the Middle East was the place to outflank and neutralize NATO. Its opportunity stemmed from several situations: the bitter Arab-Israeli conflict, the Anglo-Egyptian quarrel, Egypt's expansionist ambitions, and the U.S. attempt to draw the lines of containment just south of the Soviet border.

Arab antagonism toward Israel stemmed from the Balfour Declaration of 1917, in which Britain had pledged the establishment of a "national home" for the Jewish people in Palestine while promising the Arabs that the civil and religious rights of non-Jews would not be neglected. Zionists took this pledge as a promise to convert Palestine into a Jewish state; they considered Palestine, which had become a British mandate after the disintegration of the Ottoman Empire during World War I, to be their ancient and traditional homeland. The Arabs, meanwhile, feared that the Jewish immigration would crowd them out of what they also regarded to be their rightful homeland.

In November 1947 the United Nations partitioned Palestine into two independent states, one Jewish and the other Arab. The Arabs refused to accept this solution. On May 10, 1948, as Britain ended its mandate, the Jews proclaimed the state of Israel, and the armies of the Arab League (Egypt, Jordan, Syria, Lebanon, and Saudi Arabia) invaded the new state. In the ensuing war the Israeli army defeated the larger Arab armies, and the state of Israel became a fact of political life.

The Arabs, however, refused to recognize it as such. But Egypt, the leading Arab power, needed arms before reconfronting Israel. In September 1955 Egypt stunned the West by concluding an arms deal with Czechoslovakia, acting for the Soviet Union. Under this arrangement Egypt received a large quantity of arms, including planes and tanks. Egypt now thought that it had the means to achieve a decisive military victory over Israel. In April 1956 Egypt tightened the ring around Israel by forming a joint command with Syria, Saudi Arabia, and Yemen. In October Egypt, Jordan, and Syria announced another joint command, "the principal concern of which is the war of destruction against Israel." As Egypt solidified the encirclement of Israel and began to absorb the Soviet arms, the Israelis decided to strike before it was too late.

The Anglo-Egyptian Quarrel and Nasser's Ambitions. World War II had intensified Egyptian nationalism and heightened the demand for a withdrawal of British forces (Britain had had a presence in Egypt since 1882, and the country was even a British protectorate from 1914 to 1922). In late 1951 the Egyptian parliament abrogated the 1936 Anglo-Egyptian treaty, and in July 1952 the new military regime that took over the Egyptian government from King Farouk pressed with renewed vigor for the removal of British troops. The Eisenhower administration supported the Egyptian demand in the belief that Col. Gamal Abdel Nasser, the real power behind the military coup, and the United States were natural allies. The military was believed to be anticolonial, progressive, and committed to improving people's lives and providing Egypt with a degree of political stability. If the United States helped Nasser to evacuate British troops from their Suez Canal base, the Egyptians might in fact become allies. But once it ousted British colonial control, the new regime turned to its number-one goal: to avenge itself by destroying Israel.

The removal of British forces from Egypt did not eliminate British power from the region. Britain shifted from Egypt to Iraq, its longtime friend, whose royalist regime needed Western protection from Egypt's new military regime. Nasser did not see the Baghdad Pact as a means of containing the Soviet Union; he saw it as an instrument to preserve Western domination throughout the area and, because Iraq had always been Egypt's traditional rival for Arab leadership, he considered the pact a personal challenge as well. The pact completed Nasser's alienation from the West, for his ambitions reached beyond eliminating Israel and expelling the British. He saw himself as a modern Saladin, the champion of the Arab cause. He promoted Pan-Arabism as a way of expanding his influence and that of his country. As the former dominant influence throughout the region, the West became Nasser's target.

The Baghdad Pact was the instrument of its own destruction because it helped to bind Egypt, led by Nasser, to the Soviet Union. Its failure testified to the difficulties of containing Soviet expansion by drawing lines outside of Europe. In Western Europe the states all shared a common perception of the Soviet threat and stood united against it. Outside of Europe, U.S.-Soviet competition intersected with regional rivalries, undermining the U.S. goal of containment and providing the Soviet Union with an opportunity to expand its influence. It was in Moscow's interest to destroy the alliance along the Soviet Union's southern frontier; it was in Cairo's interest to gain a source of arms to destroy Israel and to put political pressure on the pro-Western regimes in the area. Thus Cairo received its arms, and Nasser became a hero for the Arab people. By strengthening Nasser, the Soviet Union became the Arabs' greatest friend.

The United States further upset the West's position in the Middle East in July 1956 when it retracted its offer to help finance Nasser's pet project, the Aswan High Dam. The dam on the upper Nile was intended to raise Egypt's low standard of living by irrigating new land and providing electricity for industrial development. The retraction was a heavy blow to Egypt because the American loan was a prerequisite for further aid from the World Bank and Britain, and these offers too were withdrawn. Nasser regarded these decisions as a personal slap and national humiliation. A few days later, on July 26, he announced he would nationalize the Suez Canal, which connected the Red Sea and the eastern Mediterranean, and use the revenues collected from it to finance the dam. Arab nationalists were ecstatic, and Nasser's stature, already great, reached new heights.

The 1956 Suez War and U.S. Intervention. In October 1956 the Israeli army marched into Egypt, where it quickly defeated the Egyptian forces on the Sinai Peninsula. The British and the French (who sought Nasser's downfall because of his aid to rebels trying to free Algeria from French control) intervened in Israel's behalf. They failed, however, to provide the United States with a fait accompli, the result of a quick and effective intervention. Instead, their action infuriated the Eisenhower administration, which condemned their concerted military offensive. The administration saw the invasion of Egypt as a golden opportunity to win Arab friendship. By saving Nasser, the United States could align itself with Arab nationalism; U.S. support of Britain, France, and Israel would leave the Soviet Union as the sole champion of Arab aspirations.

In short, American opposition to the invasion identified the United States with the anticolonialism of the entire underdeveloped world, and particularly with the anti-Israel and nationalistic sentiments of the Arab world. Because continued evidence of British power in the Middle East only antagonized the Arabs, the removal of this power and its replacement by American influence would be in the interest not only of the United States but also of all the Western powers. In this way the West's strategic and economic interests could be more adequately safeguarded.

At least that was the rationale for the United States humiliating its two main allies, thereby turning Nasser's military defeat into a political victory. The favorable global contrast—Washington opposing great-power intervention against a smaller state at a time when the Soviets were intervening in Hungary to suppress its aspiration for national self-determination—was a factor as well. America's opposition to the Suez invasion was the decisive factor in stopping the fighting. Given worldwide condemnation of the invasion, the British government withdrew its forces; France and Israel had little choice but to follow suit.

It is ironic in view of America's leading role in halting the attack on Egypt that the Soviet Union was to reap the benefits. After it had become clear that the United States would not support the British and French invasion, the Soviet Union threatened "to crush the aggressor." The Soviet Union risked nothing by delivering these threats to exterminate Israel and attack Britain and France, yet it received most of the credit from the Arabs for saving Nasser.

The Eisenhower Doctrine. Recognizing this development, Eisenhower urged Congress to support a new commitment to resist communism in the Middle East. A joint resolution of Congress, known as the Eisenhower Doctrine, declared in 1957 that the United States considered the preservation of the Middle Eastern nations vital to American security, and that it was prepared to use armed force to assist any state requesting U.S. help to counter military threats "from any country controlled by international Communism." Despite the fact that the Soviet Union did not border any Arab state, it was clear that this proclamation was aimed at Nasser, whose great political victory only increased his self-confidence. Supported by the Soviet Union, whose aim it was to weaken if not eliminate all Western power in the Middle East, Nasser continued his expansionist drive.

Using its new doctrine as a pretext, the Eisenhower administration in 1958 resorted to force. Lebanon had been plagued for some time with civil war between Muslims and Christians. The Muslims wanted close relations, if not union, with the United Arab Republic (composed of Egypt and Syria), and the Christians favored a pro-Western policy and the continued independence of Lebanon. Men and arms for the pro-Nasser elements were smuggled in from Syria. In Jordan, too, the situation took a turn for the worse when King Hussein dismissed his pro-Nasser government, which led to a general strike, massive street demonstrations, and riots. In response to this turmoil, the United States sent fourteen thousand men into Lebanon, and the British sent three thousand paratroopers into Jordan. The large size of the American contingent seems to have been a deliberate warning to Iraq, where nationalist officers had seized power and overthrown the pro-British monarchy, and might have been tempted to nationalize Western oil resources. But its leader quickly gave assurances that he had no such intention, and possible American intervention in Iraq was forestalled.

The Anglo-American action saved Lebanon and Jordan. But it also was intended to have another important effect: to show Nasser and the Arabs that there were limits to Soviet willingness to come to their aid. Before the intervention the Soviets again had threatened to send "volunteers" to oppose the Western "imperialists" and had carried out conspicuous military maneuvers in Soviet central Asia and other areas. The firmness of the American position and the failure of the Soviet Union to do more than denounce the intervention and call for a diplomatic settlement made it very clear that the Soviets' willingness to bail out the Arabs had its limits. This turn of events had a dampening effect on Nasser's anti-Western drive. Jordan, Lebanon, and Saudi Arabia had remained independent; Libya and the Sudan had resisted his attempts to subvert them; and, ironically, Iraq's officers briefly challenged Nasser for leadership of the Arab world—until its own leading general was himself overthrown and killed.

Meanwhile, the United States had become almost a full-fledged member of the reconstituted Baghdad Pact (renamed the Central Treaty Organization, or CENTO, after Iraq's defection). But south of CENTO's fragile line remained all the basic problems that had given rise to the turmoil after 1955: the conflicts among the Arab states, the Arab-Israeli dispute, the overshadowing competition between the United States and the Soviet Union, and, above all, the rise of Arab nationalism. The American attempt to draw another "frontier" in the sands of the Middle East had been unsuccessful. Ironically it was this attempt that had drawn the Soviet Union and Egypt together to destroy the "northern tier," permitting Moscow to jump over the line that was supposed to contain it. It was thus only a matter of time until the next war would erupt.

1967 Renewal of the Arab-Israeli Conflict. By 1967 intra-Arab rivalries, combined with domestic economic failure, had led Nasser to reassert his leadership of Arab nationalism. The result was another war. The Syrians, who had joined Egypt in a United Arab Republic, only to quit it when Nasser moved to dominate the union, now sought to displace him as the leader of pan-Arabism. They openly and repeatedly called for Israel's destruction and stepped up their terrorist raids into that country. After the Israelis retaliated, the Syrians claimed in May 1967 that the Israelis were assembling their forces for a full-scale invasion of Syria. Nasser, claiming to be the great hero of the Arab peoples, either felt compelled to act or saw in the invasion rumor his opportunity to regain his leadership of Arab nationalism. After eleven years of receiving Soviet training and arms, Nasser seemed confident that his forces could beat Israel, which this time would be fighting by itself, without the aid of France and Britain.

In preparation for the confrontation the Egyptian leader moved rein-forcements into the Sinai Desert and then demanded and obtained the withdrawal of the UN peace-keeping forces. Egyptian and Israeli forces now confronted each other for the first time since 1956. In his most delib-erate provocation of Israel, Nasser blockaded the Gulf of Aqaba, Israel's lifeline through which it received its oil and other goods. Nasser then signed an alliance with Jordan. This meant that Arab armies surrounded Israel: Syria to the north, Egypt to the south, and Jordan to the east, with its highly regarded army directed to cut Israel in two at its narrow waist. All these actions were accompanied by increasingly shrill calls for a holy "war of liberation" and the extermination of all of Israel's inhabitants.

In these circumstances war was inevitable, unless Israel was willing to accept a major political defeat—an unlikely prospect. The preservation of peace, which could be achieved primarily by Nasser's removal of the blockade, depended on the United States and the Soviet Union. Wash-ington was caught in a dilemma. On the one hand, the United States had recognized Israel's right to send ships through the gulf after compelling Israel to withdraw after its 1956 victory. On the other hand, America was, by then, deeply involved in Vietnam and therefore reluctant to take on a second conflict. Furthermore, a key question for American policy mak-ers was whether such a test would precipitate a clash with the Soviet Union, which had with great fanfare sent warships into the eastern Mediterranean, fully supported the Arabs in their aims, and continually denounced Israel as an aggressive tool of American imperialism.

For Moscow the Arab-Israeli conflict had global implications. If Western influence could be expelled from the Middle East and if the Soviet Union could establish itself as the dominant power over this oil-rich region, Europe would be weakened and perhaps even neutralized. Thus for Moscow the stakes in seeing Nasser achieve a political victory were enormous—and Soviet political support and the naval show of force undoubtedly contributed to Nasser's intransigence and helped to restore his reputation in the Arab world. If the Gulf of Aqaba blockade were successful, the Soviet Union would earn the Arabs' everlasting grat-itude as the primary force behind Egypt's political victory. Moreover, an effective blockade would demonstrate the Soviet Union's ability to inhibit the American navy and would jeopardize future American com-mitments to Israel. The Soviet Union had an opportunity to replace the West as the region's leading power.

But Moscow's ambitions were quickly frustrated in the region. Because Washington was unable to arrange a diplomatic solution, the Israelis attacked to seize the initiative in what had become an unavoid-able clash. Routing the air forces of their Arab opponents in a brilliant-ly coordinated set of air strikes during the first hours of hostilities, they defeated the Egyptian army and reached the Suez Canal in three days—two days ahead of the record they set in 1956. They routed the Jordanian army and captured half of Jerusalem and the western bank of the river Jordan. Finally, they turned on the Syrian army and eliminated the bases on the Golan Heights from which Syria launched the terrorist raids and shelled Israeli settlements. Nasser's dreams of an Arab empire, and the Soviet Union's hopes for regional hegemony, were quickly shattered.

U.S. POLICY TOWARD LATIN AMERICA

Events in Latin America further illustrate how U.S. foreign policy became driven by events in the developing world. To American leaders, revolutions based on the Cuban experience in 1958 and 1959 created a "foothold" for communism in the Western Hemisphere and thus constituted a threat to the United States. Fidel Castro's success in Cuba—and that of other charismatic rebels elsewhere—was made possible by factors such as the resentment against a history of U.S. interventions in the Caribbean and Central America, large-scale, private U.S. capital investments in and economic control of many Latin American economies; persistent U.S. support for the privileged few who, usually closely linked to American capital, sought to preserve their position by ignoring social grievances and establishing right-wing military dictatorships; and finally, the misery, poverty, and illiteracy of the majority of the people, who, although they lived in the countryside, were landless.

Latin Americans shared two aspirations that were sweeping through the developing areas: a better life for the masses and the desire of countries to determine their national destinies. The United States had exercised its hemispheric domination indirectly, usually by alliance with the wealthy land-owning governing class. Americans may have believed that they were free of Europe's taint of colonialism, but that is not what Latin Americans thought. The Monroe Doctrine had turned the entire Western Hemisphere into a U.S. sphere of influence; the United States did not have to resort to direct colonial rule. Invested American capital spoke louder than guns, and the U.S. government did not have to give political orders when a nation was a "banana republic." In contrast to their rhetorical calls for democratic rule, U.S. leaders actively supported military rulers throughout Latin America and exercised their self-appointed "international police powers"[13] to maintain stability in the region.

13. This term was coined by President Theodore Roosevelt, whose 1905 "corollary" to the Monroe Doctrine legitimized the recurring series of U.S. interventions and occupations in Latin America. See Walter Lafeber, *Inevitable Revolutions,* 3d ed. (New York: Norton, 1993), 38.

UNITED STATES

BAHAMA
ISLANDS

MEXICO

CUBA

PUERTO
RICO

CAYMAN
ISLANDS

DOMINICAN
REPUBLIC

BELIZE

HAITI

HONDURAS

JAMAICA

GUATEMALA

NICARAGUA

EL
SALVADOR

VENEZUELA

**CENTRAL AMERICA AND
THE CARIBBEAN**

COSTA
RICA

PANAMA

COLOMBIA

TRINIDAD
&
TOBAGO

VENEZUELA

GUYANA

*ATLANTIC
OCEAN*

SURINAME

COLOMBIA

FRENCH GUIANA

ECUADOR

PERU

B R A Z I L

BOLIVIA

*PACIFIC
OCEAN*

PARAGUAY

CHILE

*ATLANTIC
OCEAN*

URUGUAY

ARGENTINA

SOUTH AMERICA

FALKLAND
ISLANDS

Cape Horn

LATIN AMERICA

No single event more epitomized this pattern than the 1954 U.S. intervention in Guatemala, one of the poorest and most repressive states in Latin America. For decades, the country's large and productive agricultural plantations had been controlled by a small elite who maintained closer contacts with U.S. banks and corporations than with the landless *campesinos* who made up more than 90 percent of Guatemala's population. Thus it should have come as no surprise when democratic reforms in the country produced opposition leaders who sought to abolish this system.

The United States, though preoccupied with fighting World War II, viewed warily the spreading protests against Guatemala's dictator, Gen. Jorge Ubico. Outrage against Ubico's repressive rule led to his downfall in 1944 and his replacement by Juan José Arévalo, a popular schoolteacher and political activist who became the first democratically elected leader in Guatemala's history. Arévalo was successful at first in instituting reforms, but his supporters soon fragmented into several competing factions. As the Cold War settled in, the political climate in the country became more ideologically charged, and in the elections of 1950 a more radical leftist candidate, Jacobo Arbenz Guzmán, gained power and promised more sweeping reforms.

Arbenz, who received support from a growing Communist Party in Guatemala, attempted to take over many of the plantations and give the land, including 225,000 acres owned by the U.S.-based United Fruit Company, to the peasants. Fearing that such drastic "land reform" would provoke further uprisings elsewhere in Central America and threaten U.S. control of the Panama Canal, the Eisenhower administration supported a plan to overthrow Arbenz. After Arbenz provided the pretext needed by the United States in 1954—the importation of weapons from Czechoslovakia—the Central Intelligence Agency (CIA) executed its military coup. Within days, Arbenz was removed from power, his reforms were abolished, the military regained control of the *campesinos,* and the United States reinforced its image as an enemy of revolution in Latin America.[14]

In this context the rise of Fidel Castro became almost inevitable, and, as noted in Chapter 4, his image as a leader who directly challenged and overcame U.S. hegemony was firmly established in the early 1960s. His influence was thought to depend on two elements. The first element was how the Latin American governments would react to Castroism—whether they would undertake large-scale social and economic reforms or cling to their privileges. Public pressure for change was rising, but

14. For an elaboration, see Stephen Schlesinger and Stephen Kinzer, *Bitter Fruit* (Garden City, N.Y.: Anchor Press, 1982).

would this change be revolutionary or evolutionary? If the ruling classes remained as hostile to reform and as irresponsible toward public welfare as in the past, Castro might be able to export his revolution. Wherever there was social injustice, destruction of the *ancien régime* appeared to be the only way to have a piece of land, enough food, or a job. Revolution and a "radical solution" became the only hope for a better life.

The second element affecting the success of Castroism was the effectiveness of U.S. policy aimed at alleviating the conditions that fostered popular resentment in Latin America. Whether the United States had the will to guide this kind of revolution, however, was another matter. This task required American acceptance of noncommunist, left-wing movements and the expropriation of American property, neither of which would be easy because of the identification of reform with revolution and revolution with communism. Moreover, the United States was expected to invest billions of dollars in the Latin American economies to foster a self-sustaining rate of economic growth, to develop conditions in which private capital would be attracted to projects other than the extraction of raw materials or growth of single exportable crops, and to aid in the transformation of less-developed societies into modern, industrialized nations. In addition, Latin America's projected rapid increase of population lent urgency to development.

To meet this challenge, President John Kennedy, soon after assuming office in 1961, established the Alliance for Progress. He pledged $20 billion of primarily public money over the next decade to Latin America, and, even more significant, he emphasized the need for social change. Through the Peace Corps and other innovations, Kennedy hoped to revitalize Franklin Roosevelt's aspiration to make the United States a "good neighbor" of Latin America. Kennedy realized that, in the absence of such an effort, the possibilities of economic development were slight and the prospects of additional communist insurgencies were strong.

Castro's influence was illustrated by the U.S. intervention in the Dominican Republic. The impetus for this event was the overthrow in 1961 of Rafaél Trujillo, who had ruled as a dictator for thirty-one years. Following a brief period of political turmoil, Juan Bosch, a man of genuinely democratic convictions, was elected president. Seven months later, Bosch was overthrown by a military coup d'état whose leaders announced that they would reestablish a "rightist state." In April 1965 the pro-Bosch forces revolted against this right-wing military government. Communists were thought to be active in the movement against the junta, and Washington feared they would create a second Cuba in the hemisphere. But the rebels claimed their revolution was led by noncommunists who only sought a return to constitutional government. Before the evidence was clear that the revolution was in fact communist-

controlled, President Lyndon Johnson ordered American armed intervention.

The Dominican intervention demonstrated how obsessed the
Alliance for Progress was with Castro. Without him there likely would
have been no large-scale efforts to seek the democratic development of
Latin America. The overt U.S. intervention—the first in fifty years in
Latin America—therefore undermined the Alliance for Progress, which
had tried to persuade the region's ruling elites to undertake reforms if
they wished to avoid revolutionary violence. Latin America's ruling
classes could now relax because there was an alternative: American
intervention would save them from the consequences of their own folly
in holding onto an unjust way of life. Thus American policy south of the
U.S. border, as in other areas of the world, continued to be dictated by
the bipolar global struggle.

In Latin America, then, as in Africa and the Middle East, the globalization of containment had profound consequences. As many critics of
the policy feared, the United States gradually became immersed in civil
wars and regional conflicts far from its shores.[15] But American leaders,
bound by the logic of containment and fearful of "losing ground" to the
communists—whenever that was—stayed loyal to the policy. Their
strategy would lead to the calamitous U.S. intervention in Vietnam,
where the faltering consensus in the United States favoring global containment would be put to the ultimate test.

15. In so doing, American leaders routinely violated the democratic values they supposedly were promoting, and they turned their presumed beneficiaries—the Third World masses—against the United States.

Slogging through an abandoned rice paddy, the U.S. military carries out a search-and-destroy mission against the guerrillas. Such operations rarely worked and the Viet Cong invariably returned after the Americans left.

CHAPTER SIX

Vietnam and the Cost of Containment

The wreckage of World War II yielded to a more stable international order in the late 1940s and 1950s—but one increasingly split between two rival blocs. In this bipolar world the United States and the Soviet Union, through their allies and proxies, confronted one another indirectly in almost every region of th e world. In a series of actions and reactions they drew "frontiers" between their spheres of influence and extended their competition to remote areas of otherwise marginal concern.

By virtue of the zero-sum, all-or-nothing nature of bipolarity, both great powers always were alert to the slightest shifts in power lest such shifts upset the equilibrium to give the adversary superiority. A gain of power and security for one was perceived as a loss of power and security for the other, and the opponent's moves, even if alleged to be defensive, were interpreted to be deliberate and offensive. Similarly, developments in regions of otherwise marginal importance were ranked as significant and countered because such regions were seen as symbolically vital, and because their allegiance might tip the scales in favor of one or the other superpower. The bipolar superpower competition thus consisted of defining the frontiers around the U.S. and Soviet spheres of influence and then guarding this territorial status quo against encroachment, subversion, or defection.

VIETNAM AS A 'FRONTIER WAR'

U.S. involvement in Southeast Asia stemmed from the belief of American leaders that the seventeenth parallel dividing North Vietnam from South Vietnam represented a frontier between the free world and the communist world (see Chapter 4). Just as these leaders had decided to defend South Korea when North Korea crossed the thirty-eighth parallel, so they now decided to come to the assistance of South Vietnam. Also like the war in Korea, the Vietnam War was fought at a great distance from the United States, in a place where the frontier was very accessible to the enemy.

But that was only one of the problems the United States encountered in Southeast Asia in the late 1950s. Vietnam was a divided society: North against South; Buddhists against Catholics; lowlanders against montagnards; and peasants against urban dwellers. Moreover, loyalties were primarily local and hostility to the central government ran deep because, as in most developing countries, the government historically had been that of the colonial power, represented at the local level by the tax collector and recruiting sergeant. Transportation and communication were primitive and industrial development nonexistent. In addition, this new state had emerged from the 1954 Geneva conference that had ended the first Indochina war between France and the Vietminh forces. Thus South Vietnam had no established political institutions and a precarious economy. Because that same Geneva agreement called for a general election to be held in 1954, the communist rebels (the Vietminh, or Viet Cong) expected South Vietnam to collapse. Hanoi assumed that a majority of the twelve million South Vietnamese would vote for Ho Chi Minh, who had led the nationalist struggle against the French. When those votes were added to most of the North's fifteen million votes, the country would be reunited under communist control.

But Ho's popularity was the reason that neither the United States nor the new government in the South favored the election. The United States wanted the seventeenth parallel to be accepted as the new frontier, and the president of South Vietnam, Ngo Dinh Diem, a fervent Catholic and anticommunist, wanted to stay in power. In fact, their opposition was so decisive—whether the unsigned Geneva dec-

THE VIETNAM WAR

laration mandating the election was politically binding or not—that Hanoi's chances for a peaceful takeover of the South ended, and so did its stance of reasonableness and restraint. At the time of the Geneva settlement, approximately five to six thousand local guerrillas, presumably the Vietminh's political and military elite, had gone underground and had begun to live like peasants. About ninety thousand went north; many later infiltrated South Vietnam. In 1959 the North Vietnamese began the armed struggle in the South. The second Indochina war had started.

This war, in short, began quite differently from the Korean War. Korea had begun with a clear-cut, aggressive attack, which had aroused the American public and united the principal Western allies against the common threat. It also was a conventional war in which regular communist forces were checked by regular South Korean, American, and United Nations troops. By contrast, the French defeat at Dienbienphu in 1954 was a decisive moment in contemporary history because it demonstrated that guerrilla warfare could win against a larger, stronger, conventionally equipped army of even a major power. An internal uprising of guerrillas, directed and organized by the North, was therefore a shrewder manner of "crossing" the seventeenth parallel. It would lend the resulting struggle the aura of a civil war, which would make it less likely that the United States would come to the assistance of South Vietnam because of American doubts about the morality and wisdom of military involvement in such a conflict. Diem's increasingly autocratic rule and his failure to enlist the support of his population, especially the peasantry, through political, social, and economic reforms helped to prepare the ground for a successful guerrilla campaign and lent support to the view of the conflict as a civil war. It certainly provided the Viet Cong with fertile ground to mobilize support.

Another reason for U.S. involvement in Vietnam: the war was seen in Washington as a test of its will, and meeting the test was believed to be necessary to maintain all frontiers. Until the noncommunist states of the area became more economically developed and possessed stable political systems and military defenses, the Asian balance depended on the United States. Commitments—and the administrations of Dwight Eisenhower, John Kennedy, and Lyndon Johnson all considered the United States to be committed to the defense of South Vietnam—were interdependent. The United States could not choose to defend West Berlin and Quemoy but not Matsu and South Korea—that is, Washington believed that it could no more forgo the defense of the frontier in South Vietnam than in Greece and Turkey, in Western Europe and Berlin, or in Korea and Cuba. If one country fell, it would, in its turn, knock down the next one and so on down the line like a row of dominoes. The political and psychological impacts of an American pullout would be felt throughout the area, if not in other regions, and the series of losses would upset the balance of power. As all commitments were viewed as interdependent, being unfaithful to one risked the collapse of all. The memory of Munich and the appeasement of Nazi Germany, which had failed to avert World War II, was a stark reminder that to fight on the periphery now would prevent a bigger war later.

The assumptions underlying this viewpoint, of course, were that the world was still bipolar and that the enemy was the Sino-Soviet bloc, which the United States continued to perceive as united, despite increasing evidence to the contrary. Signs of differences between the Soviet Union and China were generally explained as tactical differences about how the "communist world" should wage its "war" against the United States, not as fundamental conflicts of national interests between the two powers. Even if these had been recognized, it probably would not have made much difference because "Red China," with its population approaching one billion and its revolutionary rhetoric denouncing "American imperialism," was viewed by Washington as far more militant and dangerous than Moscow. Ho Chi Minh and the Viet Cong were seen as puppets of China, applying Mao Zedong's guerrilla warfare tactics to destroy a noncommunist government in a country within the American sphere of influence. If they succeeded, Vietnam would be added to China's power and thus to the Sino-Soviet bloc's power; it also would be an example to other revolutionary forces in Asia and elsewhere that the United States, despite its nuclear weapons, could be defeated. As for the nature of the warfare itself, Washington saw the North's war against the South as aggression similar to North Korea's against South Korea, even if North Vietnamese forces had not flagrantly crossed the seventeenth parallel. To American military commanders the war in the South was just another variant of conventional warfare which they felt their well-trained forces and superior firepower could defeat.

There was a double irony to this pattern of thinking. First, if the United States had had diplomats in Beijing, they would have known that North Vietnam was not a puppet: historically China and Vietnam often had been enemies, and in the early 1960s the last thing Mao wanted, with China in the midst of a domestic upheaval, was to risk a confrontation with the United States. Thus the United States, not aware of the political situation or China's intentions—as was the case for China's earlier intervention in Korea—once again paid a high price for its refusal to recognize the mainland regime. Second, if the containment of China had been a key goal of the U.S. intervention, then the United States should have let South Vietnam fall. Ho was a nationalist, not just a communist, and a united communist and nationalistic Vietnam would have proven

a stronger barrier to any possible Chinese ambitions of hegemony in
Southeast Asia than a noncommunist South Vietnam governed by an
unpopular regime.

In truth, then, the Vietnam War, undertaken in the name of containment, undermined containment. The beneficiary of this effort was the
Soviet Union, America's primary enemy, which was able to focus its
resources on first catching up with and then surpassing the United States
in nuclear weapons. Because of the popular backlash to the war and to
military spending, the United States fell behind in the strategic buildup
during the 1970s. Indeed, the key domino that fell was not South Vietnam but American public opinion.

THE PERILS OF INCREMENTALISM

The massive U.S. intervention in Vietnam by President Lyndon Johnson was by 1965 inevitable because, starting with the administration of
Harry Truman, every president had deepened the involvement in Vietnam. Although Truman at first opposed France's postwar efforts to
restore its colonial rule, he changed his position to overcome French
resistance to the American plan for the revival of Germany, especially its
rearmament. After the Korean War erupted, the French war in Indochina became part of the global struggle against communism. At the time
of France's defeat at Dienbienphu in 1954, Eisenhower, though deciding
not to intervene militarily, backed the new government in South Vietnam, organized after France's defeat and withdrawal, with economic
assistance and military training for its armed forces. But this training
was in orthodox warfare, not in the unorthodox or guerrilla warfare that
already had been observed in Vietnam. Besides, the Southeast Asia
Treaty Organization (SEATO) was supposed to be the new state's security guarantee (see Chapter 4). Kennedy escalated the U.S. commitment
in the early 1960s by sending in 16,500 military advisers to help the South
Vietnamese army. Beginning in the spring of 1965, Johnson transformed
this commitment—and the conflict in general—by sending in 500,000
American troops.

Particularly significant during the years of piecemeal commitments
was that at no point did policy makers in Washington resolve some basic
questions about Vietnam: Was it vital to American security interests
and, if so, how vital? If it had been vital earlier, was it still so in the early
1960s? Could the situation in South Vietnam be saved militarily given
the nature of the Saigon government and its seeming lack of popular
support? If American forces were sent, then in what numbers? And how
could they be used effectively in an unorthodox type of war? What cost,
if any, was South Vietnam "worth" to the United States?

Because incremental U.S. commitments were made whenever conditions in South Vietnam appeared ominous, these questions were never really debated at the highest levels of the government. And if the reasons for American involvement were not clear to leaders, they were lost entirely on millions of citizens. But past American commitments foreclosed any meaningful debate except over how much force was needed to save South Vietnam.

During the Kennedy years, military advisers managed to prevent South Vietnam's total collapse, but by 1965 Johnson—who after Kennedy's assassination had concentrated on passing a major domestic reform program and getting reelected—could no longer operate on this basis and avoid the central question of what the United States ought to do. South Vietnam was about to be cut in two, and the Viet Cong would then be in a position to mop up first one part and then the other. In the face of this reality Johnson sent in 200,000 troops that year, deepening U.S. involvement and turning an incremental policy into a long-term commitment. After years of neglect and procrastination and with the situation growing worse daily, Washington had neither the time nor the inclination to make a carefully calculated decision; when the crucial decision was made, it was made by Johnson, a new president, on the advice of the Kennedy staff and cabinet he had inherited. Long-range policy had become the prisoner of a number of earlier short-range decisions made to tackle crises. Johnson's misfortune was that he could not procrastinate or make more piecemeal moves. He was stuck with the decision of whether to escalate to prevent the defeat of the South Vietnamese army or to become, as he phrased it, the first president in U.S. history "to lose a war." Each president had done just enough to prevent this defeat. Johnson's escalation was the logical culmination of his predecessors' decisions.

But perhaps even more important than foreign policy considerations was American domestic politics. Originally, in 1947, anticommunism often was used as a means of arousing the public and mobilizing popular support for Cold War policies while the nation in fact pursued more limited aims. But once an administration had justified its policy in terms of an anticommunist crusade and had aroused the public by promising to stop communism, it opened itself to attacks by the opposition party if setbacks were encountered, even if they occurred for reasons beyond America's ability to prevent them. The out-party could then exploit such foreign policy issues by accusing the in-party of appeasement, of having "lost" this or that country, and of being "soft on communism." This sort of accusation made it difficult to recognize the People's Republic of China, to build bridges to Eastern Europe, to negotiate with the Soviet Union or Cuba, and especially to discriminate between areas of vital and secondary importance to U.S. security.

Democratic administrations were more deeply affected by this political rhetoric than Republican administrations. The Democrats, who were in power when Nationalist China collapsed, were accused of "treason," of "selling out" China, and they lost the 1952 presidential election as a result. The desire to avoid accusations of being soft on communism had been one key reason why Truman advanced northward across the thirty-eighth parallel in Korea before the 1950 midterm elections and made it impossible for him to negotiate any settlement of the war that left Korea divided. The wish to avoid similar accusations made it impossible for John Kennedy, who had campaigned on a tough anti-Castro platform, to reject the Eisenhower-initiated plan to invade Cuba, even though the new president had serious doubts about it. It led the Kennedy and Johnson administrations to make their piecemeal commitments in Vietnam, lest the Democrats be charged with the "loss" of Indochina as well as China, and it influenced Lyndon Johnson to bomb North Vietnam and to escalate the war by sending in the army. Even Eisenhower, a conservative Republican president and victorious general who had led the Allies to victory over Germany, a man who hardly could be accused of disloyalty, had felt threatened enough by the right wing of the Republican Party that in 1954 he did not pull the United States out of Vietnam. Instead, he kept America in Vietnam by supporting the new South Vietnamese government.

Each president thought each step in the growing involvement in Indochina to be less costly than doing nothing and disengaging from Vietnam. In the context of U.S. politics, defeat was believed to be unacceptable. The costs of nonintervention in terms of loss of public and congressional support were calculated to be much higher than the costs of intervention.

These examples illustrate the high price the United States consistently paid for its penchant to crusade and to moralize power politics: overreaction, diplomatic rigidity, and overt or covert interventions, with the attendant loss of lives and credibility of the policy and of the United States in general. National style was a principal cause of the long delay in recognizing China and the failure to exploit Sino-Soviet differences. Worse, it was the main reason for misunderstanding Asian communism, including the war in Vietnam. It was certainly a key reason, if not *the* reason, for the protracted intervention. Because the domestic costs of losing a country to communism were so high, those in power felt compelled to intervene with the air force, navy, and army to avoid such losses. The desire to avoid accusations of appeasement, of betraying the nation's honor, and of weakening its security was keenly felt. This was especially true just before elections, and there was always an election coming up.

THE MISCONDUCT OF GUERRILLA WARFARE

During its intervention in Southeast Asia, the United States virtually ignored the political structure of South Vietnam, which was the key to the successful use of American arms. For years the United States had supported Ngo Dinh Diem, a devout Catholic whose authoritarian rule and aloofness from the mainly Buddhist population had alienated most of it. By the time the military overthrew and murdered Diem in 1963, with Kennedy's knowledge and tacit blessing, the Viet Cong already controlled much of South Vietnam; the social, political, and economic reforms needed to win the war had been neglected too long. That Diem's regime was so widely despised should have alerted future administrations; that Kennedy had said Diem had "gotten out of touch with the people" testified to the political bankruptcy in Saigon, as well as to the questionable wisdom of having begun the military intervention in the first place. Even with Diem gone, South Vietnam's governments were unable to rally popular support for a vigorous prosecution of the war against the Viet Cong.

But Saigon's succession of corrupt, reactionary, and repressive regimes apparently never reminded U.S. policy makers of Chiang Kai-shek and his Nationalist government in postwar China. At the time of China's fall, the Truman administration had decided China could not be saved, except perhaps—and it was only *perhaps*—by incurring enormous military and economic costs, which it felt the American public would not be willing to pay. In addition, these costs would have diverted the nation's resources and efforts from its area of primary interest in Europe where American security was at stake. In Dean Acheson's words, as noted before: "Nothing that this country did or could have done within the *reasonable* limits of its capabilities" could have changed the result in the conflict between Mao Zedong and Chiang Kai-shek.[1] In short, containment could not be achieved through a sieve. By attempting containment in South Vietnam, Truman's successors in Democratic administrations risked major domestic discontent. They also risked a public questioning the fundamental assumptions of the foreign policy that had led to the war.

Certainly the possibility of achieving a quick victory over the Viet Cong was remote, for guerrilla warfare is totally different from traditional warfare. The militarily weaker side resorts to guerrilla tactics because it has no other options. The aim of a guerrilla war is to capture the government from within and to do so by eroding the morale of the

---

1. Italics added. U.S. Department of State, *United States Relations with China* (Washington, D.C.: Government Printing Office, 1949), xvi.

army and by undermining popular confidence in the government, thus isolating it. To achieve this objective, guerrilla forces do not have to inflict a complete defeat on the government's forces or compel them to surrender unconditionally. Indeed, until the final stage of the war guerrillas do not even meet these forces openly, and then they do so only to apply the *coup de grâce*. A guerrilla war is therefore a protracted conflict in which the guerrillas use hit-and-run tactics—here, there, everywhere—and engage only those smaller and weaker government forces they can defeat. To cope with this strategy year in and year out, the government's troops must be dispersed to guard every town, every village, and every bridge against possible attack. Unable to come to grips with the enemy and defeat it in battle, and suffering one small loss after another, the army becomes demoralized and its mood becomes defensive.

Although such tactics gradually weaken the military strength of the army, the guerrillas' main effort is directed at the civilian population. As the weaker side of the conflict, the guerrillas aim to wrest the allegiance of the population away from the government so that, without popular support, the government simply collapses. The guerrillas do this in two ways. First, by increasing their control of the countryside, where most of the people live, and by winning battles with government forces, they demonstrate to the peasants that the government cannot protect them. The execution of village chiefs, who are often government representatives, proves this most vividly. Second, and even more important, the guerrillas exploit any existing popular grievances. Communist guerrillas do not pose as communists, and they do not usually receive support because they are communists. The populace supports them because it believes the guerrillas will oust the government with which it is dissatisfied and that a new government will meet its aspirations.

Indeed, according to Mao Zedong, guerrillas need the people "just as fish need water"; without popular support, the guerrillas would not receive recruits, food, shelter, and information on the deployment of government forces. The guerrillas gain the support of the peasantry by successfully representing themselves as the liberators from colonialism or foreign rule, native despotic governments, economic deprivation, or social injustice. In this way they isolate the government in its own country. Thus, unlike conventional warfare in which each army seeks the destruction of the other's military forces, guerrilla warfare is based on a strategy of mobilizing popular support. A government that has the allegiance of its population does not provide fertile soil for guerrillas; where social dissatisfaction exists, however, guerrillas find an opening.

This is especially the case when the combatants in such conflicts oppose foreign troops whom they believe wrongly occupy their territory and must be expelled. European powers, including the French in Vietnam, were the targets of such uprisings during the colonial period, and the United States was widely perceived as carrying on France's imperial ambitions. In such cases guerrillas are able to exploit the existing deep reservoir of hostility toward the foreign armies, along with the tactical advantage of fighting in their own familiar surroundings. Together these factors place the occupying forces on the defensive and lead to a high level of confidence and *esprit de corps* among guerrilla fighters. As one scholar observed,

> The guerrilla's self image is not of a solitary fighter hiding among the people, but of a whole people mobilized for war, himself a loyal member, one among many. If you want to fight against us, the guerrillas say, you are going to have to fight civilians, for you are not at war with an army but with a nation. Therefore, you should not fight at all, and if you do, you are the barbarians, killing women and children.[2]

Guerrilla warfare is therefore not purely military; it also is political. Although the forces under attack must try to defeat the guerrillas in the field, their principal task is to tackle the political, social, and economic conditions that breed support for the guerrillas in the first place, to regain the "hearts and minds" of the populace. Counterguerrilla warfare, then, is an extremely difficult form of war to wage—far more so than the traditional clash of armies—because the war cannot be won without thoroughgoing reforms. Yet these reforms have to be carried out in the midst of a war that is likely to last many years.

What all this means is that the United States, experienced only in "conventional warfare," found such a war extremely difficult to fight in Southeast Asia. A war that was concerned primarily with social and political reforms ran counter to the traditional American military strategy. The length of such a war caused great frustration because the U.S. government, under intense public pressure, repeatedly promised that the war would end soon, that its leaders saw "light at the end of the tunnel." When this very different kind of warfare did not yield swift and successful results, U.S. troops faced the choice of either pulling out or seeking some shortcut to victory through military escalation.

THE MILITARY BATTLEFIELD: VIETNAM

During the war in Vietnam, American policy makers misplaced their confidence in U.S. military prowess and its ability to change the guerrillas' "rules of the game." In 1965 the illusion of American omnipotence had not yet died. After all, the United States had successfully confronted the Soviet Union in Cuba and compelled it to back down. Could there really be much doubt that its well-trained generals, in command of

---

2. Michael Walzer, *Just and Unjust Wars* (New York: Basic Books, 1977), 180.

armies equipped with the newest and latest weapons from America's industry and under the leadership of that most efficient Pentagon manager, Secretary of Defense Robert McNamara, would be able to beat a few thousand "peasants in black pajamas"? With its sizable forces and its superior mobility and firepower, why should the United States have any problem finding the enemy's troops and destroying them, thereby compelling that enemy to desist from taking over South Vietnam? Characteristically, then, the emphasis was strictly military.

In Vietnam the kind of war being waged required forces to secure villages and to stay in them to root out the Viet Cong and show the villagers that Saigon did care about them. Instead, the military carried out massive search-and-destroy operations. And the guerrillas, even if driven away from the villages, returned after the helicopters had left and continued to control the countryside. Because such large-scale operations could not be launched without preparation at the base camp and usually were preceded by air strikes and artillery bombardments of the area in which the troops would land, the Viet Cong often disappeared and the whole operation ended in frustration.

American soldiers clearly did not understand the political nature of guerrilla warfare. They had been trained for conventional battle and to use maximum firepower to wear the enemy down in a war of attrition. The military was confident it could do this because its helicopters provided superior mobility and modern technology gave it the necessary firepower. The measure of success became the daily body count of communist dead.

When the war was extended by air to the North, the purpose of the bombing clearly was not military, although the United States claimed its goal was to stem the flow of men and supplies going south. The aim of the attacks was political—to persuade North Vietnam to stop the war. The gradual extension of these attacks was intended to stress that the United States meant to protect South Vietnam and would not withdraw, that the price Hanoi might have to pay for victory would be too high, and therefore that it had better desist.

But the bombing did not weaken Hanoi's will to prosecute the war, nor did it cut the supplies sufficiently to hamper the fighting in the South or greatly reduce troop infiltration.[3] Hanoi's persistence, in turn, led to increased military and political calls for more air strikes and new targets. Those who advocated intensifying the air war did not acknowledge that air power could not by itself win the war; instead, they insist-

---

3. Once again, important historical lessons were ignored. The sustained American attacks on Chinese supply lines in North Korea during the Korean War had shown that air power alone was unable to stop the flow of supplies to the fighting zone.

ed that it could if it were used with maximum efficiency. Air power, in short, came to be seen by some as an efficient, effective way of fighting the guerrillas, throttling their supply lines, breaking their morale, and finally compelling them to end the conflict at little cost in lives to the defender.[4]

This objective, however, remained unattainable. Even the more stable military regime of Nguyen Van Thieu and Nguyen Cao Ky, which sought to legitimate itself in the election of 1967, failed to implement a program of social and economic reform until 1970 when it adopted a major land reform program. It was particularly remiss in not earlier redistributing land from the usually absentee landlords to the peasants. Without such reforms, the Viet Cong grew stronger. Militarily, every increase in American forces was met by increased infiltrations of both guerrillas and conventional troops from the North to the South. Nevertheless, the U.S. government issued optimistic battle reports and forecasts of victory on a regular basis.

The 1968 Tet (or Vietnamese New Year) offensive, launched on the last day of January, was the Johnson administration's Dienbienphu. Tet showed once and for all—and Americans could see it nightly on their television sets—that, despite the repeated optimistic predictions, the enemy had again been badly underestimated. It had launched a major countrywide offensive and attacked Saigon, Hué, and every other provincial capital; a Viet Cong squad had even penetrated the U.S. embassy compound, thereby scoring a significant symbolic victory. The fighting that followed, however, was bloody and destructive of the Viet Cong. In fact, so many Viet Cong were killed that afterward the North Vietnamese army actually assumed the main burden of fighting the Americans. Nevertheless, the Viet Cong clearly had demonstrated that neither an American army of a half million men nor the far larger South Vietnamese army could give the people living in the urban areas security—and the communists presumably already controlled much of the countryside.

THE POLITICAL BATTLEFIELD: THE UNITED STATES

In Vietnam, then, American power and its effectiveness in unorthodox warfare were shown to be greatly exaggerated. Tactically, American forces had seized and retained the offensive, claiming the destruction of large numbers of enemy soldiers. But strategically the Viet Cong had main-

---

4. Secretary McNamara and his top aides confidently defended this strategy by using advanced computer models and cost-benefit calculations to predict victory, most of which were proven wrong in the context of guerrilla warfare. See David Halberstam, *The Best and the Brightest* (New York: Random House, 1972).

tained the upper hand, and the Americans were on the defensive. For example, by using about 80 percent of their forces to find and destroy North Vietnamese troops in the relatively unpopulated central highlands and frontier regions, the Americans were unable to secure and protect the 90 percent of the population living in the Mekong Delta and coastal plains. The pursuit of victory through physical attrition could not be transformed into military or political advantages. Indeed, in question was not just America's protective capacity but also its wisdom. Having left the cities unprotected, except for elements of the South Vietnamese army, allied forces had to fight their way back into the hearts of the various cities and towns the Viet Cong had infiltrated. Thus if after almost three years of American help South Vietnam was still that insecure and the enemy that strong, the wisdom of continuing the war, let alone sending further American reinforcements, was bound to be intensely debated.

As if this were not enough, many Americans perceived the war to be morally ambiguous, if not downright immoral. There had never been a clear-cut crossing of the seventeenth parallel dividing North Vietnam and South Vietnam, which made the accusation that Hanoi was an aggressor less believable. The undemocratic Saigon government and its apparent lack of popularity gave credence to the view of the war as a rebellion or civil war against Saigon's repression.[5] The massive, sometimes indiscriminate use of American firepower, which led to the widespread destruction of civilian life; the creation of thousands of refugees; and, especially, the hostility of the peasants, whose support was vital for military success—these things and more already had pricked the consciences of many Americans concerned about their nation's historic image as compassionate and humane. The tanks rumbling into cities after Tet, the divebombing of apartment houses, the civilian suffering, and the personal tragedies left television viewers—who saw only one side of the war and not, for example, the Viet Cong's deliberate slaughter of thousands of professional people and bureaucrats in the city of Hué—asking themselves if there was any point in "destroying a country in order to defend it."

Within the United States the Tet offensive aroused antiwar feelings, which had been growing throughout 1967 as the war continued, seemingly without end. Johnson's initial support eroded on both the right and the left, with the right demanding an end to the war through escalation and the left seeking an end through deescalation, if not withdrawal. The articulate opposition to the conflict expressed by a number

5. Interestingly, in 1950 the South Korean government had a similar autocratic reputation, but the attack across the thirty-eighth parallel focused attention on North Korean ambitions and justified the American intervention. No one in the United States raised questions about defending a "corrupt dictatorship."

of liberal and moderate Republican and Democratic senators, especially the chairman of the Senate Foreign Relations Committee, J. William Fulbright, lent respectability to the opposition also vocalized by many politicians, professors, students, journalists, editorial writers, and television commentators. Indeed, after Tet Fulbright and his committee became an alternative source of interpretation and policy recommendations for the president.

Thus, although the Viet Cong were virtually destroyed during the Tet fighting, the United States suffered a political defeat. The guerrilla strategy of psychologically exhausting the opponent succeeded; the American strategy of physical attrition failed. The U.S. military won all the battles, including Tet, but lost the war as the public grew tired of it. Indeed, policy makers learned quickly that during such hostilities politics go on as usual, with most domestic interest groups pursuing their specific sets of interests and preferences; butter is not automatically subordinated to guns. But, as the costs of a conflict rise in terms of lives, inflation, and taxes, public disaffection also grows. So do antiwar demonstrations and parades, some of which in the 1960s spilled over into violent clashes with the police and supporters of the war.

The Vietnam War, then, involved two battlefields. The first, in Vietnam, was bloody but inconclusive militarily. The second, in the United States, was not bloody but it was decisive politically. As the war dragged on, the nation's will to continue it declined, unlike in the two world wars (total wars) when the United States sensed that its security, if not its survival, was at stake, and thus all issues were subordinated to the prosecution of the war. In a limited war important issues may be at stake, but the security threat to the United States may not be apparent. How could the loss of South Korea or South Vietnam have diminished U.S. security? Neither North Korea nor North Vietnam could invade the United States.

The guerrillas were well aware of the two battlefields and of which one was more important. Gen. Vo Nguyen Giap, the North Vietnamese strategist who had overseen his country's victories against France and the United States, spoke of the impatience of democracies at war. He saw that a strategy in which the war never seemed to end, in which the minimum purpose was simply not to lose, would eventually erode the opponents' will to continue. As the war dragged on and as the casualties and costs mounted, the democracies would throw in the towel. It was their "home fronts" that were decisive, where the "real battle" would be won. For that reason, the Tet offensive was deliberately launched as the 1968 political primaries were about to begin in the United States, where opposition to the war had become widespread.[6]

6. See Stanley Karnow, *Vietnam: A History* (New York: Penguin, 1983), 558–566.

Disagreement over the war led two senators from the president's party, Eugene McCarthy and Robert Kennedy, to contest Johnson's renomination as the Democratic standard-bearer. Running as "peace candidates," they provided a rallying point for the growing numbers of Americans disenchanted with the war. Then in March 1968, at the end of the speech that laid the basis for the Paris peace talks, the president announced that he would not run for a second term. Lyndon Johnson's tragedy was that he had come into office seeking a "great society" in America; instead, the war destroyed him. The changing American mood was evident in the 1968 presidential campaign. Vice President Hubert Humphrey, nominated by the Democrats in Chicago after bloody clashes between police and antiwar students (many of them McCarthy supporters) and bitter disagreement among the delegates over the Vietnam platform, was mercilessly heckled during most of the campaign. As a member of the administration, he found it difficult to disavow the war; when he took his own "risk for peace," it was very late in the campaign.

In these circumstances of Democratic disunity, former vice president Richard Nixon, a career anticommunist and the Republican nominee, found it inexpedient to charge the Democrats with a "no-win" policy; instead he softened his views on the war. Indeed, in his speeches the menace abroad suddenly ran a poor second to the "moral decay" at home. Generally both candidates fell over themselves in their eagerness to abandon both anticommunist slogans and the war, offering instead hopes for an "honorable" peace in Vietnam and for "law and order" at home. Halting communist aggression was abandoned as an issue; stopping further costly foreign adventures—"no more Vietnams"—became the new issue. In Vietnam the only question was when to get out and on what terms. By not losing, the North Vietnamese had won; by not winning, the United States had indeed lost.

DISENGAGEMENT FROM VIETNAM

Before the relationships among the United States, the Soviet Union, and China could be reshaped, the United States had to unburden itself of the Vietnam War. Vietnam was a drain on U.S. resources and a political albatross for Nixon, who was reelected in 1972. But in their thinking about acceptable terms for withdrawal, Nixon and his national security adviser, Henry Kissinger, were heavily influenced by their perceptions of great-power relationships. One course open to Nixon, which would have brought him popular acclaim, was to pull out all American forces immediately on the grounds that the United States had fulfilled long enough its obligations to defend Saigon. But in the president's view the central issue was maintaining American credibility abroad.

The Nixon administration was determined that it would neither just withdraw nor accept any settlement that was tantamount to a defeat—namely, a coalition government in Saigon controlled by the communists. Nixon believed that it would not be feasible to establish a relaxation of tensions or détente with the Soviet Union and China if America's prestige—reputation for power—were tattered. Why should the Soviet Union, which was rapidly building up its strategic power, settle for parity and mutually acceptable peaceful coexistence if it sensed that America was weak and could be pushed around? Why should China tone down its revolutionary rhetoric and conduct a more traditional state-to-state diplomacy, and indeed move closer to the United States, if it could not count on American strength and determination to resist what it saw as Soviet attempts at hegemony in Asia? In short, Nixon calculated that the country had to "hang tough" in Vietnam to normalize relations with the Soviet Union and China.

Nixon and Kissinger therefore devised a twofold strategy. First, American ground troops were to be withdrawn gradually to reduce the costs of the war and make further hostilities tolerable for the "silent majority," which Nixon felt was loyal, although fatigued, and would support him in an "honorable" ending of the war. But Nixon hoped the continued involvement of some U.S. forces, especially in the air, would provide an incentive for Hanoi to negotiate an end to the war. This incentive would presumably be all the stronger if the president's strategy worked at home—that is, if it removed Vietnam as a principal issue in the next election and facilitated Nixon's reelection. Hanoi, then confronted with the prospect that the war could last longer than four more years, would have a reason to settle the war diplomatically.

The second part of the president's policy was the "Vietnamization" of the war. As American troops were withdrawn, South Vietnam's forces would receive better training and modern arms so that they could take over the ground fighting. This would counter the criticisms and pressures that had multiplied in Congress, on campuses, and elsewhere for faster U.S. troop withdrawals and for the abandonment of Saigon. But the danger inherent in the president's strategy was that the North Vietnamese would attack after American troops were withdrawn but before the South Vietnamese were ready to meet the enemy in battle.

In March 1970 Cambodia's Prince Norodom Sihanouk, who had long tolerated the communist troops and supply lines in his country, was overthrown by an anti-Vietnamese military regime that wanted communist troops out of Cambodia. When the communists moved toward the Cambodian capital to unseat the new government, Nixon decided to intervene and, without public knowledge, ordered air strikes deep into Cambodia. Once this became known, it reignited domestic dissension.

After four protesters at Kent State University were shot to death on May 4 by Ohio National Guardsmen, many campuses erupted, and dozens of colleges and universities were completely shut down. Protesters once again turned out for peaceful mass demonstrations in Washington and in other cities. The reaction to U.S. policy in Cambodia made it clear that it would be foolhardy for the president to repeat such an action.

Unfortunately, South Vietnam's decrepit army remained the key to the success of the president's strategy. In the spring of 1972, with the U.S. Army withdrawn from the battlefield, North Vietnam launched an unexpected, large-scale attack across the demilitarized zone between North Vietnam and South Vietnam. The South Vietnamese army performed poorly and only American air support staved off even worse losses.

Nixon was therefore in a quandary on the eve of a summit conference in Moscow to advance détente. The Soviet Union had supplied Hanoi with modern arms, and, whether or not it knew the date of the North Vietnamese offensive, Nixon thought the Soviet Union should have restrained its ally. As a great power, it must have known that a major South Vietnamese defeat would be humiliating to its adversary on the eve of vital negotiations from which Moscow had as much to gain as Washington. The president was unwilling to negotiate under the shadow of defeat.

With Vietnamization in danger, Nixon "re-Americanized" the war by ordering extensive bombing of the North and a blockade of North Vietnam's ports with mines. The aim was to stop the flow of Soviet and Chinese supplies. Simultaneously Nixon offered Hanoi the complete withdrawal of all American forces from Vietnam within four months if all prisoners of war were returned and an internationally supervised ceasefire were established. The communists could keep their forces in the South—a significant concession previously offered only in secret talks. Equally important, the president did not insist on the survival of Nguyen Van Thieu's government. He instead expressed hope that the U.S. withdrawal "would allow negotiations and a political settlement between the Vietnamese themselves." This new set of proposals provided a concrete and serious basis for negotiations. But Hanoi rejected the offer. It appeared to want the president to do the one thing he refused to do: guarantee communist control in Saigon. His proposal, in fact, had seemed to suggest that the North Vietnamese should do this job for themselves, if they could.

The North Vietnamese also faced a dilemma. Despite the heavy U.S. bombing and blockade, the Soviet Union had gone ahead with the summit meeting. And China no longer opposed a negotiated settlement of the war. Moscow and Beijing both gave priority to their relationships with Washington, leaving Hanoi politically isolated. Yet the North Vietnamese leaders had sought their goal of a unified Vietnam for so long, had paid such a high price for it, and had been so often cheated out of the fulfillment of their dream by their adversaries that they were suspicious of Nixon's offer and resentful of the declining Soviet and Chinese support.

But a month before the 1972 U.S. presidential election, Hanoi, probably fearing that Nixon's reelection might make him less accommodating, signaled its willingness to accept something less than a total victory. By late October Hanoi had negotiated a tentative Indochina settlement. The terms included a supervised cease-fire that would halt all American bombing and mining and bring about withdrawal of all U.S. forces within two months; separate future cease-fires were expected in Laos and Cambodia. Prisoners of war would be exchanged. A series of mixed political commissions, composed of elements from the Viet Cong, the Saigon government, and neutralists, would then be established to work out a new South Vietnamese political order leading to a new constitution and the election of a new government. Provisions and personnel were to be supplied on a one-to-one basis for both sides.

The Nixon administration felt it had achieved an "honorable peace." The North Vietnamese, after having declared for years that the Thieu government would have to go as a precondition for a cease-fire, now accepted Thieu as the leader of the government faction. Thieu remained in control of a sizable army and large police forces with which he administered most of the country and all the urban centers, leaving only minor areas and a small percentage of the population under the control of the Viet Cong and the approximately 145,000 North Vietnamese troops. The Thieu faction therefore seemed to have a good chance to compete politically and militarily with the communists after the fighting ended. But Thieu stalled in agreeing to the tentative October 1972 settlement because the United States had accepted the presence of North Vietnamese troops in areas of the South during the period of cease-fire. But even though Thieu could object, he held no veto.

When Thieu stalled, so did the North Vietnamese; both sides appeared eager to strengthen their positions as the final stage of peace talks resumed in Paris. In response, Nixon ordered some of the heaviest bombing of the North, including civilian centers in Hanoi and Haiphong. The incessant "Christmas bombings" of late 1972 continued for several days. Nixon defended the bombardment against outcries from the public and the newly elected Democratic majority in Congress. He argued that it was necessary to demonstrate American resolve against North Vietnam in the crucial final days of conflict. Simultaneously, Nixon made it clear that Thieu did not have a veto over U.S. policy.

The end of the Vietnam War came in January 1973 when the North Vietnamese returned to the negotiating table and both sides signed a cease-fire agreement at the Hotel Majestic in Paris. Twelve nations, including the United States, the Soviet Union, and China, formally approved the treaty in March. The administration could now focus its primary attention on improving relations with China and the Soviet Union, and the United States would no longer pour its resources into a war that deeply divided the country.

Two years after the Paris conference, however, North Vietnamese troops launched a final offensive against the remnants of the South Vietnamese army. Although Thieu insisted that Nixon had pledged continued U.S. support in the event of such an offensive, Nixon had resigned under the cloud of the Watergate scandal and President Gerald Ford, under great pressure from Congress and public opinion, refused to recommit American resources to Vietnam.[7] Thieu resigned on April 21, 1975, and nine days later Saigon fell to the Viet Cong as the last American officials in the city were hurriedly shuttled away by helicopter. South Vietnam then surrendered unconditionally. Twenty years after the failed Geneva accords of 1954, Vietnam was again reunited.

CONGRESS VERSUS THE 'IMPERIAL PRESIDENCY'

America's defeat in Vietnam revealed the limitations of its power and raised serious questions about its strategy of containing communism in all corners of the world. Specifically, the tragic events led lawmakers in Washington to curb presidential power in foreign policy, especially the power of the commander in chief to commit American forces to battle. Under the Constitution the president is chiefly responsible for the routine conduct of foreign policy, but the U.S. Congress shares many of these powers, including the power to "declare war." During the 1950s conservatives had wished to limit presidential authority because the president was, in their minds, not anticommunist enough, and he might, acting on the advice of the "pro-communists" in the State Department, sell the country down the river. Beginning in the late 1960s the liberals too sought to restrain the president's authority but for a different reason: in their opinion, the president, the "military-industrial complex," and the CIA were *too* anticommunist and were intent on involving the country in too many costly adventures abroad.

---

7. This scandal involved illegal activities by the Nixon administration during its 1972 reelection campaign and the elaborate means devised by Nixon to cover up these activities.

Conservative or liberal, the remedy for the "imperial presidency's" alleged abuse of its authority and its virtually solo determination of foreign policy was the same: to reassert congressional control of the formulation of external policy and to restore the constitutional balance that purportedly had been upset.[8] The president presumably would be restrained so that he could no longer, for conservatives, appease America's enemies or, for liberals, act in an interventionist, warlike manner. The abuse of power by Nixon, a conservative president who resigned his office rather than be impeached, reinforced the liberal sentiment to curb presidential powers and compel a more restrained and moderate policy.

Taking the political offensive, the U.S. Congress in 1973 passed the War Powers Act to constrain the president and assert its own constitutional authority. Under the act, which was approved over President Nixon's veto, the president is obligated to consult Congress before committing troops overseas and to report to Congress immediately afterward about the need to continue the mission. The president must terminate the mission within sixty days unless Congress agrees to extend it, a provision designed to preclude the kind of "mission creep" that occurred in Vietnam. Although rejected by later presidents as unconstitutional and rarely invoked by Congress, the War Powers Act symbolizes the national mood that blamed the war on excessive presidential power.[9]

Additional evidence of the new mood was the widespread belief that priority should be given to the nation's domestic problems. These problems became apparent in the 1960s when the "affluent society," as it was called in the 1950s, began to reveal its seamier and more violent sides, such as urban slums, air and water pollution, and the dissatisfaction of the poor and disenfranchised, who were primarily blacks and other minorities. Critics of the war wanted to spend money to improve the quality of life for all American citizens. Instead of crusading for democracy abroad, they argued, the United States should start crusading to make *America* safe for democracy. Liberal critics of the war in Vietnam quoted Edmund Burke to the effect that "example is the school of mankind." The example should be one of a democratic society protecting the rights of its citizens as its paramount task.

But such freedom could not be fully enjoyed in a nation whose excessive preoccupation with foreign affairs drained its powers and resources, both human and material. An expansionist foreign policy, it was

---

8. See Arthur Schlesinger Jr., *The Imperial Presidency* (New York: Houghton Mifflin, 1989).

9. "If events have suggested that the goal has not been reached," one scholar observed in 1990, "the [War Powers] resolution still remains as a serious legal attempt to solve an enduring dilemma." See Morris S. Ogul, "The War Powers Resolution: Congress versus the President," in *The Constitution and National Security,* ed. Howard E. Shuman and Walter R. Thomas (Washington, D.C.: National Defense University Press, 1990), 314.

charged, was unlikely to bring with it any lasting greatness, prestige, and security. Rather, as the American Founders were quick to emphasize centuries earlier, the constant expenditure of energy in adventures abroad would ruin the country's domestic base. The Cold War preoccupation was corrupting American society. Institutional imbalance was eroding constitutional processes, particularly when powerful and energetic presidents, in the name of national security, not only committed the nation to war but also sanctioned plots to assassinate foreign leaders such as Fidel Castro, lied to the American people and Congress about what they were doing or why they were doing it (intervention in Vietnam), acted covertly (bombing Laos and Cambodia, overthrowing elected regimes in Guatemala and Chile), and in various ways violated the constitutional rights of American citizens. Moreover, the large-scale diversion of the country's resources to its external commitments meant a corresponding neglect of domestic needs.

Extensive involvement in the world, in short, was tainting the American promise and vision; the priority of foreign policy over domestic policy had to be ended. This idea always had been at the heart of the old isolationism: America could take care of its own needs, serve as an example for humankind, and remain pure in a morally wicked world only if it stayed out of or minimized its political involvement in it. The consequence of assuming an active role internationally was to endanger, not protect, American democracy.

Perhaps the most revealing evidence of America's reaction to Vietnam was the reassertion of the deep-seated attitude that the exercise of power internationally was immoral and corrupting. Once power politics could no longer be justified in moral terms of democracy versus dictatorship, as in the two world wars, the sense of guilt over using power returned. To many, the Vietnam War represented a moral turning point in American foreign policy. Not surprisingly, sensitive people deeply committed to human values—and watching each day in history's first televised war the exercise of power in the form of violence—repented their former support of containment-through-power as if in giving that support they had been unwitting sinners. Fulbright, who had been a leading advocate of equating postwar foreign policy with moral mission, now attacked America's global role as evidence of an "arrogance of power."[10] He did not merely assert that the United States had overextended itself and that its commitments needed to be cut down to its capacities. Nor did he say that Vietnam had been an unwise commitment, although the basic policy of containment had been correct. He stated something far more fundamental: that all great powers seemed to

10. J. William Fulbright, *The Arrogance of Power* (New York: Vintage Books, 1967).

161

have a need to demonstrate that they were bigger, better, and stronger than other nations and that it was this arrogance of power, from which the United States then suffered, that was the real cause of international conflict and war.

In brief, it was the exercise of power per se that, regardless of a nation's intentions, made it arrogant. Power itself was corrupting; even if justified in moral terms, its use was immoral except in clear, unambiguous cases of self-defense. No idea could have been more characteristically American. Power was evil and its exercise tantamount to the abuse of power; abstention from power politics, providing an example to the world of a truly just and democratic society, was a more moral policy. America should be loved for its principles and for practicing what it professed rather than be feared for its might. Democracy and power politics were simply incompatible.

For the United States the "Vietnam syndrome" lingered until the Cold War's sudden collapse in 1989. In terms of foreign policy, it meant that the country was far less willing to commit itself to military intervention abroad. Further, the syndrome entailed a growing skepticism and distrust toward the government and its military leadership. It did not help that Richard Nixon's administration was shamed during this period by the Watergate scandal. But even without Watergate, for the first time the United States was confronted with the prospect that its power in the world had peaked. For many Americans, disillusionment with Vietnam led them to believe that their country's reputation as the world's "beacon of democracy" had been tainted, and that during the war their leaders had been guilty of misjudgment, deception, and wanton destruction of human life.

In 1972 Richard Nixon became the first U.S. president to visit the People's Republic of China.

CHAPTER SEVEN

The Era of Superpower Détente

The United States emerged from the Vietnam War with new doubts about its role in foreign affairs. Having assumed the status of a global superpower for only one generation, America found its traditional antipathy toward world politics quickly reasserting itself as the debacle in Vietnam raised serious doubts among many Americans about using anticommunism as the basis for the country's foreign policy. Before Vietnam, the United States readily asserted its power overseas; after Vietnam, the nation sought to avoid intervening in regional conflicts.

More basically, the anticommunist effort had been weakened by the increasing pluralism of the communist bloc. It was one thing to fight communism that appeared monolithic. But when communism became fragmented globally, and divided internally, the appropriate Western response became more difficult to define. Did the United States now have to distinguish among the communist states, determining which posed a true threat? More specifically, what changes in the distribution of power could America safely allow, and where, if anywhere, and against whom did it still have to draw frontiers? These questions became troublesome in the 1970s because each case would now confront policy makers with several policy options, thereby arousing intense controversy and bitter debate. In addition, anticommunism would no longer be as useful a means of eliciting popular support, not just because of the Vietnam debacle but also because the United States might well be supporting one communist state against another.

During this period the Nixon and Ford administrations pursued détente—a relaxation of tensions—because of changes in the United States and in the global balance of power. The United States had become, after Vietnam, a nation weary of its foreign policy burdens. As noted in Chapter 6, this mood was demonstrated by the attacks on the "imperial presidency" and restraints imposed on the White House by a more assertive and watchful Congress.[1] In the pre-Vietnam era of containment, Congress rarely had questioned the president's authority to use the armed forces or the Central Intelligence Agency (CIA) to carry out U.S. policy. But after Vietnam, America's self-appointed role as "global policeman" was widely criticized and emphasis shifted to the nation's own shortcomings and to its limited power. For Presidents Richard Nixon and Gerald Ford, then, détente was a course to be pursued until the United States could once again play the leading role they felt was required to protect U.S. interests against Soviet expansion.

Another change was in the U.S.-Soviet balance of power. Simply put, in military strength the Soviet Union had caught up to the United States. Before 1970, the balance between the two superpowers had long been between the U.S. Strategic Air Command (SAC), increasingly bolstered by the navy's nuclear submarines, and the Red Army. American bombers and missiles deterred the Soviet Union by threatening to destroy its cities. The Soviets gained their intercontinental capability and capacity to destroy the United States after their massive buildup beginning in 1964. From the 1950s to the late 1960s America's strategic power had been balanced not by Moscow's bomber and missile force, which had been relatively small, but by the Red Army. These powerful ground forces, it was believed, could overrun Western Europe and quickly defeat North Atlantic Treaty Organization (NATO) forces. Thus the balance of power had been asymmetric: the United States held strategic superiority and an intercontinental reach; the Soviet Union maintained conventional supe-

---

1. See Barbara Sinclair, "Congressional Party Leaders in the Foreign Policy and Defense Policy Arena," in *Congress Resurgent: Foreign and Defense Policy on Capitol Hill*, ed. Randall Ripley and James M. Lindsay (Ann Arbor: University of Michigan Press, 1993).

riority and a regional reach. But by 1970 the Soviet Union's strategic power had achieved parity with that of the United States, and the Soviets could now hold America's population, as well as Western Europe's, hostage. Moreover, this Soviet buildup showed no sign of slowing down, not even after the number of Soviet intercontinental ballistic missiles (ICBMs) matched the number of American missiles.

Even during the period of U.S. strategic superiority, Soviet leaders were willing to risk limited challenges, such as in Berlin and Cuba, but they remained cautious during confrontations. When there was resistance, the Kremlin retreated. American power, therefore, set limits as to how far the Soviets felt they could push. But because the strategic balance was now shifting, a continuation of the containment policy by means of nuclear deterrence was becoming riskier. Soviet leaders had gained a new sense of confidence in their power. Indeed, the Soviet Union now belonged to the most exclusive club in the world, and the implications of its membership were clarified when the Soviet foreign minister informed the world that, henceforth, no important issue anywhere could be resolved without the Soviet Union.

At the same time that it was strengthening its strategic power, the Soviet Union was engaging in a massive *conventional* buildup, particularly of a modern surface navy and airlift capability. Thus as the Soviet Union's ability to neutralize America's nuclear force grew, its capacity to project its conventional power beyond Eurasia also grew. The Soviet naval buildup, which by the late 1970s had produced a navy that exceeded that of the United States in numbers of combat ships, was not needed for defense. Would the Soviet Union, in these new circumstances, be content to expand its influence only on land and in nearby areas? Or would it, as a result of its new might, gain confidence and act more boldly? By contrast, would the United States, now that it had lost its strategic superiority, be more reluctant to react?

Henry Kissinger, Nixon's influential national security adviser, compared the Soviet Union's emergence as a world power to Germany's appearance on the world scene in the early twentieth century. In both cases the challengers were land powers. The symbols of their aspirations and determination to expand were the navies they built. Nothing could have carried greater symbolic weight for Great Britain and the United States, the two greatest naval powers in their respective times. Germany's emergence and desire to become a world power resulted in World War I. In this respect, how could the Soviet Union's newly gained power and its determination to pursue a *weltpolitik* (global policy) be managed peacefully so as not to threaten American security interests? Clearly, as a badge of its newly achieved equal status, Moscow also sought overseas clients, revolutionary states that would become members of the Soviet bloc. As they had been for Germany, these territories, usually of limited strategic and economic value, were geopolitically important as symbols. Thus the Soviet Union's massive military buildup raised questions not just about the military balance and its stability but also about the Soviets' ultimate intentions.

Nations that have seen their power decline normally adjust by reducing their commitments or by seeking new allies or greater contributions from current allies. They generally also seek to reduce threats to their interests through diplomacy. When it lost its strategic superiority, the United States did not curtail its obligations but sought to preserve them through détente. As a political means of managing the superpowers' adversarial relationship, this strategy was aimed at securing American interests at lower levels of tension and cost than those required by the policy of Cold War confrontation and crisis management. The U.S.-Soviet balance would still be bipolar, but it would be more complex and fluid than in the earlier Cold War era.[2]

MANAGING THE SUPERPOWER RIVALRY

One crucial question the decline of anticommunism posed for the future conduct of American foreign policy was whether, in the absence of anticommunism, the United States would dirty its hands by conducting diplomacy on the basis of traditional "power politics." When during the early Cold War *realpolitik,* based on power, was synonymous with *idealpolitik,* based on ideology, it had been easy for the United States to be a leader and to organize various coalitions against the ideological foe. The U.S. government could maintain the balance of power as long as it could disguise from its own people what it was doing and pretend it was engaged in a moral crusade. But could a nation that historically had condemned power politics adapt its outlook and style to a world in which justifying foreign policy in terms of ideological crusades was outmoded? Or would America, no longer believing it had an ideological mission, lapse into its traditional withdrawal from great-power politics?

In 1968 the incoming Nixon administration confronted a novel postwar situation: how to conduct foreign policy in the absence of a domestic consensus. In response to this dilemma the administration turned to a foreign policy based on the traditional logic of the state system. This dramatic shift away from a style that stemmed from the nation's domestic values and experiences to a balance-of-power rationale was somewhat surprising because Nixon previously had been virulently anticom-

2. The post-Vietnam international system is perhaps better understood as *bipolycentric,* meaning that the two superpowers remained dominant but that other countries, particularly those in Western Europe and East Asia, became stronger and more assertive.

munist and possessed by an inflexible moralism that rejected having anything to do with communists. But as president, he and Henry Kissinger, a German-born Jewish immigrant and Harvard professor who also became secretary of state in Nixon's second term, rejected the traditional American justification for participating in foreign affairs.

Indeed, the administrations of Nixon and his post-Watergate successor, Gerald Ford, might well be called the Kissinger era. Kissinger developed, articulated, and justified the new American grand strategy, which in many ways ran counter to the country's traditional style of foreign policy. He personally carried out much of its public as well as private diplomacy, and he provided an element of continuity amid the transfer of power in 1974. Kissinger so dominated these eight years that one observer described him as the only national security adviser and secretary of state ever served by two presidents.

THE KISSINGER PHILOSOPHY

The philosophy underlying American foreign policy during the Kissinger years (1969–1977) began with the assumption that international politics was not a fight between the "good" side and the "bad" side. All states, communist or noncommunist, had the right to exist and possessed legitimate interests. A nation, therefore, did not launch crusades against an adversary on the assumption that differences of interests represented a conflict of virtue and evil. The better part of wisdom was to learn to live with other states, to defend one's interests if encroached upon, but also to attempt to resolve differences and build on shared interests. International politics was not just conflict but cooperation as well. Differences, admittedly, would not be easily or quickly reconciled; views of national interests usually were deeply held and not easily relinquished. Summit meetings were important as part of the negotiating process, but one summit could not solve all problems, and to raise false hopes that it would was to produce the cynicism and disillusionment that would endanger diplomacy itself. Good personal relations among leaders might smooth this process, but they were not a substitute for hard bargaining, and accords basically reflected the ratio of power between the nations that the leaders represented.[3]

How then should the United States deal with a communist dictatorship whose values and practices it abhorred? The most the United States could expect was to influence the Soviet Union's international behavior in a responsible direction. American power was too limited to transform another superpower's domestic behavior. American demands would be

3. For an instructive comparison of Kissinger's approach to that of other realists, see Michael Joseph Smith, *Realist Thought from Weber to Kissinger* (Baton Rouge, La.: LSU Press, 1986).

resisted, which, in turn, would jeopardize accords on international issues that otherwise might have been resolvable. The United States, then, simply had to abandon its habit of crusading to democratize adversaries. Coexistence with a communist regime such as that of the Soviet Union was necessary if peace and security were to be preserved. The key, of course, was the balance of power, and the United States had to try to accommodate the legitimate needs of the principal challenger to that balance. Power neutralizes opposing power, and by satisfying the interests of other great powers the United States would be more likely to produce acceptance of the present international system than by perpetuating their hostility to a system in which they had little vested interest. No state could be completely satisfied, but a state could be relatively satisfied.

Kissinger's view, then, concentrated on the powerful actors in the state system. Although he brought the rhetoric and style of American foreign policy more in line with the operational norms of the international system, a fundamental continuity in policy remained in place. The Soviet-American balance remained the preoccupation; it was still the Soviet Union, as a great power, whose influence needed to be contained and its behavior moderated. This unity of rhetoric and action—the explanation of U.S. policy in terms of power, balances, spheres of influence, national interests, and the limits of American power, as well as the specific rejection of ideological justifications and crusades—represented the socialization of American foreign policy by the state system.

Kissinger, therefore, viewed détente not only as a strategy selected to secure American interests at a lower level of tensions and costs but also as a continuation of containment at a time when the United States had lost its strategic superiority and when its own citizens were questioning its extensive role in world affairs. Détente was to achieve its purpose by exploiting the Sino-Soviet split, which resulted from insurmountable differences between the two communist powers, and by using American technology and food as nonmilitary "weapons." But this political-diplomatic strategy was not utopian; it did not assume that either communist regime had become benign or that the Cold War was over. Détente was intended to be a realistic strategy for a time when, because of neoisolationism at home and the shift in power internationally, the United States no longer was in a position to compete as vigorously with the Soviet Union as in the days before the Vietnam War. Détente was the continuation of containment by other means.

EXPLOITING THE SINO-SOVIET SPLIT

When the Nixon administration came into office in January 1969, the United States had no official relationship with the communist government in China. Leaders in Beijing opposed establishing relations with the United States as long as Washington officially recognized the Nationalist regime on Taiwan. But Nixon recognized the changing strategic circumstances and considered it vital to bring mainland China, still led by Mao Zedong, into the diplomatic constellation. By calling the regime by its chosen name, the People's Republic of China (PRC), ending regular patrols of the Taiwan Straits by the Seventh Fleet, and lifting trade and visitation restrictions against the PRC, Nixon opened the way for a personal visit to China in February 1972. For the American public and Congress, long hostile to dealing with Beijing, this visit symbolized the dramatic shift in American policy. By playing the "China card," Nixon and Kissinger began clearing away mutual hostilities and defining some of the more outstanding issues and problems impeding closer Sino-American relations.

Thus détente applied not just to the relationship between the United States and the Soviet Union but also to the relationship with China. Indeed, it may be argued that détente with China was the greater U.S. achievement because of the tremendous hostility that had existed between the two countries since 1950. At least with the Soviet Union the earlier period of high tension, confrontation, and recurring crises had been balanced by mutual recognition and increasing cooperation in several areas. In any event, détente with China was a prerequisite to détente with the Soviet Union. By bringing China into the superpower balance, Nixon and Kissinger increased the Soviet Union's incentive to improve relations with the United States if it wished to avoid even closer Sino-American relations.

In executing this strategy, Nixon was able to exploit the rivalry between the Soviet Union and China because relations between these two former allies had become deeply embittered. As the capital of the first communist-controlled state, Moscow had for too long, since the early 1920s, monopolized the international communist movement and dictated its policies. Moreover, after World War II it had established control over the states of Eastern Europe. Of these states, only Yugoslavia was controlled not by Moscow but by its indigenous Communist Party. When Yugoslavia resisted Joseph Stalin's efforts to impose control, it was ejected from Stalin's empire. The birth of communist China—another state controlled by a home-grown, independent party—thus represented a serious problem for the Soviets. The Chinese leadership, while communist, was like that of Yugoslavia, highly nationalistic and therefore not likely to subordinate itself to the Kremlin. The potential for a schism, then, was built into the relationship. That the leaders of these two huge communist states shared an ideological framework did not dampen their growing policy differences toward the United States—

with Moscow generally having a more accommodating attitude and Beijing a more belligerent one. A falling out was therefore inevitable, despite the treaty of friendship signed by the two countries in 1950.

By the late 1960s both countries had allowed their treaty to lapse, leaving the Sino-Soviet split clearly visible to Western leaders. The epithets hurled between Beijing and Moscow reached a ferocity unknown since the early days of the Cold War. The Soviets compared Mao to Adolf Hitler and the Chinese to the Mongol hordes who overran Russia a millennium earlier. The Chinese, meanwhile, described the "Soviet revisionist clique" as a "dictatorship of the German fascist type" and quoted Karl Marx as saying that Russia's aim had been, and always would be, world hegemony.

As the struggle against the Soviet Union intensified, Mao and his followers were careful to avoid conflict with the United States. During the war in Vietnam, for example, China counseled Hanoi that revolutions had to be self-sufficient; it repeatedly stated that only an American attack on China would precipitate Beijing's intervention. In brief, North Vietnam should not and could not count on active Chinese assistance to help defeat American forces in South Vietnam. Rhetorically, Mao's policy was militantly anti-American, but in action it was restrained. Thus the incoming Nixon administration had a grand opportunity to exploit the Sino-Soviet tensions, to bring about closer U.S.-Sino relations and potentially lucrative economic ties, and to end a hostile twenty-year relationship that had been strategically very harmful, if not disastrous, for the United States.

But most important at the time, the Sino-Soviet split gave the United States more opportunities to bring pressure to bear on the Soviet Union. The clearly implied message to the Soviet leadership was that their obstinacy would compel Washington to align itself more closely with Beijing. To the Soviets, already fearful of China, such an alignment represented a worst-case scenario. It might encourage China to be more hostile, as well as renew tension on the Soviet Union's western front in Europe. Similarly, Beijing had for years complained about alleged American-Soviet collusion to isolate and contain China. But as the Soviet Union began to move huge numbers of troops eastward to defend its frontier with China, and on occasion let a rumor slip about the possibility of an attack on China, Beijing, apparently convinced that Nixon was pulling out of Vietnam, began to look toward detaching Washington from any possible cooperation with Moscow against China. Even more important, better relations with the United States would presumably restrain the Soviet Union from attacking China, for the Kremlin could not be sure that Washington would not support Beijing in such an event.

In the Shanghai communiqué released at the end of Nixon's historic visit to China in 1972, the United States and China declared their opposition to the hegemony of *any* power in Asia—but they clearly were referring to the Soviet Union. Thus Sino-American relations were established on a firm foundation of mutual self-interest. Moreover, the communist position had long been that Beijing would not establish any relationship with Washington before official U.S. ties with Taiwan were severed—such ties with the rival claimant to power being, Beijing claimed, interference in a domestic matter. The fact that, in these circumstances, the People's Republic of China would reverse itself and sign the Shanghai communiqué constituted evidence of its fear of the Soviet Union. As for the United States, the eagerness to attract China into an anti-Soviet coalition was reflected in America's declaration that it would gradually remove all its forces and installations from Taiwan and would not interfere in a "peaceful settlement" between the communists and Nationalists.

President Nixon's trip to Beijing in 1972 symbolized a dramatic change in Sino-American relations, ending once and for all the irrationality of a situation in which the United States for almost a quarter-century had ignored the existence of the world's most populous country, a nation with great potential power and an ideological rival of the Soviet Union. Just as Washington during the 1950s feared the Sino-Soviet coalition, and Beijing during the 1960s frequently pointed to alleged Soviet-American collusion to isolate China, so Moscow now became apprehensive of closer Sino-American relations. Such relations, Soviet leaders understood, gave the United States a persuasive lever—if used skillfully—in its negotiations with the Kremlin. The American shift of recognition from Taiwan to Beijing was long overdue. U.S. domestic politics had too long blocked a rational adjustment and exploitation of the Sino-Soviet conflict, a conflict in which tensions constantly shifted in intensity, but one that was likely to continue despite leadership changes in both communist countries. Sino-Soviet quarrels reflected historic and entrenched differences of interest more profound than mere differences of personalities.

Indeed, the succession struggle in China and the change in the presidency in the United States did not stop progress toward full normalization. On January 1, 1979, the People's Republic of China and the United States exchanged diplomatic recognition and ambassadors. This was followed by an official visit to Washington by China's future leader, Deputy Premier Deng Xiaoping, who succeeded Mao as chairman of the Communist Party two years after Mao's death in September 1976. The timing of this last step toward normalization was driven by China, which, with increasingly obsolete weapons, confronted large modern Soviet forces along its 4,500-mile northern frontier. For the United States, the final shift from Taiwan to Beijing meant ending diplomatic recognition of Nationalist China and abrogating the Taiwan defense treaty, requiring the withdrawal of the last American military personnel stationed in Taiwan. In return, Beijing accepted the American position that the Taiwan problem be resolved peacefully. (The United States could, of course, at any time resort easily to force and defend Taiwan should Beijing some day violate the understanding about the peaceful resolution of this problem.)

With recognition of the mainland came new opportunities for trade. Although at first the United States did not sell arms to Beijing in order not to provoke Moscow, it was willing to let its European allies sell China arms, such as jet fighters and antiaircraft and antitank missiles.[4] But more important than arms sales, the opening to China paved the way for rapidly accelerating commercial ties between the two countries. China looked to the West to help it modernize everything from its hotel and steel industries to exploitation of its enormous oil reserves. By the 1990s China had emerged as one of the major trading partners of the United States; its importance to Washington was revealed annually when the U.S. government extended China most-favored-nation status despite the continuation of communist rule and political repression. For the United States, access to China's vast markets proved irresistible, a fact not lost on Chinese leaders who continued to reject American calls for political reforms and moderation.

LINKING COOPERATION TO SOVIET RESTRAINT

The U.S. strategy for restraint, then, involved both communist powers. Beijing could be used to convince the Soviets to act with restraint and to show greater willingness to compromise if they wished to avoid closer Sino-American relations and collusion against the Soviet Union. Moreover, Kissinger proposed to supplement the new relationship with a network of agreements and a set of rules of mutual restraint beneficial to both powers. Key to such an arrangement was *linkage,* which was directed primarily toward Moscow. If a series of agreements and understandings on such matters as arms control and trade could be achieved, the Soviet Union would gain a vested interest in good relations with the United States. While the Soviet Union was to be faced, as before, with continued parity and a strong American military, this "stick" was to be supplemented with enough "carrots" to make a restrained foreign poli-

---

4. The United States limited its own sales to dual-purpose equipment such as radar, trucks, and transport planes, which could be put to either civilian or military use. Later, Ronald Reagan's administration, in an effort to forge stronger links with China against the Soviet Union, offered to sell Beijing arms.

cy more rewarding. Indeed, military sanctions against the Soviet Union at a time of strategic parity were becoming riskier for the United States. Fortunately, then, the linkage strategy, which offered economic rewards for restraint, was thought to be particularly appealing to the Soviets.

Linkage also had another meaning: the various U.S.-Soviet issues would be linked together diplomatically. Progress on one front would be tied to progress on another; the Kremlin could not expect to make gains on one issue that interested it but refuse to meet American interests on others. If it did so, there presumably would be a penalty exacted through U.S. resistance on issues of interest to Soviet leaders or through the withholding of benefits Moscow was seeking.

The Soviet Union was particularly vulnerable in its inability to deal with one issue: the Soviet economy, which was in serious trouble by the time Nixon entered office. After its rapid expansion in the 1950s and early 1960s, the economy saw its 5 percent growth rate head down to 2 percent by the early 1970s. The economic decline was particularly notable in those branches of industry associated with the "second" industrial revolution: computers, microelectronics, and telecommunications. In short, the Soviet Union was falling further behind the West in those industries that were most important for economic growth. Furthermore, the Soviet workplace was increasingly plagued by high absenteeism, drunkenness, corruption, and shoddy production. The implications of this decline could not be ignored; it damaged the Soviet Union's appeal as a socialist state, hampered its ability to compete with the United States, and threatened its future superpower status.

Even in agriculture the growth in Soviet production had fallen sharply below expectations and official plans. Workers on the land, like workers in the factory, were far behind their American counterparts in per capita production. The Soviet Union's continued inability to provide a balanced diet—indeed, in some years just to avoid widespread hunger—was not just the result of poor weather; it also stemmed from the ideologically determined organization of a command economy administered by a rigid bureaucracy. By contrast, the small private plots that some peasants were allowed to own produced much of the Soviet Union's poultry, grain, vegetables, and other staples.

The result of all this was that the Soviet Union was the only industrial society in which the peacetime life expectancy of males was declining and infant mortality was rising. The Soviet leader, Leonid Brezhnev, was all too aware that the failure of his predecessor, Nikita Khrushchev, to keep promises of a higher standard of living had played a large part in Khrushchev's fall from power. He had raised popular expectations and then failed to meet them. The same thing could happen to Brezhnev. In a system in which the leadership firmly maintained a monopoly on political power and control, it sought popular approval by providing jobs, as well as low-cost housing, health care, retirement benefits, and similar social services. The Soviet standard of living might not have been high by Western standards, but as long as it improved gradually the regime could claim to be fulfilling its aim of enhancing the lives of its citizens. Conversely, a decline had ominous implications; the Kremlin had to look no further than Poland for evidence of this. In 1970 the decrepit state of the Polish economy and worker dissatisfaction with food shortages and a lack of consumer goods had led to riots in several cities and the collapse of the government, which, even in a communist-controlled state, had to be replaced. Similar unrest occurred in 1980–1981 and again in the late 1980s.

Soviet concerns about the ailing economy and lack of progress in the scientific-technological sector presented the Kremlin with two choices: to look toward the West for a "technological fix" to help stimulate the Soviet economy or to attempt a basic structural reform of the country's highly centralized and rigidly bureaucratized system. Not surprisingly, the Soviet leadership chose Western technology, machinery, food, and the Western credit proffered to buy them. Structural reform was rejected because it was not only antithetical to the regime's basic ideological beliefs about private property, the profit motive, and free markets, but also contrary to the deeply vested interests of the government bureaucracies committed to central planning, a command economy, and self-preservation. Decentralization of authority—shifting power to factory and farm managers and their work forces—was judged too risky because it might threaten the Communist Party's political control. Importing Western goods and food was considered less risky than such a fundamental reform.

Trade with the United States, with its enormous mass-production capabilities, technological advances that the Soviets envied, and agricultural abundance, was especially desirable to Moscow since it also saw the benefits in broader collaboration. Because it had little to sell the United States, it offered to let Americans develop and exploit the huge Soviet deposits of raw materials, especially in Siberia. American capital to help finance this extraction would presumably be repaid in oil, natural gas, and other mineral resources in the future. The Soviets also looked to the United States for food in years of shortages, which occurred more and more frequently.

The Nixon-Ford administration believed these economic problems would give the United States leverage. Trade obviously was profitable for American industry and agriculture, but the main reason for permitting it was political. American productivity, it was hoped, would provide a powerful material reinforcement for a Soviet foreign policy of restraint and accommodation made necessary by the desire to prevent closer Sino-American "collusion," to achieve strategic arms agreements to stabilize mutual deterrence, and to gain American recognition of Soviet parity and equal status with the United States. According to Kissinger, economic relations could not be separated from the political context. The United States should not be asked to reward hostile conduct with economic benefits. In return for the expansion of trade, it was not unreasonable to require the Soviets to cooperate on key foreign policy issues. In effect, the linkage strategy would give Moscow the incentives to practice *self-containment*.

Kissinger's policy of using economic means to achieve political purposes suffered a significant setback, however, when the U.S. Senate approved offering the Soviets trade and credits only on the condition that Moscow allow more Soviet Jews to emigrate. Calling the provision, specified in an amendment by Sen. Henry Jackson and Rep. Charles Vanik, an intervention in its domestic affairs, the Soviet Union rejected the trade agreement. No great power—let alone the Soviet Union, which claimed to be a nation in which class distinctions and religious and other forms of prejudice no longer existed—would admit publicly that it mistreated part of its population and allow itself to be placed on probation by a foreign adversary in return for trade. As a result, the Soviet Union conducted its business mostly with Western Europe instead of the United States. To the extent, then, that the Soviets' primary motive for détente was economic, the lack of payoff reduced their incentives for maintaining a relaxation of tensions.

ARMS CONTROL AS THE CENTERPIECE OF DÉTENTE

Another area of potential U.S.-Soviet cooperation was in the area of strategic arms control, which over the years had assumed greater importance. The two powers had been rivals since the closing days of World War II; indeed, their rivalry reached into almost every region of the world. As a result, profound distrust and mutual fear, if not hatred, characterized their relationship. The arms race was an expression of their deep political differences. But the danger was, of course, that the arms race, fueled by continuing conflict, would at some point spill over into a nuclear war. To avoid such a cataclysmic outcome, each side built up its nuclear forces as a defense and negotiated agreements that reduced the chances of war breaking out. But as the basic conflict continued and as nuclear weapons were unlikely to be abolished, the next best tactic was to manage the nuclear balance by instituting arms control agreements and promoting mutual deterrence.[5]

During the 1960s arms control had dealt largely with issues such as the establishment of a "hot line" between the Kremlin and the White House for quick communication in a crisis, a limited ban on testing nuclear devices, and, through the United Nations, an agreement on the nonproliferation of nuclear weapons. In the 1970s these negotiations shifted to each side's strategic forces.

The Strategic Arms Limitation Talks (SALT), one of Nixon's major achievements, stood at the center of détente. SALT had four objectives. Its first was to make the arms race more predictable by establishing, documenting, and reporting the number of strategic weapons possessed by each side. Such knowledge presumably would reduce the anxiety of the arms race; uncertainty and the fear that the opponent might gain military superiority only fueled the competition.

SALT's second aim was to ensure parity. The assumption was that if the two sides had approximately the same number of nuclear warheads, or the explosives attached to ballistic missiles and bombs, neither side could launch a crippling strike against the other. More specifically, parity was a condition in which no matter who struck first, the attacked side would still have the capability to retaliate and destroy the aggressor. In the absence of nuclear superiority, the United States and the Soviet Union would each retain a sufficient second-strike capability to ensure deterrence.

The third purpose of SALT was to reduce threats to each side's deterrent forces. By the early 1970s the balance was threatened not only by the continuing Soviet strategic growth but also by technological innovations that were widely believed in the United States to be undermining the stability of nuclear deterrence. One matter of concern was the development of a new defensive weapon. The Soviets had deployed antiballistic missiles (ABMs) around Moscow and were thought to be working on a second-generation ABM for possible nationwide deployment. If ABMs could shoot down enough incoming American ICBMs and reduce the destruction inflicted on the Soviet Union to an "acceptable" level of casualties, the ABMs would undermine U.S. deterrence, which depended on its capacity to impose "assured destruction."

This defensive weapon stimulated the United States, in turn, to improve its offensive technology by developing the multiple independent reentry vehicle (MIRV)—a long-range missile with multiple warheads that separate in flight, change trajectory, and fly to assigned and dispersed

5. For an application of this concept, see Alexander George and Richard Smoke, *Deterrence in American Foreign Policy: Theory and Practice* (New York: Columbia University Press, 1974). Also see Robert Jervis, Richard Ned Lebow, and Janice Gross Stein, *Psychology and Deterrence* (Baltimore: Johns Hopkins University Press, 1985).

targets. The advantage of MIRVs was that the large numbers of warheads would be able to overwhelm any ABM defense, enabling the United States to destroy Soviet society in a retaliatory blow. But MIRVs also threatened to destabilize the deterrent balance: multiplying the warheads and providing them with greater accuracy placed a premium on attack. Whichever side got in the first blow was likely to win because it might be able to prevent any major retaliation. "Use them or lose them" could become a tempting strategy for either side. Further, MIRVs were more difficult to "count" through satellite reconnaissance and other means of verification, a problem that would later plague arms control negotiations.

The fourth reason for SALT was its importance for détente. On the one hand, the failure to arrive at an agreement or at least to continue the SALT dialogue was bound to have a debilitating effect on the overall U.S.-Soviet political relationship. On the other hand, only a relaxation of tensions could provide the diplomatic atmosphere that would enable the two nuclear giants to arrive at an arms agreement that would leave them feeling more secure, sanctify the strategic parity between them, and avoid new costly offensive and defensive arms races. SALT, in brief, became a symbol of détente.

The first set of agreements, known as SALT I, was signed by Nixon and Brezhnev in May 1972. SALT I had taken two and a half years to negotiate and incorporated two agreements. The first limited each country's ABMs to two hundred launchers, later to be reduced to one hundred each. For all practical purposes, by restricting ABMs the two powers acknowledged the dangers of strategic defense and shifted their focus to offensive weapons. Thus the second agreement froze offensive missile batteries at the number each side possessed at the time. Each side retained the right to improve its weapons within the overall quantitative agreement, thus preserving parity. Although no on-site inspection to check for violations was established, both sides pledged not to interfere with each other's reconnaissance or spy satellites, which would be the principal means of checking compliance with both accords.

The follow-up agreement, SALT II, was regarded as critical to a long-term effort to stabilize mutual deterrence. President Gerald Ford, after Nixon's resignation, arrived at the guidelines for SALT II at a 1974 meeting with Brezhnev in Vladivostok. This time each side would have an equal number of strategic weapons: 2,400 missiles and bombers; 1,320 of these delivery systems could have MIRVs. It was a complex series of agreements, carefully balancing the varying interests and different force structures of the two superpowers.

But after SALT II was signed by Brezhnev and President Jimmy Carter in 1979, the treaty became controversial in the United States. Proponents said it provided for real reductions of strategic launchers from the Vladivostok ceiling of 2,400 to 2,250. This change meant that the Soviets would have to reduce their force levels by about 150 older missiles, thereby setting a precedent for SALT III, whose main purpose was to bring about a major reduction of strategic forces. Critics noted, however, that the SALT II ceilings were so high that the agreement was the very opposite of any reasonable interpretation of the words *arms control*. Other critics asserted that, despite the equal numbers provided for both sides, the treaty would give the Soviet Union strategic superiority because Soviet missiles were considerably larger, could carry more and bigger warheads, and were becoming more accurate (though less accurate than U.S. missiles). The Soviets, therefore, would presumably be capable of destroying up to 90 percent of America's ICBMs.[6]

The debate over SALT II became moot after the Soviet Union sent troops into Afghanistan late in 1979 to shore up a pro-Soviet military regime. The U.S. Congress refused to ratify the treaty and, reversing his plans to reduce U.S. defenses, President Carter promised to counter the Soviet invasion with a U.S. military buildup. But despite heated rhetoric coming from both Washington and Moscow, the terms of SALT II were observed into the late 1980s, when efforts to reduce nuclear stockpiles accelerated again under President Ronald Reagan (see Chapter 9).

THE LIMITATIONS OF DÉTENTE

While the superpowers negotiated the size of their nuclear arsenals in the "spirit of détente," much of the outside world remained torn by internal unrest and regional conflict. Within the developing world, the ideological rivalry of the Cold War had infected many unstable governments, dividing their populations into hostile ideological camps, producing ever-greater forms of repression, and undermining their prospects for political stability and economic growth. The resulting calamity in Vietnam already has been reviewed at length. Among other Third World flashpoints, a military coup in Chile and the civil wars in Angola and Ethiopia clearly demonstrated the limitations of détente. Furthermore, the protracted Cold War struggle, merely codified by détente, led to strains within the network of military alliances the United States had created and dominated since World War II.

CHILE'S MILITARY TAKEOVER

After the declaration of the Monroe Doctrine in 1823, the United States regarded South America as within its sphere of influence.

---

6. For an elaboration of this debate, see Lawrence Freedman, *The Evolution of Nuclear Strategy*, 2d ed. (New York: St. Martin's Press, 1989), 344–395.

Although Washington gradually became more accommodating to the nationalism of its Latin neighbors, it remained sensitive to what it perceived to be radical left-wing revolutions and regimes that might bring Soviet influence close to America's shores. When in 1970 Chilean citizens elected the Marxist Salvador Allende to the presidency, the Nixon administration sought first to prevent Allende from becoming president and, when that failed, to make life difficult for him and ultimately to remove him from power through a military coup d'état engineered by the CIA. Ironically, the reasons for the Chilean coup, when it came, stemmed essentially from Allende's own actions and the domestic reactions they precipitated. By 1973 Allende's end was merely a matter of time. Indeed, Chile provided a most persuasive example of why the United States should *not* have intervened given that the outcome was largely predetermined and that, in the coup's aftermath, the U.S. role became the subject of widespread criticism.

Allende came to power in 1970 with 36 percent of the vote, only two points ahead of his next competitor in a three-way race. In the runoff vote in the Chilean Congress, he received the support of the centrist Christian Democratic Party. At the outset of his rule the opposition supported much of his program, including land reform and the nationalization of U.S.-owned copper mines, banks, and major industries such as the International Telegraph and Telephone Company (ITT), whose senior officers pressured the Nixon administration to restore their holdings in Chile. Given his early popularity, it should have been possible for Allende to work within Chile's constitutional norms with a democratic consensus. But Allende deliberately pursued a policy of polarizing Chileans, a strategy that did more to consolidate the professional middle and lower-middle classes in opposition to him than to broaden his worker-peasant base of support. As a result, his vow to maintain constitutional rule fell by the wayside; he survived only by increasingly bypassing Congress and the courts. When the Christian Democrats then joined the rightist opposition, the class polarization was at long last paralleled by the divisions between the executive and legislative branches.

The military during this period became increasingly politicized. Asked by Allende at several points to participate in his cabinet to reassure those worried about law and order, the military at first served Allende, as it had his predecessors. Later, however, the military intervened, alarmed by the rapid growth of paramilitary forces among Allende's followers, who believed in armed confrontation against "reactionaries," and the call for an insurrection in the navy by a close Allende friend and party leader. Both events apparently occurred with Allende's complicity. The country was on the verge of civil war when the military struck. It did not need American urging.

After the expropriation of American property without compensation, Washington had cut off American credit for Chile and pressured international financial institutions such as the World Bank and International Monetary Fund to follow suit. But Allende had more than made up for his American losses with credits from communist states, other Latin American countries, and Western Europe. Chile also had rich copper mines. Had Allende imitated Egypt's Gamal Abdel Nasser, he likely would have survived U.S. pressure and hostility by arousing his people's nationalist ardor. But that was why Allende did not survive; he declared himself to be president of only some Chileans—against other Chileans. Had the CIA abstained from meddling, responsibility for the Chilean coup would properly have fallen on Allende. Instead, the United States was condemned for its covert intervention, and Chile became for many critics a symbol of American imperialism.

The overthrow and death of Allende in September 1973 was controlled by a four-man junta led by Gen. Augusto Pinochet, who assumed the office of president through force and intimidation. In the years to come Pinochet emerged as a ruthless leader, but one loyal to the United States and determined to prevent Chile from enduring another socialist revolution. Despite charges that the United States was again "coddling" a foreign dictator in the name of containment, Washington actively supported the new Chilean government. In return for Washington's patronage, Chile served as a loyal U.S. client in South America through the end of the Cold War.

REGIONAL CONFLICT IN AFRICA

A second example of détente's limitations came in 1975 in Angola, a country rich in oil and mineral resources and one that geographically divided "white supremacist" Africa—Rhodesia and South Africa, which controlled South-West Africa, or Namibia—from black Africa. As a Portuguese colony, Angola had helped to protect the two racist states from black liberation movements. But as Portuguese colonialism came to an end, Angola's interim government, which was composed of three factions based on tribal allegiances, underwent a power struggle. This rivalry continued after Angola became independent, and the leftist Popular Movement for the Liberation of Angola attracted Soviet support and thousands of Cuban troops. Some claimed that the Cuban military intervention occurred after repeated South African military strikes into Angola, as well as intervention by Zaire. The Ford administration, however, believed it was the Soviets who financed the deployment of Cuban military advisers and who later provided massive numbers of jet fighters, mortars, rockets, armored cars, and ground-to-air missiles. The administration—including Secretary of State Kissinger—viewed the

Cubans as Soviet proxies and their intervention in Angola as an out-growth of Soviet expansionism.

The result was the reintroduction of great-power rivalry and confrontation into southern Africa. Rejecting U.S. military intervention, Washington provided covert arms to the faction opposing the Soviet-supported ones. But not only did this effort not match that of the Soviet Union, it also was cut off by the Senate, fearful of another Vietnam in an area that did not constitute a vital American interest. Rejecting the contention that Angola might become another Vietnam, Ford and Kissinger conceded that Angola was not a significant American interest. They emphasized, however, that Soviet behavior could not for that reason be ignored. Angola might be far away, but, in their view, it was a test case of the new superpower relationship. Soviet actions were simply incompatible with détente; the Kremlin was seeking unilateral advantage from the general relaxation of tensions. Kissinger charged that Angola was far beyond any Soviet sphere of influence and that the Soviet action constituted a military intervention to impose a regime of Soviet choice. The Soviet Union defended its behavior by asserting that support of national liberation movements, including armed intervention, was not incompatible with détente—a view rejected by the United States.

Moscow's next move in Africa came in 1977 in Somalia, the Soviet Union's closest African ally and home to its naval base at Berbera. Using Soviet-supplied arms, Somalia was supporting the Western Somali Liberation Front in the Ogaden region of northern Ethiopia. Somali troops had invaded Ethiopia to support these rebels, who claimed that this area, populated by ethnic Somalis, should be part of Somalia. Ethiopia, already facing disintegration as it confronted other rebellions and secessionist movements, especially the attempt by Eritrea to establish an independent state on the Red Sea, rejected the claim. Like other new African states, it recognized the borders existing at the time of independence—that is, borders drawn by the colonial powers. Because Ethiopia was about ten times as large as Somalia, however, and of greater strategic importance, the Soviet Union supplied Ethiopia with Soviet military advisers, twenty thousand Cuban advisers and troops, and an estimated $1 billion in military supplies to crush the Ogaden rebellion. Thus it was willing to risk alienating Somalia and losing its naval base and some air facilities facing the Indian Ocean because the stakes were even greater in Ethiopia than in Angola. The United States predictably seized the opportunity to aid Somalia after the Soviet reversal and to occupy the Berbera naval base, but even the influx of significant U.S. economic and military aid did not prevent Somalia from succumbing to its own internal collapse in the 1990s. There was irony in the Soviet rejection of its client in

Somalia in favor of another Marxist regime, which the Ethiopian government had become after the overthrow in September 1974 of Emperor Haile Selassie.

As Soviet relations with Washington worsened, Moscow saw its opportunity to enhance its influence in the strategic Horn of Africa, which was just across the Gulf of Aden from Saudi Arabia. Washington feared that the Soviet Union would gain control of the southern entrance to the Red Sea, which led to the Suez Canal and Israel, and that it would pose a threat to the important oil routes from the Persian Gulf to the West. Thus both sides traded client states and inflamed the region with massive amounts of military hardware. In no other part of the world was the spillover effect of the superpower rivalry so visible, and so disabling.

THE EROSION OF U.S. ALLIANCES

The whole concept of détente was bound to pose several problems for the United States, especially in its relationships with its allies. Alliances normally are composed of countries drawn together by common perceptions of an overriding external threat. But what cements the bonds of such relationships when that threat is no longer seen as great by the principal members of the coalition? Is it not inevitable that the strands of such "entangling alliances" become untangled? In Europe, among America's most important allies, that appeared to be the situation in the 1970s and 1980s.

In the days when all members of NATO had perceived the Soviet threat as serious, the alliance had been a reasonably cohesive organization. To be sure, NATO had become strained because its European members, although still dependent on the United States for their security, had recovered from the war and wanted a greater voice in the alliance. But the common perception of external danger had been enough to keep the bonds of the alliance close. In the era of détente, however, several member states no longer were so willing to give priority to alliance interests. Washington, for example, now negotiated directly with the Kremlin on key issues, as relations with Moscow became in some respects more important than those with NATO members. Not surprisingly, the European states also went their own way; West Germany, for example, pursued a policy of *ostpolitik,* or accommodation toward its eastern neighbors.

Economic issues also proved especially divisive among members of the Western allies. In the immediate postwar era economic policies such as the Marshall Plan had been consistent with and supported American politico-military policy. But now economic relations between the United States and Western Europe, which was rapidly forming a cohesive economic bloc, were complicating the other strands of NATO policy. As the 1970s began, Europe was no longer the weak, divided, and demoralized continent it had been after 1945. Indeed, the emerging Common Market had become an increasingly powerful economic competitor. During the Cold War the United States had been a leading proponent of European integration; a cohesive Western Europe could make a significant contribution to the U.S.-led struggle against the Soviet Union, and the competitiveness of an economically unified Europe was thought to be worth the risk. In a period of détente, however, and growing tensions between the United States and Europe, the united front that had long confronted the Soviet bloc threatened to fragment.[7]

The European-American relationship also was strained by the continued sense of vulnerability of the Europeans, fostered by their ongoing dependence on the United States for defense. To some extent, their concern reflected their fear of abandonment. As U.S. territory became more vulnerable to Soviet missile attack, many Europeans wondered if they could continue to rely on American protection. Without sufficiently large and credible nuclear forces of their own, their security was entirely in American hands. But, as Soviet intercontinental missile forces grew, what would happen if the Soviets made demands considered vital by the Europeans but not by Washington? Could the small British or French strategic force deter the Soviet Union? The U.S. management of the Berlin crises from 1958 to 1962 had not reassured the European countries—especially France and West Germany—of Washington's steadfastness as its risks and costs of defending the alliance rose. Yet Europeans also feared entrapment. They had been deeply concerned about the diversion of U.S. resources and attention away from them during the Korean and Vietnam Wars. But while Europeans worried about U.S. recklessness, the United States resented their lack of political support for U.S. ventures outside of Europe. This feeling fueled U.S. resentment over the failure of the Europeans to play a far greater role in their own defense.

The alliance was further divided by the psychological fact that, while the United States had become a global power, the European states, having shed most of their empires, had largely relinquished their former extra-European role and had concentrated on their economic growth and regional integration. As former great powers, the European states naturally bemoaned their rapid postwar decline in prestige and status and their dependence on a vigorous, self-confident, and, in their eyes, often impetuous newcomer who might disregard their counsel—advice that, the Europeans felt, was based on their greater experience and wis-

---

7. For a review of Western Europe's progress toward "functional integration" during this period, see Martin Holland, *European Integration: From Community to Union* (London: Pinter, 1994), 22–59.

dom. They became preoccupied with restraining the United States from doing anything that they perceived as rash and endangering détente, regardless of Soviet behavior.

While NATO unity weakened, the Southeast Asia Treaty Organization (SEATO) and the Central Treaty Organization (CENTO) collapsed. Indeed, the era of "pactomania" initiated under the Eisenhower administration came to an abrupt halt in the 1970s. SEATO was formally dissolved in 1975 after the fall of South Vietnam. Given that SEATO's primary raison d'être was the conflict in Southeast Asia, the conflict's conclusion, even on terms contrary to SEATO members' desires, made the demise of the organization inevitable. The Central Treaty Organization died more slowly. First, with the splitting off in 1972 of Bangladesh from Pakistan, which also had been a SEATO member, India emerged as the dominant power on the subcontinent. Pakistan, which had joined both alliances primarily to receive U.S. arms for its adversarial relationship with India, no longer had much interest in either. In the meantime, it had moved close to China, a regional rival of India. Turkey, at the other end of the CENTO's geographic reach, was grappling with domestic conflicts along with a U.S. arms embargo, which was imposed after the escalation of fighting between Turkey and Greece over control of Cyprus. In between, Iran had become the only reliable U.S. ally in Southwest Asia. The fragility of this friendship, illustrated by the overthrow of the American-backed shah and the seizure of American hostages in 1979, was ample evidence of the weakness of CENTO in its final days.

DISILLUSIONMENT WITH DÉTENTE

In the context of America's national style, it was not surprising that views of détente swung from euphoria as the 1970s began to increasing disillusionment by 1975. The United States always had wavered between such opposite and mutually exclusive categories: isolation or intervention, peace or war, diplomacy or force, idealism or realism, harmony or strife, optimism about America's destiny or cynicism about an evil world that resists reform.

The Nixon administration's overselling of détente and such slogans as "negotiation, not confrontation" reinforced the expectation that the Cold War was effectively over and that the superpowers had put their conflicts and crises and the danger of war behind them. But raising people's hopes too high was bound to lead to disappointment when events did not live up to expectations. The problem was that each administration tended to package its foreign policy in slogans that emphasized how its policy differed from that of its predecessors. And, anticipating the next election, each administration wanted to make that policy look appealing and successful. Despite the high degree of continuity of American foreign policy, the United States had indulged itself by turns in the rhetoric of containment, liberation, frontiersmanship, and détente. In addition, détente as a state of existence that combined both conflict *and* cooperation was more difficult to understand than the Cold War. It was easier to explain a relationship that was essentially one of confrontation *or* cooperation. The Cold War aroused people; détente relaxed them, as if it were the same thing as *entente,* meaning friendship. But détente means a reduction of tensions, not an absence of tensions or superpower rivalry. Expectations that it represented a harbinger of harmony were bound to produce frustration.

Indeed, it is critical to remember that in its conception détente was intended to serve as another form of containment for a period of domestic neoisolationism, superpower parity, and Sino-Soviet schism. The Cold War stick was to be supplemented by the carrot of détente, and issues were to be linked, explicitly or otherwise. The Soviet Union was to be constrained from undertaking foreign adventures by force, or the threat of force, along with the prospect that the United States could at any time withhold economic agreements desired by Moscow. The United States hoped that Moscow, enticed by Western goods, technology, and credits, would restrain itself to avoid the loss of such benefits. But whether or not the United States adopted détente as a diplomatic strategy because of the country's pervasive mood of withdrawal and its relative decline after the Vietnam War, these factors made containment of the Soviet Union at the moment it had become a global power very difficult. Détente was not a set of self-denying rules. If the Soviet Union faced favorable situations to exploit, should it shun those opportunities just because the United States was in no mood to resist? Self-restraint as a policy was asking a great deal of any major power, especially one that had just achieved strategic parity.

Within the United States, the Watergate scandal and Nixon's resignation in 1974 combined to weaken the presidency as an institution. As noted earlier, the passage of the War Powers Act in 1973 was symbolic of the shift of power from the executive to the legislative branch, and its purpose clearly was to restrain the U.S. role in international affairs. As the "Vietnam syndrome" took hold, Americans were increasingly reluctant to project the nation's power. To many, it was the exercise of *American* power, not the expansionist efforts of the Soviet Union, that was the main threat to stability. Restraint of the United States, not the containment of communism, emerged as the chief task if the world were to become a more peaceful place. The "limits of American power," the constant refrain after Vietnam, were widely proclaimed among critics of American foreign policy in the public and in the U.S. Congress.

The built-in executive-legislative conflict resulting from separate institutions sharing power always has complicated the formulation of U.S. foreign policy. World War I, America's first major experience in great-power politics after a century of isolationism, ended in a peace treaty that the Senate defeated. Congressional isolationism during the interwar period led President Franklin Roosevelt to rely on executive agreements in his conduct of foreign policy from 1939 to 1941. During the early stages of the Cold War, shared perceptions of great external threats and U.S. aims generally restrained the conflict between the two branches and increased the president's influence with Congress. But in the absence of a clear and present danger during the détente years, and amid intense disagreements about the use of American power in the wake of Vietnam, the White House and Congress pulled in different directions. Almost every policy became caught in a bitter dispute, often raising the most basic constitutional questions.

Meanwhile, the Soviet Union's conduct during this period was predictable. In the heyday of détente the United States continued to languish in Vietnam. And after renewed hostilities in the Middle East in 1973 (see Chapter 8), the United States promoted a Middle East peace settlement by making itself the arbiter between Israel and the Arabs and excluded the Soviet Union from playing a key role in the area. In this context, Moscow was especially likely to exploit America's paralysis of will and opportunities to enhance its own influence. Détente did not mean an end to the competition; it only meant competing at a lower level of tension so that the rivalry would not erupt in nuclear war. Soviet leaders had no intention of betraying their perceived historical mission to continue the revolution against Western capitalism.

Indeed, détente was a particularly favorable situation in which to promote this struggle. Détente was the product of a shift in the balance of power as a result of the new strategic parity in nuclear weapons. Note the cause and effect carefully: it was the growth of Soviet nuclear forces that induced the United States to behave with greater self-restraint. And consider the obvious corollary: the more military power the Soviet Union acquired, the more American compromises and concessions in negotiations would be offered. This perception of American behavior— and the breakdown of consensus in Washington—was nothing less than a rationale for continuing the struggle for preeminence. Strategic parity was the geopolitical status symbol of the Soviet Union's new standing in international politics. Thus the United States, despite its successful playing of the "China card" and its widening economic advantage over the Soviet Union, remained mired in the Cold War struggle that would far outlast the Kissinger era in American foreign policy.

Jimmy Carter grasps hands with Egyptian president Anwar Sadat and Israeli prime minister Menachem Begin at the signing of the Camp David accords in 1978. It would be one of Carter's final foreign policy achievements.

CHAPTER EIGHT

Jimmy Carter and World-Order Politics

In times of national self-doubt citizens often turn to an outsider who appears untarnished by past government actions and who promises a fresh approach to domestic and foreign policy making. In the 1976 U.S. presidential campaign this role was filled by Jimmy Carter, a peanut farmer and former governor of Georgia. Carter seemed to epitomize the moral virtues Americans found lacking in previous presidents. Drawing on his experience as a Sunday school teacher in his Baptist church, Carter eloquently described the country's need for moral rejuvenation and spiritual rebirth after the traumas of Vietnam and Watergate. His words struck a chord with the American people, who elected him as president over the seemingly lackluster incumbent, Gerald Ford.

Carter's world views differed profoundly from those of his predecessors. Rather than emphasizing the Cold War and East-West conflict, Carter paid more attention to global "interdependence" and the need for closer cooperation between the wealthier, more industrialized countries of the North and the poorer countries of the South. His views reflected widely perceived trends in world politics, such as greater concern about the environment and recognition of the growing importance of economic versus military power. Carter denounced U.S. interventions abroad that caused death and destruction; he also reflected the view of America's first generation of leaders that such adventures threatened democracy at home and invited tyranny. Drawing on the idealism of President Woodrow Wilson, he placed the needs of the "world society" above selfish national interests and espoused universal standards of morality as the appropriate basis of foreign policy.

In this manner Carter offered a way out of what he called the "malaise" within the United States. The best course for the country, he argued, was to reject power politics, seek renewal and purification by concentrating on domestic affairs, and build a fully free and socially just society whose example would radiate throughout the world. Power politics would be replaced by social politics; America's foreign policy would be an extension of its domestic values. In the words of a former chairman of the Senate Foreign Relations Committee, America should "serve as an example of democracy to the world" and play its role in the world "not in its capacity as a *power,* but in its capacity as a *society.*"[1] Virtue, not power, would be the hallmark of foreign policy; American influence in the world was to be derived from the nation's moral standing as a good and just society. Other nations would be attracted to the United States by its principles, not its strength.

THE SEARCH FOR CONSENSUS AND HUMAN RIGHTS

History has proven that democratic states cannot effectively conduct foreign policy in the absence of a domestic consensus. For most of its history America has enjoyed such a consensus, which has centered around the need for detachment from foreign affairs and the primacy of domestic economic and political development. In the absence of an external threat, the United States historically has wanted only to be left to its own devices. When provoked, however, its citizens have been easily mobilized and united for its foreign policy crusades. But in the wake of Vietnam and in the midst of détente, no such provocation appeared on the horizon, and the American penchant for withdrawal prevailed.

The task of re-creating consensus on foreign policy was embraced by Carter, who thought he could find it in America's self-proclaimed historical role as the defender of democracy and individual liberty. Human rights became the platform on which he expected to mobilize popular support; the liberal tradition, which former secretary of state Henry

1. J. William Fulbright, *The Arrogance of Power* (New York: Vintage Books, 1967), 256.

Kissinger was accused of having abandoned in favor of his amoral geopolitics, was to be reunited with American foreign policy. Carter pledged to condition American relations with other countries, rich and poor alike, on their respect for human rights, but he largely directed his human rights campaign toward the Third World. That was where the majority of humanity lived, where living conditions were the worst, and where population growth was the most rapid. To pursue his vision of "world-order politics," Carter would focus on the relationship between the Western industrial democracies and the poorer Third World.[2] In its preoccupation with the ideological struggle of the Cold War—in Carter's words, the "inordinate fear of communism"—the United States had neglected these impoverished areas. Indeed, the superpowers, Carter felt, by extending their Cold War to many "frontiers" in the Third World, had encouraged military dictators on both sides of the ideological spectrum, undermined the prospects of the developing countries for democracy, and further retarded their economic development. In short, the Cold War had only made the already miserable conditions in the developing countries worse.

The United States thus once more stood for something, having reclaimed its democratic heritage and a moral basis for its foreign policy. American flirtations with the Machiavellian world of great-power diplomacy during the "high" Cold War had only confirmed the Founders' dire warnings. Indeed, the United States had learned its lesson; it would no longer search for "monsters to destroy." A new foreign policy more consistent with its traditional style would be adopted. Jimmy Carter, the born-again Christian, had become the redeemer of the American way.

THE RECOGNITION OF INTERDEPENDENCE

By 1976 the nations of the world had become more interdependent, meaning that their fates were more closely connected than ever before. Shifts in economic production, the growth and movement of populations, and environmental decay did not respect national frontiers. Even in the area of national security, the continuing appeal of nuclear weapons meant that any large-scale war would affect all corners of the world—no nation was any longer "an island, entire of itself." The attraction of interdependence was its prospect of a more peaceful and harmonious world consistent with American values and an escape from the more troublesome world of power politics. Moreover, it was claimed, transnational economic and technological forces made this more coop-

2. See Stanley Hoffmann, *Primacy or World Order* (New York: McGraw-Hill, 1978).

erative world inevitable. The expansion of the global economy into a single marketplace, the perils of nuclear proliferation, and the effects of pollution and the population explosion collectively made interdependence not just an aspiration but a reality in world politics.

Four central assumptions underlay interdependence as a model for the future—and they continue to influence American foreign policy as it enters the twenty-first century.[3] First, it was asserted that, in an ironic paradox, nuclear weapons were assuring the peace. The superpowers' strategic nuclear arms were weapons of denial and deterrence, and their existence made the use of conventional arms less likely because of the danger of escalation of hostilities. Thus the likelihood of major war between the superpowers, even among their allies and friends, was minimal. When wars occurred, however, as in the case of Vietnam, the conflicts were likely to last a long time and to be expensive in terms of lives lost, money, and increased social divisions—in short, the costs might be excessive in relation to the combatants' goals. Thus future Vietnams were unlikely, especially after the disastrous American experience.

The second and related assumption underlying interdependence was that economic or welfare issues (collectively referred to as low politics) had become at least as important to national security as military protection (high politics). This had occurred not only because security seemed more assured but also because the democratic societies of the West had become more and more preoccupied with economic growth rates, consumerism, and ever-higher standards of living. The developing countries, too, were bent on modernizing and on satisfying their own people's expectations for a better life, an effort that Carter promised to support generously. The key issues were economic and social, in his view, and by their nature they promoted such values as social justice and human dignity rather than violence and destruction.

Third, under conditions of interdependence nations could not fulfill their socioeconomic goals by themselves. Western societies, for example, ran largely on oil imported from non-Western countries, which, in turn, sought Western capital, technology, and food. All countries, rich and poor alike, suffered from cyclical downturns in the world economy and prospered when these cycles reversed themselves. Thus nations no longer completely governed their own destinies, and no government by itself could meet the aspirations and needs of its people for a better life; only cooperation would enhance each nation's prosperity. More specifically, whereas in zero-sum military matters one nation's increase in power was seen by its adversary as a loss of power, on positive-sum eco-

---

3. For a detailed examination and application of this concept, see Robert O. Keohane and Joseph S. Nye Jr., *Power and Interdependence*, 2d ed. (New York: HarperCollins, 1989).

nomic issues each country's welfare was dependent on the existence of prosperity in other countries. Precisely because nations were vulnerable to one another, they needed to work out problems together. Such cooperation required a greater willingness to resolve disputes peacefully and a higher degree of mutual understanding and international harmony.

Fourth, and very important, great-power coercion was said to play a minimal role in resolving welfare issues, again in strong contrast to the primary role it might play in security issues. Even if coercive threats were effective once or twice, their frequent use would only alienate countries whose support was needed on other issues. Although many of the nations with which the United States had to deal were comparatively weak militarily, they were not helpless or without leverage of their own. Their economic troubles would require commitments of American aid; their social problems would send thousands of refugees to American shores and cities. Furthermore, they possessed commodities that, if production were shut off, would hurt the consuming nations. And together they had considerable political influence. The traditional way of calculating power—by adding up human resources, industrial capacity, military strength, and other factors—did not reveal this.

It was not surprising that this vision of transnational interdependence strongly influenced the Carter administration's policy. Carter came to power just after South Vietnam's final collapse, when the United States was sick and tired of the war and the power politics that presumably had been responsible for the country's involvement. Many of the administration's top officials, who as leaders or members of the bureaucracy under Lyndon Johnson or Richard Nixon had participated in the decision making about the war, shared the widely felt sense of shame about that conflict. They felt guilty about the apparent abuse of American power, as well as about other misuses (such as covert political interventions). Henry Kissinger's balance-of-power approach, therefore, was dismissed as obsolete; the world had moved beyond the days when this "European" approach seemed relevant. The incoming administration claimed that it would be more sensitive to the "new" realities of a more complex world and no longer a prisoner of the old Cold War myth of superpower competition and confrontation, which had led to U.S. support for right-wing dictatorships in the name of freedom.

East-West matters, then, no longer were regarded as a central concern except in the sense of East and West working together for arms control to reduce the superpowers' nuclear arsenals, to prevent the outbreak of a catastrophic war, and to reduce the spread of nuclear weapons to nations that did not yet possess them. As for détente, it remained a prerequisite for doing "good works" in the developing areas of the world.

This image of the post–Vietnam War world, with its distaste for national egotism and the use of power, represented more than the reassertion of an older and more "moral" American approach to foreign policy. To many it signified the ultimate transformation of world politics.

ECONOMIC STATECRAFT IN WORLD POLITICS

When social and economic strength supplemented military power as the foundation of national security in the 1970s, the instruments of foreign policy changed as many countries increasingly turned to the tools of "economic statecraft" in advancing their foreign policy goals.[4] For example, the United States often dangled the "carrots" of trade and technology (see Chapter 7) before Soviet leaders to induce their compliance in arms control negotiations. Other instruments included international organizations, particularly the United Nations, where Third World countries had become numerically dominant and where their proposals for closer North-South collaboration would attract worldwide attention. Regional organizations such as the European Community, Organization of American States (OAS), and Organization for African Unity (OAU) brought their leaders together to devise common strategies for political stability and economic growth. Flows of foreign aid, in both military and economic forms, increased dramatically during this period. These growing volumes of aid served the interests not only of the recipients but also of the donors themselves, who competed for political influence among developing countries. Finally, and perhaps most dramatically, the petroleum "weapon" was used by what in traditional power terms were small, weak Middle Eastern states against the powerful Western industrialized countries whose economic prosperity was vulnerable to interruptions in the oil flow.

THE NEW INTERNATIONAL ECONOMIC ORDER AND NONALIGNMENT

Before Carter's rise to power, Western leaders often had argued that the causes of the persistent poverty in so many of the developing countries were of their own making: the fragility of nationhood; inefficient farming techniques, resulting in widespread hunger; high birth rates, which defeated the most valiant efforts aimed at economic growth; large defense budgets, often used to prop up dictators and repress citizens; and, all too often, widespread inefficiency and corruption. The develop-

4. For an elaboration, see David Baldwin, *Economic Statecraft* (Princeton, N.J.: Princeton University Press, 1985).

ing countries rejected the argument, however, that they were responsible for their failure to modernize. They pointed to the external system—the international economy—in which they were the sources of raw materials for Western industry, as the culprit. When demand declined, which occurred frequently as Western industries found substitutes or synthetics, the prices of developing country exports fell. As prices declined, so did the ability of the developing countries to earn foreign exchange with which to import manufactured goods. This in turn prevented development of their own industries and urban centers, widely viewed as the catalysts of greater prosperity, higher levels of education and literacy, and improved living conditions.

In short, the earnings of the world's poorest countries often declined while the cost of goods from industrialized societies steadily rose. In addition, when these countries were able to develop some industry and export to the West, they often ran into protective tariff barriers. Thus even when the developing countries worked harder, it was of little use; the structure of the international economy was biased against them and kept them in a subordinate position as suppliers of cheap raw materials for the rich Western states and as consumers of their finished products. Third World countries seemed condemned to poverty and to continuing political weakness.

Third World leaders viewed their countries as dependencies. They may have gained political independence, but they remained chained economically to the Western industrialized economies. Indeed, their status remained *neocolonial* because their economies were geared not to the needs of their own markets but to those of the developed countries' markets. That is why, they claimed, they remained impoverished despite decades of working hard and large infusions of foreign aid. Their dependent status in the international system hindered their ability to grow economically. Their integration into the global economy only benefited the dominant Western nations and left them further behind.

The developing countries argued not just that the Western-controlled international economic order gave an advantage to the strong over the weak; their main point was that they were poor because they had been exploited by the West. They had been plundered during the colonial days, and this plunder continued as they sold their resources cheaply on the international market. In this context their demand for a "new international economic order" was a claim for a redress of past wrongs. The rich nations, having used their power unfairly to take from the poor countries what rightfully belonged to those countries, the argument went, were obligated to make restitution in the name of past abuses. The transfer of wealth from the West to the Third World was therefore seen as repayment of a moral debt, and as an overdue investment in the ravaged economies of the poorer nations.

Among Third World countries the demands for a new international economic order included calls to stabilize commodity prices, link those prices to Western inflation rates, increase foreign aid, and establish preferential tariffs so that they could sell their products in Western markets. They felt they had the resources Western industry needed, and they vowed to press their demands through collective action. Toward that end, and recognizing their numerical superiority in the United Nations, the developing countries organized themselves into a cohesive bloc, the Group of 77 (G-77), as a vehicle to make their voices heard. As for their relations with the two superpowers, they reaffirmed their earlier adherence to "nonalignment" in the Cold War and to freedom from superpower interference.

While nonalignment was the geopolitical buzzword for much of the Third World, in reality the bias of many of these countries toward the Soviet Union was clearly visible. The Soviets had charged all along that the poverty and misery of the non-Western world were the results of Western capitalism and imperialism. Still, it seemed odd to find Vietnam, Afghanistan, North Korea, and Cuba accepted as "nonaligned" nations and odder still that the 1979 conference of these countries was held in Havana. Furthermore, the support given by the developing countries to most Soviet positions in the UN General Assembly raised doubts about their independent status. These states routinely voted against the United States in the General Assembly and openly criticized American actions in the United Nations Conference on Trade and Development, which had been established in 1964 to promote greater cooperation between rich and poor countries. But, oddest of all, when Vietnam, after its victory in the war, was cruelly driving its Chinese population out of the country, usually in boats that would not survive long ocean journeys, its behavior was not condemned.

In reality, this unofficial coalition between the Soviet Union and the nonaligned nations was largely cosmetic. The nonaligned countries were, above all, nationalistic; they had not fought for national independence only to lose it to Soviet imperialism. Yet it was a sign of the times that this coalition existed and that only a small number of Third World governments criticized the direction of the nonaligned movement and defended American policies.

FOREIGN AID AND NORTH-SOUTH RELATIONS

While often critical of U.S. policy and supporting Soviet positions, the leaders of developing countries frequently criticized both superpowers for their Cold War preoccupations and their alleged neglect of the poorer nations of the world. Far from neglecting them, however, the United States, the Soviet Union, and other industrialized countries gave them attention and resources in the form of foreign aid wholly disproportionate to the Third World's power. The reason was the bipolar distribution of power, which conferred on these new nations, most of which were fragile both economically and politically, greater leverage than their strength and influence warranted. Confronted by two great powers competing for their allegiance and loyalty, the Third World countries could lean first toward the communist states, thereby attracting Western economic and military aid and political support, and then toward the West, thereby attracting similar assistance from the Soviet Union or China.

The developing countries' exploitation of this "foreign aid rivalry" continued throughout the Cold War. Even many wealthy states outside the superpower competition, particularly those in Scandinavia and later along the Pacific Rim, offered billions of dollars in aid to further their own designs for international development. As the era of "low politics" took hold, affluent states began to view foreign aid as an obligation. It was not a question of *whether* they would contribute foreign aid, but how much, to whom, for what purposes, and under what terms. As time went on, each wealthy state devised a program of foreign aid that promoted its own national interests as well as those of recipient states.[5]

By the late 1970s, however, many industrialized states had become disappointed with the results of previous assistance efforts. The passage of two decades had revealed that the optimistic expectations of "instant development" had underestimated the difficulties of modernization. Moreover, foreign aid had not even been successful in winning friends and gaining influence within developing countries. As a result, not only did American aid fall to its lowest point by 1980—less than half of 1 percent of the gross national product (GNP)—but the emphasis shifted from capital development to technical assistance and a bigger role for private enterprise, including multinational corporations.[6] In surveys Americans consistently identified foreign aid as their least favorite government program.

In any event, prospects for the developing countries grew worse as the Cold War dragged on. With few exceptions they were still impoverished. The optimism had faded that foreign aid would propel their modernization or, later, that "trade, not aid" would permit them largely to earn their own way and to finance their own development. Food shortages and

5. See Steven W. Hook, *National Interest and Foreign Aid* (Boulder, Colo.: Lynne Rienner, 1995). Also see Steven W. Hook, ed., *Foreign Aid toward the Millennium* (Boulder, Colo.: Lynne Rienner, 1996).

6. In 1979 U.S. aid was only 0.2 percent of GNP, behind the aid given by Sweden, Norway, the Netherlands, France, Britain, West Germany, and other donors.

famines in Africa and southern Asia were stark reminders of what could happen. Thus the expectation of the former colonial states that they could realize their dreams of better and more rewarding lives for their peoples was unfulfilled. Illiteracy, starvation, and disease continued to coexist with dreams of national dignity and material welfare. For a variety of complex reasons, the billions of dollars in annual support from the North had little or no impact in the Southern Hemisphere. Despite the creation of an elaborate development aid "regime," gaps between the world's richest and poorest populations only widened.[7]

OIL AS A 'WEAPON'

It was in the context of yet another Arab-Israeli war in 1973 (described in the next section) that the Organization of Petroleum Exporting Countries (OPEC) quadrupled oil prices, from $3 to $12 a barrel, and its Arab members embargoed shipments of oil to the United States and the Netherlands, both supporters of Israel. The oil companies, which were supposed to be such powerful multinational corporations that they dominated the countries in which they operated, were shown to be without much power. Indeed, they were at the mercy of the governments of the countries in which they operated. The so-called imperialist states, whose governments were presumably controlled and directed by the capitalists, did not mobilize to squash the governments that were said to be their puppet regimes. Confronting a vital threat to their well-being and security from countries that had no military power to speak of, the industrial democracies did not even debate the issue of military intervention. As noted, this was the era of "low politics," in which economic and social issues took precedence over security issues. The Western countries instead talked of accommodation and acquiesced. Had this event occurred a few decades earlier, they would not have hesitated to resort to force rather than face the possibility of being destroyed economically.

OPEC's action at the time was widely viewed in the Third World as symbolic of a general protest against the industrialized countries. The organization became a kind of vanguard for the world's poorest nations. They shared a mood of anger, resentment, and revolt which clearly was directed against the North, particularly the United States. But ironically, the effects of the quadrupling of oil prices were felt most keenly by developing countries by threatening their plans to industrialize and handicapping their efforts to grow more food using technologically intensive, petroleum-based agricultural techniques.

7. See Robert E. Wood, *From Marshall Plan to Debt Crisis: Foreign Aid and Development Choices in the World Economy* (Berkeley: University of California Press, 1986).

Despite the increased suffering brought on by the steep rise in oil prices, the Third World countries did not form a coalition with the United States, Western Europe, and Japan to force lower oil prices. This can be explained in part by their fear of irritating OPEC, in part by their hope for promised but largely undelivered OPEC economic help (most went to fellow Muslim nations, where it was spent on arms), and in part by their desire to imitate OPEC. But the basic reason was that the Third World, as noted, identified emotionally with OPEC. The organization's action was widely perceived by these countries as "getting even" for past exploitation. It gave them a good feeling that for once the weak had turned the tables and made the strong suffer. (The German word *schadenfreude* says it best: pleasure received from seeing someone suffer who deserves it.)

The sharp rise in oil prices left no country untouched. In the United States and among its principal industrial allies, high oil prices slowed economic growth, brought on unemployment, created "stagflation" (simultaneous inflation and recession), lowered standards of living, created large Western imbalances of trade, and sharply lowered the value of the dollar. The energy crisis of the 1970s did not merely cause occasional inconveniences such as long lines to buy gas or higher prices at the gasoline pump; it profoundly upset entire economies and changed ways of life, as evidenced by smaller cars and lower speed limits in the United States. Moreover, the energy crisis raised the question of whether the Western states, which had paid for welfare programs by means of rapidly growing economies, could still afford such programs. Would they have to reduce defense expenditures in order to continue such programs? Or would they have to cut social expenditures to maintain strong defenses? Plenty of "guns" and "butter" no longer appeared affordable.

When Mao Zedong once said that "power grows out of the barrel of a gun," he would have been equally correct had he referred to a barrel of oil, an irreplaceable commodity that cannot be recycled. Large-scale capital investments and many years are required to explore, find, and drill for new oil. Similarly, new technologies to exploit solar energy or shale oil also require enormous investments of time and money. Other energy sources such as nuclear power are controversial or are, like coal, deemed environmentally undesirable. Thus no short-run substitute is readily available for economies that have long depended on relatively cheap oil and have neglected the development of alternative energy sources.

Is it any wonder, then, that the developing countries were delighted and held high hopes in the wake of the oil shocks of the 1970s? Indeed, OPEC's actions gave rise to three expectations: first, that OPEC would use its leverage to raise the prices of natural resources from the other

Third World countries; second, that the other commodity producers would follow OPEC's example by organizing their own cartels; and, third, that the OPEC "petrodollars" would flow to the Third World in the form of foreign aid. But to the chagrin of these countries, none of the three expectations materialized. OPEC fragmented as its members reverted within a decade to their previous patterns of undercutting the cartel oil prices.[8] And its example was not adopted by producers of other commodities, who remained consumed by their own competition for Western markets. Finally, OPEC profits were not shared with developing countries in the form of aid. After being deposited in New York banks, they were lent instead to many developing countries (particularly Mexico and Brazil) at market rates, which the borrowers could not repay, thus contributing to the debt crisis that afflicted much of the Third World in the 1980s.

CONTINUING STRUGGLES IN THE MIDDLE EAST

Four years before Carter took office, in the waning days of the Nixon administration, tensions in the Middle East had erupted in warfare that threatened to draw in both superpowers. In 1973 Egypt and Syria attacked Israel on the highest of all Jewish holy days—Yom Kippur, or the Day of Atonement. Egypt, which was ruled by Anwar Sadat, the Egyptian nationalist who had succeeded Gamal Abdel Nasser, attacked because it had become increasingly frustrated by Israel's continued occupation of Egyptian territory up to the East Bank of the Suez Canal, which Israel had captured in the Six-day War in 1967. The Egyptians achieved initial success in crossing the Suez Canal and driving into the Sinai Desert. Fearing that it would lose influence in the Arab world by remaining neutral, the Soviet Union delivered offensive arms to the Arab states. When indeed the Egyptian and Syrian armies proved successful in the opening round of fighting, the Soviets began a huge airlift of war materiel and opposed any cease-fire calls that were not linked to a pullback by Israel to the 1967 frontiers. Moscow also called on other Arab governments to join the war and approved the OPEC oil embargo.

U.S. INTERVENTION AND NUCLEAR CRISIS

The United States, under President Nixon, responded with its own massive airlift of military supplies in the face of enormous Israeli fighter plane and tank losses. Once Israel had recovered from its shock and had driven the Syrians back from the Golan Heights, its forces concen-

---

8. See Daniel Yergin, *The Prize: The Epic Quest for Oil, Money, and Power* (New York: Simon and Schuster, 1991).

THE MIDDLE EAST

trated on Egypt, crossed the Suez Canal to the West Bank, and moved to cut off supplies to the Egyptian forces on the East Bank and to encircle them. At this point the United States and the Soviet Union agreed on a cease-fire resolution in the UN Security Council. But the shooting continued, and the Israelis drove to encircle and destroy the Egyptian army on the eastern side of the Suez Canal.

Sadat then asked the United States and the Soviet Union to use their own forces to impose their cease-fire resolution. The United States declined to intervene with its forces, but the Soviet Union threatened to do so unilaterally. Thus the two superpowers now confronted one another, and American military forces were placed on a worldwide nuclear alert. Moscow backed off, however, and the United States, also eager to avoid an escalation, pressured Israel to end its military advance. These moves assured the cease-fire.

For Henry Kissinger, the urgency of reaching a Middle East settlement was obvious, and the time seemed favorable. He campaigned actively for a settlement, engaging in "shuttle diplomacy" as he crisscrossed the Middle East mediating the dispute. Indeed, Sadat was the first Egyptian leader to declare his willingness to accept the existence of Israel and make peace with it on the basis of the 1967 frontiers. Moreover, an Arab-Israeli peace would prevent an American-Soviet confrontation that could escalate into a superpower war. Each Arab-Israeli war had held the possibility of such a confrontation; in 1973 that possibility had become almost real. Kissinger also was determined to avoid the past pattern of an Israeli military victory, which could not be translated into an acceptable political settlement, and an Arab defeat, which left the Arabs humiliated, resentful, and more determined than ever not to accept Israel's right to exist and use oil as a weapon against the West. But when Ford left office, Kissinger's designs for a comprehensive peace settlement in the Middle East remained on the drawing board.

CARTER'S MIDDLE EAST BREAKTHROUGH

In 1976 the incoming Carter administration viewed the Middle East situation with alarm. Resentment from the Yom Kippur War remained sharp, with both sides acquiring new and more advanced weapons systems in its aftermath. Carter therefore proposed that all parties resume the negotiations that had begun at Geneva after the 1973 war.

In the final days of the Ford administration, Kissinger had fashioned his strategy to bring the Arabs and Israelis together step by step and exclude the Soviets; only at the final conference would the Soviet Union be invited for symbolic reasons. But Carter decided to approach the Soviets and enlist their cooperation in achieving a peace settlement. Moscow had influence with the more militant Syrians and within the Palestine Liberation Organization (PLO), which had formed to press the cause of renewed statehood for Palestine. The Soviets, therefore, could cause a lot of trouble and block negotiations. If Moscow participated in the peace negotiations, however, it would retain a degree of influence in the Arab world if and when a peace treaty were signed, the possibility of a superpower clash would be reduced, and détente with the United States would be strengthened, a prerequisite for a U.S. focus on the developing countries.

The two superpowers reached agreement on resolution of the Middle East conflict late in 1977, but neither Jerusalem nor Cairo was happy with the Soviet-American accord. Israel did not want to face all its enemies again simultaneously, and Egypt already had broken with Moscow, which now favored Syria, Egypt's rival. Thus Israel and Egypt decided to bypass Moscow and Washington and negotiate directly. In a dramatic and internationally televised visit to Jerusalem in November 1977, during which he addressed the Israeli Knesset (parliament), Sadat extended recognition to the Arabs' archenemy. The mood afterward was euphoric; a comprehensive peace, a peace with all of Israel's Arab enemies, seemed near.

The mood did not last long, however. Sadat apparently believed peace was achievable easily and quickly because he had taken the significant psychological step of reassuring the Israelis that his peace offer was genuine, not a trick. Israel would withdraw to its 1967 frontiers from the Sinai, the West Bank, Syria's Golan Heights, and Jordan's East Jerusalem and would recognize the Palestinians' legitimate rights. In return for their land, the Arabs would sign a peace treaty and Israel would gain the legitimacy and peace with security it had sought since birth. The Israelis always had asserted that if only the Arabs would negotiate with them directly, implying recognition, they would be willing to return the territories taken in 1967. In fact, Israel had specifically disclaimed annexationist ambitions. After the 1967 war its Labor government had accepted UN Resolution 242 committing Israel to the withdrawal from the captured land (or, given some adjustments for security reasons, from almost all of these areas).

But Israel's new coalition government was led by Prime Minister Menachem Begin, leader of the principal opposition party, Likud. He proposed an Israeli withdrawal from the Sinai Desert, but offered the Palestinians on the West Bank and in the Gaza Strip only autonomy, or self-rule, not self-determination. Moreover, Begin referred to the West Bank by its ancient Hebrew names, Judea and Samaria, and he claimed that it was not occupied territory to be returned but liberated territory to be kept as a part of the Greater Israel of which he had long dreamed. He left no doubt that he expected to establish Israeli sovereignty over both the West Bank and Gaza, each of which contained large Arab populations. In the meantime, the Israeli government announced that Jewish settlements in the Sinai and West Bank would remain, and it encouraged more settlements.

When, to no one's great surprise, bilateral negotiations broke down, the United States reentered the negotiating process. Carter felt that Sadat was offering Israel the security and peace it had so long sought, and that if this opportunity were not seized the result would be politically disastrous for Israel and economically disastrous for the West. The president thought three conditions were necessary for a solution in the Middle East. First, Israel had to abide by UN Resolution 242 and return most of the Arab territory it had captured in 1967. Only minor adjustments for security reasons could be allowed. Second, because the key to peace was the Palestinian issue, the Palestinians had to participate in the peace-making process. Carter himself declared that the Palestinians had a right to a "homeland," a deliberately vague term but one that nevertheless carried great symbolic weight. Third, in return for such Israeli concessions, the Arab states had to commit themselves not only to ending their state of hostilities with Israel but also to signing a peace treaty.

Begin was at odds with the first two conditions. He reinterpreted UN Resolution 242 to mean that Israel was not required to withdraw from the West Bank and Gaza. He also was opposed to a Palestinian state, which he—and indeed most Israelis—felt would endanger the existence of Israel. Moreover, he promoted his own plan for Israeli settlements in the occupied lands. Since 1967, however, the United States had consistently opposed these settlements as illegal. The Carter administration repeated this while it watched in disbelief as the Israeli government, in the middle of the peace process, actively encouraged new settlements on the land the Arabs claimed to be theirs. Washington was convinced that the Israelis were acting in bad faith in the midst of peace negotiations.

Repeated American efforts to halt this policy were in vain. By contrast, Sadat appeared reasonable and conciliatory. He had with great courage provided the psychological breakthrough with his trip to Jerusalem. He had shown sensitivity to Israel's security needs and had been willing to accept Israel's demands for a peace treaty and the subsequent normalization of relations—not after twenty-five years, or even five years, but immediately. The stalemate continued.

As the three-year interim Sinai agreement was about to run out in October 1978, Carter gambled and invited Begin and Sadat to meet with him at Camp David, the Maryland presidential retreat. The invitation was a gamble because had this summit meeting produced no results, the president's prestige, already low, would have been even more seriously impaired, American mediating attempts would have run their course, and Israeli-American relations would have been set back even further. But the president showed persistence and skill and after twelve days of patient negotiations emerged with a series of agreements, including a commitment by the two leaders to sign a peace treaty within three months.

Sadat made most of the concessions. He did not gain a commitment to an eventual Israeli withdrawal from the West Bank and Gaza Strip, or full Palestinian self-determination. The Israelis, however, promised to recognize "the legitimate rights of the Palestinians," to permit West Bank and Gaza Palestinians to participate in future negotiations on these areas and ratify or reject a final agreement, and to halt temporarily new Israeli settlements on the West Bank. In return, Israel gained a separate peace treaty with the strongest of its Arab neighbors; without Egypt the others could not by themselves take on Israel. Thus for a seemingly small investment Israel had gained the enormous dividend of a real sense of security.

Sadat hoped that a peace agreement would start momentum for further agreements with Israel. The first Arab reaction to the Camp David accords, however, was negative. Jordan, and even Saudi Arabia, joined Syria, Iraq, Libya, Algeria, and South Yemen in condemning Sadat, who became more isolated than ever. Under these circumstances, Carter's courageous personal intervention—his trip to Egypt and Israel—produced the necessary diplomatic breakthroughs and brought peace between these two long-term enemies. Yet the treaty finally produced did not bring a stable peace to the area. Israel quickly resumed and accelerated its settlements policy in the West Bank; the Arab states, except Egypt, became more hostile to American "meddling" in the region; the key Palestinian issue remained unresolved; and all sides continued to import large volumes of military hardware in preparation for the next conflagration.

THE COLLAPSE OF CARTER'S FOREIGN POLICY

Jimmy Carter's embrace of world-order politics in the late 1970s coincided with the Soviet Union's achievement of nuclear parity and many Americans' "crisis of confidence" in their government, brought on by a series of domestic problems. Thus, while the new Carter administration was deemphasizing the East-West conflict and focusing on North-South cooperation, the Soviet Union, perceiving the global balance of power to be shifting in its favor, saw opportunities to exploit and expand its influence militarily in the Third World.

The East-West struggle was not just an old, bad memory. It was still very much alive, even if the United States preferred not to compete actively and told itself that containment no longer seemed relevant in the face of the diffusion of power in the world, growing nationalism in the developing countries, and the shift in emphasis from power politics to world-order politics. The Soviets showed that they shared neither the belief that international politics had changed nor the view that military force had become an increasingly irrelevant instrument of policy. By 1979 the Soviet Union was estimated to be heavily outspending the United States on its military forces by at least 25 percent, perhaps by as much as 50 percent. Given an economic base believed to be about half that of the United States, this disproportionate spending on "guns" at the cost of "butter" for the Soviet people suggested that these forces were intended for more than just defense. In the Third World the Soviet

Union used its growing political-military involvement to exploit hostility among developing countries toward the North and to offer its model of communism and centrally directed industrialization for the developing countries to emulate.

During the "high" Cold War, the United States often had erred by overemphasizing East-West relations. Indeed, some of its mistakes, particularly with regard to China, were costly. But experience also had shown that grave danger lay in ignoring or downplaying these relations. It was one thing to learn from the past and correct errors. It was quite another to dismiss the very nature of international politics, whose chief characteristic is its strong sense of historic continuity. In the last half of Carter's presidency this lesson was painfully learned. His restraint in foreign affairs and appeals to universal moral standards were followed in rapid succession by the Soviet invasion of Afghanistan, a Marxist revolution in Nicaragua, and the seizure of American diplomats as hostages in Iran. These three concurrent events, along with a second energy crisis, seemed to offer strong testimony to the limitations of world-order politics and raised the question of whether the Nixon and preceding administrations had been so wrong in giving priority to American-Soviet competition, in emphasizing military power, or in thinking that the East-West struggle could not be divorced from North-South relations.

THE SOVIET INVASION OF AFGHANISTAN

Divisions within the Carter administration between adherents of détente and hard-liners continued to fester. This division was symbolized by Secretary of State Cyrus Vance, on the one hand, and National Security Adviser Zbigniew Brzezinski, on the other. After Soviet troops and tanks poured into Afghanistan in late 1979, Vance's influence waned and Brzezinski's rose. The Soviet-inspired coup that had occurred a year earlier in Afghanistan had been overlooked, but the 85,000 Soviet troops that entered the country during the last week of 1979 were hard to ignore. Fierce resistance by Muslim citizens to radical and antireligious reforms appeared to threaten the Soviet-supported regime.

Among their other concerns, the Soviets feared that the Islamic fundamentalism then sweeping Iran and Pakistan might engulf Afghanistan, which lay between these two countries, creating an insecure situation on the Soviet Union's southern border where approximately fifty million Soviet Muslims lived. In response to the situation, Moscow invoked the Brezhnev Doctrine, which asserted that once a nation had become socialist, it was not to be surrendered to counterrevolution (as the Soviets defined these terms). The march of history toward socialism was inevitable and irreversible. Earlier, this doctrine had been invoked only in Eastern Europe—in Hungary in 1956 and Czechoslovakia in 1968. Now the Red Army was to ensure history's progress outside of the Soviet sphere in a Third World country.

The Soviets expected no more of an American response than a condemnation of the Soviet action as deplorable, but no action. Clearly the Soviets believed that vital security interests were at stake and did not give much thought to American reactions. In truth, the Soviets felt there was little to lose. Carter, to rescue the SALT II treaty in the Senate, had promised to increase defense spending and modernize American strategic forces. And the Soviet Union had received few of the trade, technology, and financial benefits it had expected from détente; indeed, it had been denied most-favored nation commercial status, which China had received. Nevertheless, such a disregard for American reaction, implying contempt for American power, was rather new.

For Carter and Vance, who had pinned so much of their hopes for world-order politics on superpower cooperation, the Soviet invasion was a shock. Chagrined, Carter called the Afghanistan invasion the greatest threat to world peace since World War II and said, "[the Soviet action] made a more dramatic change in my opinion of what the Soviets' ultimate goals are than anything they've done in the previous time I've been in office." No president in the postwar era has testified more dramatically to his own naiveté.

The president, swinging with events, then became a hard-liner. He stepped up military spending, halted high-technology sales, embargoed grain shipments, and imposed a U.S. boycott on the Olympic Games scheduled for Moscow in the summer of 1980. The Senate, meanwhile, refused to ratify the SALT II treaty. Most important of all, Carter announced his own doctrine: the United States would henceforth consider any threat to the Persian Gulf to be a direct threat to its own vital interests. It would be one of many steps in Carter's anguished transition to a more aggressive, militaristic, and Cold War-oriented foreign policy.

Détente thus came to an end in 1980 as superpower relations disintegrated. Carter undoubtedly had been correct that not all regional conflicts were tests of superpower strength and credibility. In truth, however, few purely regional quarrels existed outside the context of global Cold War. Détente ultimately collapsed because of a series of regional conflicts that the administration had attempted to isolate from the American-Soviet rivalry—only to find that it could not do so. As Soviet activities in the Third World showed, the Soviet Union did not consider this rivalry over. Quite the opposite: it took advantage of America's post-Vietnam reluctance to act and its illusion that Third World problems could be separated from the superpower competition.

History also was unkind to President Carter in Central America, where decades of economic distress, military dictatorship, and ideological polarization spawned a variety of revolutionary movements. These often were directed not only against the reigning rulers but also against the United States, whose support for dictators in the name of containing communism engendered widespread resentment throughout Latin America and the Caribbean. The United States, the self-proclaimed protector of the region under the Monroe Doctrine, was widely viewed by many as more of a menace than a supportive patron. Carter hoped to change this perception by reforming U.S. policy and establishing a new reputation as a truly "good neighbor."

In Nicaragua, Carter opposed the long-standing military dictatorship of Anastasio Somoza, whose family had ruthlessly controlled the country for nearly five decades (after the departure of U.S. Marines from the country). Carter's reversal of American policy was consistent with his overall effort to shift attention from Cold War concerns to internal social and economic problems in the Third World. Continuing U.S. support for right-wing dictatorships, he felt, would certainly doom U.S. interests in the region and throughout the developing world. Popular resentment and anger would eventually lead to the overthrow of such dictatorships, and American identification with the status quo would only alienate the new rulers. Unlike in Vietnam, the argument went, the United States had to place itself on the "right side of history." Thus the Carter administration favored social and political change and tried to identify U.S. policy with such change rather than oppose it.

The rebellion against Somoza accelerated in the late 1970s despite the leader's increasingly brutal use of the Nicaraguan National Guard. His overthrow also was encouraged by the Organization of American States, which called for a democratic government and the holding of free elections as soon as possible. As a result of all these forces, Somoza's regime finally collapsed in 1979.[9] At first, Carter favored the coalition of anti-Somoza forces led by the Sandino Liberation Front (known as Sandinistas), which during Somoza's days were domestically supported by such elements as the Catholic church, the educated middle class, and the business community. In its first years under the coalition, Nicaragua received allotments of $90 million in foreign aid from the United States and promises for long-term support. "If you do not hold me responsible for everything that happened under my predecessors," Carter told

9. For a more thorough treatment, see Anthony Lake, *Somoza Falling* (Boston: Houghton Mifflin, 1989).

Nicaragua's new leader, Daniel Ortega, "I will not hold you responsible for everything that happened under your predecessors."

The new regime in Nicaragua, however, did not live up to Carter's expectations. The broad-based anti-Somoza coalition rapidly dissolved as the Sandinistas centralized authority within a nine-member directorate. Free elections were delayed, the press was (again) censored, and other political restrictions were imposed by the junta, which turned increasingly to Marxist-Leninist models for building a self-sufficient communist state. In addition, the Sandinistas offered to assist their allies in El Salvador, where a similar civil war was erupting between its military dictatorship and left-wing guerrillas. The Salvadoran dictatorship responded by sending "death squads" into the impoverished countryside and murdering suspected insurgents. When their victims included three American nuns, the Carter administration rescinded U.S. aid to El Salvador and watched as the civil war became bloodier. Nicaragua and El Salvador remained battle zones into the mid-1980s and became a central preoccupation of Ronald Reagan's presidency.

The unrest in Central America further demonstrated the limitations of Carter's efforts to redirect American foreign policy. To some degree, he was captive to the unstable conditions that had developed in the region before and during the Cold War. No immediate reversal of American policy, however well intentioned, was likely to counteract the bitterness and resentment that had developed for so long toward "*yanqui* imperialism." Far from engendering newfound trust between the United States and Central America, Carter's efforts instead provided an opening for anti-American forces to assume power and translate their resentment into revenge. As Carter attempted to purify American foreign policy, he discovered that the outside world was continuing to pursue the same *realpolitik* he had eschewed. Ideological tensions only increased during his tenure, despite his best efforts to focus on areas of cooperation between the United States and its Latin American neighbors.

AMERICA 'HELD HOSTAGE' IN IRAN

The low level to which American credibility and power had fallen was symbolized by the storming of the American embassy in Tehran in November 1979 by a mob of militant students, who seized fifty-two American embassy workers. This occurred after the ousted, pro-American shah, who was suffering from cancer, was admitted to the United States for medical treatment.[10] The newly installed revolutionary

---

10. The shah died a few months later in Egypt. For a review of his long and intimate relationship with the United States, see Mrak Gasiorowski, *U.S. Foreign Policy and the Shah* (Ithaca, N.Y.: Cornell University Press, 1991).

authorities, hoping to create an Islamic theocracy in Iran, gave the unprecedented action their blessing and support.

The seizure of American hostages paralyzed Carter, and his subsequent efforts to gain their safe release became high public drama. Nightly, U.S. television networks exposed the American public to pictures of crowds, like well-rehearsed choruses, chanting their hatred of America, the "Great Satan," as it was called by the Ayatollah Ruhollah Khomeini, Iran's chief religious leader and *imam*, or leader, of all Shiite Muslims. "Death to America" was the battle cry as Carter was burned in effigy on the streets of Tehran.

Carter, who had stressed human rights in his election campaign and who had pointed to the shah, among others, as an example of his predecessors' amoral, if not immoral, policy, was as usual caught between conflicting views. The disagreements in Washington were such that the fall of the shah and Khomeini's triumph were greeted with relief. But as had happened so often before, the Carter administration's understanding of Khomeini was superficial, consistent with its own hopes of what would happen. Yet perhaps Carter's confusion was understandable, for, after all, who in Washington or any other Western capital in that secular age would have given serious consideration to the strength of a religious movement and the possibility that it would transform Iran into a medieval theocracy? The possible emergence of an Iran dominated by the clergy was so alien to all Western thinking that it was not taken seriously. There was no precedent for such a reaction to efforts at modernization.

In the 444 days following the taking of the hostages, the world watched as the Carter administration tried one means after another to gain their release. Among other things, appeals were made to the United Nations and the International Court of Justice and a series of economic sanctions was applied. But all was in vain. The holding of the hostages was a symbolic act of defiance and revenge for the shah, who was portrayed by the new regime as an American puppet who had cruelly exploited Iranians in behalf of U.S. interests. As the administration's patience wore thin, it attempted a rescue mission in the spring of 1980. The mission was called off, however, when three of the eight helicopters malfunctioned in a desert sandstorm. Even worse, one helicopter collided on the ground with the refueling aircraft for the flight out of Iran, killing eight servicemen and injuring five others. To a nation on edge, the mission's failure dramatically symbolized the apparent helplessness of the United States, as well as the low level of readiness, competence, and reliability of its armed forces. Secretary of State Cyrus Vance resigned in protest of the mission, revealing deepening divisions within the Carter administration over foreign policy.

Fortunately, two events helped to gain the hostages' release on January 20, 1981, the day Carter left office. The first was the Iraqi attack on Iran in the fall of 1980. The war suddenly made the U.S. economic sanctions, especially the freeze on Iranian money in U.S. banks, painful for Iran because its military forces were largely American equipped. The need for spare parts and the cash to buy them and other goods grew as oil production in Iran fell to almost nothing. The second event was the November 1980 victory of Ronald Reagan, the former governor of California, in the U.S. presidential elections. Because he had run on a tough foreign policy platform and had denounced the Iranians as "barbarians" and "kidnappers," the Iranians expected harsher measures from Reagan, including military action.

In these circumstances diplomacy finally proved successful. The fifty-two hostages were released just after Reagan's inauguration in a gesture fraught with symbolism. A humiliating chapter in American history, coming so shortly after the Vietnam trauma, had ended. In the exuberance of the welcome that the ex-hostages received on their return to America, one could almost hear the refrain "never again," for, in a real sense, America itself and the U.S. government had been taken captive and held hostage. Combined with national frustrations over Afghanistan, Nicaragua, and the second oil crisis of the decade, which was precipitated by the turmoil in Iran, the Iranian debacle deepened the perception of an American "decline." Reagan vowed to reverse this trend upon his assumption of the presidency in January 1981.

THE TRIUMPH OF REALISM OVER IDEALISM

As we have seen in this chapter, the Soviet invasion of Afghanistan, the Sandinista revolution in Nicaragua and its spin-off rebellion in El Salvador, and the hostage crisis in Iran collectively undermined Carter's attempt to promote world-order politics on the basis of global interdependence, universal standards of morality, and peaceful cooperation. Along the way, these events dispelled much of the post-Vietnam malaise and led to a demand for a more vigorous American foreign policy. In this respect, Leonid Brezhnev, Daniel Ortega, and the Ayatollah Khomeini may have done the United States a favor, just as German submarine attacks on U.S. ships (World War I), a Japanese attack on Pearl Harbor (World War II), and a Soviet seizure of power in Czechoslovakia (Cold War) had served to mobilize the nation when the public mood was one of disengagement and relaxation. After America's years of withdrawal, the challenges of 1979 and 1980 may have been necessary to demonstrate that isolation from the unsavory realities of world politics, far from rendering such realities inconsequential, perhaps encouraged their spread and resulted in sustained assaults on U.S. interests and prestige.

Carter sensed this shift in mood as he took a harder line toward the Soviets during his final year in office. For example, he elevated the stature of Brzezinski. And on Capitol Hill the U.S. Congress enthusiastically approved Carter's requests for a large increase in American defense spending. Thus began the process of national rearmament that Ronald Reagan would oversee and accelerate well into the 1980s. In all of these efforts Carter was strongly supported by the American public, which drew a connection between his previous condemnation of power politics and the calamities that befell his administration in its final two years.

Paradoxically, it was not the *recognition* of Carter's moralistic values but their *repudiation* that pulled the country out of its post-Vietnam "malaise." The widely perceived consequences of American introspection and self-doubt, which included humiliations and challenges to its interests on virtually every continent, mobilized public opinion and political consensus where appeals to universal moralism had fallen short in previous years. The American style of foreign policy, it appeared, seemed to require more than good intentions; support for democratic values and global progress could not be sustained at the cost of American national interests.

Carter was clearly anguished by the spreading challenges to his foreign policy. For weeks he refused to leave the White House while he considered ways to get the hostages home from Iran; in December 1979 he refused to light the White House Christmas tree while the hostages remained in captivity. Moreover, the downward spiral of events took a visible physical toll on the president, who was forced to reconcile his most basic spiritual beliefs with the unavoidable challenges of overseas competition. In response to these challenges and to the shift in American public opinion away from world-order politics, Carter abandoned many of his foreign policy beliefs and programs.

Reagan received the full benefit of this shift in mood. For decades, he had taken a hard line toward the Soviet Union. Although inflation and the weak state of the U.S. economy may have been important factors in Reagan's election, the fact remains that because of OPEC and the collapse of the shah, the domestic economic issue was inseparable from American foreign policy and the U.S. position in the world. Whereas Carter was forced to acknowledge that the events of 1979 and 1980 undermined his idealistic world view, Reagan was able to argue that they confirmed his realism. "Historical forces" were not moving in the direction of transnational cooperation, as Carter had claimed previously; they had never diverted from their consistent path, which was plagued by conflicting interests and tests of strength.

Ronald Reagan, often called the "great communicator," promoted hard-line policies toward communist countries during the early 1980s.

CHAPTER NINE

The Revival of Superpower Confrontation

Just as Jimmy Carter's rise to power reflected the introspective American mood of the Vietnam-Watergate era, Ronald Reagan captured the more assertive national spirit of 1980. A former movie star and pitchman for General Electric, President Reagan was known neither for his intellect nor for long hours spent in the Oval Office. The contrast with his predecessor was widely apparent. Whereas Carter's world view emphasized the complexities of interdependence, Reagan's was unabashedly one-dimensional. Whereas Carter pored over background reports and anguished over policy choices, Reagan literally dozed through high-level meetings. But he brought to the office two characteristics that were to help transform American-Soviet relations: strong anticommunist instincts and a powerful ability to mobilize public opinion. Both characteristics served him well.

Reagan attempted to restore the country's battered stature and the national pride of Americans by reviving the notion that an active U.S. role in world affairs was essential to world peace. Soviet leaders, he felt, had exploited détente, the Vietnam syndrome, and Carter's conciliatory gestures to advance America's global strategic interests. As Reagan's supporters saw it, a clear line could be drawn from Carter's idealism to the Soviet invasion of Afghanistan, the Sandinista revolution in Nicaragua, and the seizure of American hostages in Iran. Believing the United States must match the Soviet nuclear and conventional military buildup of the 1970s, Reagan proposed a massive buildup of U.S. armed forces. A concerned Congress approved his proposals to double American defense spending in his first term. This included matching recent Soviet deployments of intermediate-range nuclear missiles in Europe with a new round of North Atlantic Treaty Organization (NATO) deployments.

Reagan often boasted that he was blessed with the luck of the Irish. Indeed, he certainly had the good fortune to take office as the torch was being passed in Moscow from the old guard to a new generation of reformers ultimately led by Mikhail Gorbachev. The reduced tensions between the superpowers, so unexpected at the beginning of the decade, often have been attributed to Gorbachev, who took over the Kremlin in 1985, during Reagan's second term in office. The new Soviet leader was said to be the first enlightened ruler since the 1917 Revolution. His generation of Soviet elites hailed from urban rather than rural backgrounds and had some exposure to foreign countries; it was thus more aware of the failings of the Soviet system and critical of its internal defects. Had Brezhnev or his two immediate successors survived, Gorbachev's domestic and foreign policy changes might not have occurred. Nor would the Cold War likely have ended on terms that were as peaceful or as beneficial to the West.

To some, the collapse of the Warsaw Pact and the Soviet Union in 1991 was a fait accompli, a historical inevitability no matter who was the president of the United States in the 1980s. The ossified Soviet system already was in an advanced stage of decline; its internal problems were growing severer daily and its hold on its clients in Eastern Europe and beyond was becoming more tenuous. Thus Gorbachev—or any leader of the country—had to implement drastic reforms in the Soviet Union's political and economic system; permit the restive populations in Warsaw, Prague, and East Berlin to express themselves; and adopt a more cooperative posture toward the United States. These measures would, in this view, only magnify the deficiencies of the Soviet system and hasten its self-destruction.

But this interpretation of events, which minimizes the roles of both Reagan and Gorbachev, does not quite tell the full story. It fails to rec-

ognize the crucial part that Reagan played in raising the costs of the
superpower competition and in forcing the Soviet Union to reform its
system. The U.S. military buildup, which actually began in Carter's last
year, required greater Soviet investments in arms at a time when the
dwindling resources of the Soviet Union were needed for domestic priorities. Moreover, new NATO missile deployments in Europe negated
the strategic advantages of recent Soviet installations. The president's
proposals for a Strategic Defense Initiative further worried the Soviets
because, whether or not it succeeded in creating a missile-proof shield
over the United States, the research might lead America to a quantum
leap in technology at a time when the Soviet Union was struggling with
growing economic problems at home. Finally, the Reagan Doctrine of
supporting guerrillas against Soviet-backed Marxist regimes further
increased the costs of Soviet expansion.

In short, the Brezhnev foreign policy, which at first had appeared so
successful, had become counterproductive: it had provoked a strong
American reaction, held NATO together, and left the Soviet Union surrounded by enemies (including Japan and China). Reagan had increased
the strains on the Soviet Union so much that it could no longer muddle
through. Moreover, he had eliminated any flexibility that Gorbachev
might have had and forced him to retrench abroad, cut military spending, and subordinate foreign policy to domestic affairs. Initially thought
to be reckless and widely condemned as a cowboy (especially in Europe)
because he appeared trigger-happy, the president left office in January
1989 with the superpower relationship on the best terms it had been
since 1945. Thus, despite some setbacks and a huge federal budget deficit
that helped to make the United States, once the world's largest creditor
nation, its greatest debtor, Reagan left office with the highest public
approval of any postwar president.

REAGAN'S RHETORICAL OFFENSIVE

When Reagan came into office, the national disillusionment with
détente was widespread and the term *Cold War II* was heard often. The
president's longtime hostility toward communism in general and the
Soviet Union specifically fit the new post-détente mood. He denounced
Soviet communism as "the focus of evil in the modern world" and
announced to Americans, "There is sin and evil in the world, and we're
enjoined by Scripture and the Lord Jesus to oppose it with all our
might."[1] Soviet leaders would "lie, steal, cheat, and do anything else to

---

1. Remarks to the National Association of Evangelicals, March 8, 1983, in *The Russians
and Reagan,* ed. Strobe Talbott (New York: Vintage Books, 1984), 113.

advance their goals," warned Reagan.[2] Opposition to the Soviet Union was, therefore, a religious as well as a political imperative. Reagan spoke of the march of freedom and democracy leaving "Marxism-Leninism on the ashheap of history." Of Eastern Europe he said, "Regimes planted by bayonets do not take root"—that is, the communist regimes had no legitimacy. The United States could not accept the "permanent subjugation of the people of Eastern Europe," he asserted.[3] In making the point that democracy and freedom were the waves of the future, the president was not just giving the Soviets a dose of their own medicine, for the Soviets regularly denounced the United States and forecast the "inevitable end" of Western capitalism. More important, he was questioning the legitimacy and longevity of communism as a social and political system in Eastern Europe and the Soviet Union.

Many American critics dismissed Reagan's predictions about communism being swept aside by the tide of democracy as empty rhetoric. By the end of his second term, however, as noncommunist tyrannies were being swept away and communist regimes were being exposed to greater demands for liberties from within, Reagan's prediction looked less like right-wing rantings than accurate insights into historical development. While far from being a political theorist, Reagan was a spirited polemicist whose expectation of communism's demise in Europe was fulfilled under his watch.

The harsh denunciations of the Soviet Union were not mere statements of the president's personal ideology; they served two tactical purposes. First, they were intended to remobilize American public opinion after the years of détente. Reagan, to whom détente had all along been an illusion based on the unwarranted belief that the Soviets had changed their character, sought to arouse American opinion for the longer term. Second, the president's war of words was intended to send the Soviet leaders a message, one that probably was heeded all the more because the Soviet leadership was in the throes of a geriatric crisis. First, Soviet leader Leonid Brezhnev died in late 1982; his successor, Yuri Andropov, died just over a year later in early 1984; and his successor, Konstantin Chernenko, in ill health when he took over, died just over a year later in 1985. Gorbachev, who had risen rapidly to the top of the Communist Party hierarchy, now became the Soviet Union's fourth leader since Reagan had assumed office. Reagan's blunt declarations were intended to send the new Soviet leadership the signal that the Vietnam syndrome was a thing of the past, that America's will to resist Soviet expansion was

---

2. *New York Times,* January 30, 1981.

3. Address to members of the British Parliament, June 8, 1982, in Talbott, *Russians and Reagan,* 89–104.

back. But the president hoped to avoid confrontations and possible military clashes by sending signals that were intentionally sharp so that the Soviet Union would not act, as it had during the 1970s, in the belief that America would not react. Minor U.S. military actions against small Soviet proxies such as Libya and Grenada—actions that the United States could not lose and were not costly—were intended to drive this message home. In that sense, the tough words were essentially a substitute for riskier deeds.

The early Reagan years may have been characterized by rhetorical confrontations, but there were no direct encounters or crises. In policy terms they were quiet years. Despite his reputation for machismo, the president was operationally cautious. Indeed, to the extent the Soviets saw him as a leader spoiling for a fight, they were no doubt strengthened in their conviction that they needed to act with restraint. Reagan's foreign policy was basically a return to the containment policy of the immediate postwar years. The primary emphasis was on East-West relations, on the Soviet Union as a communist expansionist state, and on the need to contain that expansion, including in the Third World, by force if necessary.

THE U.S. MILITARY BUILDUP AND OPPOSITION TO ARMS CONTROL

The 1970s in the United States were rife with antimilitary sentiment, neoisolationist hopes, and cries for domestic priorities and reductions of the defense budget. Indeed, those years witnessed "the most substantial reduction in American military capabilities relative to those of the Soviet Union in the entire postwar period."[4] American defense expenditures had fallen to the 1950 (pre–Korean War) low of 5 percent of the nation's gross national product (GNP) at a time when the Soviet Union, despite having an economy only half the size that of the United States, was spending substantially more than the United States on defense.

By 1981 any president would have been concerned about Soviet intentions and capabilities. Carter's defense secretary, Harold Brown, already had noted that "as our defense budgets have risen, the Soviets have increased their defense budgets. As our defense budgets have gone down, their defense budgets have increased again." And Reagan had once asked, "What arms race? We stopped, they raced."

After a decade and a half of Soviet efforts to exploit America's Vietnam-induced isolation and a weakened American presidency, the Sovi-

4. John Lewis Gaddis, *Strategies of Containment* (New York: Oxford University Press, 1982), 320–322.

et Union possessed the strategic and conventional forces needed to project its power beyond Eurasia. It was in the context of Soviet perceptions of a changing "correlation of forces" that the Soviets had exploited Third World situations to increase their influence by means of military advisers and arms, proxies such as the Vietnamese in Cambodia and the Cubans in Africa, and, of course, their own troops in Afghanistan.

The Reagan administration was especially worried about the state of America's deterrent forces. The vulnerable land-based Minuteman intercontinental ballistic missiles (ICBMs) and the aging B-52 bombers and Polaris submarines had been built in the 1950s and mid-1960s. American strategic forces needed to be modernized to ensure their continued deterrent capability. At the center of the administration's rearmament program was the MX (missile experimental) ICBM with ten warheads. Highly controversial because it appeared to have the same first-strike capability attributed to Soviet ICBMs, the MX would, it was feared, create a mutual hair-trigger situation that could lead to a nuclear war that neither side wanted. Each would feel it had to take that risk because if it failed to strike first, its ICBMs might be destroyed.

Even more disturbing was the administration's talk of nuclear warning shots, "protracted" nuclear war, nuclear "war fighting," and "prevailing" in a nuclear war. The Reagan administration, more than its predecessors, speculated about such scenarios publicly, particularly Secretary of State Alexander Haig. Thus the administration's five-year, $1 trillion defense program (which actually totaled almost $2 trillion over Reagan's two terms) stimulated enormous controversy. It conveyed the impression that by relying too much on military strength the administration was flirting with disaster, and it reinforced the impression that the United States was largely responsible for the arms race. The momentum of the Soviet Union's arms program since the mid-1960s and its impact on the balance of nuclear and conventional balances often appeared forgotten in the uproar over the administration's rearmament program.

This uproar was intensified by Reagan's strong opposition to arms control, the centerpiece of both Nixon's and Carter's policies toward the Soviet Union. Rejection of the SALT process reflected the Reagan administration's strong distrust of the Soviets and its conviction that past arms control efforts had led to America's relative decline. It announced that it would postpone any arms negotiations until the United States could "negotiate from strength." But postponing new arms control talks proved difficult because public opinion equated arms control with disarmament and even more so with a sincere search for peace. The pressure on the administration therefore grew. When negotiations finally began in 1982, the administration claimed it was shifting the emphasis from arms limitation—setting ceilings on launchers—to drastic reductions. Thus it changed the name of the process from SALT (Strategic Arms Limitation Talks) to START (Strategic Arms Reduction Talks). The administration's real motive for this change, however, was to make its approach politically appealing at home, to deflect domestic criticism, and to weaken the newborn nuclear freeze movement while the buildup continued. The initial arms control proposals, then, were clearly propagandistic and meant to be rejected by Moscow, thereby winning time for the administration.

That is how many Americans saw it too, and Reagan therefore inspired a widespread "peace movement" in the early 1980s. Its adherents ranged from academics to religious leaders, especially the Catholic and Methodist bishops, who questioned the morality of nuclear deterrence, a policy based on the threat to use nuclear weapons in order to prevent their use. Both sets of bishops condemned not only the use of nuclear weapons, but also their very presence in the arsenals and military doctrines of both superpowers. Yet if such weapons could not be used even in retaliation, how could deterrence be made credible? Was the goal of peace moral but the means of preserving it immoral? In the meantime, antinuclear books and films became popular, climaxing in an ABC-TV movie entitled *The Day After* which depicted the nuclear devastation of an average American city.

In addition to decrying the immorality of nuclear deterrence, the peace movement asserted that nuclear war would mean the end of civilization, the "last epidemic" as a doctors' organization phrased it. This theme was supported strongly by new scientific arguments that the smoke produced by the many fires caused by nuclear attacks would shut out sunlight, plunging the world into darkness for several months and causing a prolonged freeze, or "nuclear winter," leading to the extinction of most plant and animal life. Regardless of who "won" a nuclear war, climatic catastrophe would follow and spread over the globe.[5]

Despite their widespread appeal, the arguments and revelations of the antinuclear movement contained little new. By 1980 the horror of nuclear war had been common knowledge for thirty-five years—that was, after all, why the United States had adopted a deterrent strategy. And it was the suicidal nature of nuclear arms that had encouraged the belief that nuclear deterrence would prevent an all-out Soviet attack on the United States and preserve peace among the superpowers. Moreover, although deterrence could fail, it had a historical record. The superpowers had not exchanged as much as a rifle shot in Europe where they confronted one another; their nuclear power and their mutual fear of sui-

5. See Carl Sagan, "Nuclear Winter and Climatic Catastrophe: Some Policy Implications," *Foreign Affairs* (winter 1983–1984): 257–292.

cide had given Europe thirty-five years without hostilities, its longest period of peace in the twentieth century. Indeed, nuclear weapons had eliminated war among *all* the great powers, not just the superpowers.[6]

Although the antinuclear movement appeared to confuse the issue of threatening nuclear force to bolster deterrence with its use, that did not stop the movement from gaining enormous momentum by 1982. The danger of nuclear war appeared to be the nation's first concern. In New York City three-quarters of a million people turned out for the largest political gathering in American history. For those demonstrators and the others marching, meeting, and debating the nuclear issue across the country, the ultimate goal was to eliminate nuclear weapons, but the immediate goal was to achieve a nuclear freeze. Proposals for a freeze on the testing, production, and deployment of nuclear weapons to stop the arms race were passed (or almost passed) by many town-hall meetings and by voters in ten of the eleven states on whose ballots the proposals appeared in the midterm 1982 election. Congress, especially the Democratic House, reflected this antinuclear mood, and, after coming within two votes of endorsing a nuclear freeze in 1982, it endorsed a modified version of the freeze in 1983. In 1984 all Democratic presidential candidates but one came out in favor of a freeze.

THE STRATEGIC DEFENSE INITIATIVE

Reagan first introduced his Strategic Defense Initiative (SDI) in the midst of the controversy about arms control. The proposal was quickly dubbed "Star Wars" by its critics because of its reliance on sophisticated space-based technologies glimpsed only in movies, such as lasers and particle beams. SDI was intended to render nuclear missiles "impotent and obsolete," presumably protecting America's population. According to official descriptions, SDI would be a layered defense using different technologies to destroy attacking missiles during each phase of the ballistic trajectory. Mutual assured survival would replace mutual assured destruction. Was it not better to save lives on both sides, the president asked, than to kill the population of the aggressor in revenge for a first strike?

For the president the SDI plan served several purposes, the first of which was domestic and political. Criticized for increasing the defense budget while cutting social services and assailed for being a warmonger, Reagan was able to seize the initiative with SDI. Instead of always defending himself, he could pose as a man of vision who would end the

---

6. See John Lewis Gaddis, "The Long Peace: Elements of Stability in the Postwar International System," *International Security* (spring 1986): 99–142.

threat of missile attacks and ensure that the population of the United States, of the Soviet Union, and, indeed, of the world would survive. He had gone arms control advocates one better, not by stabilizing the balance of offensive missiles but by banishing their life-threatening potential. As for the antinuclear movement, using SDI Reagan stole its thunder. He may have been the nation's most conservative postwar president and he did promote a large-scale rearmament program, but on nuclear issues he was an abolitionist who often spoke of a world devoid of nuclear weapons as his ultimate goal. Reagan dismissed the distinction between stabilizing and destabilizing nuclear weapons, as he did the role they had played in deterring war. He clearly was uncomfortable with the deterrent strategy to which all of his predecessors had been committed, and he condoned the addition of new nuclear stockpiles only as a means to hasten arms control efforts. At the Reykjavík (Iceland) summit in 1986 Reagan had come close to agreeing with Gorbachev to the total elimination of all nuclear weapons within a ten-year period.[7]

Second, SDI's utopian side was matched by a more pragmatic consideration: if it worked it would outflank the Soviets. For years the Soviets had invested heavily in first-strike missiles, which also were the basis for the Soviet claim to superpower status. SDI now threatened the value of this Soviet investment in ICBMs and claims to equality with the United States. What would be the point of a Soviet attack if its missiles could not penetrate the defensive shield above the United States?

Third, although defense of the population and elimination of all ICBMs were the fundamental and long-term goals of SDI, it could potentially defend U.S. ICBMs in the future. A defense against missiles would relieve the American fear that its ICBMs were vulnerable and increase Soviet uncertainty that they could launch a successful first strike. Thus there would be no point in a Soviet strike at all. SDI could make mutual deterrence—the reciprocal hostage relationship—safer.

SDI was denounced by critics for many reasons: it would be enormously expensive; it would accelerate the arms race; it would have to work perfectly the first time it was needed; it would tempt a Soviet first strike if the Soviets felt they were on the verge of becoming "nuclear hostages" to an unassailable United States. In short, SDI would only lead to new arms races, offensive and defensive, in which the defensive technologies, even if they gained the upper hand, would do so only temporarily. Moreover, the system would be so expensive that it would threaten U.S. budgets for other strategic and conventional forces. Therefore, it was doubtful that the United States or the Soviet Union would be

---

7. Ironically, it was Reagan's refusal to postpone research on SDI that undermined that agreement.

any more secure. Arms reductions through bilateral negotiations were the better course.

But if the critics were correct, why did the Soviets denounce Reagan's "arms race in space"? Why, after previously walking out of all arms control negotiations, were the Soviets so eager to resume talks? Clearly SDI worried them; they really were as fearful of an American first strike as the Americans had been of a Soviet first strike since the early 1970s. The Soviets perceived SDI to be part of an offensive, not defensive, strategy, a prelude to an American strike that would be launched once China's population could be protected. They also were aware that SDI research and development would result in American technology taking a huge step forward at a time when Soviet technology already was behind. With its domestic economy in shambles, the Soviets could not afford to accelerate the arms race on so great a scale.

The Soviets thus were eager to delay, if not stop, the deployment of SDI. The United States, meanwhile, continued to worry about the Soviet first-strike capability. A compromise seemed the obvious solution: a drastic cut in Soviet ICBMs in exchange for SDI, or at least a delay of SDI. Reagan, however, refused to turn SDI into a bargaining chip and trade it for Soviet ICBMs. After he walked out of the Reykjavík negotiations, no strategic arms control agreement was possible. Such a deal became possible only after Reagan left office. Nevertheless, he approved the more modest START I agreements signed by his successor.

THE REAGAN DOCTRINE IN THE THIRD WORLD

Although Reagan refocused the attention of American foreign policy on the East-West struggle, the Third World remained a matter of concern. Among Reagan's top priorities on taking office was a reversal of what he saw as Soviet gains during the 1970s in, among other places, Angola, Ethiopia, Yemen, Afghanistan, and Cambodia after the Vietnam War. The Soviets and their allies had been using force to make inroads in these areas—direct force in Afghanistan, indirect force through proxies elsewhere. And in Central America the Marxist Sandinista government in Nicaragua consolidated its power and sought to extend its influence to neighboring countries, especially El Salvador.

Past administrations had been committed to containment and had not hesitated to intervene to save a friendly regime from being attacked from outside or from within by the Soviet Union or its friends. But, except for episodic efforts such as Harry Truman's effort to "liberate" North Korea or John Kennedy's Bay of Pigs operation in Cuba, it had never been the official policy of the U.S. government to unseat Soviet-supported regimes. Dwight Eisenhower's administration had spoken of the "liberation" of Eastern Europe and the global "rollback" of communism but had never acted on those words; containment remained a fundamentally defensive doctrine. The new Reagan policy, however, was offensive.

Dubbed the "Reagan Doctrine," it aimed to undo the results of recent Soviet expansion. Afghanistan, Angola, and Nicaragua had established Marxist governments that had not yet consolidated their power, and all faced resistance movements. The Soviets had justified their Third World expansion with the doctrine of "national liberation" and then asserted that communism was irreversible once a society had become Marxist. Reagan now adopted his own national liberation strategy against governments that had not come to power by means of democratic processes. In his eyes such regimes lacked legitimacy. Moscow had placed them in power and, unlike his predecessors (with the partial exception of Jimmy Carter in Afghanistan, where a U.S. program of largely covert assistance for resistance fighters already was in progress), he refused to accept Moscow's claim that the civil wars were over once governments were in place. The domestic conflicts were not over until popular governments, acceptable to the people (and presumably to Washington), were in power. In short, the Reagan Doctrine set out to disprove the claim of the Brezhnev Doctrine that once a nation had become part of the Soviet bloc it could never leave.

The president's version of national liberation was not applied to all Third World states—only to some of the Soviet Union's recent acquisitions. The doctrine was based on certain assumptions: that the Soviet Union had become overextended in the 1970s; that the global balance of military power, after favoring Moscow in the 1970s, was shifting back to the United States; that the Soviet Union's most critical problems were domestic; that, except for Afghanistan, only peripheral Soviet interests were involved; that the Soviet Union would not want to risk a confrontation with the United States; and that a democratic tide was sweeping across the Third World. In practice, the Reagan Doctrine amounted to little more than bleeding the targeted governments and especially Moscow; if they wanted to stop the hemorrhaging, they would have to negotiate a political solution with the insurgents. The insurgencies were not strong enough to overthrow the Marxist regimes, but with American help they could keep the wars going.

ROLLBACK IN THE DEVELOPING COUNTRIES AND DEMOCRATIC REFORMS

As noted, the Reagan administration turned Marxist ideology on its head by arguing that "historical forces" were on the side of Western democracy and capitalism, not socialism. For evidence, the administration pointed to Latin America, where during the Reagan years (1981–1989) Argentina, Bolivia, Brazil, Guatemala, Honduras, Peru, and Uruguay had become, at least nominally, democratic, in addition to El Salvador, Grenada, and Haiti. Whatever the reason for this phenomenon—administration policy, global social and political trends, economic development, or sheer coincidence—the administration expressed its optimism that this was part of an irreversible process. The Soviet bloc, by denying human freedom and dignity to its citizens, was running against the tide of history.

Drawing on the traditional hemispheric preoccupation of the Monroe Doctrine, Reagan identified Central America, South America, and the Caribbean as vital U.S. interests and vowed to turn back any outside (that is, Soviet) incursions into America's backyard. To demonstrate his resolve, Reagan intervened directly on the tiny Caribbean island of Grenada, where a military coup had led to the installation of a Marxist regime in 1983. The U.S. military operation, which ostensibly was designed to liberate American medical students from the island, took longer than expected because of logistical problems and a considerable amount of bungling by U.S. Army, Navy, and Marine forces. But it achieved its main objective of eliminating the Marxist regime.

The U.S. invasion of Grenada was intended to raise the risks and the costs for the Soviets and Cubans should they continue to try and extend their political and military control in the Western Hemisphere, as well as elsewhere. Asserting that it had intervened to prevent Grenada from becoming a "Soviet-Cuban colony," the administration called Grenada a "warning shot" that actually was targeting the Sandinista regime in Nicaragua. The administration was convinced that the Sandinistas harbored ideologically motivated ambitions beyond their own frontiers. Because they also accepted support from Havana and Moscow, Washington saw them as a continuing source of instability and tension for the vulnerable states in the region. The Sandinistas' pledge to confine themselves to Nicaragua was regarded with skepticism by those who recalled their earlier pledges to promote political pluralism, a mixed economy, and a nonaligned foreign policy.

What the Reagan administration sought in Nicaragua was to undo the Sandinistas' increasing monopolization of power and return the country to its immediate post-1979 state when the popular anti-Somoza revolution had produced a new coalition government composed of the major groups that had helped to overthrow the dictator, including religious groups, entrepreneurs, and large segments of the middle and working classes. Once in power, however, the Sandinistas began to consolidate their hold on government, gradually suppressing the voices of criticism. They postponed general elections, censored the news media while building an army larger than Somoza's, restrained activities by other political parties, extended control over worker and peasant organizations, and strengthened their police and security apparatus. They also turned toward Cuba and the Soviet Union for diplomatic support and economic assistance. But the question was not how *Marxist* the regime would become as it turned against the Catholic church, the business community, professional organizations, trade unions, and student groups that had helped it to depose Somoza. The question was how *dictatorial* it would become and how closely it would align with Havana and Moscow.

The United States, which initially supported the new regime in Nicaragua with foreign aid, was increasingly distressed by its consolidation of power and militaristic behavior. Thus after Reagan took office, he authorized the formation of an anti-Sandinista army known as the "contras." Trained by U.S. military advisers in neighboring Honduras, the soldiers staged a series of military offenses against the Sandinista regime from Honduras, which received increased U.S. military assistance for these purposes, even though Reagan encouraged the public to view the contras as an indigenous, independent army of "freedom fighters." Later, however, this policy backfired against the Reagan administration and dealt a serious blow to its credibility at home and abroad.

The Reagan administration also placed the Central American country of El Salvador, a country the size of New Jersey with a population of six million, within the context of the superpower conflict. Adapting the Eisenhower administration's domino theory of communist expansion to Latin America, Reagan expressed concerns that the Sandinista revolution in Nicaragua would spread to El Salvador, and ultimately the rest of Central America. Furthermore, the threat was defined as applying to the wider U.S. position throughout the world. "If Central America were to fall," the president asked, "what would the consequences be for our position in Asia, Europe, and for alliances such as NATO? If the United States cannot respond to a threat near our own border, why should Europeans or Asians believe that we are seriously concerned about threats to them?"[8] Specifically, Reagan alleged that the Nicaraguan government was shipping weapons to rebels in El Salvador, and he proposed increased U.S. arms transfers to El Salvador to match the reported Sandinista arms transfers.

Whether El Salvador was the right place to take a stand against Soviet communism and its proxies, or whether the revolution should have been allowed to follow its natural course, was energetically debated in

---

8. Ronald Reagan, "Central America: Defending Our Vital Interests," *Current Policy* (U.S. Department of State), April 27, 1983.

the United States. Critics of the administration's plans, especially the Democrats in opposition, argued that the Nicaraguan arms were not the principal cause for the civil war but, rather, the appalling domestic social and economic conditions and political repression. As was the case throughout the Third World (see Chapter 5), the seeds of revolution often were sown in poverty and despair, the byproducts of despotic rule. In the view of these critics, the United States should not support the privileged few who had long exploited the poor. Social justice demanded nonintervention; so perhaps did self-interest if the United States wished to avoid being identified with the losers, as it had been so many times before. The Vietnam War frequently was cited as a reminder of the dangers of supporting the wrong side—an unpopular political elite whose vested interest lay in the preservation of the status quo. In any event, no purely military solution was possible.

Locating a moderate center in El Salvador was the key to the Reagan administration's effort to mobilize support domestically and achieve success. In the Third World the United States often had appeared trapped between reactionary forces, on the one hand, whose rigid commitment to the status quo only intensified revolutionary sentiment and endangered American interests, and radical forces, on the other, which tended to be Marxist and to look to Havana and Moscow. The administration was saved from this trap in El Salvador by Napoléon Duarte, who was in power for most of the Reagan years and sought to pursue democratic reforms while preventing the radical left from capturing power. Duarte strengthened the Reagan case for assistance to El Salvador because Reagan could rightfully claim that the United States was not supporting the right wing as an alternative to the radical left. Washington hoped, by sending Duarte economic and military aid and by encouraging domestic reforms, it could avoid both another Cuba in Central America, as well as another Vietnam. The fighting, however, continued.

The Salvadoran precedent of support for a democratic center was widely recognized after the events of 1986 in the Philippines, where the United States had long supported the dictator Ferdinand Marcos. But his despotism, economic mismanagement, transparent corruption, and the military's abuses had fueled public discontent and a rebirth of the communist guerrilla force called the Nationalist People's Army. In the absence of basic reforms, it appeared that the guerrillas might defeat the poorly trained and badly led Philippine army. Nevertheless, Marcos refused to heed suggestions for reform and, to prove his legitimacy, called for snap elections. He was confident that he could manipulate and control such elections as he had done before, but in this case the opposition proved overwhelming. The opposition candidate, Corazon Cojuangco Aquino, was the widow of the popular opposition leader

Benigno Aquino, who in 1983 had been assassinated at the airport in the capital of Manila upon returning from exile in the United States. After the assassination, Corazon Aquino, whose tempered manner and conciliatory approach attracted worldwide support, became both a symbol of democracy and a rallying point for the opposition. When it became obvious that he would not win the election, Marcos tried to alter the results with widespread fraud, but, because the election was closely monitored by international observers and the news media, the fraud was clearly visible. Thus Marcos lost his legitimacy even while "winning" another term. The United States encouraged him to step down. When top army commanders defected, Marcos fled to Hawaii and Corazon Aquino became president.

Also in 1986 the Reagan administration helped the Haitian people to oust Jean-Claude "Baby Doc" Duvalier, who had succeeded his father as dictator of the Western Hemisphere's poorest state. The United States first advised Duvalier not to use force against protesting crowds and then furnished him with an airplane to flee to France. Previously, the U.S. government had backed the military juntas in Haiti in the name of communist containment and often had looked the other way as vicious dictators tortured, killed, and otherwise silenced their enemies, real or imagined. The Reagan administration now declared its new policy: "The American people believe in human rights and oppose tyranny in whatever form, whether of the left or the right."[9] Under this variation of Carter's human rights policy, the United States would support those struggling for democracy and oppose not just radical Marxist regimes but also pro-American military dictatorships.

And it did so. In 1987, after considerable turmoil in South Korea which had flared on and off for years, the military government was persuaded to promise free elections for the presidency. Administration pressure on South Korea, a key U.S. ally and beneficiary of U.S. aid, had encouraged the long-awaited transition. Similar pressure on Chile resulted in an election that displaced its military leader, Gen. Augusto Pinochet, and opened the way for the establishment of democracy.

WAS THE REAGAN DOCTRINE A SUCCESS?

Although the Reagan administration invoked its claim of a global pro-democratic tide to support the resistance movements in Afghanistan, Angola, and Nicaragua, the insurgencies it supported in the name of spreading freedom often fell considerably short of that virtue. Indeed, the administration's emphasis on human rights in many cases was compromised by the absence of moderate factions that had any

9. "President Reagan's March 14 Message to Congress," *New York Times,* March 15, 1986.

chance of taking power. For Reagan it became a matter of identifying and supporting the lesser of evils. In Afghanistan the opponents to Soviet rule were Islamic fundamentalists, who, if they won, were more likely to establish an Iranian-style theocracy than a democracy and to fragment the Muslim world further. Still, that they were a genuine resistance movement could not be doubted. In Angola, Jonas Savimbi, the rebel leader representing Angola's largest tribal group, was trained in the People's Republic of China and was quite willing to rely on racist South Africa for help. And in Nicaragua some of the principal contra commanders were former members of Somoza's detested National Guard. Reagan was ultimately pragmatic in these cases; he supported all opponents of the Soviet Union in order to weaken it.

The contrasts between Afghanistan and Nicaragua were, in this respect, instructive. In Afghanistan the resistance to the Soviet-imposed government had genuine popular support. The so-called freedom fighters fought courageously and successfully against the Soviet army despite their general lack of modern weapons. As a result, many nations were sympathetic to the rebels; in fact, the Muslim states were largely united in their condemnation of Moscow. As for the United States, unlike its support for the contra war in Nicaragua, which most states in Latin America and elsewhere opposed, its covert assistance to the Afghan resistance was not condemned by neighboring states. Moreover, at home it had congressional and popular support.

Lack of congressional and public support for the Nicaraguan contras left Reagan with only one option when the presidents of Costa Rica, El Salvador, Guatemala, Honduras, and Nicaragua agreed to a regional peace plan in 1987. He had to support the Contadora initiative because if the plan failed and if its failure could be clearly attributed to the Sandinistas' unwillingness to open up Nicaragua to genuine democratization, as stipulated by the peace plan, he might regain support for further financial assistance of the contras. But the Democratic-controlled Congress remained disenchanted with the contras, whose ties to the U.S. government were obvious despite administration denials, and used the peace plan as a reason not to fund any more military aid. Such assistance, it was claimed, would only thwart efforts to bring peace to Nicaragua and the region. Thus the administration's plan to overthrow the Sandinistas seemed doomed to failure. This appeared even more certain after the five Central American presidents, over the protests of the United States, called for the disbandment of the contras, most of them in Honduras, and for general elections in Nicaragua. But there was no enforcement provision, so the contras remained a viable force.

Under continuing international pressure, Sandinista leader Daniel Ortega finally agreed to hold multiparty elections in 1990. Ortega and his military aides had consolidated power during their ten years in office and expected to exploit their control of the government, including the police and army, to ensure an electoral victory that would give them international legitimacy and eliminate any possible rationale for further U.S. assistance to the contras. Like Marcos in the Philippines, they certainly did not expect to lose the general election and to relinquish their power. But lose they did. Despite Sandinista control of the government and efforts to intimidate opposition candidates and rallies, as well as the holdup of congressionally approved funds for the opposition, Ortega lost to Violeta Chamorro, widow of the anti-Somoza newspaper editor whose assassination had rallied the Sandinista-led revolution that brought down the dictator Somoza.

It was unclear who should have received the credit for the defeat of the Sandinistas: the five Central American presidents led by Costa Rica's Oscar Arias, the Nicaraguan people who had the courage to vote against an oppressive regime, or the Sandinistas themselves for believing they could survive an unpopular draft and a mismanaged economy in a relatively free election. But there was no doubt of the consequences. For the Salvadoran guerrillas, the loss of Nicaraguan political support and military assistance constituted a serious setback to their campaign to overthrow the government or negotiate a favorable settlement that would give them a share of the power. For Fidel Castro, who had served as an idol for the Sandinistas and a source of help and support, it meant further isolation as he was the only remaining revolutionary in Latin America. As for Nicaragua, the solid defeat of the Sandinistas gave that country a second opportunity to build a democracy, to reintegrate the contras into the fabric of Nicaraguan society, to reconcile political opponents, and to reestablish cordial relations with the United States.

Whether the results of the Nicaraguan elections were attributed to the Reagan Doctrine or not, the doctrine had to be judged at least a partial success. It was a cost-effective means of putting pressure on Moscow, which had to spend an estimated $10–20 billion a year (compared with less than $1 billion annually for the United States) to preserve the gains it had achieved in the 1970s. In 1988, therefore, a number of the regional conflicts in which the United States and the Soviet Union had been engaged came to an end. In Afghanistan, Gorbachev, realizing that the war was an unending drain and a political embarrassment, decided to withdraw Soviet forces. In Angola, after years of fruitless negotiations, the Cubans agreed to pull out their forces, and the South Africans agreed to pull back their forces and grant independence to neighboring Namibia, which they had governed since World War I. These arrangements were followed by a settlement of the Angolan civil war and a largely effective effort by the United Nations to hasten the region's democratic transition. In Cambodia the Vietnamese agreed to withdraw their army, which had invaded that country earlier and overthrown the pro-Chinese Pol Pot regime, responsible for the genocide of over one million of its own eight million people. Gorbachev had to resolve these regional quarrels because by 1987 it had become clear that he needed to conserve his resources for investment in the stagnating Soviet economy. The prerequisite was an armistice in the Cold War so that the Soviet leader could greatly reduce spending on the huge Soviet military establishment and unpromising foreign policy involvements. But the Soviet Union did not suffer a set of total defeats or the United States a series of unqualified triumphs. In Afghanistan, Angola, Ethiopia, Mozambique, and Cambodia, Marxist regimes retained power. The United States had compelled the Soviet Union, Cuba, and Vietnam to withdraw, but it had not achieved its declared goal of replacing Marxist regimes with democratic governments.

ABUSES OF THE REAGAN DOCTRINE: THE IRAN-CONTRA SCANDAL

In one area of its execution the Reagan Doctrine tarnished the president's reputation among the public. In 1987 Reagan's competence, integrity, and sense of judgment were laid open to question when it was revealed that profits from secret arms sales to Iran, now an anti-American Islamic theocracy, had been used to fund the Nicaraguan contras from late 1984 to 1986, a period when the U.S. Congress had expressly forbidden the use of U.S. funds for this purpose. In fact, in an end run around Congress the administration had shifted the conduct of the contra war from the Central Intelligence Agency (CIA) to the National Security Council (NSC) staff. Both operations were reputedly run by the CIA director, William Casey, and his point man in the NSC, Oliver North, a marine lieutenant colonel.

Referred to in the later congressional investigation as the only "five-star" lieutenant colonel in the U.S. military, North supervised the arms sales made to Iran in the hope that U.S. hostages, seized in Lebanon by pro-Iranian terrorists, would be released. He also directed the raising of private funds for the contras from tax-exempt organizations and from wealthy U.S. citizens and foreign governments. Moreover, North commanded a vast network of arms dealers, ships, and airplanes to supply the contras, for whom he also provided tactical intelligence and advice on how to conduct the war. The NSC thus became a "shadow government," which, in turn, organized the secret campaign to direct and fund the contra war effort. When the operation was discovered, the NSC attempted a coverup to minimize the president's role in these events— relevant documents were shredded or smuggled out of NSC offices.

Moreover, throughout the operation the administration kept any knowledge of what it was doing from Congress; indeed, it lied to Congress. To make matters worse, as the story broke the president first denied knowledge of many of the details of these events, making it appear as if his deputies had taken the foreign policy of the United States into their own hands.

Public opinion polls showed that most Americans thought Reagan was lying, and the congressional hearings held made it plain that he was actively involved and informed, especially on the contras. Thus he suddenly reversed directions and claimed that he knew about everything except the diversion of funds, but he argued that the congressional restrictions did not apply to him or his staff. The secrecy with which the Iran and contra operations were carried out, however, suggested that the administration knew very well that it was breaking the law even though when Congress had first forbidden military assistance, the administration had claimed repeatedly that it was obeying the law. All the participants, once they were caught, claimed to be acting only out of patriotic motives; in several cases, however, their patriotism seemed well greased by private gain.

Reagan damaged himself badly by this affair. He was, after all, the presidential candidate who had accused his opponent, Jimmy Carter, of weakness in dealing with the Iranian hostage situation. Under his own leadership, Reagan had vowed, the United States would "never negotiate with terrorists," let alone sell them weapons. He had consistently projected an image of toughness and confidence, and he had claimed that the nation could "stand tall" again. Many Americans shared this new sense of patriotism and regarded the president as the man who would make them proud again and who could—and did—stand up to the Soviets. But Reagan almost did the impossible by making Carter's hostage policy look good; Carter had not sent arms to Khomeini in the hope that U.S. hostages would be returned in exchange. Even President Reagan's admirers and supporters were puzzled. They knew that if congressional investigators had been able to find a "smoking gun" linking the scandal to the Oval Office, Reagan might, like Nixon before him, have faced impeachment for his violation of federal laws. As it was, he survived the crisis and left office with a clouded reputation, and the Iran-contra scandal haunted the administration of Reagan's successor, George Bush.

ALLIANCE POLITICS IN THE LATE COLD WAR

The Reagan administration's early attacks on détente, its preoccupation with rearmament, its reluctance to engage in arms control negotiations, and its vigorous pursuit of the Reagan Doctrine exerted great pressure on the Soviet Union throughout the 1980s. This pressure exacerbated the already strong tensions within the Warsaw Pact countries, where long years of political repression and economic stagnation had left people increasingly frustrated and restive.

Along the way, the renewed Cold War also strained the Western alliance and provoked public demonstrations from Washington to Bonn. Old questions resurfaced about the status of Western Europe as a potential superpower battleground, about the dominant role of the United States in NATO, and about the freedom of each member of NATO to pursue its own foreign policy. But the most important confrontation came over the issue of new Soviet missile deployments, which compelled the United States to propose its own series of new installations of intermediate-range missiles in Europe. With both alliances wavering, the outcome was very much in doubt: Would NATO disintegrate first because of its members' internal differences? Or would the Warsaw Pact succumb to its own deficiencies and to the mounting pressure from the West?

Thus the 1980s was a decade of great volatility on both sides of the iron curtain. What few people anticipated, however, was that this latest round of alliance posturing was a prelude to resolution of the post–World War II division of Europe. The curtain was falling rapidly on the Cold War.

POLAND AND THE RISE OF SOLIDARITY

The first crack in the Soviet empire came in Poland, where in 1980 a labor union, asserting first its economic rights and then its political demands, led the Soviet-backed communist government to impose martial law. This crackdown, reminiscent of past actions in Eastern Europe, further inflamed East-West hostilities.

It was ironic that it was in Poland, a so-called people's democracy and a communist state that purported to represent and protect the interests of the working class, where a truly spontaneous workers' revolution against their exploiters occurred and threatened the Communist Party's monopoly of power and control. Stimulated by a failing economy stemming from poor political leadership, inefficient bureaucratic planning, and mismanagement, Polish workers demanded the right to form their own independent trade union, which would have the right to strike. Such a demand was unheard of in a communist country where the party claimed to embody the workers' aspirations. In wanting their own union, the Polish workers rejected this claim and challenged the basis of the party's legitimacy.

After strikes brought down the government, the new political leadership recognized the right of the workers to form their own union, called Solidarity. In effect, this eliminated the party's monopoly of power. Solidarity then began to issue its demands—demands that were not only economic but also political. As the party-controlled government retreated before each demand, the demands increased and the party withdrew further in the face of threatened strikes. With each success, Solidarity grew more militant, publicly asserting that it was "the authentic voice of the working class" and announcing support for other East European workers who might wish to form independent unions. Domestically, it favored free parliamentary elections, free speech, and a voice in government policy, including the running of the economy. Although the Soviets accused Solidarity of provocative behavior—seeking "political power"—they refrained from invading Poland.

This restraint contrasted sharply with earlier Soviet behavior in Hungary (1956) and Czechoslovakia (1968), where the Soviet army had intervened when the Communist Party's monopoly of power was threatened. And Poland, the nation through which every Western invader of Russia had marched and through which the Soviet Union had projected its power into the center of Europe since 1945, was geographically far more critical than those two countries had been. As the situation grew more intolerable in Moscow's eyes, the danger of the Polish "disease" spreading to other East European states, perhaps even to the Soviet Union, led the Soviets to hold very visible Warsaw Pact military maneuvers in hope of frightening the Poles. The Soviet Union could afford neither a weakening nor a collapse of its hold on central and Eastern Europe, nor a dilution of controls at home.

But the risks and costs of intervention also were great. The Soviets recognized that Solidarity was not just a trade union seeking better working conditions; it also represented a well-organized mass movement. In suppressing Solidarity, the Soviets faced the real possibility of a clash with units of the Polish army, the costs of occupation, and the difficulties of pacifying the population and getting it to work. In addition, the cost of paying off Poland's $27 billion debt to the West would be a drain at a time when the Soviet economy was in trouble; it would become more difficult to maintain the separate détente with America's European allies; and the possible establishment of a better relationship with the new U.S. administration would be jeopardized. No less important, Reagan could exploit a Soviet invasion of Poland to rally the NATO allies. Thus for more than a year Moscow demonstrated remarkable restraint. When the move against Solidarity finally came, it was the Polish military and police who arrested the union leaders and imposed martial law in Poland.

Whether Moscow ordered the intervention or the Polish government acted on its own to forestall Soviet action, there can be little doubt of increasing Soviet pressure on the Polish authorities to crack down on what the Soviets called "counterrevolutionary" elements. Solidarity, by winning the sympathies of almost ten million members, about one-third of the population, was a living refutation of the party's claim of representation; it symbolized the bankruptcy of communism. Unable either to produce a decent standard of living or to tolerate a minimal degree of freedom, communism in Poland had forfeited its legitimacy. The lesson was not lost on other parts of Eastern Europe, where the struggle by Solidarity served as an inspiration and a precursor of greater challenges to come.

THE MISSILE DEBATE IN EUROPE

In Western Europe one almost heard a collective sigh of relief that the Red Army had not invaded Poland. The Polish army's crackdown was considered a domestic affair, not a matter over which détente was to be sacrificed. This reaction reflected anxieties in the region about the growing hostilities between East and West, with the Western Europeans finding themselves trapped in the middle. Indeed, it had become apparent in the early 1980s that the Western Europeans wanted to pursue an independent political policy while still counting on the United States for their defense; they wanted, it was said, to "uncouple" themselves politically from Washington but to remain "coupled" to it militarily. But even the military relationship was called into question when West European opinion appeared to go back on a decision, collectively agreed to by the United States and Western Europe, to meet the threat of new intermediate-range Soviet missiles (SS-20s) with a new generation of NATO missiles (Pershing IIs) to be deployed in Western Europe.

Since the beginning of NATO the Europeans had wanted the alliance strategy to emphasize deterrence. Europe had had more than enough wars in the twentieth century. The NATO army, therefore, was to serve as a "plate glass" that, once the Soviet invasion occurred, would sound the alarm and call in the U.S. strategic forces. The army's purpose was not to fight a long war like World War II, even when it was reinforced by 300,000 American soldiers. The presence of the troops emphasized America's stake in Europe and clarified to Moscow that any attack would result in war with the United States. The fear of nuclear retaliation by the United States, it was reasoned, would deter the Soviet Union from invading Western Europe.

After the first Soviet missile test in 1957, the key question had been: Would the United States risk its own survival for the defense of Europe? Some observers had said no, but most had been uncertain, although U.S. strategic forces at the time had been superior to those of the Soviet Union. After the 1970s and the emergence of strategic parity, the answer to this question had grown even more doubtful. It had been one thing for the United States to attack the Soviet Union when the Soviets could not attack the United States, or when America had a vast strategic superiority; it was quite another to do so when the Soviet Union could retaliate fully. Was America's strategic deterrence still credible? Washington's standard reply was yes, but in Western Europe there was more doubt than ever that this was really so.

The intermediate-range nuclear force (INF) deployments were supposed to reassure the allies, who were troubled by the Soviet SS-20s. Instead of being strengthened by new American resolve, however, the NATO "marriage," in the words of the French foreign minister, came close to a divorce. Huge crowds throughout Western Europe (except in France) demonstrated for months against the proposed deployment of the new missiles, with the greatest opposition in West Germany. There the Protestant churches, the universities, the Social Democratic opposition party, and a new political movement, the pro-peace and pro-environment Green Party, were all opposed to the deployment. The street demonstrators' accusations were many: America was stoking the arms race; America intended to fight a war limited to Europe, America was the aggressive party in the Cold War. Moscow was not considered the chief threat. It was Washington, which had defended Western Europe since 1949 and had not yet deployed a single Pershing II, that was charged with being the bigger menace to peace.

Certainly the demonstrators did not represent the majority opinion in their respective countries. In all NATO countries support for the alliance remained generally strong; so did faith in deterrence. Nevertheless, the peace movement reflected widespread concern about Reagan's antidétente foreign policy and an increased fear of war. The Soviets shrewdly exploited the protests. By repeatedly saying they were eager to negotiate the issue, the Soviets appeared reasonable and put the United States on the defensive.

Reagan felt compelled to respond to the demonstrations in Europe and to the Soviet initiative. He proposed a "zero option" whereby the United States would not deploy any of its Pershings and cruise missiles if the Soviets dismantled all of their intermediate-range missiles, which had a maximum range of 1,500 miles, including the SS-20s. It sounded good; all such missiles were to be eliminated. What could be more beneficial for peace and more moral than doing away with a whole class of dangerous weapons? The United States, however, did not expect Moscow to accept this offer. The zero-zero option was a public relations move; by turning it down, the Soviets would enable the U.S. deployment to go ahead as a clearly necessary and defensive move, the street demonstrations would decline, and the blame for the American missile buildup in Europe would be placed at the Kremlin's door.

The intra-NATO "missile crisis," however, had by then done considerable damage to the alliance. For many Europeans the protests against deployment expressed their concern about Reagan's foreign policy and, more generally, their desire to reduce the risk of war. For many Americans the protests were a reminder that Europeans did not appear ready to take the measures necessary for their own defense. Although their combined population and industrial output exceeded that of the Soviet Union, America's European allies were still unwilling to raise the size of their conventional forces. They wanted to continue relying on the American strategic deterrent at a time when the superpowers strategically neutralized one another.

In the United States, demands began for the withdrawal of some or all American forces from Europe over a period of several years. Most of the American defense budget allocated for hardware and maintenance was not spent on strategic forces; half went for the upkeep of the more expensive conventional forces whose primary mission was the defense of Europe. When the NATO alliance had been formed, the European nations still vividly remembered their attempts to appease a totalitarian regime, the defeats and suffering of World War II, their postwar collapse, and their need for American protection against the new threat from the East. By the 1970s and 1980s the memory of having appeased Nazi Germany was fading; indeed, the story of the appeasement was not even a part of the history or consciousness of the new generation that had grown up in a peaceful Europe. Protected by the United States, that generation, like many older Europeans, had seemingly forgotten the realities of international politics and took peace for granted.

Only in France, which had deployed a growing independent deterrent force, was the popular historical association of national independence and pride in the nation's armed forces still alive. There were no massive antinuclear and anti-American demonstrations. French Socialist president François Mitterrand told the West German parliament in 1983, "I'm against the Euromissiles. But I notice two terrible simple things about the current debate: Pacifism is in the West and the Euromissiles are in the East. I consider this an unequal relationship."[10] Such an imbalance, he predicted, would ensure war, not avoid it.

But elsewhere in Western Europe, defense apparently had become an American responsibility. Parties that formerly were stalwart defenders of NATO, such as the British Labour Party and the West German Social Democrats, now deserted the alliance. Given the changes in the four decades after World War II, one had to wonder whether, if NATO had

10. Quoted in Flora Lewis, "Missiles and Pacifists," *New York Times*, November 18, 1983.

been proposed in the 1980s, there would have been an alliance at all, and
if so, which countries would have joined it.

NATO THREATENED FROM WITHIN

By the mid-1980s one thing had become very clear: the intermediate-range nuclear weapons issue was not primarily a military issue but a critical political one. The decision to deploy the new generation of ground-based nuclear missiles in Europe had been an alliance decision. But Moscow refused to accept *any* American deployment and rejected the principle of superpower equality. The Soviet purpose clearly was to manipulate Europe's fear of war and to encourage divisiveness among the NATO allies, especially between Europe and the United States. Would the alliance survive? The Soviets had no reason to compromise in separate arms control negotiations on this issue; they had every reason to test the strength of the European peace movement in the hope of aborting the American deployment. The Soviets could deploy their missiles and target every European capital, but the United States could not deploy missiles in Europe that could hit the Soviet Union. What Moscow had was not negotiable; what NATO had was.

For NATO, Moscow's attempt to undermine the alliance through the missile debate was the most serious issue it had had to confront since German rearmament in the early 1950s and the Berlin crisis after 1957. Both issues had threatened the future of the alliance, its ability to face down intimidation and remain united. Above all, they had included a struggle for West Germany, NATO's strongest European member, whose territory bordered the Soviet bloc. Moscow obviously wanted to detach West Germany from NATO, and Washington wanted to keep that country within the alliance. Given the political stakes for each superpower, should it have been surprising that American-Soviet relations reached a low point in the early 1980s, regardless of who the leaders were? Neither side was willing to compromise in what it regarded as a fundamental test of wills. Despite considerable pressure on Reagan to be more accommodating, he insisted on going ahead with the deployment. When that began during the winter months of 1983–1984, was it really surprising that Moscow walked out of all arms control negotiations in order to raise the fear of war in Western Europe and to push it into a greater neutralism and pacifism?

For a time, however, the missile crisis faded as the deployment continued. Then in a complete turnabout, Gorbachev accepted the earlier Reagan proposal for the complete elimination of intermediate-range missiles for both powers. The Soviet leader needed a relaxation of international tensions in order to give priority to domestic affairs and rebuilding the Soviet economy. The administration's determination had paid off. It had not abandoned the deployment, nor, when the Soviets responded by walking out of all arms control negotiations, had it delayed deployment, despite widespread calls to do so. Unable to achieve Soviet goals with threats, Moscow capitulated.

The "zero-zero" solution was a significant achievement that meant trading about 1,400 Soviet warheads for just over 300 U.S. warheads. This move eliminated an entire class of weapons rather than—as in SALTs I and II—placing limits on their deployment. Moscow also accepted intrusive verification procedures to monitor the agreement. More fundamentally, in retrospect the Soviet turnabout was the first sign that the Soviet Union needed a cease-fire in the Cold War. U.S. resolution had paid off, undermining not the NATO position but that of the Warsaw Pact.

It was clear, however, that Europeans' confidence in the United States had weakened severely since Vietnam. During the Nixon-Ford détente years Europeans had complained about possible U.S.-Soviet deals at Europe's expense; during the Carter years, of vacillation and weakness; and during the Reagan years, of too much machismo or "Ramboism." Europe's fear of war also had risen. Not Soviet behavior but the arms race itself was seen as the critical danger, as was "provocative" American behavior in remote regions that could ignite a head-on clash in Europe. These attitudes translated into growing public doubts about the value of NATO.

The European members of the alliance remained unwilling to reexamine the assumption they had accepted for more than forty years— namely, that the Soviet Union was the naturally dominant Eurasian power against which Western Europe could not mobilize sufficient counterbalancing power without outside help. Such an assumption was demeaning for states that had for centuries been the leading international actors but that, by the 1980s, found themselves the dependents of an overseas protector. Ironically, their growing skepticism toward NATO coincided with its victory over the Warsaw Pact.

At home, many Americans by the late 1980s had recaptured much of their confidence in America's mission of defending and, where possible, advancing democratic values. Although Reagan's talk of a turning of the communist tide and the inevitable global sweep of democracy was at first widely dismissed as self-serving propaganda, such were the emerging trends in his final year as president.

FROM CONFRONTATION TO CONCILIATION

Although the tensions of the 1980s ruptured the cohesion of both alliances, in the end, as Reagan left office in January 1989, U.S.-Soviet relations were better than they had been since the two had been allies against Nazi Germany during World War II. How could that be? How, in a few years, could such a profound transformation of superpower relations have occurred?

The rapidity of the change in the two superpowers' relationship was astounding. The Cold War had spanned more than four decades, exceeding the time that elapsed from the beginning of World War I (1914) to the end of World War II (1945). The transformation of superpower relations was even more surprising because the 1970s had been a period of great confusion and self-doubt for the United States. Having withdrawn from Vietnam without victory—some would say defeated—the United States was domestically divided. The Watergate scandal had undermined public trust in the presidency. The U.S. economy and that of the other Western nations had suffered oil shocks and stagflation in 1973 and 1979—the year the Somoza government fell to the Sandinistas in Nicaragua; the Iranians seized the U.S. embassy and fifty-two American hostages; the Soviets invaded Afghanistan; the Vietnamese, after invading Cambodia in December 1978, established a pro-Soviet government there, and a pro-Soviet communist faction seized power in Grenada. It was a decade to deflate any country's self-confidence. By contrast, the Soviet Union had appeared confident and optimistic about the future course of international politics.

Soviet policy was at a high point in the 1970s. The Soviet Union had attained strategic parity and a conventional capability to project Soviet power beyond Eurasia; and it sought to gain a geopolitical advantage to exploit America's mood of withdrawal. The Soviet leadership saw the Soviet Union's growth of military power as part of a shift in the "correlation of forces" from West to East. That strength would allow Moscow to exploit opportunities it saw in the Third World to weaken the West while simultaneously deterring American military countermoves. Leonid Brezhnev and his colleagues believed that the more military power they acquired, the more America would have to be accommodating. In addition, by encouraging Third World governments to adopt Marxist-Leninist one-party governments, Moscow believed that Soviet gains would be irreversible and cumulative. Convinced that the United States was a declining power, Moscow calculated that Washington had no choice but to adjust to these new circumstances and accept the consequences.

The apparent successes of the Soviet Union were, however, deceptive for two reasons. The first was the failure of the Soviet economy. Its economic growth rate, 5 percent in the 1960s and only 2 percent by the early 1970s, had stagnated by 1980. Capable only of producing a plentiful supply of weapons, the Soviet economy could no longer supply basic goods and public services. By the late 1980s the Soviets were importing many necessities and basic foodstuffs were being rationed. After harvests failed repeatedly in the 1970s, grains and produce had to be imported from the United States and other countries. The centralized Soviet economy was nearing a breakdown. Gorbachev, who when first appointed general secretary in 1985 had believed that economic growth could be stimulated by more discipline in the workplace, less worker absenteeism and drunkenness, and higher productivity, by 1987 realized the severity of the crisis he faced. The second reason for the Soviet turnabout was the cost of Brezhnev's foreign policy. With a gross domestic product (GDP) half that of the United States and a military budget that the CIA then estimated at 16 percent of GDP (compared with 6 percent for the United States and 3 percent for Western Europe), the civilian economy was starved. In fact, later Soviet figures showed that military spending was between 25 percent and 30 percent of Soviet GDP.

Outside the Soviet Union, Moscow's unrelenting arms buildup and expansionist activities in the Third World had produced fear and suspicion of Soviet intentions. The result was the very encirclement the Soviet Union had long feared. In Asia the growing Soviet threat allowed the United States to play divide-and-rule, attracting China to the West in a major shift of power. Thus the Soviet Union, like Germany at the turn of the century, had created its own worst nightmare and increased its sense of vulnerability.

The United States played no small role in this scenario. American-supplied weapons raised the price of the Afghanistan intervention, placing victory out of reach, and prolonged the civil war in Angola. Although the administration did not succeed in overthrowing the Sandinistas in Nicaragua, the Soviet effort to sustain the latter was the only bargain in an otherwise unending financial drain. The imperial outposts that had looked so promising only ten years earlier had now lost their luster, and support for proxies such as Cuba, Ethiopia, and Vietnam had become prohibitively expensive. Gorbachev had no choice but to see what Marxists always had prided themselves on recognizing: objective reality. The Soviet Union, hampered by a structurally unsound economy, looking at a resurgent U.S. economy (despite its rapidly increasing federal and trade deficits), and surrounded by a Western coalition of NATO, Japan, and China, was forced to recognize the need for rapprochement with the United States.

The Soviet weakness and consequent desire to end the Cold War first became apparent in 1987 when the Soviet delegates walked back into the INF talks they had earlier walked out of and accepted virtually the entire package of U.S. demands. Even more significant, in a series of pronouncements Gorbachev and his supporters contradicted long-held Soviet doctrine and positions by stating that: (1) the "all-human value of peace" would now take precedence over the class struggle, meaning that the unilateral pursuit of advantage to extend socialism could jeopardize the peace; (2) Soviet (and American) security could not be achieved unless there was "common security," suggesting that if one side armed and then the other responded in kind, as in the past, the initiating side would be left less, not more, secure; (3) force and the threat of force should no longer be instruments of foreign policy; (4) security should be achieved by political means—that is, resolving disputes by compromise; (5) in the future "reasonable sufficiency" would be the new standard by which the Soviet Union would judge the military strength it needed; (6) Soviet forces along the iron curtain would be reorganized in a "nonoffensive defense" so that NATO, whose war plans called for no advance eastward, could feel reassured; and (7) negotiations between NATO and the Warsaw Treaty Organization would likely reduce the levels of troops and arms and, wherever asymmetries favored one side, the stronger power—such as the Soviet Union in tanks and personnel carriers—would reduce to the level of the weaker side rather than the opposite.

In the Third World Moscow deemphasized the revolutionary struggle for national liberation and raised questions about the future of socialism in the developing countries. In addition, by withdrawing from Afghanistan and helping to resolve several other regional conflicts, Gorbachev reduced Soviet foreign policy costs and diminished the likelihood of new conflicts with the United States and the chances that the current ones would undermine the emerging improvement in U.S.-Soviet relations. More broadly, Gorbachev sought to deprive the American-led coalition encircling the Soviet bloc of an enemy. His "charm offensive," including visits abroad, was very effective in Europe, especially in West Germany where "Gorby" rated far higher as a statesman and peacemaker than either Reagan or his vice president and successor, George Bush. The Soviet leader also normalized relations with China in 1989. Among two of the many dramatic moves made to improve the Soviet image, Moscow confessed that its intervention in Afghanistan had violated Soviet law and international norms of behavior, and, after years of denying accusations that it had violated the 1972 ABM treaty, admitted the violation.

Gorbachev therefore changed priorities and launched his program of *glasnost* (openness) and *perestroika* (restructuring) to revitalize Soviet society and the economy. He realized that the two were intimately related: without more openness in Soviet society, without harnessing the energies of the Soviet people, long used to suppression and obedience, the Soviet economy would not recover from its stagnation. Thus Gorbachev advocated strengthening civil liberties—more freedom in the press, arts, literature, scholarship, and even in the reexamination of the darker side of Soviet history, long kept secret. He also called for decentralizing the economy, cutting back on the pervasive role of the Moscow-based central planning bureaucracy, and permitting the profit motive and market forces a greater role in stimulating production, including a degree of private ownership and entrepreneurship. And he urged the removal of the Communist Party from the daily management of the economy and other sectors of Soviet life, permitted real but limited competition in party and legislative elections, and allowed the Soviet parliament to assert itself, plus a host of other reforms.

But despite Gorbachev's exhortations and reform efforts, there was strong resistance from the nineteen million party and government bureaucrats who had a vested interest in the status quo. Change threatened their jobs, status, and privileges. Opposition to Gorbachev was further fueled by the fear that the loosening of central controls would be harmful, if not fatal, politically. It was the Russians who in the Soviet Union, as in czarist Russia, had controlled most of the levers of power and were particularly concerned that such a devolution of power away from Moscow might result in more political self-determination by the hundreds of non-Russian nationalities. Economic decentralization would then spill over into political decentralization. In other words, the fundamental structural reforms required by the Soviet Union might threaten not only the party's sole control of power but also Moscow's imperial control over its own vast country. The ongoing unrest in the Baltic republics (Estonia, Latvia, and Lithuania), especially the demands for independence, and similar agitation in Georgia and the central Asian republics, were in this respect very worrisome. This uneasiness was compounded by the successful efforts of the countries of Eastern Europe to throw off their communist yokes. Quite contrary to Marxist analysis, the political system determined the fate of the economy rather than the other way around. The Soviet political system had become the greatest obstacle to economic modernization. That was why, preoccupied at home, Gorbachev needed to end the Cold War.

To many, the dismantling of the Berlin Wall in 1989 symbolized the end of the Cold War.

CHAPTER TEN

Ending the Cold War: Negotiating the Terms of Peace

The implosion of the Soviet bloc already had begun by the time George Bush became president in January 1989. Mikhail Gorbachev's reforms were rapidly undermining the Communist Party's hold in Moscow, the Baltic states were demanding independence, and the first streams of East Europeans were making their way across the iron curtain with the reluctant assent of their crippled political leaders. Many analysts (including George Kennan, father of the containment policy) proclaimed that the Cold War was effectively over.

Others suggested more cautiously that it was coming to a close, perhaps.

President Bush, a lifelong politician who lacked Ronald Reagan's flamboyance and his convictions, was otherwise a capable and pragmatic leader. His experience as director of the Central Intelligence Agency (CIA), ambassador to China, and U.S. representative to the United Nations left little doubt that he was competent in foreign affairs. When he became president, Bush said he would not use the term *Cold War* to characterize America's relationship with the Soviet Union. He referred instead to a period of U.S.-Soviet relations "beyond containment" in which the principal task would be to integrate the Soviet Union into the "community of nations." In 1990, however, after referring to the "Revolution of '89" in his State of the Union address, Bush said the changes in Eastern Europe had been so striking and momentous that they marked "the beginning of a new era in the world's affairs." This proclamation, though grandiloquent, proved to be an understatement.

In truth, very few observers, including the most experienced and perceptive analysts of international relations, anticipated the sudden collapse of the Soviet system. Most predicted either a prolonged stalemate, a gradual convergence of the capitalist and communist systems, or, more gloomily, an apocalyptic military showdown. The suggestion that one of the two superpowers would simply default and disappear from the world map without a shot being fired and virtually without preconditions would have been rejected as sheer fantasy. Napoleonic France and Nazi Germany had not just disappeared; they had to be defeated on the battlefield.

For Bush, the principal task of American foreign policy would be to manage this historic transition as smoothly as possible and to ensure that the Warsaw Pact's demise would not be overwhelmed by an even greater cataclysm. If that were accomplished, Bush looked forward to a harmonious new era in which the attributes of the Western political and economic system would be extended into the former communist bloc and provide the basis for global stability and prosperity.

BUSH'S MANAGEMENT OF THE SOVIET COLLAPSE

With the benefit of hindsight, what were some of the signs that the Cold War was drawing to a close? At first, the Bush administration was not sure what to believe. In the context of forty years of Cold War and of previously dashed hopes that the Cold War was ending, the administration—and especially the president—tended to be cautious. If Gorbachev were to fall and be replaced by a hard-line conservative, the United States did not want to be caught off guard. Nevertheless, Secretary of

State James Baker, a holdover from the Reagan team, acknowledged that Soviet "new thinking" in foreign and defense policies promised possibilities that ten years earlier would have been unimaginable.[1] Uncertainty about Soviet reforms was all the more reason to seize the opportunities represented by Gorbachev. Thus, after a period of hesitation, the Bush administration followed Reagan's lead and embraced Gorbachev, whose continuation in power was deemed good for the United States.

Events, already moving rapidly, only accelerated both within the Soviet Union and beyond as the 1980s ended. In these circumstances, predicting what lay ahead for the Soviet Union was risky business because the changes had come so quickly and had been so unexpected. The year 1990 witnessed growing upheaval in Moscow as the communist system, seventy-three years after its inception, began to crack. It became apparent that the Soviet Union was operating from a position of grave weakness, that Gorbachev's foreign policy amounted to a diplomacy of retreat and damage control. The result was that regardless of who held power in Moscow, the United States had a golden opportunity to exploit its advantages. Any ruler of the Soviet Union, if the nation survived essentially intact, would face debilitating domestic constraints on the conduct of foreign policy.

As the "victorious" power in the Cold War, the United States had to give thought to its terms of peace: What kind of post–Cold War world did the United States wish to see? It had, therefore, to define its own goals. Even if Gorbachev did not survive, the United States needed to take advantage of the time he was in office to codify Soviet concessions and ensure that future Soviet foreign policy would be as irreversible as possible. Granted, American influence on Soviet internal affairs was limited, and the ultimate success of *perestroika* (restructuring) depended on events in the Soviet Union. But if the United States were responsive to Gorbachev's policies and proposals, it could support and assist the process of domestic reform and bolster his position in the Kremlin. Washington's principal recourse, therefore, was to lend its support for the peaceful reform of the Soviet state given that both superpowers were moving beyond the Cold War toward an unknown future.

Although the Soviet Union's negotiating position was weak—a problem that was to worsen as Eastern Europe defected, ethnic nationalism grew, and communism as a political and economic system was directly challenged inside the Kremlin—the country had not surrendered unconditionally. Nor had the United States won a total victory as it had in World War II against Germany; it could not impose its terms on

1. See James A. Baker III, with Thomas M. DeFrank, *The Politics of Diplomacy* (New York: Putnam, 1995), ch. 5.

Moscow. Moreover, a victory that humiliated the loser would result in a peace built on sand. World War I had ended with a victor's peace imposed on Germany, but it had lasted only as long as Germany remained weak. After World War II both Germany and Japan were treated in a more conciliatory fashion. Neither, therefore, had been bent on revenge. For a durable peace, the Soviet Union, too, had to find the emerging international order hospitable. Thus the two powers engaged in complex negotiations about the terms on which the Cold War was to be ended, as well as about the construction and shape of the new balance of power.

The final resolution of the Cold War depended basically on the fulfillment of three conditions: the dismantlement of Joseph Stalin's empire in Central and Eastern Europe, the detachment of Leonid Brezhnev's Third World outposts, and a reduction in arms and a stable nuclear balance. When these conditions were fulfilled, Bush was thrust into the tenuous position of managing the disintegration of the Soviet Union and directing the transition of U.S. bilateral relations toward the largest successor state, Boris Yeltsin's Russia.

DISMANTLING STALIN'S EMPIRE

Events in China during the summer of 1989 served as a prelude to the autumn uprisings in Eastern Europe and suggested that the erosion of communism's appeal and legitimacy had extended to the world's most populous communist state. As in Moscow, dissidents in Beijing were granted greater freedom to express their grievances in public and to exercise some degree of political freedom. After they erected a miniature Statue of Liberty in Beijing's Tiananmen Square, however, the communist government moved in with tanks and brutally squashed the growing rebellion. The worldwide television audience that witnessed these events was understandably horrified by what it saw. But China's decrepit regime dismissed the condemnation of foreign governments and intensified its crackdown on pro-democracy activists. When their time came, the East Europeans were inspired by the Chinese example to accelerate their revolution and guarantee that it could not be turned back.

One key sign of Soviet willingness to end the Cold War was its acceptance of Eastern Europe's rapid moves away from Communist Party control. The conquest and subsequent Stalinization of Eastern Europe, together with the division of Germany, had split the continent after World War II. This division was at the heart of the Cold War confrontation, and only self-determination for Poland, Hungary, Czechoslovakia, and other Eastern European states could end it. Events in the region were critical because each of the major wars of the twentieth century had broken out there. The disintegration of the Austro-Hungarian

Empire had led to the eruption of successive Balkan wars and World War I; Germany's absorption of Austria and Czechoslovakia and its invasion of Poland had sparked World War II; and the de facto Soviet annexation of Eastern Europe had led to the Cold War.

American foreign policy during World War II had been sensitive to Soviet security concerns in Eastern Europe, but the United States also had been committed to national self-determination. President Franklin Roosevelt had presumed that after the war Soviet security could be compatible with democratic freedoms. Where communist parties did well, they could be included in coalition governments, reflecting the popular will. Critical to the president's thinking was the knowledge that smaller countries living in the shadow of the Soviet Union would take its security concerns into account in formulating their foreign policies. Roosevelt's thinking reflected that of a traditional great power: small nations living within a superior power's sphere of influence do not have to have governments that reflect the latter's ideological and political values. They *must*, however, be willing to make a virtue out of necessity: to make the best of their geographic situation, to be aware of their constrained freedom and maneuverability, and to acquiesce to the wishes of the regionally dominant power. Finland provided the most concrete example of this relationship.

But Soviet ideology defined security in Marxist terms. Security could be ensured only if potential class enemies were kept out of power altogether. The governments bordering the Soviet Union therefore had to be communist. Even coalition governments in which the Communist Party controlled the major levers of power—the military and police forces—were unacceptable. Eastern Europe, then, was to become a sphere of dominance, with each country having not only communist governments controlled by Moscow but also ideological conformity. As for the Soviet troops stationed throughout Eastern Europe, they were intended not merely to protect these states from perceived Western threats, but also to assure Soviet dominance and adherence to Soviet-style socialism. Without this military presence and occasional Soviet interventions, these governments, unpopular with their people, would not have survived as long as they did.

Could Moscow now separate its ideology from its definition of security? That was the main question in 1989. The initial answer to that question came when the Communist Party in Poland was unable to form a government after its disastrous showing in the free June elections in which the Solidarity movement claimed overwhelming popular support. Because the communists had been repudiated, Solidarity, which had in effect received a mandate to govern, was asked to organize the government. Poland thus formed its first noncommunist—indeed anticommunist—government in the post–World War II era. The military forces, including the security police, were left in communist hands, however, to reassure Moscow about the future course of Poland, a country the Germans had twice marched through in the twentieth century to invade the Soviet Union. In addition, Lech Walesa, Solidarity's leader and spokesman, announced that Poland would remain a member of the Warsaw Pact—just the kind of political sensitivity that Roosevelt had had in mind.

Gorbachev appeared willing to accept such a noncommunist Poland and a more traditional sphere of influence in Eastern Europe for several reasons. One was his preoccupation with worsening domestic matters. Another was that Eastern Europe had not proved to be a security belt. Instead, it had added to Soviet *insecurity*. Its people were sullen and resentful of the Soviet-imposed regimes, and they had not forgotten that earlier efforts to rid themselves of these regimes had been suppressed militarily. Gorbachev did not want to be confronted with an explosive situation, which, among other things, would be a major, if not fatal, setback to the reemerging détente with the West. The installation of more acceptable and legitimate governments would avoid this confrontation and thus enhance Soviet security. Furthermore, given the strains on the Soviet economy, he could not afford continued subsidies to Poland and the rest of Eastern Europe, all of whose economies were in trouble. It made eminent sense, therefore, to unburden his straining economy and "dump" Eastern Europe on the West, especially German bankers. Finally, by accepting a more modest sphere of influence, he could resolve a principal issue that had precipitated and prolonged the Cold War.

The dominoes continued to fall throughout 1989. In Hungary the parliament dropped the word "People" from the country's formal name, and the Communist Party renamed itself the Democratic Socialist Party in order to survive a Polish-style disaster in the upcoming multiparty elections. (Even so, the party was able to keep only 30,000 of its original 720,000 members.) Similarly, Czechoslovakia dropped "Socialist" from its name, and the East German Communist Party also sought to shed its Stalinist skin to better compete in the 1990 elections. In a decision of critical importance, the Hungarian foreign minister opened his country's borders with Austria on September 10, 1989. A free fall then ensued when 200,000 East Germans, mostly young skilled workers vital to its industry, fled their country—via Czechoslovakia, Hungary, and Austria—for West Germany. These events demonstrated vividly that communism had lost its grip on the Eastern Europeans. Indeed, the events of 1989 suggested that the legitimacy of all communist regimes throughout the area was in doubt. Even those who had grown up under communism rejected its philosophy and were now able to say so openly. The direction of these events became obvious during what Zbigniew Brzezinski called the "terminal crisis of Communism."[2]

To make the best of the situation, Gorbachev announced that socialist countries had no right to intervene in each other's affairs; each country was responsible for its own destiny. The clear implication was that the Brezhnev Doctrine was dead. To make the point clearly, in late 1989 Gorbachev paid a symbolic visit to Finland, a country that always had been sensitive to Soviet security interests yet had maintained a relatively autonomous democracy. He presented Finland as a model of a relationship between a big and little country that were neighbors but had different social systems. Gorbachev also visited East Germany to observe its fortieth anniversary as a communist state. There he restated the new doctrine of nonintervention that further propelled the Warsaw Pact's demise. The process gained even more momentum after Moscow and its four Warsaw Pact allies that had jointly invaded Czechoslovakia in 1968 condemned that invasion as "illegal" and pledged a strict policy of noninterference in each other's affairs. Moscow issued its own declaration of repentance.

Gorbachev's actions were most keenly felt in East Germany, where the exodus of its youth threatened to depopulate the country of sixteen million and undermine its hopes for the future. Mass demonstrations finally led to the removal in December 1989 of its despotic communist leader, Erich Honecker. In what was a genuine people's revolution, Soviet troops stood by instead of propping up the regime, and the new party leader promised radical changes, including free elections in May 1990. Among the first reforms, all restrictions on travel and emigration were lifted, inciting hundreds of thousands of East Germans to scale the Berlin Wall in the hours after that announcement. Altogether, 1.5 million East Germans poured across the wall that first weekend to celebrate. As for the wall itself, entire sections were leveled with sledgehammers, and fragments were taken home as souvenirs. From its construction in 1961, the wall had been the symbol of what the Cold War was all about— tyranny versus freedom. Its collapse on November 9, 1989, exactly fifty-one years after Adolf Hitler unleashed his storm troopers against German Jews, thus symbolized more than any other event the end of the Cold War.

After the fall of the Berlin Wall, the winds of change swept over Czechoslovakia. What was happening there also had great symbolic importance, although it was not widely noted at the time because of the tumult elsewhere. The great powers had inflicted tremendous injustices on Czechoslovakia, the only central European democracy before World

2. Zbigniew Brzezinski, *The Grand Failure* (New York: Scribner's, 1989).

War II. It was betrayed by France and England in their efforts to appease Hitler in 1938 and, a decade later, was violently transformed into a communist nation by the Soviets. Its efforts to humanize Czech communism during the Prague Spring of 1968 were crushed by Soviet tanks. The collapse of the communist regime in Prague, therefore, also was a sign of the times.

Everywhere in Eastern Europe—in what Ronald Reagan had once called the "evil empire"—people were saying openly just how evil that empire had been. They demanded not just the reform of communist parties but their removal from office, ending what many of them viewed as a forty-year-long foreign occupation. They also called for free elections and interim governments composed mainly of noncommunists. Only in Bulgaria and Romania did the local communist parties manage to run under new names, promising that they had reformed, and easily win the first free elections after the collapse of the Soviet-supported governments.

The United States responded by expressing support for the governments seeking to liberalize, and President Bush provided a visible show of support by visiting Poland and Hungary in 1989. Beyond this effort, however, the Bush administration did not want to arouse Soviet security concerns. Gorbachev, therefore, sought a tacit understanding with Bush. The Soviet leader would continue to support, if not encourage, the transformations in Eastern Europe, and he would not resist the changes even if they went further down the road to "decommunization" than he would have preferred. In return, the United States would not exploit the geopolitical transformation then under way in the Soviet empire, nor would it jeopardize Soviet security or humiliate Moscow more than already was being done by the popular rejection of communism among its Warsaw Pact allies. Bush also agreed to make concessions—on trade, for example—to help Gorbachev rebuild the Soviet economy and to show some tolerance for his internal problems. Because it was in Washington's interest to manage the changes in the Soviet Union and Eastern Europe peacefully, the Gorbachev-Bush bargain held. This deal even applied for a time to the Baltic republics. Gorbachev considered them part of the Soviet Union and forcefully resisted the secession of Lithuania. The United States, which had never recognized their annexation, did not overtly support their independence movement at this pivotal moment.

The path of nonviolent transformation was chosen not only by the East European rulers but also by the masses. For forty years the Soviet-imposed regimes had exploited and oppressed their peoples. Thus violence from below would have been natural as these regimes relented. Instead, the transitions to democracy were almost unnaturally peaceful.

Revolutions—for that was what was going on in Eastern Europe—are rarely so orderly. After all, 1989 was the bicentennial celebration of the French Revolution, an act of popular liberation that degenerated into a reign of terror. But, as everyone seemed to understand, such violence in the liberation of Eastern Europe would jeopardize the whole process of change.

In Eastern Europe only Romania fell into violence because the regime used force in its attempt to stay in power. Hundreds of people were killed as its dictator, Nicolae Ceausescu, sought in vain to buck the trend in the rest of Eastern Europe. But he failed, as army units defected to the opposition and fought his security forces. Captured as they attempted to flee, Ceausescu and his wife, Elena, were executed after a hasty trial on Christmas Day. With that single exception, it was nonviolence that prevailed. Czechoslovakia's new president, the playwright Vaclav Havel, set the tone by calling on his fellow citizens to act with dignity, honesty, and honor. The slogan of the demonstrators massed in the streets of Prague was "we are not like them."

Equally important, Washington thought it best to allow Eastern Europe's evolution to occur within the broader European context. Even before the 1989 revolutions the members of the European Community (EC) had decided to revive its movement toward a single market. It was a wise move given the likelihood that U.S. economic problems as well as a diminished Soviet threat would lead America to shift its attention to the domestic arena. The European Community also was mindful of stiffening American economic competition, as well as that of other countries, especially in Asia. A single market and currency, the coordination of foreign and security policies, and other cooperative efforts spelled out in the Maastricht accords of 1993 represented steps toward a competitive European economy and a possible European confederation.

If the task of helping Eastern Europe was now an additional motive for an enlarged role of the European Community, renamed the European Union (EU) at the Maastricht summit, another and perhaps more important issue was the rebirth of the "German problem." For more than forty years East and West had lived with a divided Germany. Each side preferred a partitioned Germany because such an arrangement would ensure that Germany would not initiate another war. The "terminal crisis" of communism in Eastern Europe, however, ended this division. Thousands of East Germans poured into West Germany every month, further crippling the East German state, its economy, and its social cohesion. Moreover, as the East German government's authority waned, the calls in East Germany for unification grew stronger every day. To everyone's surprise, the East German election held in March 1990 (earlier than planned given the mounting crisis) was won by the followers of West German chancellor Helmut Kohl, thereby ensuring reunification. The large votes for the Christian Democrats and the Social Democrats, both tied to their West German counterparts, amounted to a death sentence for the German Democratic Republic and an endorsement of a "buyout" by the richer and more powerful West Germans.

But a reunited Germany, even a democratic one, posed all sorts of problems and potential instabilities. In fact, the collapse of the Warsaw Pact and the inevitable, increasingly imminent, reunification of Germany meant constructing a new European balance of power. To make a united Germany acceptable to Moscow, the West insisted that it be a member of NATO. It offered Moscow two reassurances, however. First, no Western armies, including German troops assigned to NATO, would be stationed on former East German territory in view of Moscow's certain opposition to the presence of NATO troops on the Polish border. Second, during a three- to four-year transition period, the 380,000 Soviet troops already in East Germany would remain there. Germany also would guarantee its neighbors' borders, renew West Germany's pledge that it would not seek to acquire nuclear weapons, and agree to limit its armed forces to 370,000, below West Germany's 474,000 in 1990 and well below the 667,000 level of the two Germanies.

Gorbachev's initial opposition was based on memories of the German defeat of czarist Russia in World War I and of the 20 million Soviet lives lost repelling the German invasion in World War II. He insisted that a reunited Germany be a neutral, disarmed state. But this was unacceptable to virtually everyone else, and it probably was not even thought to be the best solution by Moscow. The real question was whether a united but neutralized Germany would become once more a nationalistic, dangerously destabilizing force on the continent. Pushed even by his former allies to accept a reunited Germany restrained by the NATO alliance, Gorbachev proposed that Germany be a member of both the Warsaw Pact and NATO. This too was rejected as merely another formula for neutrality. George Bush, who played an active role in the negotiations, felt confident that Moscow eventually would agree to his terms, which were favored by all members of the Western alliance, the West German government, the new East German one, as well as most Warsaw Pact members. The Soviets, having obviously lost the Cold War, were thought to be in too weak a bargaining position to insist on anything else.

But Gorbachev, weak or not, continued to resist the Western solution. He realized that when it came, the collapse of East Germany would spell the end of a major Soviet Cold War goal, hegemony over Europe by neutralizing West Germany. Indeed, all the Soviet Union's gains in World

War II had been lost. Even more humiliating, a reunited Germany would likely emerge as the financial and economic center of Europe, the dominant power in Eastern Europe, and the principal source of capital and machinery for the Soviet Union.

In July 1990, only four months after declaring that German membership in NATO was "absolutely out of the question," Gorbachev bowed to the inevitable, accepting a reunited Germany in NATO. His acceptance was made easier by the promise of $8 billion in German credits to help the failing Soviet economy. Nevertheless, like his acceptance of a larger number of U.S. troops than Soviet troops in the new Europe, Gorbachev's acquiescence to German membership in NATO was tantamount to Soviet surrender. Although it had none of the drama of VE Day and VJ Day, which marked the end of the war in Europe and in the Pacific in 1945, history will note July 16, 1990, as the day the Soviet Union gave up, effectively ending the Cold War. Indeed, the American insistence on Soviet acceptance of Germany's admission to NATO appeared in large part driven by the need to clarify this issue.

The reemergence of modern Europe's central problem—that of Germany—was imminent. What kind of security arrangements could be established to contain German power in the new post–Cold War Europe? The two superpowers agreed on a framework for ending the division of Germany. First, merger of the two governing Christian Democratic parties was scheduled for October 1, and formal German reunification was set for October 3. Second, in November the reunification issue would be submitted for formal approval to the thirty-five-nation Conference on Security and Cooperation in Europe (CSCE).[3] Finally, an all-German election of an all-German parliament was set for December 2.

The new year would start therefore with the convocation of the new parliament and the formation of the new government. As for the future, the reunited Germany would assume the role of Europe's most powerful economic actor and, like Japan, the other country vanquished in World War II, would quickly become a principal actor in the newly emerging multipolar international system. The world hoped, however, that Germany's preponderant size, population, and economic power would be directed not toward fulfilling selfish interests but toward serving as a catalyst for political stability and economic growth throughout Europe and, indeed, within the Soviet Union itself.

---

3. The CSCE, now known as the Organization on Security and Cooperation in Europe, comprised sixteen NATO countries, seven Warsaw Pact states, and twelve neutral countries. It was founded in 1975 in Helsinki, Finland, where its signatories promised to respect existing frontiers (including the East German-Polish border) and to respect human rights.

Ending the
Cold War:
Negotiating
the Terms
of Peace

DETACHING BREZHNEV'S THIRD WORLD OUTPOSTS

The second precondition to ending the Cold War was Soviet cooperation in resolving regional conflicts in the developing world. As noted earlier, Soviet support for Marxist regimes and insurgencies hindered U.S.-Soviet relations for decades. But now the Soviet Union's desire to avoid trouble with the United States was likely to prevent further expansionism.

Gorbachev's reversal of Soviet expansionism was dramatic. The Soviets withdrew from Afghanistan and later admitted that the invasion had been a mistake, a result of their foreign policy's overreliance on force. In Angola, after prolonged negotiations failed to achieve the exit of fifty thousand Cuban troops from that country in return for South Africa's withdrawal from Namibia, a deal was struck under which the Cubans would withdraw in return for the independence of Namibia.[4] In Southeast Asia, with Soviet encouragement, Vietnam withdrew from Cambodia. Its forces had invaded Cambodia to overthrow its murderous Khmer Rouge government, which had slaughtered more than one million of its own population of eight million. In both Angola and Cambodia, the backing of the Cuban and Vietnamese operations in support of Marxist governments had been costly to the Soviet Union both economically and in terms of credibility. Moscow wanted to cut its losses from these seemingly unending struggles; its overseas empire was proving unmanageable.

Even in the Middle East, Moscow moved, initially, toward rapprochement with Israel—it had broken diplomatic relations in 1967—and later toward the reestablishment of relations. It also supported the U.S. objective of an Israeli-Palestinian treaty and raised the possibility of increased Jewish emigration from the Soviet Union to Israel. Instead of supporting the more radical parties and obstructing American peace efforts, the Soviet Union indicated that it preferred a new course of partnership with the United States.

But in one important area, Central America, the Soviets continued to supply arms to anti-American forces despite soothing words about seeking peaceful settlements. Soviet arms shipments to the Nicaraguan government, although reduced, continued; shipments from Cuba and Eastern Europe made up the difference. Soviet-made weapons also reached the Salvadoran guerrillas, who launched a number of attacks in the capital city of San Salvador in 1989.

The Bush administration strongly protested these policies of support as "Cold War relics," calling these countries "Brezhnevite clients" during

4. South African troops had frequently attacked Angola in pursuit of guerrilla forces operating in Namibia, one of the last African colonies to gain independence.

the informal summit meeting that Gorbachev and Bush held in December 1989 off the Mediterranean island of Malta. Gorbachev denied sending weapons to Central America, but Bush would have none of it. Cuba and Nicaragua were Soviet clients. Washington clearly expected Moscow, which elsewhere had pressured its proxies to resolve their internal and regional differences, to do the same in the Western Hemisphere. Undoubtedly, Cuba's Fidel Castro, who had denounced the Soviet Union's retreat from Marxism-Leninism and considered himself one of the few true remaining communists, would resist counsels of restraint. Even without Soviet arms shipments, Cuba and Nicaragua had enough weapons to ship to the Salvadoran guerrillas.

The more critical issue was the February 1990 election in Nicaragua, which, as noted in Chapter 9, held out the promise of easing regional tensions in Central America. Gorbachev prevailed on the Sandinistas to permit free elections like those held in Eastern Europe. When the Sandinistas lost the elections, which were closely monitored by the United Nations and the Organization of American States, the Soviet Union lost yet another overseas client. National reconciliation, disbanding the contras, rebuilding the economy, ensuring a democratic and more just society, and reestablishing good relations with the United States were to be the central tasks of Nicaragua's new government.

The only remaining source of real friction between Washington and Moscow was Cuba. Castro swore that socialism would continue to be practiced on his island even if it had been "betrayed" by Gorbachev and even if it were abandoned virtually everywhere else. Moscow discontinued its massive annual subsidies to Cuba in 1991, which were largely in the form of petroleum and other necessities, announcing that future economic relations between the two countries would be on a trade-only basis. The Soviet military training brigade also would be withdrawn. The Soviet Union, itself seeking economic help from the West, was responding to the Bush administration's insistence that it would not consider providing such assistance while Moscow continued to provide Castro with the equivalent of $5 billion annually. Thus the Soviet retreat from the developing world continued.

REDUCING ARMS AND STABILIZING THE NUCLEAR BALANCE

The third condition for ending the Cold War was a reduction in superpower arms and a stable nuclear balance. A consistent U.S. goal in the evolving new superpower relationship was to provide for a stable security environment through appropriate arms control agreements. More specifically, U.S. policy had three objectives. The first, especially in view of Gorbachev's uncertain tenure, was to reach agreements to reduce strategic and conventional arms; once achieved, such arms reductions would be politically and economically difficult to reverse. The second objective was to reduce the likelihood of surprise attack, a goal that was pursued by both sides through a variety of confidence-building measures. And the third objective was to reduce the burden of defense spending and to realize a "peace dividend" to be spent on domestic needs. (For Gorbachev, this financial benefit was probably the driving force behind all his arms proposals. As the U.S. budget deficit grew, Bush also wanted to see a reduction in defense spending.)

From the beginning of the SALT process, SALT III was intended to cut drastically the strategic arsenals of both powers. Renamed START (Strategic Arms Reduction Talks) by the Reagan administration to emphasize more ambitious reductions—a 50 percent cut—the treaty was aimed at cutting Soviet land-based missiles, which, with their multiple and accurate warheads, were the principal threat to the survival of American intercontinental ballistic missiles (ICBMs). In short, reductions per se were not the objective; the aim was *stabilizing* reductions. By the time Reagan left office, the START negotiations were substantially completed. Each side had agreed to a ceiling of 1,600 delivery vehicles, an aggregate of 6,000 strategic weapons, and a ballistic missile warhead limit of 4,900. Although the overall cut in strategic forces was closer to a 30 percent reduction, the most destabilizing forces—ballistic missiles with multiple warheads—were reduced by 50 percent.

The chief obstacle from the very beginning was the Strategic Defense Initiative (SDI), or the American plan to defend its territory from incoming nuclear missiles (see Chapter 9). The Soviets insisted that they would not reduce their ICBM force until they knew whether they would have to cope with American strategic defenses. But Reagan clung to his vision of SDI, and therefore the Soviets refused to sign the START treaty. To break the deadlock, Moscow announced in 1989 its willingness to sign the treaty on the condition that the United States abide by the 1972 antiballistic missile (ABM) treaty. While the two issues were finally severed, at least formally, START's fate again depended on Washington's decisions about SDI development. The program had lost its main advocate with the end of the Reagan presidency, however, and faced great technical difficulties and increasing congressional disenchantment at a time of a huge federal deficit. Thus support for SDI steadily eroded, and it no longer posed an obstacle to arms control negotiations.

As for conventional forces, after 1987 Gorbachev had talked repeatedly about a shift from an offensive to a defensive military doctrine, as well as sizable military budget cuts as the Soviet Union scaled its forces back to "reasonable sufficiency." He promised and carried out unilateral reductions of Soviet forces, including the withdrawal of troops and tanks facing NATO. For Warsaw Pact forces to shift to a strategy that could repel an attack but not launch a massive surprise attack on NATO was obviously very much in the West's interest. Such a shift would greatly relieve Western fears stemming from the Soviet Union's sizable forces and Soviet military doctrine, and it would be a tangible sign that Soviet intentions had fundamentally changed.

The conventional arms reduction negotiations, or Central Front Europe (CFE) negotiations, sought to reduce Soviet forces in Eastern Europe and American forces in Western Europe to 275,000. CFE also sought equal numbers of tanks, armored personnel carriers, artillery pieces, and combat aircraft for the two military alliances. But events in Eastern Europe were moving so fast that in January 1990 President Bush called for a further U.S.-Soviet troop reduction in central Europe to 195,000, with 30,000 more American troops outside of that area. Surprisingly, Gorbachev accepted the U.S. proposal, even though this cutback would, for the first time since the war, leave the United States with more troops in Europe than the Soviet Union. Militarily this was unimportant, but politically and psychologically it provided further evidence of Soviet weakness. In any case, the 195,000-troop ceiling was unlikely to be the last word on reductions because of strong domestic pressure in the United States to cut U.S. forces further to about 75,000.

Such reductions appeared possible because by 1990 the Soviet-led alliance, organized to protect the Soviet-imposed socialist systems, had fewer systems to defend as Eastern Europe defected from the Warsaw Pact. In these circumstances Moscow could no longer count, if it ever could, on the armies of Czechoslovakia, Hungary, Poland, East Germany, Bulgaria, and Romania for any joint military action against the West. In 1990 Moscow agreed to withdraw its forces from Czechoslovakia, Hungary, and Poland by the end of 1992. But this pledge became irrelevant as the Warsaw Pact died shortly afterward, to be formally buried in 1991.

Would NATO also disappear? That was unlikely, at least in the short run, because the alliance continued to have several functions. One was to continue to guard the West against the possibility of a renewed Soviet (or, later, Russian) threat. There remained widespread concern that Gorbachev might be overthrown by the old communist guard, which could then reimpose Soviet hegemony in Eastern Europe.[5] Another function of NATO, not spoken of openly for diplomatic reasons, was to restrain the new Germany. After twice calling on American power to defeat Germany, Europeans were unsure that they alone could manage a

5. Even after the attempted coup in August 1991 against Gorbachev, which led to the Soviet Union's own demise, Russia, the successor state, retained significant military power.

unified Germany. Retaining NATO would keep American power in Europe. Finally, the United States wanted the alliance to serve as an institutional link through which it could influence the shape of the emerging new order in Europe as the European Union moved toward greater economic and political integration.

Bush's arms control initiatives continued even after the Soviet Union itself dissolved in late 1991. Under the rubric of the START II negotiations, Bush carried on with Russian president Boris Yeltsin. At their June 1992 summit meeting, the two sides agreed to even deeper cuts in nuclear arms, among them the most destabilizing multiple-warhead missiles which had become a headache to strategic planners in Moscow and Washington. The agreement called for both sides to be down to about three thousand missiles by the year 2003, or sooner if the United States could assist the financially strapped Russians in dismantling their weapons.

ENDGAME: THE COLLAPSE OF THE CORE

In 1990–1991 there was no question but that the Soviet Union itself was undergoing a rapid and profound transformation. With the disintegration of its economy, the political regime lost its legitimacy and was further weakened by internal conflicts between Moscow and a number of Soviet republics. Demands for autonomy, if not independence, erupted in many areas, and ancient ethnic feuds reemerged. These events threatened the integrity of the Soviet state and compelled the regime to move Soviet tactical nuclear warheads out of the Baltics and the volatile southern republics to parts of Russia it considered more secure.

In addition, the Communist Party was showing growing signs of disintegration and was losing its authority to impose decisions on the nation. In the Baltics it was faced with the Lithuanian Communist Party's defection from the Soviet party and its identification with Lithuania's demand for independence. In Azerbaijan the Soviet army had to be deployed not only to restore order between the Azerbaijanis and Armenians, but also to prevent the communist government from falling into the hands of the Azerbaijani popular front—much as communist regimes in Eastern Europe had fallen to the opposition groups. In several cities and regions, party officials had to resign because of popular outrage over their corruption and privileges. Indeed, in Moscow, Leningrad, and other cities the emerging democratic political opposition inflicted embarrassing defeats on the communists by winning majorities in local elections.

Gorbachev, alert to popular disenchantment with the party, gradually shifted his base of power from the Communist Party (whose conservative apparatus continued to resist his reforms) to the elected Supreme Soviet and the presidency, a post he held in addition to that of general secretary of the party. He went even further by calling on the party to give up its seventy-year constitutional monopoly of power, although he clearly considered the party to be the most capable of guiding the nation through its turmoil. For the party to remain the political vanguard, however, it would have to earn the Soviet people's trust. And to do this, the party would have to restructure itself. Gorbachev even suggested that at some future point rival political parties might be established.

Equally revolutionary was Gorbachev's embrace of the free market as an alternative to the failed communist economy. Having repudiated Lenin, Gorbachev now dumped Marx as well. Thus seventy-three years after the Bolshevik revolution, the Soviets reversed themselves; markets would replace bureaucracy, and capitalism would succeed socialism. But Gorbachev, however revolutionary his rhetoric and declarations, hesitated to implement his reforms because they would surely propel the flow of power away from Moscow and the central government he headed. A social explosion might occur as well if the withdrawal of subsidies to industry and to Soviet citizens for rent, food, health care, and education resulted in sharp rises in inflation and unemployment. Moreover, Gorbachev could not discount the old guard's opposition, and he clung to the notion that a communist system could exist alongside a Soviet transition to free markets.

In principle, then, the party had renounced both its political-economic dictatorship and its intellectual heritage, but the real question was whether it had happened too late. Could a political system that no longer enjoyed sufficient political authority or popularity because of five years of growing economic shortages, which now included even bread and cigarettes, take the tough measures required to implement wholesale economic changes? Had Gorbachev become the captain of the Soviet *Titanic* as the party increasingly lost control to the Supreme Soviet, the legislatures of the republics, municipal governments, popular fronts, and increasingly assertive workers' unions, all of which sought a greater devolution of power and policy?

The strongest challenge to Gorbachev's power came from Boris Yeltsin, a former Communist Party leader who in May 1990 was elected president of the Russian republic. Russia occupied two-thirds of the territory of the former Soviet Union and had almost half of its population and most of its oil, natural gas reserves, and coal. Yeltsin was quick to sense the popular disaffection with the power and privileges of the Communist Party. Once Gorbachev's protégé, Yeltsin became his fiercest critic and arch rival because the Soviet leader had not, in Yeltsin's judgment, moved quickly enough to change the system.

COMMONWEALTH OF INDEPENDENT STATES, 1992

On the day after his election by the Russian parliament, Yeltsin challenged the system by proposing Russia's economic autonomy and a radical decentralization in which republic law took precedence over Soviet law and the president of the Soviet Union would have no greater authority than the presidents of the fifteen republics. Indeed, not only would Russia claim sovereignty and determine the prices of its natural resources, but it would make its own agreements with the other members of the Soviet Union. And just to make his challenge clear, Yeltsin announced that he would seek to make the Russian presidency a popularly elected office, which he won overwhelmingly. By being elected president of the Soviet Union's largest republic, Yeltsin acquired a legitimacy Gorbachev never had.

A few weeks later, Yeltsin, together with the reformist mayors of Moscow and Leningrad, resigned from the Communist Party. Their resignations were symptomatic of growing national disenchantment with the party and Gorbachev's declining popularity. Next, the Ukraine, the Soviet Union's second largest republic and its "breadbasket," with a population of more than fifty million, declared its sovereignty and that its laws were above those of the Soviet Union. It also claimed an independent foreign policy role by stating it would be a neutral state; it would not participate in military blocs; and it would ban the production and deployment of nuclear weapons on its territory. The Ukraine's action was followed by a similar declaration from Belarus, a small but geographically vital republic located between Ukraine and the Baltic states. Eventually all of the Soviet Union's fifteen republics issued sovereignty declarations, asserting either outright independence or more cautious assertions of their rights. Gorbachev's Soviet Union crumbled around him, piece by piece.

By late 1990 Gorbachev had become more and more irrelevant in domestic affairs. Yeltsin was setting the pace and scope of change by supporting the drive for independence of the Baltic republics and by proposing a five-hundred-day plan for the transformation of the Russian economy into a market economy. Gorbachev found himself maneuvering between the increasingly radical forces on the left and the forces of reaction on the right, represented by the traditional instruments of Soviet power—the military, secret police, and Communist Party bureaucracy—which had survived all his attempts at reform. They were the elite and therefore had a strong vested interest in the status quo. In the meantime, Gorbachev had his hands full just trying to hold the union together, to stem the republics' nationalism. Thus he shifted his original direction and aligned himself with the forces of "law and order." He dismissed many of his former liberal allies in the struggle for *glasnost* and *perestroika,* began cracking down on the Baltic republics, and reimposed censorship.

Gorbachev's new allies, however, tried to limit his power and enhance their own because they felt he was leading the country to chaos and anarchy. Moreover, they despised him because he had retreated from Eastern Europe and had given up the Soviet Union's World War II gains. In response, Gorbachev swung back to ally himself once more with the reformers. He made his peace with the republics and promised the presidents of the nine republics who agreed to stay within the union, including Yeltsin, to turn the Soviet Union into a new voluntary federation that all republics would have the right to join or not join. They also would be free to choose their own form of government and exercise most of the power over their natural resources, industry, foreign trade, and taxes. He promised a new constitution and a newly elected central government.

But just as the new All-Union Treaty was about to be signed, the hard-liners struck. Fearing that their power was waning and that it soon would be too late to do anything about it, they launched a coup in August 1991, arresting Gorbachev while he was on holiday. But the coup plotters failed to understand the effects of the six years of Gorbachev's policies. Led by the popularly elected Yeltsin, who showed enormous courage, the people of Moscow rallied behind Gorbachev, resisting those who would reimpose the old dictatorship. When units of the military and secret police opposed the coup, it quickly collapsed. This event proved to be the death blow to the Soviet Union.

All the republics now wanted their independence from Moscow and central authority. The three Baltic republics were let go and their independence was recognized by Moscow. At this point, seven of the twelve remaining republics, including Russia, planned to stay together in a loose confederation because they were still economically interdependent, although the agriculturally and industrially important Ukraine would not commit itself to creating a "common economic space" and a single currency, the foundation of a free-market economy.

What was absolutely clear in these times of uncertainty was that the old regime had disgraced itself by the coup attempt. Statues of Stalin and Lenin were unceremoniously removed from public squares. The old imperial flag designed by Peter the Great once again flew over the Russian parliament, the center of the resistance to the coup. Leningrad was renamed St. Petersburg, its prerevolutionary name, in accordance with the wishes of its citizens. Many said that it also was time to remove Lenin's body from the mausoleum in Red Square. But the major victim of the failed coup was the Communist Party. Yeltsin took sweeping measures against the Russian Communist Party, closing all of its offices and newspapers. Gorbachev, acknowledging the mood of the country and trying to salvage some of his authority, ended the party's role as watchdog of the military, secret police, and government bureaucracy, and disbanded its leadership. For all practical purposes the Communist Party as a governing body was dead. It could no longer block the path to democracy and radical economic reform. The revolution of 1917 had been undone in a stunning sequence of events.

The republics, however, were still grappling with their future. At the moment of decision the seven republics that had endorsed the new union would not commit themselves, leaving its fate in the hands of their national parliaments. When the Ukraine voted on December 1, 1991, for independence and instantly became Europe's fourth largest country, it became clear that nothing could stop the process of Soviet disintegration. With even a weak confederation now dead, Russia was left as the successor state to the Soviet Union. Indeed, this status had become overwhelmingly clear when the central government declared bankruptcy in November 1991 and Russia assumed its debts and promised to fund what remained of the central government's ministries. In capitalist language, this act constituted a leveraged buyout of the former Soviet Union. Russia also claimed the Soviet Union's permanent seat on the UN Security Council.

The Soviet Union was formally buried on December 8, 1991, when, in an act of desperation to stop the complete disintegration of the nation, the presidents of the three Slavic republics—Russia, Ukraine, and Belarus—representing 73 percent of the population and 80 percent of the territory of the Soviet Union, decided to establish a commonwealth and invited other republics to join. The new Commonwealth of Independent States (CIS) assumed all the international obligations of the Soviet Union, including control over its nuclear arsenal. Coordinating bodies would be established to decide on cooperative policies in foreign affairs, defense, and economics. Later, the commonwealth agreement was signed by eleven of the remaining twelve Soviet republics after the defections of the three Baltic states; the twelfth republic, Georgia, was consumed by civil war. On December 25, 1991, the red hammer-and-sickle flag that had flown over the Kremlin was lowered for the last time, seventy-four years after the Bolshevik revolution. The Soviet Union had disappeared from the world's map.

DID THE UNITED STATES 'WIN' OR THE SOVIET UNION 'LOSE' THE COLD WAR?

Throughout his presidency George Bush was dogged by the notion that he lacked a coherent vision of the future of world politics. Further, he was criticized for what seemed to be an overly cautious approach to U.S.-Soviet relations, his continuing embrace of Gorbachev after the Soviet leader lost legitimacy, and his resistance to immediate deep cuts in American defense spending. Bush, the lifelong government bureau-crat, manager, and caretaker, presumably lacked the panache to seize such a profound historic opportunity.

Twenty-first century historians probably will be kinder to Bush because a careful review of his performance reveals how skillfully he manipulated one of the crucial turning points in history, not only to the advantage of the United States but also in the interests of global stabili-ty. The three-year free fall of the Soviet system was by no means a cer-tainty when Bush arrived in office, and its peaceful course was without precedent. In assisting Gorbachev when he urgently needed outside sup-port, in insisting on German unification on Western terms, and in exploiting the opportunity for drastic nuclear disarmament, Bush suc-cessfully navigated the United States and its allies through a complicat-ed phase of international relations toward their ultimate victory in a protracted conflict of global proportions. Bush was chastised for adher-ing to the most "prudent" approach to world politics, but history may suggest that prudence was precisely the approach the world required.[6]

Immediately after the Cold War ended, the question was raised whether the United States had "won" the war and whether its contain-ment policy had been successful. Or was it more accurate to say that the Soviet Union, plagued by internal problems of its own making, had "lost" the Cold War? This question—not one conducive to a definitive answer—sparked a contentious debate among scholars, journalists, and policy makers.[7] But it was not merely an academic exercise, for the answers to these questions would reveal the central lessons of the Cold War, which in turn would figure in the establishment of guidelines for future American foreign policy.

THE CONTENDING ARGUMENTS IN PERSPECTIVE

Advocates of the view that the United States had "won" the Cold War claimed that the Western system of political, economic, and military organization was simply more durable than that of the Soviet Union and its allies. Furthermore, the U.S.-led containment policy successfully combined pressure and patience to overwhelm Soviet capabilities.[8] In other words, containment had worked much as George Kennan predict-ed it would nearly fifty years earlier, preventing Soviet expansion through the selective application of Western resistance. Conversely,

---

6. A more thorough review of Bush's performance is provided by Michael Beschloss and Strobe Talbott in *At the Highest Levels* (Boston: Little, Brown, 1993).

7. For a review of these arguments, see Michael J. Hogan, ed., *The End of the Cold War: Its Meanings and Implications* (New York: Cambridge University Press, 1992).

8. See John Lewis Gaddis, *The United States and the End of the Cold War* (New York: Oxford University Press, 1992), 193.

those believing that the Soviet Union had instead "lost" the war diminished the role of the containment policy. If the United States had "won," it was merely because the Soviet Union's flawed system made its demise inevitable. Its excessive centralization of power, bureaucratic planning, and supervision of every detail of Soviet life, economic and otherwise, as well as its command economy and ideological oppression, contributed to its undoing.[9] Furthermore, for some neo-Marxists the Soviet Union's demise reflected its perversion of Marxist ideals and principles, not the bankruptcy of the political theory.

Both views call for a closer look at the Soviet experience in converting the aspirations of the 1917 Russian Revolution into practice. Seventy years after the revolution, the Soviet standard of living was so low that even Eastern Europe, with its own economic problems, appeared affluent by contrast. According to the former Soviet Union's own statistics, about 40 percent of its population and almost 80 percent of its elderly citizens lived in poverty. One-third of its households had no running water. Indeed, the Soviet Union was the only industrialized society in which infant mortality had risen and male life expectancy had declined in the late twentieth century. In Zbigniew Brzezinski's words, "Perhaps never before in history has such a gifted people, in control of such abundant resources, labored so hard for so long to produce so little."[10]

The Soviet economy, which was supposed to have demonstrated the superiority of socialism, sputtered for decades and then collapsed. Deliberately isolating itself from the global capitalist economy, the Soviet Union intended to build an economy that was self-sufficient and productive, assuring a bountiful life for the workers and peasants who so long had been deprived. Instead, the centralized command economy meant no domestic competition among firms, and its self-exclusion from the international economy ensured that it remained unchallenged by foreign competition. The Soviet economy thus became a textbook case of what free traders have long argued are the results of state control: inefficiency, lack of productivity, unresponsiveness to consumer needs, and technological stagnation. And there was nothing in the writings of Karl Marx, which had more to do with revolution than communist government, that provided a solution to this central problem.

Soviet communism was efficient only in producing military hardware. But this, ironically, also contributed to its defeat. As a state with few natural protective barriers, frequently invaded throughout its histo-

9. See Walter Laquer, *The Dream that Failed* (New York: Oxford University Press, 1994), 50–76. Also see Charles W. Kegley Jr., "How Did the Cold War Die? Principles for an Autopsy," *Mershon International Studies Review* (summer 1994): 11–41.

10. Zbigniew Brzezinski, *Game Plan* (Boston: Atlantic Monthly Press, 1986), 123. Also see Brzezinski, *The Grand Failure* (New York: Collier Books, 1989).

ry, first Russia and then the Soviet Union kept sizable standing forces for its defense. Its twentieth-century experiences with Germany did nothing to relieve the longtime Russian sense of insecurity, fueled by the Marxist conception of politics as a constant struggle and its perception that enemies were everywhere. But whether Soviet expansionism stemmed from a defensive preoccupation with security or from an offensive ideological goal of aggrandizement, Moscow's drive for absolute security left other states feeling absolutely insecure. It is no wonder, then, that such insecurity drove all of the Soviet Union's great-power neighbors (Western Europe, on one side; Turkey, Iran, China, Japan, and South Korea, on the other sides) to accelerate their own defense spending. Furthermore, many Soviet accomplishments, such as its inroads in the Third World, considered at the time as setbacks for the United States, were actually setbacks for Moscow. Cuba in the 1960s, Angola and Ethiopia in the 1970s, and Afghanistan in the 1980s gave the Soviet system a bad case of indigestion. The logic, then, of this thesis—the more the Soviet Union expanded, the greater the cost—was that the U.S.-led containment policy was not an essential ingredient in stopping Soviet expansion. Indeed, it was precisely where containment *failed*, providing an opening for Moscow, that the Soviet Union's burden became too great to bear.[11]

Strobe Talbott, *Time*'s Soviet expert and later a deputy secretary of state in the Clinton administration, asserted that the Soviet threat was a "grotesque exaggeration" and claimed in retrospect, "The doves in the great debate of the past 40 years were right all along."[12] The Soviet "meltdown" in the Cold War was self-inflicted "not because of anything the outside world has done or not done or threatened to do." Thus American and Western policies had little to do with the Soviet defeat in the Cold War since its cause was purely internal. Characteristic of the revisionist view that has followed every major American war, Talbott's analysis was: that there really had been no major danger to this country; that the nation's long, intense, and dangerous involvement in the post–World War II world had not been necessary; and that the containment policy, instead of playing a key role in the defeat of America's adversary, had merely prolonged the Cold War. Soviet power "was actually Soviet weakness," and the conflict itself "distorted priorities, distracted attention and preoccupied many of the best and the brightest minds in government, academe, and think tanks for nearly two generations." Thus it would have been better to have avoided the "grand obsession" with the "Red Menace," to have remained isolated from the power politics that diverted resources from domestic reforms to military

---

11. John Mueller, "Enough Rope," *New Republic*, July 3, 1989, 15.
12. Strobe Talbott, "Rethinking the Red Menace," *Time*, January 1, 1990, 66–71.

preparations and war. Gorbachev, Talbott claimed, not only helped to show that the Soviet threat was not what it used to be, but "what's more, that it never was."

Soviet communism, a far cry from the worker's utopia envisioned by Karl Marx, surely deserves some of the credit it has been given for abetting its own collapse. But to conclude from this that the containment policy was not necessary, or, if necessary, was not a key ingredient in the Soviet Union's demise, is to differ from the conclusions drawn by its potential victims. As the United States attempted to withdraw from Europe after World War II, countries such as Iran and Turkey, followed by those in Western Europe, pleaded with the United States to help them. The collapse of the former great powers of Western Europe left the Soviet Union as the potential hegemon throughout Eurasia. All countries saw their independence and national integrity at stake; America's continued presence was their only protection. Had the United States retreated into isolationism, as it did after World War I, the countries on the periphery of the Soviet Union would have been exposed to Soviet control.

Western Europe remained the pivotal strategic stake throughout the Cold War. The Soviets repeatedly tried to intimidate these nations, to divide them (especially West Germany from the United States), and to drive the United States back to its shores. But the containment policy made Moscow cautious about expanding its power. From this perspective, the ancient rule of states is a prudent one: power must be met by countervailing power. A balance among states is the only guarantee that they will retain their independence and preserve their way of life. Without containment, the inefficiencies of the Soviet system might not have mattered as much; the Soviet Union would not have had to engage in a costly, ongoing arms competition.

Containment, however, was not aimed just at blocking Soviet domination of Western Europe and the rest of Eurasia; it also was intended to win time for the Soviet leadership to reexamine its goals and moderate its ambitions. Thus the American strategy in the Cold War rested largely and correctly on a tactical assumption of Soviet behavior. As George Kennan had explained years earlier, the United States had

it in its power to increase enormously the strains under which Soviet policy must operate, to force upon the Kremlin a far greater degree of moderation and circumspection than it has had to observe in recent years, and in this way *to promote tendencies which must eventually find their outlet in either the breakup or the gradual mellowing of Soviet power. For no mystical, messianic movement—and particularly that of the Kremlin—can face frustration indefinitely without eventually adjusting itself in one way or another to the logic of that state of affairs.*[13]

13. Italics added. George Kennan, *American Diplomacy, 1900–1950* (Chicago: University of Chicago Press, 1951), 127–128.

In retrospect, these words were prophetic. The Cold War experience demonstrated the virtue of patience in foreign policy. While interpreting the Soviet threat as the country's paramount concern, Kennan foresaw no quick fixes and recommended no immediate solutions to the problem. To the contrary, he anticipated a prolonged, low-intensity struggle along several distant frontiers. The conflict would be settled most effectively—and most peacefully—through the gradual exposure of contradictions within Soviet society. Soviet communism, in his view, would ultimately *self-destruct* under the weight of these contradictions. In the meantime, the United States would have to pursue a "long-term, patient, but firm and vigilant containment of Russian expansive tendencies." From Truman to Bush, that is just what U.S. presidents did.

The importance of the containment policy becomes even more evident when it is contrasted to an earlier period of American foreign policy. If the principal causes of the Cold War were the structure of the postwar state system and the Soviet style in foreign policy, then America's national style made its own contribution. By failing to take a firm stand against Soviet policy during World War II, after it had become evident from repeated episodes that it was impossible to accommodate Soviet interests in Eastern Europe and Asia, the United States has to accept some of the blame for the Cold War that followed. This is not to say that the United States passively accepted Soviet expansionism, but only that it did not oppose Stalin early enough, that it continued to cling to its hope for postwar amity with the Soviet Union despite Soviet behavior in the late stages of the war, and that after hostilities had ceased, it dissipated its strength immediately in a helter-skelter demobilization. Stalin respected American power and was a cautious statesman, but when President Roosevelt informed him that American troops would be withdrawn from Europe after two years, Stalin did not need to concern himself about American protests against Soviet actions in Eastern Europe. Protests were one thing, action another. Not until after the war did the United States act and draw the lines beyond which Soviet expansion would not be tolerated.

The American containment policy, then, played a critical role in the defeat of the Soviet Union. If the United States had not resisted Soviet expansion, Moscow, believing that communism represented the wave of the future, would have become more assertive and aggressive; perceived weakness always invited efforts to expand. For example, when Khrushchev claimed that the balance of power had turned in favor of the Soviet Union, he precipitated a series of crises in West Berlin and Cuba that stretched from 1957 to 1962. And later, when Brezhnev's Soviet Union did attain strategic nuclear parity while also fielding a sizable army and building a growing navy, it exploited America's "Vietnam syndrome," using its own forces and sponsoring clients in Southeast Asia, Africa, Latin America, and Afghanistan. U.S. policy compelled Soviet caution and moderation. If the United States and its allies, especially NATO, had not opposed Soviet expansionist efforts through constant pressure, there would have been no need for Gorbachev to reassess his predecessors' policy and seek an accommodation with the West.

EXCESSES OF THE CONTAINMENT POLICY

Containment was not, of course, a flawless policy. Once the Cold War started, U.S. misperceptions, like those of Soviet leaders, fed the superpower conflict. For example, Washington frequently exaggerated Soviet military capabilities. Fears of Soviet superiority—the bomber gap in the 1950s, the missile gaps a few years later, the ABM gap in the mid-1960s, and "the window of vulnerability" in the early 1980s—propelled the arms competition already well under way. In addition, the U.S. emphasis on anticommunism meant American policy often was insensitive to the nationalism of the new nations. As a result, the Middle East Treaty Organization (METO) and Southeast Asia Treaty Organization (SEATO) alliances proved weak reeds for containing communism, alienating important states such as Egypt and India which shifted toward the Soviet Union, aggravating regional rivalries, and aligning the United States with discredited regimes such as Nationalist China and Iran. Indeed, in the name of anticommunism Washington often supported authoritarian, right-wing regimes in the Third World; it saw no democratic alternatives to the regimes it backed other than left-wing pro-Soviet or pro-Chinese ones, which were unacceptable.

The U.S. government also consistently exaggerated the monolithic nature of international communism. The fall of Nationalist China, the Korean War, and the communist Chinese intervention in that war transformed the containment policy—which originally was limited to responding to Soviet moves in the eastern Mediterranean and Western Europe—into global anticommunism. The events of 1949 and 1950 led to virulent anticommunism in the United States, with the Republicans (notably Sen. Joe McCarthy) accusing the Democrats of being "soft on communism" and engaging in paranoid witch hunts. Future Democratic administrations therefore would not be able to exploit the growing differences between the Soviet Union and China; instead, seeking to avoid being charged with the "loss of Indochina," as they had been with the "loss of China," Democratic administrations intervened militarily in Vietnam.

The American penchant for crusading, already vividly demonstrated in two "hot" wars, was not to be denied in the Cold War. Its failure to distinguish between vital and secondary interests—or to discriminate between different communist regimes—resulted in a war that the United States could not win, dividing the country deeply and undermining the domestic consensus that had been the basis of the Cold War. Ironically, Vietnam destroyed the aggressive mode of American anticommunism, and U.S. policy shifted back toward a more passive containment of Soviet power—but this time in a de facto "alliance" with China. Finally, as noted in Chapter 9, the overzealous pursuit of the Reagan Doctrine resulted in the Iran-contra scandal, which raised new doubts about the extent to which the U.S. government would go to fulfill its mission of defeating communism.

A FINAL APPRAISAL

Its shortcomings aside, the American containment policy must be pronounced, on the whole, a success. The expansion of American power and influence in the world has, despite the excesses of the Cold War, been associated with the promotion of democracy. America's World War II enemies, once dictatorial, are today stable, free, and prosperous societies. And its allies, particularly in Western Europe, have benefited from the opportunity to integrate their economies and pursue cooperative foreign relations.

If one looks at the societies "liberated" by the Soviet Union during World War II, the contrast is striking. No East European country, until Gorbachev, was granted self-determination by the Kremlin; earlier attempts by East Germany, Hungary, Czechoslovakia, and Poland to move toward greater freedom were crushed by Soviet forces or their proxies. East Germany had to build a wall across Berlin and a barbed-wire fence along its entire border with West Germany to prevent its citizens from escaping. It was symbolic, too, that in the summer of 1989, when the pro-democracy movement in China was culminating, student leaders erected a "goddess of democracy" modeled after the Statue of Liberty. After the movement was violently crushed by the authorities, this goddess became the symbol for its sympathizers all over the world.

Over the four decades of the Cold War the United States acquired many authoritarian allies, mostly in the Third World, which weakened Washington's moral standing and laid open its foreign policy to the charge of hypocrisy. It would have been preferable, of course, to have democratic allies, but that was not always possible in a world in which most developing countries had never been democratic in the Western sense of the term. Security, both internally and globally, was bound to conflict with democratic development, as today the values of economic growth and human rights frequently clash. Which value was to be given priority presented a difficult, often agonizing choice both for American leaders and for the leaders of developing countries.

The basic fact remains, however, that the principal thrust of American foreign policy after World War II, as before the war, was to preserve a balance of power that would safeguard democratic values in the United States and other like-minded states. Indeed, this has been a consistent policy since World War I, whether the threat has come from the right or the left. American policy makers in the twentieth century have opposed both types of regimes, for they have threatened not just U.S. security but, more broadly, the international environment in which democratic values can prosper. And this was the crux of American opposition to the Soviet Union: that its great power constituted a threat to Western values and democratic political institutions. Communism, especially as reflected in the Soviet Union that Gorbachev inherited, was antithetical to individual freedoms, whether of speech or religion, to multiparty competition and genuine political choice, and to a distinction between state and society. It was America's power, not simply its democratic ideals, that protected these values.

Indeed, the end of the Cold War was witness not only to the end of the Soviet challenge but also to the defeat of the second totalitarian challenge to Western-style democracy in this century. The Nazis will be forever identified with the concentration camps of Auschwitz, Bergen-Belsen, and Treblinka, where they systematically murdered millions of people, including 6 million Jews, and with the unleashing of World War II, which, before it was over, cost the lives of 17 million soldiers and 34 million civilians. Just as the Nazi system was epitomized by Hitler, the Soviet system remains identified with Stalin and his cruel collectivization of the Soviet peasantry, the deliberate starvation of the Ukrainian peasants in the early 1930s, and the purges and other crimes that claimed the lives, conservatively estimated, of 20 million people and imprisoned and deported 20 million more. Stalin, not Hitler, was the great mass murderer in history; he also was in power twice as long.[14] Thus, while the "decommunization" of Eastern Europe and the collapse of Soviet power were to be celebrated, the defeat of the two regimes that had been the greatest suppressors of human rights had global significance.

Although the U.S. victory in the Cold War coincided with America's own economic woes, the country still had reason to be proud of its overall record. During the nearly half-century of Cold War in which the United States led the Western coalition, there had been no nuclear war, Soviet expansionist ambitions had been checked, and democracy had

14. See Edvard Radzinsky, *Stalin* (New York: Doubleday, 1996); Paul Johnson, *Modern Times*, 2d ed. (New York: Harper and Row, 1992), ch. 8; and Robert Conquest, *The Great Terror* (New York: Oxford University Press, 1990).

emerged in a steadily growing number of countries. Then, after winning the Cold War, the U.S. government refused to gloat, seeking instead to attract the former Soviet bloc as a partner in the process of economic and political reform. While this process would be as complex, difficult, and potentially dangerous as that of containing communism, it would gradually extend the domain of European cooperation and produce a degree of stability not seen before in the twentieth century.

Victims of the "ethnic cleansing" in the former Yugoslavia, these refugees are being evacuated by the UN from Srebrenica, a Moslem enclave in Bosnia-Herzegovina.

CHAPTER ELEVEN
Old Tensions in a New Order

The winding down of the Cold War in the early 1990s gave rise to a new sense of euphoria in the West. The world seemed to stand on the verge of a new era. This hope, admittedly, was based in part on the Soviet Union's collapse and the anticipated replacement of the Cold War rivalry with Russo-American cooperation in maintaining the peace. But much of the euphoria was based on more fundamental expectations that the very forces that historically had fueled international politics were themselves being transformed.

Two such forces, part of a broader trend toward global integration (see Chapter 13), were democracy and free-market capitalism. Both were expected to spread to Eastern Europe and across the former Soviet Union. The extension of democracy would greatly facilitate international stability since democracy was equated with peaceful behavior. Nuclear weapons had made war suicidal and thus prohibitive. War among the great powers, then, was fated to become obsolete, just as dueling and slavery, once widely accepted, had become unthinkable in modern soci-

eties. Given the high costs of even conventional warfare, war also might
become obsolete among developing countries, where most violent conflicts were occurring. As one commentator saw it,

What we may be witnessing is not just the end of the Cold War, or the passing of
a particular period of history, but the end of history as such: that is, the end point
of mankind's ideological evolution and the universalization of Western liberal
democracy as the final form of human government.[1]

Responding to the force of free-market capitalism, industrialized
societies began to join together, as transnational economic, financial,
and technological forces wove a widening and deepening web of *interdependence*. Economics, which tied nations together in a cooperative
search for prosperity, was the wave of the future. George Bush, the first
president to preside over this presumably more harmonious new era,
labeled it a "new world order," a gesture he was to regret after the 1991
war with Iraq and other developments abroad. Bush, however, was part-
ly right. The Cold War was over. The Soviet Union had disappeared,
along with the Warsaw Pact whose troops had withdrawn from their forward positions in central Europe. And Germany, at long last, was reunited. All these vast changes, moreover, were accepted peacefully.

It was not long, however, before questions were raised about how
"new" the new era really was. Globally, the jockeying for power and
strategic advantage continued. Iraq's August 1990 invasion of Kuwait,
stemming from its designs on the Persian Gulf oil fields, was the most
obvious provocation. But other simmering regional and civil conflicts
would soon erupt. Meanwhile, the United States remained concerned
about the sluggish reform movement in Russia, lest the country slip
back into its old dictatorial ways and expansionism. American leaders
also grew increasingly anxious about China's growing military strength
and assertiveness after the Sino-American partnership, which in large
measure was directed against the Soviet Union, became null and void.

One might have expected the United States to feel triumphant after
its victory in the Cold War. After all, "the Soviet Union wasn't just beat-
en on points, it was dismembered. Communism wasn't just relegated to
second place, it was utterly delegitimized. And all with remarkably little
bloodshed."[2] But even after its quick and brilliant battlefield victory over
Baghdad, America seemed apprehensive and weary of its international
burdens. In part, this could be explained by the growing signs that the
old order had not altogether disappeared. While for the moment armed
interstate conflicts had virtually ceased to exist, civil wars were breaking
out in many areas and the United States soon was embroiled in human-

1. Francis Fukuyama, "The End of History?" *National Interest* (summer 1989): 4.
2. Owen Harries, "My So-Called Foreign Policy," *New Republic*, October 10, 1994, 24.

itarian interventions in faraway places unfamiliar to most Americans. Even in areas close to the United States such as Haiti, there was strong opposition to placing the lives of American soldiers at risk over issues that were not widely perceived as vital, whatever the administration's rationales and rhetoric.

Rather than foreign conflicts, many Americans were deeply anxious about the country's economic future as smokestack industries fell to foreign competition and the high-technology sector faltered in the late 1980s. It was not hard to understand the implications: the loss of America's historic economic vitality meant a decline in the country's status and power in the world. The accompanying rise of other industrialized states meant a loss of jobs and a loss of opportunities to improve America's wage structure and standard of living. As never before, the country had become aware of its dependence on exports for employment and economic growth.

As a result, even before the Bush years were over debates began about the future role of the United States in the world. Of central concern was how much attention and resources should be devoted to foreign policy when, for all practical purposes, the nation no longer was confronting any formidable military threats, and "rogue states" were not likely to confront the United States directly. Typically, America had under such circumstances detached itself from great-power politics. Isolationism, to be sure, never meant that the United States would not intervene within "its" sphere of influence to the south. But it did mean distancing itself politically and militarily from the affairs of the great powers in Europe and Asia. Thus in the wake of the Cold War there was widespread support for withdrawal from what for most of the twentieth century had been a demanding and exceedingly troublesome world beyond the Western Hemisphere.

This appeal was strong, but it was widely realized that America would find it difficult to maintain a purely defensive position. After all, a new era of intense global economic competition had dawned, computer technologies were uniting the far reaches of the globe, environmental problems were growing severer, and weapons of mass destruction were falling into unknown hands. For all of these reasons, a revival of American isolationism was out of the question.

An alternative to isolationism was closely related to America's self-image as the "city on the hill." The American people believed their nation to be an exceptional one whose foreign policy had to pursue a moral course, even if other nations did not. It was America's duty to make the world better for its inhabitants. Did then the United States not have a responsibility to be actively involved in creating a "new world order" that represented America's values? Should not the country support and encourage democracy in those areas where its influence could be brought to bear? Such a policy could be carried out through the United Nations, which for so long had played such a critical role in the American vision of its global role.

Or, as yet another course, should the United States continue to pursue a "realist" policy, one primarily concerned with potential and long-term threats from other great powers? Realism was appealing to Americans because it seemed to foreswear moral crusading and frequent interventions in regional disputes. In short, realism restrained the crusading impulse and balanced it with more mundane considerations common to all states such as security, international stability, and prosperity. The pursuit of these interests did not require American foreign policy to abandon American ideals and moral values; it meant adapting them to the reality of a world of regional conflicts marked by mass killings, cruel mistreatment of civilian populations, and flagrant atrocities against human rights not seen since World War II. It was significant that realism finally had taken root in American soil, where such an approach long had been rejected as a vestige of the "old world." But historical experience in the twentieth century had taught Americans otherwise.

Each of these courses for America's post–Cold War foreign policy competed for favor in Washington in the early 1990s. But beyond a recognition that some new grand strategy was called for, few agreed on what it should be. Into this void came the closely contested presidential campaign of 1992. Bush's standing had been extremely high after the Desert Storm victory in the Persian Gulf—so high, in fact, that most top Democratic prospects for the presidency opted not to run. This left the field wide open for Arkansas governor Bill Clinton, who captured the nation's introspective mood and promised to concentrate on domestic problems rather than foreign policy. This position was summed up in the poster displayed in his campaign headquarters: "The economy, stupid!" Capitalizing on the broad public support for his domestic platform, Clinton, who claimed no foreign policy experience, defeated Bush and independent Ross Perot, who effectively split the vote among conservatives.

After a fumbling start, during which the issue of gays in the U.S. military dominated national attention, Clinton slowly settled into the presidency. His popularity ratings crept upward as the economy showed signs of sustained recovery. This good news was offset, however, by a steady stream of international crises that stole the president's attention from his domestic priorities and vividly demonstrated that history hardly had "ended." To the contrary, history may have *resumed* after a half-century in which Cold War bipolarity froze many domestic and regional rivalries in place. Violent conflicts erupted in many disconnected parts of the world, each with complex origins and no clear path to a peaceful solution. Their relationships to U.S. national interests varied widely and were difficult to discern. But by the time Clinton was reelected in November 1996, one thing was obvious: American foreign policy could no longer be relegated to the back burner.

WAR AND PEACE IN THE MIDDLE EAST

One of the trouble spots was the Middle East. Ample and inexpensive oil flows from the Persian Gulf powered the twentieth century's Industrial Revolution. But after the OPEC oil embargo of 1973 and a second oil "shock" in 1978, the West acutely felt its dependence on Middle East oil and recognized its vulnerability to future disruptions of oil flows. After the Cold War, the absence of superpower rivalry left a power vacuum that one regional leader, Iraq's Saddam Hussein, attempted to fill. Hussein's bid for hegemony in August 1990, which occurred while Bush was still in office and before the Soviet Union finally collapsed, effectively produced the first post–Cold War world crisis. Meanwhile, the peace process between Israel and its Arab neighbors inched forward between spasms of violence and political crisis. A comprehensive Arab-Israeli peace was nearly achieved before political upheavals within the region and violent attacks by militants on both sides threatened to destroy the peace process.

IRAQ'S CHALLENGE IN THE PERSIAN GULF

At least $80 billion in debt from his eight-year war with Iran and unable to compel OPEC to raise its oil prices to replenish his treasury, Saddam Hussein ordered his battle-tested army to invade his other oil-rich neighbor, the emirate of Kuwait, on August 2, 1990. The Iraqi army quickly overran the largely undefended Kuwaiti capital. With his troops poised on the border of Saudi Arabia and many Arab neighbors afraid of him, Hussein sought to intimidate the Persian Gulf oil kingdoms and assert his dominance over the entire region, goals he had failed to achieve in his costly eight-year war against Iran in the 1980s.

At the time, there really was no one in the Middle East to oppose Hussein's bid for power. Egypt, traditionally the leader of the Arab states, had lost that status when it made peace with Israel. Moreover, in an era in which "petrodollars" produced political and military power, Egypt, without oil reserves, was weaker than the Persian Gulf states. Syria, another frequent rival for Arab leadership, was left isolated with the disappearance of its patron in Moscow. Thus Saddam Hussein reasoned that by establishing Iraq as the dominant power in the region, he could launch his campaign for regional hegemony against the moderate Persian Gulf oil kingdoms and rival Arab states.

THE PERSIAN GULF, WITH KEY OIL FIELDS AND PIPELINES

As Iraqi forces massed near Saudi Arabia's border in the summer of 1990, the possibility that Hussein might soon control 40 percent of the world's oil reserves and dictate the terms of OPEC production forced the industrial powers to act. Aware that their economic growth depended on stable oil prices and uninterrupted supplies, Japan and the Western powers froze Iraqi assets in their countries and those of the deposed government of Kuwait. This was accompanied by an embargo on Iraqi oil and other UN-sponsored economic sanctions, to be enforced by a naval blockade of the Persian Gulf. The two key questions were whether Iraq's customers would honor the embargo long enough to bankrupt the Iraqi economy, and whether Hussein ultimately would succumb to the economic sanctions or allow his people to suffer indefinitely, as Fidel Castro had done in Cuba. Meanwhile, the United States proceeded with its largest troop buildup, dubbed Operation Desert Shield, since the Vietnam War; 250,000 troops were deployed to deter an Iraqi attack on Saudi Arabia. Bush hoped the prospect of war with the diverse UN coalition, composed mainly of U.S., British, and French forces, as well as those from several Arab states, would persuade Hussein to withdraw from Kuwait and restore its government. If the prospect of war did not deter Hussein, coalition forces would be large enough to force the Iraqi army out of Kuwait.

The stakes were clear in this confrontation: possible Iraqi control over oil production and prices, threats to moderate Arab regimes and Israel, and a direct challenge to the post–Cold War balance of power. Having rhetorically accepted the challenge, the United States could not afford to back off. If it did so, it would endanger its security, its economic growth as well as that of its major trading partners, and its status as the world's lone superpower after the Cold War. If it neglected its Arab allies and Israel in their moment of peril, they might not trust the United States again. Thus the stage was set for a showdown.

The United Nations gave Hussein a deadline of January 15, 1991, to withdraw from Kuwait. If he refused, force would be used to eject him. The unanimity within the UN Security Council was remarkable and clearly demonstrated how great-power politics had changed with the end of the Cold War. Previously, the council's five permanent members—the United States, the Soviet Union, Great Britain, France, and China—had agreed on virtually nothing and the two superpowers had vetoed any call for collective action. But with Mikhail Gorbachev clinging to power in the Soviet Union and seeking accommodation with the West, members were able to identify common problems and take collective actions. Hussein, hoping to disrupt this marriage of the great powers, instead provided a rationale for the United Nations to test its long-dormant system of collective security. As his tactics became more desperate and ruthless—including a barrage of long-range "Scud" missiles into Israeli cities—they infuriated world opinion and stiffened the resolve of the UN coalition.

The unprecedented UN solidarity was not matched within the U.S. Congress, however, which insisted that President Bush gain its assent before he used force. Many members of Congress, still haunted by memories of Vietnam, argued that economic sanctions would be sufficient to dislodge Iraq. Their arguments were shared by thousands of peace activists, who held candlelight vigils and public demonstrations to denounce the impending war. With the UN deadline nearing and the U.S. troop deployment increasing to nearly 500,000, Congress held a historic debate about the Iraqi challenge and narrowly approved the military operation. When the January 15 deadline passed with Iraqi forces still in Kuwait, the United States and coalition partners transformed Operation Desert Shield into Operation Desert Storm.

The massive air and land assault sent Hussein's forces fleeing for cover. In an air war that lasted five weeks, allied air forces flew more than 100,000 sorties, devastating Iraqi targets from the front lines to Baghdad. In the first phase they took out Iraqi command-and-control posts, air fields, communications centers, and other military installations. In the second phase they destroyed bridges and roads to stop all supplies from reaching the Iraqi forces in Kuwait. Cut off, these Iraqi forces were then subject to constant pounding. Their poorly concealed tanks and armored personnel carriers were destroyed by laser-guided U.S. missiles, which either killed the Iraqi soldiers or left them stranded in the desert. Only in the final phase did the coalition's tank forces launch their ground attack across the Saudi border.

The results of this military response exceeded the expectations of the most optimistic military planners. Within one hundred hours, the coalition forces had surrounded the Iraqis, most of whom swarmed in for relief at the beginning of the ground assault. Once feared as the world's fourth largest fighting force, these troops were only too glad to surrender and receive food and water from the coalition tank commanders. Facing almost no opposition, the coalition convoys rolled toward Kuwait City, past burning oil fields set ablaze by Iraq's retreating forces. When the first wave of liberation forces, mostly from Arab countries, reached the Kuwaiti capital, they were greeted and embraced by cheering mobs. The Gulf War had lasted forty-three days. More than 100,000 Iraqis were killed in the blitzkrieg, while coalition casualties were limited to less than 200. Hussein was forced to revoke his annexation of Kuwait and withdraw what was left of his occupation force.

The war, however, did not result in Hussein's removal from power; that had not been the goal of the United Nations. Indeed, had the tank columns rolled on to Baghdad, the coalition likely would have come apart. The Arabs wanted to end Hussein's threat to his neighbors, but they were against his overthrow. And Washington wanted no part of governing a nation in civil war, which appeared likely in the wake of Hussein's defeat. Iraq's Kurds and Shiite Muslims, constituting the majority of the country's population, rebelled in separate regions against their ruler, a Sunni Muslim. But they were not strong enough to defeat the remnants of Hussein's Republican Guard, many of whom were saved at the last moment by the abrupt cease-fire.

Despite Hussein's undisguised brutality toward his own people, and contrary to their own public statements, the United States and its allies did not want to see Iraq disintegrate. They expected Iraq to maintain its pivotal role in the Middle East balance of power, a role not possible if Iraq were partitioned. More important, they did not want the surrounding countries, especially Iran and Syria, to carve up the country in their own bids for regional dominance. The United States was charged with inciting Iraqi dissidents to unite against Hussein, then ignoring the rebels once they were engaged in battle. But the realities of the regional power balance overrode those criticisms.

After the war Hussein defied a series of international demands, making it clear that despite the coalition's victory he would remain a threat. In late 1994 he displayed his capacity to disrupt the region at will when he again massed troops on the Kuwaiti border, this time to protest continuing UN sanctions against Iraq. The United States responded by mobilizing its remaining forces in the Persian Gulf and deploying thousands of new troops to the region. Again, Hussein backed down and ordered his Republican Guards to return to their bases. In 1996 Hussein sponsored attacks against the Kurdish populations of northern Iraq, a region declared off-limits by the United Nations and occupied by a U.S.-led relief force. After the United States responded with aerial strikes against Iraqi military installations, Hussein withdrew once more. His economy ravaged by economic sanctions, he remained passive until Iraq was allowed to renew oil production in December 1996, a step urgently needed so that Iraq could pay for shipments of food, medicine, and other necessities.

Despite the coalition's spectacular success in routing Iraq from Kuwait, Saddam Hussein remained firmly in power and demonstrated repeatedly his ability to create havoc. He recognized his importance to the strategic interests of the Western powers, and he openly exploited his freedom to inflame the Persian Gulf region at the time and place of his choosing.

ISRAEL'S BELEAGUERED PEACE PROCESS

After the war with Iraq, and with American prestige at an all-time high, the Bush administration judged the time right for a major effort to gain a comprehensive peace between Israel and its neighbors. The oil kingdoms owed Washington a favor for saving them from Saddam Hussein. Syria, deprived of Soviet patronage and protection, sought favor with the United States. Moreover, shortly after the Gulf War Israel's hard-line Likud government, which had a somewhat cool relationship with the United States, was replaced by a more accommodating Labor Party government. Yet, despite the favorable conditions, American leaders had to make many trips to the region to mediate the differences among states.

The unexpected breakthrough came in September 1993 when the Palestine Liberation Organization (PLO) and Israel agreed to mutual recognition. In a historic agreement the PLO abandoned its call for the destruction of Israel and renounced terrorism. In return for Palestinian recognition of the right of Israel "to exist in peace and security," Israel would withdraw from the Gaza Strip and the West Bank town of Jericho and allow the Palestinians to govern themselves. It was assumed that, over time, Palestinian control over education, health, social services, taxation, and tourism would be extended over the West Bank except in the areas settled by the Israelis. It also was assumed that the Palestinians would keep order, police themselves, and, in particular, end the *intifada* (holy war) against Israel and its supporters. If these expectations were realized, the two sides eventually would discuss whether the Palestinians would be allowed to establish a state of their own.

Why did these two deadly enemies finally decide to negotiate their differences? For one thing, the end of the Cold War had deprived the PLO of a strong political supporter—the Soviet Union. For another, the Gulf War had left the organization almost broke; PLO leader Yasir Arafat had made the disastrous decision to support Saddam Hussein against the oil kingdoms that had provided the PLO with most of its finances. Even earlier, however, the spontaneous outburst of the *intifada* among West Bank Palestinians, frustrated by the continued Israeli occupation and Arafat's inability to solve their problems, had demonstrated his declining influence. In response, Arafat had declared in 1988 the establishment of a Palestinian "authority" in the occupied areas, thereby suggesting a two-state solution instead of Israel's elimination. For their part, the Israelis were tiring of the constant conflict and the costs— physical, economic, and human—of the six-year-old *intifada*. But more than that, they too were worried about the increasing support among Palestinians for extremists. If Israel could achieve a stable peace, the country's economy, aided by the large influx of skilled Russian immigrants who were fleeing the antisemitism that was flourishing once more in their homeland, would prosper. Thus talks with the PLO had become inevitable and the hope was that these would lead to a comprehensive peace agreement.[3]

Despite the opposition of extremists in Israel, the Middle East peace process moved forward in 1994 when Israel resolved its differences with Jordan. Under the terms of this second agreement, both countries

---

3. See Anthony H. Cordesman, *Perilous Prospects: The Peace Process and the Arab-Israeli Military Balance* (Boulder, Colo.: Westview Press, 1996).

GOLAN HEIGHTS AREA: Occupied by Israel since 1967. Unilaterally annexed by Israel in 1981.

WEST BANK AREA: Unilaterally annexed by Jordan in 1950. Occupied by Israel since 1967. Status to be determined.

GAZA STRIP: Occupied by Israel since 1967. Status to be determined.

SINAI PENINSULA: Returned to Egypt by Israel in 1982.

ISRAEL AND OCCUPIED TERRITORIES

acknowledged the right of the other to exist, bringing their de facto state of war to an end. In addition, Jordan's King Hussein and Israeli prime minister Yitzhak Rabin agreed on the boundaries between the two states and divided control over underground water reservoirs and other natural resources; they also established the basis for bilateral trade and tourism.

The United States again played a key role in brokering the treaty. Secretary of State Warren Christopher, though criticized for his lack of attention to such trouble spots as Bosnia and Haiti, was credited by both sides with hastening the agreements through his repeated, often unpublicized trips to the region. As part of the treaty, the United States agreed to forgive Jordan's foreign debt, which played a key role in securing the country's cooperation given its continuing economic distress. Bill Clinton, suffering from a series of domestic setbacks, welcomed the opportunity to preside over the signing of the accord at the White House.

Syria was another story. Earlier, Clinton had failed to bring Syria into the peace process, even after visiting Damascus and meeting personally with Syrian leader Hafez al-Assad, long considered by the U.S. government to be a primary sponsor of international terrorism. Assad conceded little to Clinton while enjoying the enhanced prestige and legitimacy that attended the presidential visit. The fact that Clinton would go to Damascus without a set of previously negotiated agreements spelling out Syrian contributions and concessions to the peace process suggested an unwillingness to pressure Assad and wishful thinking that Syria's strongman would reciprocate American goodwill—an unlikely occurrence.

The United States had hoped that Israel and Syria would agree on a peace accord that would incorporate Syria and Lebanon, Syria's satellite, and produce peace on the northern border of Israel. Since the 1967 Six-day War, Israeli troops had occupied the Golan Heights region connecting the three countries as well as a strip of southern Lebanon. Both areas had served as staging areas for attacks by Islamic militants on Israel. If Syria could be brought into serious negotiations and would cooperate in order to regain the Golan Heights, the elusive goal of a comprehensive treaty with all of Israel's neighbors, as well as the PLO, would be within reach. But despite news reports that Rabin and Assad both privately endorsed the principle of a return of the Golan Heights to Syria in return for Syria's recognition of Israel, no such agreement was concluded.

The overall progress toward Arab-Israeli peace was shattered by violence and tragedy. On November 4, 1995, Rabin was assassinated by a Jewish extremist who admitted killing Rabin in order to halt the peace process. After mourning the loss of its leader, Israel was shocked by another wave of violence in the midst of an election campaign to select

a new leader. In the spring of 1996 Palestinian terrorists staged four suicide bombings in nine days, killing more than sixty Israelis and wound-
ing more than two hundred. In the subsequent vote, the Israelis, suddenly doubtful about the peace process, elected a new prime minister,
Benjamin Netanyahu, head of the rival and more conservative Likud
Party and an outspoken critic of the peace process. Netanyahu pledged
to bring "peace with security" to Israel, meaning that he would not support further concessions to the Arabs without explicit guarantees that
Israel's security would be protected on all fronts.

When these guarantees were not forthcoming, Netanyahu delayed the
withdrawal of Israeli troops from the West Bank and from Hebron, a city
in the heart of the occupied territories. As each side accused the other of
trying to scuttle the agreements, a new round of bloody attacks occurred
in the spring and summer of 1996. Each massacre and the inevitable
counterattacks that followed diminished the prospects for a Middle East
settlement. With the peace process on the verge of collapse, Israel, under
great pressure from the United States and other countries, agreed in January 1997 to withdraw from Hebron, a concession that at least tem
porarily restored the lost momentum. But Netanyahu's insistence on
building new Jewish settlements in East Jerusalem, home to many Palestinians, led to another round of violence. Thus despite the best efforts of
the United States, a resolution of the Arab-Israeli conflict remained elusive.

RUSSIA'S IMPERILED REFORMS

The collapse of Soviet rule, which was widely hailed by foreign
observers and many Russians in 1992, exposed deep fault lines within the
former Soviet Union and across its vast periphery. Just as the breakup of
the Ottoman and Austro-Hungarian Empires contributed to the onset
of World War I, and just as the dismantling of the European colonial
empires after 1945 had set off violence between and within many new
states, the same potential for violence attended the end of the Soviet
empire.

The fall of the iron curtain and the Berlin Wall released forces of
nationalism across Eastern Europe and the former Soviet Union.
Czechoslovakia broke up, peacefully, into the Czech Republic and Slovakia as each ethnic group sought its own state. To the south, a Hungarian
political leader claimed that he was "in spirit" responsible for all Hun-
garians, including sizable numbers living in Romania, Slovakia, and Serbia. To the west, in Germany, where East and West had just been reunited, many Germans became openly critical of the country's open immigration policy and hostile toward the waves of refugees that flowed in

from the Balkan Peninsula, where a religious war had erupted (see next section). Further resentment was directed at the large volumes of German aid flowing to Eastern Europe and Russia, which slowed economic growth in Germany and across the European Union. Finally, across Western Europe, nationalist groups gained prominence and political power.

A new layer of potential conflict appeared after the Soviet Union fractured into fifteen republics, all claiming sovereignty, with the Baltic states of Estonia, Latvia, and Lithuania reclaiming their pre–World War II independence. Since the Russians had long controlled both the czarist and communist states, ethnic Russians were left scattered throughout the Commonwealth of Independent States (CIS), the loose amalgamation of non-Baltic republics. In addition to the Russians, more than a hundred other nationalities that had composed the Soviet Union inhabited its vast frontiers. This intermingling of nationalities inflamed the hatreds between the Russians and the peoples they had long dominated, particularly Muslims living in the southern tier of CIS states. In Russia it gave xenophobic nationalists and former communists, bent on destroying the liberal state and market economy the reformers were trying to create, a strong emotional issue with which to bring down the centrist regime of Boris Yeltsin. Moldova and Georgia (a non-CIS state) were facing secessionist movements; Ukraine was internally divided between its own ethnic group and a sizable Russian population; Belarus, Turkmenistan, and Uzbekistan came under dictatorial rule; Tajikistan was engulfed in civil war; and Armenia and Azerbaijan fought a costly war over an enclave seen as the rightful possession of both states.

After the Soviet Union disappeared from the map, Russia remained a potentially formidable military power with the ability to destroy the fragile political arrangements that were emerging in the early 1990s. The Russian government continued to command an army of more than 1 million soldiers, 200,000 of whom remained outside its borders within the CIS. Boris Yeltsin, Russia's elected president, instituted ambitious political and economic reforms, but they proved difficult to impose on a society that never had been exposed to democracy or the free market. Prominent communists, elected under the old Soviet constitution, still dominated the legislature and state bureaucracy, and they blocked Yeltsin's reform efforts. Also opposed to Yeltsin's efforts were Russian nationalists who shared the communists' resentment at the loss of empire and status and a powerful "mafia" that exploited the vast black market in Russia's largest cities.[4] George Bush had succeeded in manag-

4. See Stephen Handelman, *Comrade Criminal: The Theft of the Second Russian Revolution* (New Haven, Conn.: Yale University Press, 1994).

ing the Soviet Union's fall; Bill Clinton faced the equally treacherous task of assisting its peaceful transition to democracy and a freer market economy.

Yeltsin clearly was caught in the middle. In October 1993 an attempted parliamentary coup failed when Yeltsin, supported by security forces and the army, succeeded in dissolving the parliament (and destroying its meeting place). But the elections that followed only made matters worse: the new parliament was dominated by extremists from both the left and right. The most outspoken nationalist, Vladimir Zhirinovsky, pledged to restore the old Russian empire, even suggesting that he would gain the return of Alaska. As conditions worsened across the country, many Russians welcomed his appeals and openly longed for the more "orderly" system under Stalin and Brezhnev.

In the United States and Western Europe questions were raised about the continuing flow of Western aid to Russia. Should the new Russia be left to wallow in its economic misery, perhaps to emerge some day as a resentful state as Germany did after World War I? Or should Russia's former adversaries furnish the support the nation needed to grow economically and become politically stable—just as American helped Germany after World War II? Western powers finally agreed that Russia should receive economic assistance, but only as long as the money was used effectively. They demanded that Yeltsin's political reforms move forward, that Russian leaders stop subsidizing inefficient or mafia-controlled industries, and that the rate of inflation be held in check. Even though faced with their own economic problems, Western leaders promised more than $30 billion in aid to Russia. Meanwhile, the International Monetary Fund (IMF) approved an additional $10 billion in low-interest loans to Russia—a transparent effort to revive Yeltsin's standing as he campaigned for reelection.

In December 1994 Yeltsin's internal problems mounted after he felt compelled to deploy thousands of troops to the province of Chechnya in southern Russia. The Islamic territory, which had long struggled against Moscow's hegemony, had declared its independence after the collapse of the Soviet Union three years earlier. When Chechen leaders declared that "our independence is forever," Yeltsin sent Russian troops to the Chechen capital, Grozny, and the Russian air force bombed residential neighborhoods. As the assault continued, however, the poorly organized and under-equipped Russian troops faltered against the more determined Chechens. Yeltsin then escalated the Russian offense in defiance of protests from the United States and other major powers. In defending their actions, Russian leaders diminished the significance of Chechnya as an oil producer, although its annual production of more than 10 million tons was a vital resource. More important to Russia was the dangerous precedent that Chechnya, a relatively small territory located in the Caucasus Mountains, would set for other dissatisfied regions if its demands for independence were met. But nothing the Russian troops did was sufficient to overcome the Chechen fighters, whose defiance in the face of a stronger enemy was reminiscent of the Afghan *mujahidin*. The Chechens stood firm, and their rejection of Russian hegemony led to elections in January 1997 and an even more explicit declaration of independence.

The attempted suppression of Chechen independence was only one of several Yeltsin policies that drove the leader's public approval ratings down to single digits. Another was economic reform. For most Russians, living conditions continued to deteriorate as doubts about the durability of Yeltsin's reforms spread across the country. Russia's gross national product (GNP) fell by nearly 20 percent in the first four years of reform, and the rampant inflation of 1993 and 1994 consumed much of the national savings. Russian soldiers went unpaid for months and, in some cases, relied on the charity of private citizens for survival. But with his $10 billion in IMF credits, a quarter of which were made available immediately, Yeltsin restored many social programs and launched an aggressive Western-style political campaign. By the time national elections were held in September 1995, Yeltsin regained enough support to defeat his communist and nationalist challengers.

In facing the communist Gennady Zyuganov in the runoff election, Yeltsin made an expedient move that sealed his reelection but would later backfire, producing an even greater threat to his presidency. Alexander Lebed, a former general turned populist, won 15 percent of the votes in the general election, a distant third place but suggestive of a significant pool of support. As the runoff neared, Yeltsin saw his opportunity and embraced Lebed, offering him the post of national security adviser if he swung his support to the Russian president. Lebed agreed, and the makeshift alliance between the two men proved unbeatable for Zyuganov. Unfortunately for Yeltsin, Lebed then pursued his own agenda in Russian foreign and domestic policy. He personally brought the Chechnya war to a close and openly criticized Yeltsin's growing tolerance of the Russian mafia, composed of former Communist Party leaders who benefited from the black market and controlled many government programs. When Lebed quickly surpassed Yeltsin in popularity, he became a serious threat to Yeltsin and what remained of the president's reforms. Yeltsin then fired Lebed in October 1996, which allowed the former general to become an outspoken critic of the Yeltsin presidency.

Throughout this ordeal the Clinton administration clung to Yeltsin as the best and perhaps only hope for peaceful reform in Russia. Although the two leaders argued over the possible expansion of North Atlantic

Treaty Organization (see Chapter 12), they agreed on the basic designs of
the new Russia and on their mutual need for close relations. To a large
extent, however, the amity between Washington and Moscow only
inflamed Yeltsin's domestic opponents, including a large segment of the
general public. Furthermore, the American effort to preserve Russia's
reforms were overshadowed by Yeltsin's struggle to keep his own house
in order. Western leaders were restrained in condemning Yeltsin over
Chechnya and other issues, fearing that his overthrow would only lead
to a more repressive regime. Finally, the power vacuum threatened to
engulf Yeltsin, who underwent heart surgery late in 1996 and remained
inactive for months afterward. His controversial reforms were difficult
enough to sustain under the guidance of a vigorous, forceful leader; they
would be doubly difficult in the midst of a chaotic struggle for succession.

'ETHNIC CLEANSING' IN THE BALKANS

Yugoslavia's violent disintegration in the early 1990s served as a
frightening example of what could occur when the cessation of Cold
War–imposed restraints unleashed nationalistic rivalries. Yugoslavia,
like most of Eastern Europe after World War I, was a diverse state composed of several national and religious groups: mainly Serbs (Eastern
Orthodox), Slovenes and Croats (Catholic), and Bosnians (Muslim).
The dominant Serbs, who controlled the capital of Belgrade, the national government, and the formidable armed forces, opposed the country's
disintegration. After the republics of Slovenia and Croatia declared
independence in 1991 and were immediately recognized by the European
Union, the Yugoslav army forcefully intervened in both territories.[5]

Serbian troops inflicted great damage on Slovenia and Croatia, but
they were unable to prevent the secession of the two new states, both of
which were promptly admitted to the United Nations. The Serbs then
directed their military campaign to the heart of Bosnia-Herzegovina,
the most multinational of the former Yugoslav territories, which also
had declared its independence from Belgrade. Bosnia's challenge to the
Yugoslav state, also condoned by the Western powers, was unacceptable
to Serbs both in Belgrade and within Bosnia itself. In the brutal campaign that followed, the Bosnian Serbs, fueled by their patrons in Belgrade, pursued a self-described policy of "ethnic cleansing" which consisted of driving the primarily Muslim population from their communities in order to expand Serb territory. The Serbs burned and looted

---

5. For an account by the former U.S. ambassador to Yugoslavia, see Warren Zimmerman,
Origins of a Catastrophe: Yugoslavia and Its Destroyers (New York: Times Books, 1996).

villages, tortured non-Serbs in concentration camps, systematically raped Islamic women, and besieged the Bosnian capital, Sarajevo, for three years, depriving its citizens of food, water, and electricity.

These actions appalled outside observers and drew widespread condemnation. Many Americans, including presidential candidate Bill Clinton, called in 1992 for military intervention in Bosnia. They asserted that by looking on passively while the Serbs committed such flagrant aggression, the United States and the Europeans were undermining the very principle that had supported their war against Iraq: the inviolability of frontiers. According to the prevailing expectations of the post–Cold War world, no borders were to be changed by force. Indeed, aggression simply "would not stand," as President Bush had stated at the height of the Persian Gulf crisis. Horrified onlookers charged that the systematic expulsion of Muslims constituted genocide, which was explicitly prohibited by the UN Charter, and they called on all countries to act immediately to prevent mass slaughter on the basis of ethnic or religious differences.

Opponents of outside intervention countered that the Balkan conflict was a civil conflict, not an international war, despite the recent establishment of new states recognized by the United Nations. Furthermore, military intervention to separate the combatants and preserve order was said by the Pentagon to entail a massive commitment of between 200,000 and 400,000 troops, heavy fighting, and extensive casualties. Such a military presence in the treacherous mountain territory likely would be required for many years, and no coherent "exit strategy" was evident. But, most important, the conflict appeared to be contained within the Balkan peninsula, posing little or no security threat to the great powers, including the United States. The Bush administration, in generally adopting this cautious view, sought to promote a diplomatic solution to the crisis. Once elected, Bill Clinton also soon perceived the public's widespread resistance to large-scale U.S. military intervention and supported a diplomatic solution, preferably mediated by America's allies in Western Europe.

The international arms embargo imposed on Yugoslavia in the early days of the conflict favored the Serbs because the Yugoslav army—well equipped from its years of association with a communist dictatorship— supplied the Serbs in Croatia and Bosnia with weapons from its arsenal; the Muslims and Croats were unable to acquire sufficient arms to protect themselves. European leaders opposed lifting the embargo, arguing that it would only broaden the violence and endanger their own peacekeeping forces, which were providing humanitarian aid to the residents of so-called safe havens in the remaining Muslim-held areas. Thus the arms embargo continued into 1995, along with a broader economic boycott against the Serbian regime in Belgrade, which claimed to be independent of the Bosnian Serbs.

When President Clinton occasionally advanced proposals for multilateral military action—and for lifting the arms embargo against Bosnia—he was strongly opposed by most Western European governments and many influential members of the United Nations, including Boris Yeltsin's Russia, a traditional ally of the Slavic Serbs. Within the Defense Department, most experts opposed a military response because, in their view, air strikes would have to be complemented by the deployment of large U.S. ground forces. Domestic issues were of greater concern to Congress than the seemingly intractable problems in the Balkans. In short, many Americans asked the same question: If the Europeans did not feel sufficiently threatened by events in Bosnia to intervene, why should the United States, an ocean away?

For all of these reasons, Clinton was unwilling to assert himself and demand action within the North Atlantic Treaty Organization (NATO) as his predecessor had done in Kuwait. Rather, he wavered, sometimes threatening to intervene with air power and to lift the arms embargo, at other times retracting these positions, citing allied unwillingness to go along as his reason for inaction. He knew that if the United States intervened unilaterally, the war would soon become "America's war." Like President Lyndon Johnson in Vietnam, he might become stuck in military quicksand, jeopardizing his domestic priorities, stimulating a peace movement, and endangering his reelection chances in 1996.

Meanwhile, the United Nations—which, in effect, meant the United States and its European allies—pressed forward with a plan to partition Bosnia along ethnic lines. The scheme would have given the Serbs nearly 50 percent of Bosnia—a notion the United States opposed and considered immoral because it appeared to reward aggression. But the plan was supported by European leaders with troops in Bosnia who otherwise would have been forced to fight the Serbs, suffering serious casualties. In response, the Serbs played hard-ball—after all, the Western allies were divided and paralyzed— and negotiations over the plan foundered as the Serbs continued shelling Muslim enclaves that the United Nations had promised to protect. The United Nations provided the besieged Muslims with medicine and food in an effort to mitigate the impact of the Serb assaults. But the Serbs continued to test the limits of the organization's patience by sustaining their attacks on population centers. Only the threat of UN-authorized air strikes against Serb positions in the mountains surrounding Sarajevo, to be carried out by NATO warplanes, temporarily brought relief to that city and other safe havens. Serb defiance resumed, however, when the relatively few and ineffective air strikes demonstrated that the United Nations and NATO did not have the will to stop them. Indeed, the limited air strikes only provoked the Serbs and increased their determination to push on as they watched cracks widen within the anti-Serb coalition.

For a brief period late in 1994 it appeared that the tide was turning against the Serbs. After the Muslims and Croats joined forces and established a combined federation within Bosnia-Herzegovina, Serbian leaders in Belgrade broke with their kinsmen and imposed their own arms embargo against the Bosnian Serbs—a move clearly designed to persuade the United Nations to lift its economic sanctions against Belgrade. The United States then announced that it no longer would enforce the arms embargo against the Muslims and Croats. This move, dictated by Congress, essentially told the Europeans that if they insisted on depriving the besieged Bosnians of weapons, they would have to enforce the embargo themselves. The United States could, of course, take this position because no U.S. soldiers were exposed to the consequences of its action.

But the embargo remained largely intact as the Serbs regrouped and retaliated near the safe haven of Bihac in northwestern Bosnia, one of the last Muslim-Croatian strongholds in the region. To deter future air attacks, the Serbs seized hundreds of UN peace-keepers and held them hostage for several weeks. By early 1995 the Serbs had accomplished their goal of displacing the Muslims from their homes throughout Bosnia. Furthermore, they had succeeded in humiliating the United Nations by demonstrating that its peace-keeping forces never had a peace to keep and that the Serbs could overrun UN-protected safe havens with impunity. The Serbs then announced a ban on UN military escorts of humanitarian convoys, making it impossible for aid to reach Sarajevo and other cities and depriving the United Nations of its principal reason for being in Bosnia at all. In a final turn of the screw, the Serbs overran the Muslim safe havens of Srebenica and Zepa in July 1995. While UN peace-keepers watched, they separated Muslim families and herded onto buses thousands of men and boys, who later were executed and buried in mass graves. Several weeks later Serbian troops again shelled downtown Sarajevo, the heart of Bosnia, and killed thirty-seven civilians at a crowded marketplace.

The discrediting of the United Nations mirrored the impotence of NATO, whose leaders earlier had stated their intention to play a critical military role in the Balkan conflict. The alliance that had for forty-five years deterred a Soviet attack on Western Europe appeared paralyzed before the Serbs in the post–Cold War world, when the alliance no longer was held together by a common enemy and the organization was searching for a new role. NATO members knew, however, that continued defiance by Serbia eventually would have to be resisted, and NATO was in a better position to respond than the unwieldy United Nations.

Suddenly in late 1995 a shift in the regional balance of power transformed this situation. The Croatian army, showing surprising strength, launched a successful ground attack against the Serbs, depriving them of many of their earlier territorial gains. Muslim forces joined in the counteroffensive, which produced a new flood of refugees, this time Serbs fleeing the Croats and Muslims. Recognizing the shifting power balance and outraged by the most recent Serb atrocities, NATO then launched a sustained bombing campaign against Serbian munition dumps, bridges, and air defenses that further weakened the Serbs. By this time, the economic sanctions against Belgrade had taken their full toll and forced Serbian president Slobodan Milosovic to assert his dominance over the Bosnian Serbs, who empowered him to negotiate on their behalf.

In this new climate, American leaders late in 1995 seized their opportunity to negotiate a deal among the Balkan rivals. Despite the violence and the hatreds that had deepened, they realized that each of the factions had strong reasons to end the fighting: for the Serbs, to consolidate the Bosnian Serb gains before they were lost or reversed and to end the crippling economic sanctions; for the Croats, to secure their independent state and the safety of their nationals in other areas; and for the Muslims, to relieve the suffering of their people and to create a Bosnian state with strong Muslim representation. Forced to negotiate face to face at an American military base in Dayton, Ohio, leaders of the three factions signed a complex agreement in November 1995 that led to a ceasefire in 1996. Under the Dayton Accords, nearly sixty thousand NATO troops were deployed to the region as part of Operation Joint Endeavor. Once in place, they separated the armed factions, protected civilian populations, and delivered economic assistance to the war-ravaged Bosnian communities. Meanwhile, Bosnian leaders began to create a new government led by a three-member presidency, one from each ethnic group, to be chosen by the Bosnian people in national elections.

Although the Dayton Accords provided a framework for reconciliation in Bosnia, implementing them would be difficult at best. All three factions harbored deep resentments from the war, and the elections held in September 1996 brought Serb and Croat representatives to power who openly called for the annexation of their respective territories in Bosnia and the creation of a Muslim mini-state around Sarajevo. The third, Muslim member of the presidency, Alija Izetbegovic, received the most votes and thus became chairman of the three-member presidency. His calls for a "Greater Bosnia" led by Muslims were predictably rejected by the other leaders.

Shortly after his reelection in November 1996, President Clinton extended the NATO mission in Bosnia through June 1998, a move that surprised no one. NATO troops would continue to separate the combatants in three zones supervised by the United States, Great Britain, and France, respectively. Clinton argued that the troops were needed to buy time for the new civilian-led government to take full control. In addition, NATO forces were assigned to oversee the disarmament of Bosnia's warring factions and, if this failed, to provide weapons and training for Muslim and Croat forces in order to create a balance of power in the region. The United States and Western European governments then formally put the Bosnians on notice: continue the peace process or face the suspension of Western aid, the reimposition of economic sanctions, and the withdrawal of the NATO peace-keeping force.

Left open to question, however, was the ultimate exit strategy of the NATO mission. Could it successfully provide the basis for long-term peace in the Balkans and leave the country to a patchwork national security force? Or, more likely, would it be forced to extend its mission repeatedly and acknowledge the permanent partition of Bosnia? If so, would the Western powers agree to police another Cyprus or Korea indefinitely? Even the Clinton administration would not guarantee the success of this mission. Interestingly, the only aspect of the Dayton Accords acceptable to critics was the provision for prompt NATO withdrawal if the Bosnian factions could not come to terms.

The Yugoslav debacle revealed critical shortcomings in the system of collective security that was supposed to guarantee peace in the post–Cold War era. The United Nations was shown incapable of harnessing a united response to aggression, much less ending and punishing such transparent "ethnic cleansing." This failure of the United Nations reflected the failure of the Western great powers. NATO, until forced into action, was deeply divided by a crisis in which none of its leading members, even though horrified by the human tragedy and outraged by the Serbs' conduct of the war, felt their vital interests to be at stake. Given this record, it was doubtful that the externally imposed peace of 1996 would provide a basis for long-term reconciliation. More likely, it would simply give all sides of the conflict time to prepare either for the partition of Bosnia or for the next round of bloodletting.

THE PLIGHT OF 'FAILED STATES'

Since World War II the number of nation-states in the world has grown dramatically, from 55 in 1946 to nearly 190 by 1996. Most of these new countries were created from former European colonies in Africa and southern Asia. Others, such as the detached Czech Republic and Slovakia, emerged after the Cold War in Eastern Europe, and still others were carved out of the former Soviet Union.

This proliferation of nation-states, part of a longer-term process of "self-determination" which received its impetus from President Woodrow Wilson after World War I, dramatically changed the face of world politics during the late twentieth century. The new countries, often located in the world's poorest areas, received large volumes of foreign aid from wealthier nations and accepted their help in the complicated task of "state building." Yet despite some progress in their living conditions, these developing countries remained hostile to the industrialized North. In the United Nations, the new states united with other developing countries to form a majority in the General Assembly, which served as a forum for expressing their grievances against industrialized states and a vehicle to promote a "new international economic order."

During the Cold War, many developing countries served unwittingly as "theaters" of the superpower conflict, thereby illustrating a popular aphorism in Africa that "when two elephants fight, the grass suffers." The ideological nature of these conflicts polarized the developing countries and often pitted neo-Marxist revolutionaries against right-wing military juntas, which became more repressive when challenged for power. In many cases, both sides received modern weaponry from the superpowers or their allies, which further fueled the regional conflicts.

The propensity of the superpowers to intervene in these regional flashpoints abruptly ended in the aftermath of the Cold War. In this respect the end of the Cold War was welcomed by the most impoverished nations, which were still reeling from the punishing economic distress in the 1980s, widely labeled the "lost decade" of development. In the mid-1990s, however, these same countries discovered that their social and economic problems actually had *worsened* since the dissolution of the Soviet Union and the subsequent preoccupation of the United States with its own needs. Many developing countries witnessed the same revival of ethnic violence and political unrest that occurred in the Balkans, and their populations continued to suffer from the malnutrition, poor medical care, and inadequate education that had persisted since their release from colonial domination. Contrary to widespread expectations, the accommodation between Washington and Moscow produced lower levels of development aid for the world's poor; indeed, the United States all but eliminated its foreign aid program for "non-strategic allies."

Some observers suggested dismantling what was left of the most desperate developing countries and putting them under UN trusteeship. Such a response was highly unlikely, but it revealed the depths to which many of these countries had fallen. Indeed, in many areas the post–Cold War era witnessed the emergence of the "failed state":

From Haiti in the Western Hemisphere to the remnants of Yugoslavia in Europe, from Somalia, Sudan, and Liberia in Africa to Cambodia in Southeast Asia, a disturbing new phenomenon is emerging: the failed nation-state, utterly incapable of sustaining itself as a member of the international community. . . . [T]hose states descend into violence and anarchy—imperiling their own citizens and threatening their neighbors through refugee flows, political instability, and random warfare.[6]

These crises raised serious questions about the political arrangements that created these countries in the first place, particularly those in Africa whose tribal-based populations transcended the artificial state boundaries drawn by the departing colonial rulers. For the United States, which previously had sought support from these states to counter Soviet influence in the region, the spreading unrest and the plight of their impoverished people were suddenly remote to its strategic self-interests. But Americans could not escape the disturbing scenes of warfare and starvation that appeared on their television sets daily—scenes that seemed to cry out for action by the world's richest and most powerful country. Yet what form, if any, this help should take remained unclear.

SOMALIA

One of the first such states to arouse international attention was the impoverished country of Somalia, located along the Horn of Africa at the entrance to the Red Sea. During the Cold War, the Soviets had supported its ruler because its larger neighbor to the north, Ethiopia, was aligned with the United States (see Chapter 7). But when a pro-Soviet military regime came into power in Ethiopia, Somalia's ruler switched sides as well. Gen. Muhammad Siad Barre, despite his ruthless oppression of the Somali people, became a loyal client of the United States. All of this perversely made sense in the context of Cold War rivalry. But when the Cold War ended and Barre was overthrown, Somalia descended into a civil war between rival factions which fought for succession. The government effectively ceased to function and chaos prevailed. When the rival militias prevented farmers from planting new crops, disrupted the activities of nomadic traders, and killed most of the nation's livestock, famine and widespread starvation followed.

After months during which the world looked the other way—toward the plight of the Kurds in Iraq, the civil wars in the Sudan and Liberia, and the war in Bosnia—media attention compelled a Western response through the United Nations. More than 27,000 troops, at first mainly American, were dispatched in late 1992 to provide order and food. After they had accomplished the mission of Operation Restore Hope, the

6. Gerald B. Helman and Steven R. Ratner, "Saving Failed States," *Foreign Policy* (winter 1992–1993): 3. Also see I. William Zartman, ed., *Collapsed States* (Boulder, Colo.: Lynne Rienner, 1995).

American forces were to be withdrawn and replaced by UN forces drawn from various nations.

The problem, however, was that once UN forces were withdrawn, the "warlords" would resume their struggle for power, leading to renewed killing and hunger. Thus the UN mission was changed in 1993 from one of humanitarian relief to one of rebuilding Somalia's political and economic structures. But the country's principal warlord, Gen. Mohammed Farah Aidid, who controlled Somalia's capital of Mogadishu, resisted the enlarged UN mission because it called for his own removal and disarmament. In the fighting that followed, twenty-four Pakistani peace-keepers were ambushed and killed. Later more UN troops were killed, including U.S. soldiers who were deployed to capture the elusive general. As the number of U.S. casualties mounted—and after one dead soldier was dragged through the streets of Mogadishu before cheering crowds and television cameras—demands for the withdrawal of U.S. troops began. Clinton responded by accelerating their departure, and the United Nations announced in late 1994 that the failed peace-keeping effort would be suspended in the spring of 1995.

The critical downfall of the Somali operation was that the international peace-keepers, initially dispatched for the humanitarian purpose of feeding the people, ignored the political situation that had created the hunger in the first place. The hunger had not stemmed from a natural disaster; it was man-made. Indeed, it should have been clear from the beginning that resolving the anarchic political situation was a prerequisite to resolving the humanitarian crisis. But because that was not clear, what was believed at the outset to be a short mission ended up taking two and a half years, underlining the point that there was no such thing as an apolitical, purely humanitarian mission. A lasting solution to the Somali conflict could be achieved only by an internal reconciliation, and this would have to be undertaken by the Somalis themselves. Thus a worthy, moral effort to help Somalia turned into an open-ended and unachievable commitment. In the mid-1990s Somalia remained in the grip of civil war. But the withdrawal of foreign troops, and the diversion of the world's attention to other trouble spots, seemed paradoxically to increase the chances that a home-grown and lasting solution could be reached.

CENTRAL AFRICA

In the aftermath of the Somalia debacle, the world was confronted with an even more grotesque humanitarian nightmare in the African state of Rwanda. Over a period of less than three months in 1994 violence between the Hutu tribe, which dominated the government, and the minority Tutsi population had resulted in more than 500,000 casualties, mainly Tutsi. This death toll far exceeded that in Bosnia, where the killing of about 200,000 Muslims by the Serbs had been labeled genocide. Since the multilateral response proved unworkable in Somalia, a concerted peace-keeping effort in Rwanda was out of the question. Thus the United Nations was largely silent in the face of the Rwandan tragedy. The responsibility for outside intervention fell on the French government, which considered francophone Africa part of its sphere of influence even after its colonial control had ended.[7] But by the time French troops intervened in Rwanda, it was too late. Rwanda's rivers were choked by slain bodies, many horribly hacked to death with machetes. The subsequent victory of the Tutsi army and the establishment of a Tutsi-led government then provoked one of the world's greatest human migrations. Fearing vengeance, the Hutus virtually emptied Rwanda— half a million fled to Burundi, another half million to Tanzania, and a million to Zaire. This relentless flow of refugees overwhelmed local and international efforts to help and led to widespread deaths from starvation, cholera, dehydration, and exhaustion.[8]

The regional conflicts in Africa widened in 1996 and 1997 with no end in sight. Violent attacks and reprisals between the Tutsi-led government of Burundi and the majority population of Hutus raised the prospect of another Rwandan-style bloodbath. The fighting there provoked yet another exodus of refugees, mostly to eastern Zaire, where the corrupt regime of the ailing dictator Mobutu Sese Seko battled its own insurgency. Thousands of Hutu refugees were trapped in the crossfire between rebel forces, led by Laurent Kabila, and Mobutu's army. Mobutu had virtually no support among Zaire's civilian population, and, unlike during the Cold War, he could not count on military assistance from the U.S. government, which declared during the rebellion that "the era of Mobutuism is over." Thus the rapid advance and victory of the rebel forces in May 1997 was inevitable. Upon seizing control of the capital of Kinshasa, the new regime immediately restored the country's original name—Congo—and sought international recognition. It was unclear, however, whether the new regime would be any more democratic than Mobutu's dictatorship.

These events in Africa proved how complex and difficult the process of political development was in countries recovering from colonial rule and the subsequent intervention by the Cold War superpowers. Further, they revealed the inability of outside actors—whether governments or relief organizations—to prevent horrible atrocities and humanitarian

7. Although Rwanda was a Belgian colony, it had been incorporated into France's sphere of influence after its independence.
8. For a personal record of this trauma, see Fergal Keane, *Season of Blood: A Rwandan Journey* (New York: Viking, 1996).

nightmares. In fact, many critics charged that foreign aid programs primarily were designed to promote the self-interests of the donors themselves, not to relieve suffering in developing countries, and that relief agencies like CARE, UNICEF, and the U.S. Agency for International Development were most concerned with enhancing their own stature. "Crippled societies are just another marketing opportunity for those looking to get rid of free food," observed Michael Maren, a former relief worker in Somalia. "As long as there are aid workers willing to risk their lives to move the commodities, or the world is willing to send troops to move the food, anarchic societies are not an obstacle."[9]

HAITI

The Clinton administration was confronted with yet another crisis in the failed state of Haiti, the poorest country in the Western Hemisphere. Ruled by the U.S.-backed Duvalier dictatorship until 1986, the Haitian people had their first experience with democratic elections in 1990 when they elected the Reverend Jean-Bertrand Aristide to the country's presidency. But Aristide's proposed reforms, including his plans to demilitarize the country and redistribute wealth, resulted in his overthrow six months later by the military. With Aristide in exile in the United States, Haiti's military leaders, ruled by Gen. Raoul Cédras, launched a campaign of terror across the island, killing, torturing, and imprisoning those who had fought for reforms and who continued to resist the new rulers. As a result, thousands of Haitians constructed makeshift boats and fled to the United States. In his final months in office, President Bush announced that the United States was unprepared to accommodate these "boat people" and ordered the U.S. Coast Guard to turn them back. His decision angered many human rights groups, as well as candidate Bill Clinton, who declared that as president he would allow the Haitians to seek asylum in the United States.

But just as in other areas of foreign policy, Clinton's position on Haiti changed once he took office. Suddenly he shared Bush's reservations about absorbing the mass emigration of Haitians. Thus, while continuing to demand Aristide's return to Haiti and denouncing the military rulers, Clinton announced that he would not allow Haitian refugees to enter the United States. Instead, a UN-sponsored economic embargo was imposed on Haiti, but it proved to have little effect on the political and social crisis.

In July 1993 Clinton and the Haitian leadership reached an agreement that would have brought about Aristide's return to power in exchange

---

9. Michael Maren, *The Road to Hell: The Ravaging Effects of Foreign Aid and International Charity* (New York: Free Press, 1997). Also see Steven W. Hook, *National Interest and Foreign Aid* (Boulder, Colo.: Lynne Rienner, 1995), and Steven W. Hook, ed., *Foreign Aid toward the Millennium* (Boulder, Colo.: Lynne Rienner, 1996).

for amnesty for Cédras and other military leaders. But when the 270 U.S. and Canadian peace-keepers arrived on the U.S.S. *Harlan County* to oversee the transition back to civilian rule, they were greeted at the waterfront by armed demonstrators who denounced their arrival. The ship then beat an ignominious retreat. An angry and disappointed Aristide publicly condemned the Clinton administration's reversal and was joined by many liberals on Capitol Hill, including members of the Congressional Black Caucus who saw a racial bias in Clinton's acceptance of Cuban refugees, while Haitians, of African origin, were turned back in open waters.

The tentative American response to disorder in Haiti became a symbol of the Clinton administration's general lack of resolve in foreign policy. The *New York Times,* which supported most of Clinton's domestic initiatives, expressed dismay at his reversals in handling the deepening crisis in Haiti. "After months of vacillating from one policy to another, America faces the troubling prospect that Mr. Clinton is drifting into using troops in Haiti because he wants to compensate for other policy embarrassments and does not have a better idea."[10] Clinton also was condemned by conservatives, aghast at his retreat at the first sign of opposition by a weak and corrupt military regime and at the squandering of U.S. prestige, which had been elevated by America's Cold War victory and its more recent spectacular military defeat of Iraq.

The turmoil in Haiti continued into the fall of 1994 even while Haitian refugees were being diverted to an overcrowded settlement camp on the Guantánamo naval base in Cuba, then to temporary facilities as far away as Panama City. Clinton finally concluded that the Haitian problem could only be resolved by U.S. military intervention, and he issued a public ultimatum to the Cédras junta. His threat of war was widely denounced in the United States, where congressional opponents demanded time to debate and vote on the impending invasion, but Clinton had gone beyond the point of no return. Yet even as American jets were taking off toward Port-au-Prince, he dispatched to Haiti a high-level mission, headed by former president Jimmy Carter, to confront Cédras, offer him a final opportunity to leave peacefully, and prevent a military clash. Cédras accepted the offer, but only after being notified that the invasion was in progress.

Thus the military assault on Haiti was transformed into a "semi-permissive occupation" by twenty thousand American troops that extended well into 1995. As in Somalia, the United States was thrust into the role of state builder. Aristide was returned to power, and he was succeeded peacefully the next year by René Préval in elections that, although close-

10. "Which Haiti Policy?" (editorial), *New York Times,* July 7, 1994.

ly monitored, were widely boycotted by Haiti's political parties and largely illiterate citizens. Stability on the island was largely dependent on the presence of U.S. troops, a steady stream of Western foreign aid, and the deployment in March 1996 of six thousand UN peace-keepers, whose mission later was extended until May 1997.

LESSONS FROM THE REGIONAL CRISES

The American public's response to Clinton's efforts in each of these cases was overwhelmingly negative. The failed states of Somalia and Haiti became synonymous with failed American foreign policy; many members of Congress and the public openly doubted that the United States had vital interests in these areas. The terms of the Haitian settlement—recognition of the military junta, amnesty for Cédras, and a comfortable retirement for him and his henchmen, whom Clinton consistently had denounced as criminals—were viewed as excessively generous, granted only because Clinton needed a face-saving alternative to invasion. While Haiti was a "success" in that no American soldiers were killed in combat (in contrast to Somalia), few Americans celebrated this latest show of force.

Most important, widespread rejection of American actions in Somalia and Haiti—coupled with Clinton's rebuke in the 1994 congressional elections—assured the demise of humanitarian intervention in areas marginal to U.S. self-interests. Recognizing this, Congress cut deeply into the U.S. foreign aid budget and closed dozens of foreign embassies, consulates, and missions. Although the United States continued sending nearly $5 billion worth of aid to Israel and Egypt every year, along with new aid commitments to Russia and Eastern Europe, it reduced or eliminated aid to the poorest countries of Africa and Latin America.

These experiences taught the United States that, at the very time that there were fewer restraints than ever on U.S. intervention, its leaders must pay attention to the interests at stake in any conflict—as well as the cost, level of public support, likelihood of success, and presence of a coherent exit strategy. These preconditions became part of the so-called "Powell doctrine," named after Gen. Colin Powell, who emerged as the most popular American leader of the mid-1990s. Powell, chairman of the joint chiefs of staff under Bush, insisted that American troops not be jeopardized in open-ended military engagements. In his view, Somalia was a reckless operation with predictable consequences and Bosnia was a whirlpool just waiting to drown American forces. In the early days of the Persian Gulf crisis, Powell urged Bush to extend the economic sanctions against Saddam Hussein rather than unleash Operation Desert Storm. But once Bush declared that his patience with Hussein had ended, Powell sought to defeat Iraq quickly with overwhelming force, then quickly withdraw American forces from the region even before Hussein and most of his Republican Guards were captured.

Collectively, the regional conflicts described in this chapter shattered the vision of a harmonious "new world order" that had prevailed after the Cold War. The crises—deeply rooted in ethnic, religious, and cultural divisions that predated the Cold War—defied easy explanation and could not be placed neatly into a single "paradigm" of world politics, despite the best efforts of the Clinton administration to do so (see Chapter 12). In the absence of such an orienting principle, both aspects of America's national style of foreign policy—its missionary zeal and its detachment from "foreign entanglements"—expressed themselves. But the ambiguous new order demanded a firm restatement of American purpose that would reconcile the competing requirements of global leadership and self-restraint. As Henry Kissinger observed in 1994,

Indiscriminate involvement in all the ethnic turmoil and civil wars of the post–Cold War world would drain a crusading America. Yet an America that confines itself to the refinement of its domestic virtues would, in the end, abdicate America's security and prosperity to decisions made by other societies in faraway places over which America would progressively lose control.[11]

This was the central dilemma of American foreign policy in the mid-1990s. But as described in the next chapter, American leaders were deeply divided and thus unable to resolve the dilemma. The result was a protracted political struggle in Washington, where Clinton's attempt to establish a new grand strategy based on a revival of liberal internationalism was challenged by those who sought a more modest role for the United States based on tangible self-interests.

11. Henry Kissinger, *Diplomacy* (New York: Simon and Schuster, 1994), 833.

Opening-day crowds get their first taste of McDonald's food in Beijing. The world's largest McDonald's opened in the Chinese capital in April 1992, symbolizing the integration of the global economy.

CHAPTER TWELVE

New Frontiers of American Foreign Policy

The regional conflicts described in Chapter 11 denied the United States the luxury of neglecting foreign affairs and focusing instead on domestic problems. The post–Cold War era had quickly become more chaotic than expected, and it soon became apparent that the United States would have to play a strong role in world affairs long after the Soviet Union had disappeared.

In trying to move beyond its piecemeal response to these events, the Clinton administration reconsidered the basic tenets that guided American foreign policy in the past. It recognized that, along with the armed struggles that had erupted in many areas, broader trends were at work that demanded even greater attention from Washington. For example, the global marketplace was providing vast opportunities for Americans, along with new sources of competition for jobs and investment. More people lived under democratic rule than ever before, but dozens of new democracies faced internal challenges and revolts by dissatisfied groups.

The global environment, meanwhile, continued to deteriorate, spurred on by the accelerating pace of industrialization and population growth.

These trends collectively defined the new frontiers of American foreign policy, which for so long had focused on the singular task of containing communism. This chapter reviews the Clinton administration's response to these trends, which raised the profile of foreign *economic* policy, elicited new "grand strategies" for the Pentagon and State Department, and, by the end of Clinton's first term, produced a bitter power struggle between the White House and Congress.

THE POLITICS OF GEOECONOMICS

On the campaign trail in 1992, Bill Clinton made the U.S. economy the centerpiece of his bid for the presidency. He laid out a program of domestic reforms and emphasized that, without a strong and growing economy accompanied by declining budget and trade deficits, the United States could not afford to play an influential role in world politics. As Clinton and others acknowledged during this period, the "decline" of the U.S. economy during the Cold War had been inevitable.[1] The overwhelming strength of the U.S. economy just after World War II, when it accounted for half of global production, stemmed from the wreckage of the Western European and Pacific economies. And its strength lasted only until these economies recovered: the U.S. share of global production measured about 22 percent in the early 1990s, just where it stood before World War I. Thus the country's predominance after World War II was a historical aberration. Its *relative* economic decline was not a harbinger of economic collapse. On an absolute basis the U.S. economy continued to grow.

From this perspective, the deep-seated fears of many Americans about the economy were unfounded. But the United States did face many daunting economic problems, a number of which were self-inflicted. For example, many long-complacent American industries were unprepared for the sudden burst of overseas competition. In the public sector the U.S. government had built a military superior to any other and funded growing social and entitlement programs, but it had resisted tax increases to pay for the new programs, which led to enormous budget deficits. Because almost every sector of American society bore some responsibility for the problems confronting the U.S. economy in the 1990s, Clinton argued that resolution of the problems would require an aggressive national effort. In focusing on domestic problems that

---

1. Concern over the national decline, unusual for a great power but typically American, was reflected in the strong public response to Paul Kennedy's *The Rise and Fall of the Great Powers* (New York: Random House, 1987).

went beyond fiscal matters—to include social divisions, deteriorating schools and hospitals, and widespread public cynicism toward government—Clinton confronted a series of issues that had deep historical roots and thus would be very difficult to overcome.

THE COURSE OF AMERICA'S ECONOMIC TROUBLES

In the aftermath of World War II, American leaders rarely raised the issue of affordability when responding to a foreign country or a regional crisis that was of "vital interest" to the United States. A few occasionally asked whether the United States could afford a Marshall Plan or expanded military programs. But in the words of President John Kennedy, America could "bear any burden" thought necessary. The nation was wealthy enough, citizens assumed, to support a high standard of living at home and an activist presence abroad. The 1950s and 1960s were decades of unprecedented economic growth in the United States. Wages rose rapidly as trade unions grew powerful and negotiated sizable annual raises paid by industries that apparently could afford them while still earning handsome profits. Meanwhile, in the 1960s Kennedy and Lyndon Johnson vastly expanded the welfare state in their effort to build a "Great Society," leading to the establishment of new entitlement programs, as well as higher costs for older programs such as Social Security. Some newer programs, such as Medicare and Medicaid, started small but grew rapidly as their responsibilities multiplied.

The bubble burst for the U.S. economy in the early 1970s. The enormous expense of the Vietnam War combined with the dramatic rise in oil prices produced high inflation, interest rates, and unemployment, putting a brake on the generation-long economic expansion. The economy ceased to grow rapidly and "stagflation" set in. Meanwhile, the war-ravaged industrial economies of Western Europe had recovered and new competitors in East Asia were entering the global marketplace. After the Vietnam War, it was obvious that the United States no longer could afford an unlimited supply of both guns and butter. It had to make choices. Richard Nixon first responded in 1971 by suspending the gold standard and ending the U.S. dollar's role as the basis of the world's monetary system; he also lowered tensions with Moscow and transformed China from an adversary to an ally to lower the cost of foreign policy.

In the late 1970s Jimmy Carter tried to revive the economy by reducing military spending and keeping taxes in line with growing entitlement programs (see Chapter 8). But a second oil shock in 1978–1979 produced a new burst of inflation, punctuated by double-digit interest rates and unemployment. The resurgence of Soviet expansionism and anti-

American revolutions in Iran and Nicaragua then forced Carter to reverse his military cutbacks. Ronald Reagan accelerated expansion of the military in the early 1980s and cut taxes, thereby fulfilling two campaign promises. But despite his efforts to reduce domestic spending on social programs and to crack down on "waste, fraud, and mismanagement," government expenditures continued to mount.

Free spending is usually followed by a free fall. The long-term expectation of Reagan's supply-side economics was that the U.S. economy, stimulated by lower taxes, would grow as rapidly as it had during the 1950s and 1960s. But the American economy had changed greatly since the 1960s. American agriculture was the most bountiful in the world, yet by the mid-1980s its overseas markets were shrinking. Other industrialized countries and many developing states such as India, China, Thailand, and Indonesia became food exporters. More important, traditional American smokestack industries such as steel and automobile manufacturing were caught off guard as the newly industrialized countries produced superior goods at less cost and thus increased their shares of the American market. In addition to the growing budget deficits recorded in Washington, which surpassed $100 billion in the early 1980s and reached $290 billion by 1992, a string of trade deficits plagued the U.S. economy. Its annual trade deficits with Japan and China alone averaged $80 billion in the mid-1990s.

Reasons for the twin deficits were similar to those for the overall deterioration of American industry: low capital investments in nonmilitary research and development; the preoccupation of corporate leaders with quarterly profits and dividends to the detriment of long-term growth; and the decline of the American labor force, a byproduct of lower educational standards. In addition, there was a lack of corporate enterprise. During the 1980s capital investment and modernization took second place to merger mania and hostile company takeovers. Even though this shuffling of paper was profitable financially for a small group of investment bankers and lawyers, it did not add one whit to economic growth. As for American consumers, despite the stagnation of their disposable incomes they continued to spend freely, often with credit cards, thereby draining the economy of an essential pool of national savings. Finally, much of American industry was moving overseas, especially to developing countries, where it could gain access to new markets and where wages were lower. Industry considered these policies rational, but they contributed to growing unemployment in the United States and other problems that could not be attributed simply to economic cycles. It appeared that "structural problems"—a euphemism for intensified global competition—threatened the U.S. economy, and they would not recede on their own.

But not all of the blame for America's economic lethargy could be directed inward. The economies of Western Europe and East Asia were expanding rapidly, in large measure by violating the terms of the "liberal international economic order" promoted by the United States under the Bretton Woods regime (see Chapter 3). Members of the European Community (now called the European Union) may have opened their internal markets, but they discouraged exports from overseas through high trade barriers such as those enacted through their Common Agriculture Policy. The Japanese government also assisted in the expansion of its key industries, particularly automobiles and consumer electronics, by providing them with generous tax breaks, research funding, and protection from foreign competitors.[2] These practices incited charges of neomercantilism from the United States, Japan's primary export market, which was unable to sell its products in Tokyo at competitive prices. Relations between the two countries suffered as a result, especially after the Cold War when Japan's strategic role as an East Asian bulwark of containment had lapsed. The People's Republic of China, whose communist government was perversely fueled by capitalist expansion, also got into the act, flooding international markets while restricting imports. Most troubling to American leaders and workers, the East Asian version of "industrial policy" became a role model for newly industrialized countries far beyond the Pacific Rim.

RESPONSES BY THE CLINTON ADMINISTRATION

The superior production capacity of the United States underwrote its victory in World War II and its successful Cold War campaign against the Soviet Union. But economic stagnation in the 1980s and 1990s raised the critical question of whether the economy could still support a foreign policy that maintained 300,000 U.S. soldiers in Western Europe, defended Japan and South Korea, policed the Persian Gulf and the Middle East, and retained its traditional sphere of influence in Latin America. Could the United States do all this while supporting ever-growing domestic programs and keeping up with interest payments on the national debt, the fastest-growing area of federal spending?

On taking office, Clinton declared that for America to compete more effectively with the outside world the U.S. government would have to "reinvest" in its domestic base—that is, take a more active role in reforming the national health care system, improving the quality of American schools, and restoring the country's basic infrastructure such as roads and bridges. Furthermore, he sought to ease the antagonism

---

2. See Chalmers Johnson, *MITI and the Japanese Miracle* (Palo Alto, Calif.: Stanford University Press, 1982).

that existed between the federal government and many large industries. Toward this end Clinton met in 1993 with leaders from the U.S. automobile industry and proclaimed a "new partnership" between the federal government and auto makers. These two groups would act as allies rather than adversaries in promoting economic growth, much as their counterparts had done in Japan. In promoting his own version of industrial policy, Clinton was prepared to play by many of the same rules as his competitors.

Among Clinton's other priorities in foreign economic policy was expansion of the U.S. role in regional trading blocs. The early 1990s witnessed a wave of regional economic integration, much of it based on the success of the European Union (EU), which had linked its member states together in a single economic market.[3] By removing barriers to trade and investment within the blocs, by encouraging the movement of workers and services across national borders, and by standardizing health and safety regulations, these states hoped to increase economic efficiency and raise overall levels of production and commerce.

The first such achievement for the United States was the passage in 1993 of the North American Free Trade Agreement (NAFTA), which united the economies of the United States, Canada, and Mexico. Proposed and negotiated by the Bush administration, NAFTA was aimed at reducing or eliminating the tariffs that had limited trade among the three countries. American critics of NAFTA charged that it would encourage U.S. manufacturers to relocate their factories in Mexico, where labor was far cheaper, thereby crippling American firms and their surrounding communities. Others claimed NAFTA would reward Mexico's one-party government for neglecting its impoverished population, as it had in the past. NAFTA supporters countered that in Mexico the treaty would stimulate economic growth, relieve poverty, and move the country toward democracy, all while creating new markets for American goods. They further argued that trade with Canada, the largest export market for the United States, had been severely limited by cross-border restrictions. Finally, they proclaimed NAFTA to be consistent with the laissez-faire principles of free markets that the United States had long espoused. In the end, pro-NAFTA forces prevailed; the treaty passed narrowly in Congress and went into effect on the first day of 1994.

---

3. The European Union expanded to fifteen member states in 1994 when Austria, Finland, and Sweden voted to accept membership. The twelve other members of the EU are Belgium, Denmark, France, Germany, Great Britain, Greece, Ireland, Italy, Luxembourg, the Netherlands, Portugal, and Spain. In the late 1990s, EU members pledged to increase their number still further, and they explored membership possibilities with Cyprus, Slovenia, and several other countries in Eastern Europe.

In yet another step toward regional economic integration, the United States joined in 1994 the eighteen-member Asia Pacific Economic Cooperation (APEC) forum. The Pacific market had emerged as the most dynamic area of economic exchange for the United States; it was growing faster and producing more jobs than Europe. According to Clinton, Asian export markets had become the "lifeblood" of U.S. economic growth. Political divisions ran deep among many APEC members, however, which limited progress on economic reforms. But the loosely knit trade bloc provided potential avenues for political as well as economic cooperation, and it was significant that leaders of the region's most powerful states—including the United States, Japan, and China—became enthusiastic supporters of APEC. Economic integration already had moved forward among Asian states in 1992, when Brunei, Indonesia, Malaysia, the Philippines, Singapore, and Thailand—all members of the Association of South East Asian Nations (ASEAN)—committed themselves to creating a free-trade area by 2003.

Overall, this "pactomania" in global trade relations contributed to the market-driven world economy sought by the United States throughout its history. A further step in this direction was taken late in 1994 when Congress ratified the latest General Agreement on Tariffs and Trade (GATT), approved by most other member states earlier in the year.[4] The agreement reduced tariffs on most products sold overseas and was hailed by Clinton as the "largest tax cut in world history." Passage of GATT, which had seemed assured, briefly was placed in doubt after several members of Congress criticized its provisions for a World Trade Organization (WTO) to monitor trade practices and enforce compliance. The criticisms were silenced, however, after Clinton assured Congress that the United States would not surrender its sovereign authority to the WTO. In fact, the United States would be in a strong position to use the WTO as a vehicle for its own economic program. After Clinton's Republican rivals finally endorsed the agreement, it was ratified easily and the WTO became a fixture of world politics.

ECONOMIC COLD WAR AGAINST CUBA

Economic sanctions have long been standard instruments of foreign policy—and a central element in the American struggle against the communist government of Cuba. Fidel Castro survived the collapse of his patron in Moscow, but with the Cuban economy in a shambles he sought to stimulate economic growth by appealing to foreign investors.

4. GATT, part of the Bretton Woods system described in Chapter 3, has set the terms of international trade through several rounds of negotiating, the latest occurring in Uruguay.

Fearing that Havana's new sources of outside capital would undermine U.S. sanctions, the Clinton administration announced new measures to penalize foreign companies dealing with Cuban properties, including Cuba's telephone system which was owned by American firms before the 1959 revolution.

Congress approved these "extra-territorial" sanctions (affecting third parties) after Castro ordered an attack on two private American planes that crossed into Cuban airspace in February 1996, leading to the death of four Americans. But the Helms-Burton law, named after its congressional sponsors, Republican senator Jesse Helms of North Carolina and Republican representative Dan Burton of Indiana, not only angered Castro but also infuriated many U.S. trading partners, particularly Canada, who declared that they would not allow Washington to impose its sanctions on them. They ignored the U.S. embargo and exploited Castro's recent openness to foreign investment. In doing so they were joined by large segments of American public opinion which opposed the policy of economic isolation that clearly had failed to force cooperation from Castro and that gave foreign investors free reign on the island. Clinton, however, concerned primarily with winning Florida from the Republicans in the 1996 elections, signed the Helms-Burton law under political pressure from Republicans and a strong Cuban-American lobby based in Florida.

Critics of the American policy had argued that a flood of U.S. investment would likely drown Castro faster than the economic boycott, which had failed to exact any concessions from him for over four decades. Why risk major disputes with allies and trading partners, these critics had asked, over a secondary foreign policy objective? But Clinton had no convincing answers to such questions because, clearly, foreign policy was being subordinated to domestic politics. His position on Cuba, to be sure, represented the exception to his general rule of allowing U.S. economic concerns to guide American foreign policy. Other interest groups had to be satisfied politically.

CHINA'S ECONOMIC BOOM AND POLITICAL CHALLENGE

The dispute over Cuba demonstrated that the era of geoeconomics often would depart from the "harmony of interests" envisioned by Scots economist Adam Smith. Territorial disputes, ideological conflicts, and political power struggles remained facts of life in a world still dominated by nation-states. Nowhere was this more evident than in American relations with China, one of the world's fastest-growing economies in the 1990s. Even after Richard Nixon's recognition of the communist government in Beijing, the United States frequently condemned its repressive system of rule and its systematic violations of human rights, particularly its crackdown on pro-democracy activists after the 1989 Tiananmen Square uprising. Clinton's predecessors had linked China's most-favored nation trade status, which provided it with open access to American consumers, to its progress in respecting human rights. But officials in Beijing insisted that their domestic behavior would not be tailored to satisfy American concerns and demands. Their defiance grew stronger as the Chinese economy boomed in the 1990s. Thus Clinton, who was well aware of the economic value of Sino-American trade, was trapped by American policy.

When push came to shove, Clinton backed down on his political demands and announced in 1994 that human rights no longer would be linked directly to U.S. trade with the Chinese. Instead, he argued that the carrot of continuing trade would better elicit reforms in China than the stick of trade sanctions. His decision to pursue "comprehensive engagement" with China, which angered human rights groups, sent a message that the United States would henceforth consider its economic self-interests above humanitarian concerns in making foreign policy decisions. China's treatment of its political dissidents became even more oppressive after the new policy was announced, but this did not deter Clinton from maintaining closer economic ties with Beijing. Yet China's deplorable human rights policy remained a sore point for congressional critics, nongovernmental organizations such as Amnesty International and Human Rights Watch, and even the State Department, which through its annual survey of human rights kept up a steady barrage of criticism of China.

Sino-American relations became further strained in 1995 over China's unfair trading practices, especially its infringements of international copyright and patent laws. A trade war was narrowly avoided. Then, in March 1996, a military confrontation nearly erupted in the Taiwan Straits over elections on the island. Chinese leaders still considered Taiwan a part of China and feared that the first democratically elected leaders would demand political independence. Beijing resorted to gunboat diplomacy as the elections approached, holding live-fire war games in the Taiwan Straits and "testing" intermediate-range missiles that landed close to Taiwanese ports. As this attempt to intimidate Taiwan continued in the days before the election, Clinton responded by deploying two aircraft carriers to the region as a show of support for the U.S. ally. Despite all the commotion offshore, the elections were held and the reformist leader and incumbent president, Lee Teng-hui, became Taiwan's first freely elected leader. In the election's aftermath, the Chinese and American fleets withdrew from the area. But the latest round of brinkmanship added to the tensions created by the trade disputes and human rights issues.

Early in 1997 an even more important issue loomed on the horizon: the scheduled Chinese takeover on July 1 of Hong Kong—one of the four Asian "tigers" whose population of 6 million was dwarfed by China's 1.2 billion but which represented nearly 20 percent of the Chinese gross national product. Many residents of Hong Kong feared communist control and moved away, creating large and often wealthy enclaves in some Western cities such as Vancouver, Canada. Others stayed in Hong Kong, expecting the Chinese government to preserve its market-driven economic system as it did those of other "development zones" along the Pacific coast in order to fund its massive social programs in the interior regions. After the British government agreed to release its former colony, the fate of Hong Kong was placed squarely in the hands of Chinese leaders. "Almost every problem China faces will be more difficult to solve if Hong Kong's well-being is undermined either in 1996 or in the years beyond," warned Hong Kong's mayor.[5]

In the meantime, other matters continued to aggravate Sino-American relations in the mid-1990s. Among them was the proposed sale of Chinese nuclear technology to Pakistan, thereby flouting U.S. antiproliferation policy. Once again, officials in Beijing curtly dismissed the American complaints, as they did earlier when China considered a similar sale to Iran, thought by the United States to be a sponsor of international terrorism. The question in Washington: How much longer would Clinton remain passive in order to avoid rupturing Sino-American relations and hurting American business? In the meantime, comprehensive engagement took on a predictable pattern: the United States would openly criticize Chinese behavior in both political and economic areas, China would dismiss Washington's allegations, and business would continue as usual.

China's future course became even cloudier after the death in February 1997 of Deng Xiaoping, the reformist leader who had effectively succeeded Mao Zedong twenty years earlier. Deng, who had formally retired in 1990 but remained China's symbolic leader, maintained the Communist Party's iron grip over its political system. He approved the 1989 crushing of the Tiananmen Square revolt and the subsequent roundup and persecution of pro-democracy demonstrators. But, at the same time, he also opened the Chinese coastline to foreign investment and greatly expanded Chinese exports, measures that produced the economic boom that brought higher living standards to most Chinese citi-

5. Christopher Patten, "Hong Kong, July 1st," *The World in 1997* (London: *Economist*, 1996), 66.

zens by the 1990s. As its economy and self-confidence grew, so did Chinese military spending and its regional assertiveness—in the Taiwan Straits; in the export of sophisticated military technology to "rogue states," as defined by Washington; and in the rejection of outside complaints about its abuse of human rights.

Deng himself did not recruit a single successor, preferring instead a collective leadership led by President Jiang Zemin, also the secretary general of the Communist Party; Premier Li Peng, the head of government; and others. These leaders had different visions of China's future—some preferring political as well as economic reform, others taking a harder line toward both domestic opponents and potential foreign adversaries, including the United States. Complicating matters further, these contenders for power were themselves elderly; China's younger generation had been shut out of the party leadership for decades. Thus a repeat of the Soviet Union's experience of 1981–1982, when three aged leaders died in rapid succession, seemed likely—without a Gorbachev-like figure waiting in the wings.

All this raised more doubts about the long term direction of China. A growing number of observers predicted a "coming conflict with America" and argued that Beijing had come to see the United States "not as a strategic partner but as the chief obstacle to its own strategic ambitions."[6] According to this view, as China became stronger economically and militarily and as its leaders appealed increasingly to nationalism as a substitute for communism, it would seek to take what it considered to be its rightful place as Asia's primary power, supplanting American influence, and as one of the world's leading powers. Its relationship with the United States was based primarily on its economic need for technology and investments. Yet despite this Chinese need, the United States and China increasingly would clash. The more optimistic view adopted by the Clinton administration also was held by the American business community, mesmerized as it was by the prospect of the virtually unlimited profits to be made in a country with more than one billion people. Clinton believed the growing economic ties between the two countries favored the political status quo, which considered military conflict an unacceptable threat to the trade on which both economies heavily relied.

Clinton made another pragmatic shift in U.S. policy when he lifted Washington's twenty-year trade embargo against Vietnam. The president was persuaded by economic projections indicating that trade between the United States and Vietnam would triple to more than $8

---

6. Richard Bernstein and Ross H. Munro, "The Coming Conflict with America," *Foreign Affairs* (March–April 1997): 19.

billion by 1999 if the embargo were lifted. Again, he used the argument that closer economic ties between the two countries, which still had deep ideological differences and lingering disputes over a quarter-century after the Vietnam War, would contribute more to the resolution of differences and disputes than political and economic isolation. As in the case of China, his support for American material interests over idealistic crusades again pleased business leaders while angering human rights groups. Their protests, however, were difficult to sustain as the American economy flourished in the mid-1990s.

'PREVENTIVE DEFENSE' AS GRAND STRATEGY

Just as global influence was dependent on a sound domestic base, the reverse also was true: to remain attentive to domestic needs, the United States required a stable international order. Yet, as described in Chapter 11, Clinton's economic focus did not signify the end of international crises, nor the end of America's traditional interests as a great power. To the contrary, events overseas became only more complex, unpredictable, and potentially dangerous for the United States. While the Clinton administration initially responded to the series of regional conflicts on an ad hoc basis, it searched for a new "grand strategy," or general guide for action, to bring coherence to its actions throughout the world.

In Washington and around the country many people questioned whether the United States really *needed* an explicit grand strategy in the wake of the Cold War. After all, the U.S.-Soviet rivalry and the bipolar balance of power had been unique in history. Communism had represented an unambiguous challenge to American principles, institutions, and the security of its allies. And George Kennan's containment strategy served as an equally clear response. Once the Soviet Union had vanished, the simplicity of superpower bipolarity gave way to an uncertain distribution of power: either unipolar, with the United States as the world's "sole remaining superpower," or multipolar, with the emerging power centers—the European Union, Japan, China, and several newly industrialized countries—becoming more influential in world politics. In either case the regional conflicts that erupted in the 1990s derived from many sources, with little or no relation to each other and often with remote connections to U.S. self-interests. Consequently, according to a prevalent view, the United States should consider each foreign problem independently and respond on a case-by-case basis.

The United States, however, obviously could not pursue a coherent foreign policy in the dark. No great power can survive in the absence of a clear statement of purpose. Vital interests must be recognized and articulated. Priorities must be set, budgets prepared, and resources deployed in a systematic fashion. Furthermore, allies must be reassured and adversaries put on notice by a government speaking with one voice. Otherwise, policy vacillates and drifts, each arm of government moves in separate directions, and public support is impossible to sustain. Most troubling, challengers to the status quo will inevitably seek to exploit the void that results when a great power leads by improvisation.

But what would serve as this new grand strategy? Clinton, preoccupied first with his domestic agenda and then with the spate of regional conflicts, put off a definitive answer to this question. Instead, he left it to his top aides to frame their own responses. The Pentagon at first was unable to clarify its strategy at a time when its budget and human resources had been reduced substantially by a Congress whose top priority was downsizing government and lowering the federal deficit. Les Aspin, Clinton's first secretary of defense, accepted many of the cuts, which he personally endorsed as part of his "bottom-up review" of the Pentagon, completed in 1994. Aspin identified many areas in which the army, navy, and air force duplicated tasks such as in the area of intelligence gathering, and mapped out reductions in the U.S. troop divisions that were still deployed around the world. Meanwhile, Congress approved the closure of nearly one hundred military bases, of which more than fifty were permanently shut down by 1997.

Aspin's successor, William Perry, tried to restore the Pentagon's strategic mission, and he announced in May 1996 that "preventive defense" had become the new orienting principle for the armed forces. "Preventive defense may be thought of as analogous to preventive medicine," Perry said. "Preventive medicine creates the conditions which support health, making disease less likely and surgery unnecessary. Preventive defense creates the conditions which support peace, making war less likely, and deterrence unnecessary."[7] In promoting this strategy, Perry echoed the UN's 1992 *Agenda for Peace*, which devoted a full chapter to "preventive diplomacy," and the earlier 1990 Charter of Paris, signed by most European leaders, which sought "new forms of cooperation . . . [for] ways of preventing, through political means, conflicts which may emerge."

Perry likened the new strategy to the Marshall Plan, which provided assistance to European allies after World War II and dampened the prospects that the region would again erupt in violence. He then described a series of policies the United States would pursue as part of preventive defense: reducing nuclear stockpiles and preventing prolifer-

7. William Perry, speech to John F. Kennedy School of Government, Harvard University, May 13, 1996, U.S. Department of Defense, Washington, D.C. He elaborated on this strategy in "Defense in an Age of Hope," *Foreign Affairs* (November–December 1996): 64–79.

ation, countering the spread of chemical and biological weapons, supporting the spread of democracy in foreign countries, helping foreign
governments to create civilian-led armed forces, and promoting "confidence-building" measures between countries such as state visits and the
sharing of intelligence. All of these measures would presumably create a
more stable international system, thereby reducing the need for deterring global threats and making the actual use of American armed forces
less likely.

But as Perry later acknowledged, preventive defense failed to capture
the attention of the American people. Yet this was to be expected; the
strategy seemed abstract, hypothetical, and remote from the sense of
invulnerability that was widely shared by Americans after the Cold War.
True to its historic form, the public sought to avoid "foreign entanglements" unless its own security were threatened directly. Many Americans thus turned against the growing peace-keeping role assumed by the
United Nations, which had tripled the number of such missions since
the Cold War and increased the number of blue-helmeted troops
deployed overseas from less than ten thousand to more than seventy
thousand. And in Washington Clinton supported a new round of military base closings in 1997, along with deeper cuts in defense spending—
all in the interest of balancing the federal budget, the president's primary concern.

NATO'S UNCERTAIN FUTURE

A crucial element of any grand strategy is the management of
alliances. For the United States after the Cold War, this applied most
directly to the North Atlantic Treaty Organization (NATO), which had
achieved its stated mission of preventing Soviet expansion into Western
Europe and which, as a result, had outlived its original mandate. A
British secretary general of NATO had once summed up the alliance's
function as "keeping the Americans in [Europe], the Russians out, and
the Germans down." Apparently, these purposes were still considered
valid despite the Soviet Union's collapse, the Warsaw Pact's disintegration, and the Cold War's demise. For many American and European
leaders, NATO had to be retained to keep a strong and stabilizing American presence in Europe. It also was needed to prevent a resurgence of
German military power, including the possibility of nuclear armament,
and to deter any future threat by Russia against central and Eastern
Europe. Finally, NATO was seen as a guarantee against another German-
Russian collision (like that before World War I) or further collusion (like
that before World War II).

For all of these reasons the preservation of NATO was widely supported even after the defeat of its declared enemy. But instead of declar-

ing victory, NATO found reasons for projecting itself into a very different future. It found an immediate rationale for its continued existence
in the anxieties felt by former member countries of the Warsaw Pact,
which were eager to become part of the "West" but were not offered
immediate membership in the European Union. The issue therefore
became not whether the alliance should disband, but whether it should
expand eastward. Some NATO members felt that because abolition of
the Warsaw Pact had created a power vacuum in central Europe, this was
the time to move NATO forward, while Russia was weak. Others dis-
agreed, arguing that such an expansion would undermine the alliance's
already fragile cohesion, negate its sense of common purpose, and drag
NATO members into a host of "out-of-area" conflicts in which they had
little vested interest.

The decision to expand was further complicated by the issue of
Russian involvement. The most common suggestion was that NATO
expand gradually, beginning with Poland, the Czech Republic, and
Hungary (which does not even border any NATO country) and then
add new members as events warranted. But such an incremental expansion would likely antagonize the Russians, historically alarmed at the
prospect of "encirclement" by hostile neighbors. Moreover, if the Eastern European states but not Russia were incorporated into NATO, the
process would inflame Russian nationalism and isolate the moderates,
pushing Russia to possible rearmament and the diversion of resources
badly needed to ensure the success of its political and economic
reforms.

Clinton and other NATO leaders arrived at a compromise solution.
Under the rubric of a "Partnership for Peace," the former Warsaw Pact
members and the CIS republics were invited to become auxiliary members of NATO. By May 1994 eighteen of these countries had agreed to
join the partnership. As auxiliary members, they were allowed to participate in some NATO deliberations and training exercises, but key strategic decisions were left to the original members. If the larger collabora-
tions proved successful, NATO officials suggested, these auxiliary states
might at some future date become full-fledged members of the NATO
alliance. Russian president Boris Yeltsin at first rejected the partnership
concept, but later insisted that if Russia were to join, it should receive
preferential treatment given its greater military strength, its former role
as a superpower, and its status as a permanent member of the UN Security Council. NATO rejected this demand, arguing that Russia should
assume the same role as other partnership members while long-range
negotiations over the alliance's future continued. Yeltsin reluctantly
agreed to these conditions and accepted a muted Russian role in the
Partnership for Peace.

But this fragile arrangement began to unravel after NATO members agreed to consider an accelerated schedule for Polish, Czech, and Hungarian entry into the alliance. Yeltsin protested this plan at a December 1994 meeting of the thirty-five-member Organization on Security and Cooperation in Europe (OSCE), whose purpose was to control conflict in Europe.[8] Exploiting the tensions within NATO, Yeltsin warned all Europeans, from both east and west, about subjecting themselves to American military control which always had been a central element of the NATO alliance. He then declared that a "Cold Peace" was emerging between Moscow and Washington which would thaw only after the proposed eastward expansion of NATO was suspended. Later, he called NATO's expansion a direct blow to Russia's security and one designed to squeeze Russia out of Europe and strategically isolate it.

The United States and its NATO allies again dismissed Yeltsin's thinly veiled threats, which they attributed largely to the Russian leader's need to appease domestic nationalists at a time when his hold on power was threatened. Instead, they moved forward on their plan to include the three Visegrad states into NATO by 1999, the fiftieth anniversary of the alliance's founding, and to leave the door open for other new members. In response, Russia again modified its stance; instead of blocking NATO expansion it asked to negotiate a separate treaty with the alliance and a guarantee against the West's placement of nuclear weapons in Eastern Europe. The two sides reached an agreement in May 1997, although NATO officials declared that Russia was given a "voice, not a veto" over NATO policy.

Left unclear, however, was the future mission and structure of the enlarged NATO. During the Balkan crisis, before the Dayton Accords, the Americans and Europeans continually quarreled over tactics as well as a strategy for ending the war in Europe's "backyard." For the United States, the expansion of NATO was likely to mean new financial burdens because it would have to modernize Eastern European armies and equip them with Western arms, as well as extend U.S. defense commitments to Russia's frontier. The expansion of NATO also was linked to some rather basic assumptions that both Germany and Russia at some future point would revert to their past behavior. But was it likely that Germany, the continent's most powerful state with a prominent role in Europe and the world, would revert to the nationalistic and expansionist course it had pursued from 1870 to 1945? Germany had been rooted democratically since World War II and was no longer the militaristic nation it had been in its more autocratic past. Moreover, it was highly integrated into West-

8. The OSCE was composed of mainly European states, as well as the former Soviet states, the United States, and Canada.

ern Europe and the Atlantic community, and its current government favored strengthening both ties.

Furthermore, was Russia, suffering from a faltering economy, political uncertainty, and a demoralized and declining military, really a threat to its neighbors? Would Russia reassert itself as an imperial or communist threat? Could it also do this so quickly that NATO needed to expand well before such a threat might emerge, thereby perhaps generating the very outcome it was seeking to prevent? Moreover, would NATO's expansion not violate the implicit agreement reached between Washington and Moscow in 1990 that NATO would not exploit the dissolution of the Warsaw Pact, the withdrawal of Soviet troops, and Mikhail Gorbachev's agreement to German reunification?

One need only think about how Washington would react if the Soviet Union had won the Cold War, and Moscow had offered Mexico and other Latin American nations membership in the Warsaw Pact, explaining that the expansion was not directed against the United States. NATO's offer not to station nuclear weapons in the territories of the new Eastern European members was hardly reassuring, since it was an offer that could change with circumstances and contradicted the past policy of deterring an attack precisely by stationing Western forces on the soil of the nations to be defended. The question thus remained whether NATO's expansion would continue to be seen in Moscow as a provocative act, jeopardizing Russian-American relations, as well as the security of Europe, as Russia moved closer to China and pursued policies that might disregard future American interests. But confronted with the inevitable, Yeltsin sought the face-saving NATO-Russian charter and reaped the rewards of his acquiescence: billions of dollars in continued economic aid from the West.

A NEW PUSH FOR ARMS CONTROL

Among the central components of William Perry's strategy of preventive defense, arms control assumed a critical role. He believed that reductions worldwide in the number of weapons—both conventional and nuclear—would improve the chances that regional conflicts could be prevented or contained. This had been the conventional wisdom in Washington throughout the post–Cold War period, but Perry declared arms control to be a pillar of American national security. In January 1996 Congress ratified the START II agreement, which George Bush and Boris Yeltsin had signed three years earlier. START II required both countries to reduce the number of their long-range nuclear warheads to between 3,000 and 3,500 by the year 2003, a two-thirds cutback in such warheads since the peak of the Cold War. In addition, it banned long-range nuclear weapons with multiple warheads, one of the most destabilizing components of the nuclear arms race.[9] And in March 1997 Clinton and Yeltsin agreed to move forward on START III, an agreement to reduce nuclear stockpiles by another thousand on each side. (Whether the Russian Duma would approve either START II or III, given its opposition to NATO's expansion, remained to be seen.)

In addition to the bilateral START process, the United States pursued multilateral efforts to control weapons. In September 1996 Clinton signed the Comprehensive Test Ban Treaty (CTBT) which banned the testing of nuclear weapons. The agreement also was approved by the other declared nuclear states—Russia, China, France, and Great Britain. (Only India opposed the CTBT, advocating instead a worldwide ban on nuclear weapons that was unacceptable to the nuclear powers.) Clinton also signed the Chemical Weapons Convention, negotiated by the Reagan and Bush administrations and signed by 163 countries. The convention, which went into effect in April 1997, was designed to prevent a recurrence of the chemical warfare that had occurred in the world wars and more recently in Iraq, which had used nerve gas against its Kurdish population in the 1980s. The United States also supported renewing the Treaty on the Nonproliferation of Nuclear Weapons, and it advocated stronger restrictions on the export of missile technology, particularly to "rogue states" that threatened regional security.

But in promoting arms control, Clinton faced opposition from the U.S. Senate, which had the power to ratify or reject the new treaties. Many Republican leaders expressed doubts about the use of arms control in protecting American interests and raised old concerns about the reliability of foreign governments in respecting the arms treaties. In practice, these congressional leaders used the treaties as leverage in gaining concessions from the White House in other areas, many of which had little or nothing to do with arms control. Senate ratification of the chemical weapons ban, for example, was assured only after Clinton agreed to restructure the State Department—something Congress had been demanding for several years. Further complicating matters, many foreign governments questioned the credibility of the United States in the area of arms control. After all, it maintained the world's largest nuclear arsenal, and since the collapse of the Cold War had virtually cornered the world's conventional arms market.

Meanwhile, the Clinton administration scaled back funding for "strategic defense," or antimissile technology, and instead sought to pre-

---

9. The Russian government delayed consideration of START II amid concerns about NATO expansion and the possible deployment of missile defense systems in the United States. But Yeltsin promised to observe its provisions, much as the United States complied with SALT II even after it was rejected by the U.S. Senate following the Soviet invasion of Afghanistan.

vent threats to the United States through arms reductions or, as during the Cold War, through nuclear deterrence. Perry argued that Ronald Reagan's "Star Wars" program could not guarantee the safety of Americans in the foreseeable future, and with the disappearance of the Soviet Union there was no credible prospect of a long-range missile attack against the United States.[10] His arguments were strengthened by a July 1996 study by the Congressional Budget Office which found that building such a system would cost $116 billion over twenty years, more than ten times the amount estimated by supporters of strategic defense. Within the Pentagon, there was little support for a hypothetical nuclear "shield" that could undermine existing arms treaties and tempt American adversaries to accelerate their nuclear programs. Instead, military leaders sought funding for other needs such as troop readiness and munitions.[11]

Clinton's concerns about nuclear proliferation were reflected in his response to provocations in 1994 by North Korea, China's close ally whose Stalinesque dictator, Kim Il-Sung, threatened to build nuclear weapons in defiance of North Korea's earlier pledge to respect the terms of the nuclear nonproliferation treaty. The prospect of nuclear weapons in North Korea was disturbing to the United States and much of the world for several reasons: the possibility that such weapons might stimulate an arms race in East Asia—South Korea and Japan could not ignore such a threat to their security; the encouragement such weapons might give other radical anti-American regimes, such as Iran, to build their own nuclear bombs or to obtain help from regimes like North Korea; and, above all, the role such weapons would likely play in undermining the nuclear nonproliferation treaty and setting loose the forces of mass destruction.

The Clinton administration vowed that North Korea would not be allowed to become a nuclear power and insisted on delaying negotiations with the North Korean government until after it permitted inspection of its nuclear facilities. In addition, the administration threatened to impose economic sanctions against North Korea. Kim responded by declaring that such sanctions would be regarded as an act of war and by deploying troops to the border with South Korea. For several weeks a reprise of the Korean War of the 1950s became a possibility. Moreover, the North Korean standoff raised a number of questions about the role China might play in any conflict, and it heightened concerns in Japan and other Pacific Rim states about their own security.

10. By 1997 all nuclear weapons had been removed from the ex-Soviet republics of Belarus, Kazakhstan, and Ukraine—an accomplishment that received little public notice but was considered a top priority of the Clinton administration.

11. See Joseph Cirincione, "Why the Right Lost the Missile Defense Debate," *Foreign Policy* (spring 1997): 39–55.

All this presented an additional challenge to Clinton, who dispatched Jimmy Carter to North Korea for personal meetings with its dictator. After several discussions in June 1994, Carter announced that Kim had agreed to limited inspections of his nuclear program. It became clear, however, that he already had diverted enough plutonium to build at least one nuclear bomb. The United States announced that North Korea had agreed to "freeze" its nuclear program. But the price for maintaining peace with North Korea, not as a nonnuclear state but as an infant nuclear power, was incredible: nearly $5 billion to be paid by the United States, South Korea, and Japan for the construction of two nuclear power generators that would not yield plutonium; a free supply of oil for eight to ten years (since China was no longer willing to supply oil at "friendship" prices); and diplomatic relations with the United States and Japan.

What had the United States received in return for reviving North Korea's failing economy with free oil, ending its diplomatic isolation, and building its nuclear reactors gratis? It had received only promises to allow inspections within eight years and shut down the plutonium reprocessing plant—promises North Korea had made years earlier and then violated. In short, North Korea's nuclear program remained intact but "frozen." It would keep any weapons it already had while buying time to build more if it decided later to up the ante. And Washington had to assume that Sung's successor—his son Kim Jong-Il, who assumed power upon his father's death in July 1994—would respect the agreement.

The North Korean episode demonstrated the lengths to which the United States would go to promote arms control in the post–Cold War era. The determination of Clinton and Perry in this regard reflected their view that, beyond the inherent and often inevitable conflicts of interest that exist among nations, the mere presence of weapons can incite international crises. Unfortunately, history provides little evidence that this is the case. What could cause greater harm to the United States, and the state system in general, is the denial of political differences and the coddling of America's enemies while arms control is pursued as an end in itself.

PROMOTING DEMOCRACY AND SUSTAINABLE DEVELOPMENT

By the time the Cold War collapsed, urgent global problems such as environmental decay, rapid population growth, and growing gaps between rich and poor were demanding immediate attention. These problems, which had taken a backseat to the superpower rivalry, were fused with the effort to consolidate global democratic reforms and became part of a distinct post–Cold War global agenda. Clinton, who called for greater attention to global problems as a presidential candidate along with a heightened emphasis on economic issues, seized on these aspects of "low politics" once in office. In doing so, his variant of liberal internationalism recalled various aspects of President John Kennedy's Alliance for Progress and Jimmy Carter's world-order politics, both of which emphasized cooperative North-South relations, human rights, and the interdependence of all countries in the modern world. For the first time, Clinton argued, such an approach could be undertaken in the absence of superpower tensions.

DEMOCRATIZATION

Long before Clinton took office, the United States had sought to promote the expansion of democratic rule overseas. The roots of this long-time American quest can be traced to Thomas Jefferson's "empire of liberty," to the widespread presumption of America's "manifest destiny," and to Woodrow Wilson's pledge to make the U.S. role in World War I a mission "for democracy, for the right of those who submit to authority to have a voice in their own government, for the rights and liberties of small nations . . . and to make the world itself free." The renewal of this democratic crusade after the Soviet Union's collapse, then, was merely continuation of an existing practice. "No national security issue is more urgent, nowhere is our country's imperative more clear," Clinton declared on the campaign trail in 1992. "I believe it is time for America to lead a global alliance for democracy as united and steadfast as the global alliance that defeated communism."[12] Once in office, Clinton's top aides put these principles into practice. Echoing George Kennan, containment's intellectual founder, National Security Adviser Anthony Lake asserted in 1993,

The successor to a doctrine of containment must be a strategy of enlargement— enlargement of the world's free community. . . . We must counter the aggression— and support the liberalization—of states hostile to democracy. . . . The United States will seek to isolate [non-democratic states] diplomatically, militarily, economically and technologically.[13]

Secretary of State Warren Christopher cited U.S. involvement in Eastern Europe, southern Africa, the Middle East, and Latin America as evidence of the administration's determination to match its words with deeds. Indeed, the massive commitments of Western aid to Russia and its neighbors—at a time when the popularity of U.S. foreign aid had

12. Bill Clinton, "A Strategy for Foreign Policy," *Vital Speeches of the Day,* May 1, 1992, 421.
13. Anthony Lake, "From Containment to Enlargement," Department of State Dispatch, September 27, 1993, 658–664.

descended to record lows—were viewed as a critical component of this effort. Christopher justified the continuing priority of global democratization in 1995 in words that clearly captured the idealistic strain of American foreign policy:

> At bottom, support for democracy and human rights, setting an example, and standing up for what we believe in are vital parts of U.S. leadership. Other nations have long followed America's lead in part because our nation has a proven willingness to stand for something larger than itself. From the time of the American Revolution, people everywhere have looked to the United States for inspiration in their struggle for freedom and a better life. We are committed to carrying on that tradition because it is right and because it is our greatest source of strength in the world.[14]

As in the case of preventive defense, Clinton faced an uphill battle in arousing public and congressional interest in his democratization campaign. Many Americans simply questioned whether the effort was actually vital to U.S. security and economic interests. Further, the targets of the democratization strategy were disbursed throughout the world, often in remote areas with no tradition of representative government. Internal revolts had upended democratic regimes in many countries, which succumbed to ethnic rivalries and military rule. As one critic observed, capturing all of these concerns, "It remains unclear that 'enlarging' democracy actually qualifies as a paramount American interest. In any event, the objective is difficult—at times impossible—to translate into immediate policy while the process of democratization works in uncertain ways."[15]

In rejecting these concerns, Clinton, like his predecessors, appealed to the crusading impulse that long had animated American leaders. The United States, which always had portrayed itself as the world's "beacon of democracy," could not stand by while countries sought to consolidate democratic institutions in the face of internal upheaval. Driven by this logic, the United States was propelled into its Haitian intervention (see Chapter 11). It also identified "rogue states"—Iran, Iraq, Libya, Syria, North Korea, and Cuba, among others—which it felt threatened the foundations of democratic rule. It then isolated them through economic sanctions, diplomatic exclusion, and occasional military coercion. "Real zero tolerance requires us to isolate states that refuse to play by the rules we have all accepted for civilized behavior," Clinton told the United Nations in September 1996.

Like his predecessors criticized for their selective drive to contain communism, Clinton confronted charges that the United States had

---

14. Warren Christopher, "America's Leadership, America's Opportunity," *Foreign Policy* (spring 1995): 26.

15. Richard Haass, "Paradigm Lost," *Foreign Affairs* (January–February 1996): 44.

pursued double standards in its most recent campaign of democratization. Violations of human rights by the Chinese government, for example, were frequently subordinated to the greater objective of expanded economic ties. Saudi Arabia and Egypt, loyal friends of the United States—one the source of oil, the other a strong supporter of Arab-Israeli peace—were ruled by repressive governments. But surely America's interest lay in supporting these undemocratic regimes rather than seeing them fall to militant, anti-American Islamic governments. Meanwhile, in several Eastern European countries many former communists were being elected to leadership positions, demonstrating that the ballot box was no guarantee that leaders favorable to the United States would come to power. Finally, the disintegration of Yugoslavia and Czechoslovakia and the rise of ethnic, religious, and nationalist passions in and among the former Soviet states meant that pluralism and tolerance of diversity were not always produced by the introduction of democracy. In countries that maintained authoritarian rule through their armed forces, elections were largely a sideshow.

But the United States would not be denied its self-appointed democratic mission. After all, it had succeeded in defeating fascism during World War II and the world's most powerful communist state in the Cold War—campaigns not undertaken merely to resurrect a stable balance of power but to liberate world politics from the scourge of power politics. In this context, obstacles to democratization in the more benign setting of the 1990s did not appear insurmountable.

SUSTAINABLE DEVELOPMENT

Beyond his policy to support democratization overseas, Clinton embraced the global effort to promote "sustainable development" in the former Third World, a loosely knit concept that combined political reforms, environmental protection, population control, and broadly based economic growth. Chronic problems in developing countries, where most of the world's people lived and where population growth was most rapid, could no longer be ignored by the industrialized nations. Their problems were becoming *transnational* in scope, spilling into neighboring countries and threatening global security. Solving these problems, then, would require cooperative action and sacrifice on an equally universal scale—and strong leadership by the United States.

Plans to promote sustainable development preceded Clinton's arrival into office in 1993, and they originated from many sources outside the United States. The impetus for sustainable development came in June 1992 during the United Nations Conference on Environment and Development, at the time the largest single gathering of world leaders in history. The Earth Summit's concluding statement, *Agenda 21*, constituted a call to arms to pursue this goal. The eight-hundred-page manifesto called for annual spending of more than $125 billion in dozens of areas such as pollution control, education, health care, poverty relief, technology transfer, and the empowerment of women. According to the preamble of *Agenda 21*, "peace, development, and environmental protection are interdependent and indivisible."[16]

Many of these provisions had been rejected earlier by George Bush, who was more concerned about his fading reelection prospects in the summer of 1992 and virtually had to be dragged to the Earth Summit. Bush provoked worldwide criticism at the conference by refusing to sign the Biodiversity Convention, designed to protect endangered species hard-hit by accelerating development in the Third World. To Bush, the treaty unfairly restricted the access of American companies to the tropical forests of Latin America and Asia, and it imposed excessive demands (more than $200 million initially) on wealthy countries to aid equatorial states that would lose revenue if development halted in these sensitive areas. The United States stood alone in opposing the treaty, which was approved by 153 other governments.

Bush's defiance of the Earth Summit and the estrangement of the United States from the revived environmental movement provided strong ammunition for Clinton, who made the U.S. stance one of the few foreign policy issues of his campaign. Once elected, Clinton adopted *Agenda 21* as a prototype for his environmental proposals of 1993 and 1994. Vice President Al Gore, an outspoken environmentalist, was designated to oversee the effort.[17] In the State Department a new position was created—Under Secretary of State for Global Affairs—symbolizing the administration's concern for these issues. Finally, Clinton signed the Biodiversity Convention along with the UN Convention on the Law of the Sea, which was adopted in 1982 despite objections by the United States, and he restored funding for the UN Fund for Population Activities which had been suspended by Bush and Ronald Reagan.

In 1994 the Clinton administration set forth its *Strategies for Sustainable Development,* which proposed multilateral efforts in six areas: protecting the environment, stabilizing world population growth, protecting human health, providing humanitarian assistance, encouraging economic growth, and "building democracy."[18] In all of these areas the

16. United Nations Conference on Environment and Development, *Agenda 21* (New York: United Nations, 1992).

17. Gore outlined his environmental views in *Earth in the Balance* (New York: Plume, 1993).

18. U.S. Agency for International Development, *Strategies for Sustainable Development* (Washington, D.C.: U.S. Department of State, 1994), 4.

United States pledged to work closely with the United Nations and other international organizations, as well as a growing number of private groups. These programs were brought together in the Peace, Prosperity, and Democracy Act of 1994, a wide-ranging bill supported by Clinton and a Congress then dominated by the Democratic Party.

For a brief time, it appeared that Bill Clinton's "pragmatic neo-Wilsonian" foreign policy, as it was described by Anthony Lake, would be enacted into law. But this was not to be. Clinton's window of opportunity slammed shut in November 1994 after midterm congressional elections reversed the political tide and brought an entirely different agenda to Washington. By the time Clinton was reelected in 1996, sustainable development had virtually disappeared from the lexicon of American foreign policy, the Biodiversity Convention was languishing in the Senate, and the United States was rapidly dismantling its foreign aid program. American self-interests once again became preeminent, while "assertive multilateralism" gave way to unilateral action by the United States.

DOMESTIC CHALLENGES TO CLINTON'S FOREIGN POLICY

It was not upheavals abroad that provoked the challenge to Clinton's foreign policy. The backlash began at home, within the U.S. government, for reasons only marginally related to foreign policy. Despite the administration's progress in reducing the federal deficit and stimulating economic growth, public opinion polls suggested widespread distrust of the federal government. The extremism of regional militia groups—epitomized by the destruction of a federal office building in Oklahoma City on April 19, 1995—served as a potent expression of growing public disenchantment with "business as usual" in Washington. On another and more personal level, this sentiment was directed toward Clinton himself. Beset by scrutiny of his role in the Whitewater land development venture while governor of Arkansas, charges of sexual harassment, and other "character issues," Clinton was viewed with skepticism by the general public.

This widespread distrust was accompanied by the revival of the Republican Party in many state governments, particularly in the South, where a historic realignment in state legislatures had been under way for more than a decade. While many observers expected Republican Party gains in the midterm elections, few predicted that the elections of 1994 would produce a historic resurgence of the Republican Party—its first claim to majority status in both houses since 1954. The Republicans, who held just 176 of the 435 House seats before the elections, won 231 seats to capture majority control. On the Senate side, the Republican Party increased its share from 43 to 52 of the 100 seats—a solid, if not veto-proof, majority. Thus the final two years of Clinton's term would feature a reversal of the pattern of divided government experienced by Reagan and Bush: now a *Republican* Congress would offset a *Democratic* White House.

Republican leaders pursued a foreign policy very different from that adopted by Clinton. In general, they sought a more modest role for the United States since the Soviet threat had disappeared and since no other power comparable to the Soviet Union had emerged in its absence. In their view, American policy should be based on tangible self-interests rather than ambiguous global concerns, and on strong military defenses rather than on foreign aid and a reliance on international organizations. This divergence of views resurrected the historic and unresolved debate over the country's world role, a debate that to a large extent had been suspended during much of the Cold War. Thus both aspects of the American style of foreign policy—detachment from the "outside world" and moralistic crusading by the United States—found expression in the debate.

Congressional Republicans followed the lead of Sen. Jesse Helms, an outspoken critic of Clinton's foreign policy who became chairman of the powerful Senate Foreign Relations Committee in January 1995. Within five months Helms introduced legislation for a "new" State Department which included major cutbacks in foreign affairs spending, particularly U.S. foreign aid (Helms charged aid was being poured into a "rathole" overseas). He further demanded the establishment of an "America Desk" in the State Department to ensure that diplomatic activities directly contributed to U.S. national interests. Finally, he recommended increases in U.S. military spending as a more appropriate means to achieve these interests in the post–Cold War world.

By the end of 1995 Helms was holding much of U.S. foreign policy hostage—including nearly four hundred foreign service promotions, thirty ambassadorial nominations, more than a dozen treaties and international agreements, and many daily functions of the State Department. Until Clinton agreed to the Republicans' demands, the Foreign Relations Committee indefinitely suspended its normal operations. With the committee out of business, many routine operations of U.S. foreign policy ceased. Much of the State Department's Washington-based staff was furloughed and the handling of the nearly thirty thousand visa applications received daily was temporarily halted. The U.S. government stopped paying utility bills at many foreign embassies, and funds to operate the State Department's computer and cable services were suspended. "As a result," the *New York Times* reported, "the day-to-day foreign policy business on Capitol Hill has ground to a halt."[19]

Clinton supported the general idea of reorganizing the State Department, an idea previously endorsed by five former secretaries of state. But he claimed that Vice President Gore's "national performance review," which was designed to streamline the federal government and which included an audit of the State Department, responded to Republican budgetary concerns. Congressional efforts went far beyond structural refinements, Clinton argued, and instead sought to redefine the general course of U.S. foreign policy—an authority he believed was firmly lodged in the White House.

The showdown between the White House and Congress not only reflected national ambivalence about America's post–Cold War role; it also demonstrated once again how limited the president's foreign policy powers are when the United States is not at war or faced with an imminent crisis. In more tranquil periods, Congress holds sway, primarily through its "power of the purse" which prevents new foreign ventures sought by the president from being launched. Thus the political balance of power *within* the United States becomes a key determinant of its foreign policy.[20]

Returning to the campaign trail in 1996, Clinton again spent most of his time addressing domestic reforms. This time he faced Republican Bob Dole, who resigned from his Senate seat and position as majority leader to engage full time in the campaign. Although Dole criticized Clinton's foreign policy, particularly his haphazard response to regional crises, Clinton ignored his complaints. In his calculus, foreign policy had no "constituency" among the American people in peacetime, so his efforts were better directed toward issues that could win him votes: welfare reform, deficit reduction, economic competitiveness, and the "war against crime." And on these issues, Clinton sounded more like a Republican than a Democrat, a reflection of his strategy to reduce Dole's running room and dominate the "vital center" of American politics. It proved an effective strategy, assuring Clinton's reelection by a wide margin.

In pursuing this campaign strategy, however, Clinton missed an opportunity to clarify his vision of America's future world role. Still shaken by the Republican victories of November 1994, Clinton chose a policy of political expedience and allowed public opinion polls and focus groups to determine his stand on many issues. What little ideo-

19. Elaine Sciolino, "Awaiting Call, Helms Puts Foreign Policy on Hold," *New York Times*, September 23, 1995, 1A.

20. For an elaboration, see Robert J. Lieber, ed., *Eagle Adrift* (New York: Longman, 1997), chs. 1–6.

logical fervor he demonstrated in his first term had been all but extin-guished. Thus when Congress demanded the ouster of UN Secretary-General Boutros Boutros-Ghali of Egypt, Clinton willingly complied.[21] When Congress expressed doubts about the Chemical Weapons Convention, Clinton removed the treaty from the table until after the elections. And when Congress demanded a larger defense budget than was requested by the Joint Chiefs of Staff, along with deep cuts in foreign aid that greatly reduced the U.S. contribution to sustainable development, Clinton again conceded. Rarely in American history had a president so passively relinquished his control over American foreign policy.

As he prepared for his second term, Clinton was given an opportunity to overhaul his foreign policy team. Many of his top aides had tired of their roles in the first Clinton administration or were unable to overcome the internal scandals and morale problems that plagued their agencies. Thus a game of musical chairs ensued. Secretary of State Christopher, who retired, was replaced by Madeleine Albright, the former UN ambassador. Defense Secretary William Perry resigned from his post, which he had accepted only reluctantly after the resignation of Les Aspin. To succeed Perry, Clinton nominated former senator William S. Cohen, a Republican from Maine whose selection clearly was designed to appease congressional leaders. National Security Adviser Anthony Lake was chosen to replace John Deutch as head of the Central Intelligence Agency, and Lake was replaced by Samuel Berger, his former deputy.[22]

Albright became the first female secretary of state in American history, a factor Clinton said influenced, but did not determine, her nomination. More important, as a refugee from the former Czechoslovakia who had escaped the tyranny of both Adolf Hitler and Joseph Stalin, she personified the democratic values that had long shaped American foreign policy. "We have a responsibility in our time, as others have had in theirs, not to be prisoners of history, but to shape history," Albright declared in February 1997. Her assertive and articulate style contrasted sharply with that of Warren Christopher, who was thought to be more of a tactician than a visionary. Albright's promotion presaged a more active American role in world politics. But whether the United States could indeed escape the bonds of history—including its own spasmodic style of foreign policy—remained to be seen.

21. The United States, though alone in its campaign to prevent Boutros-Ghali from seeking a second five-year term as secretary general, exploited its veto power in the UN Security Council to kill the candidacy. To replace Boutros-Ghali, the United States championed the nomination of Kofi Annan, from Ghana, who was then elected by the world body.

22. Lake was opposed by leading Republicans and ultimately gave up his candidacy for the CIA post, which later was filled by George Tenet, the agency's former deputy director.

President Bill Clinton, surrounded by leaders from the world's richest nations, delivers the Denver Summit of the Eight's final communiqué, June 22, 1997.

CHAPTER THIRTEEN

America at the Millennium

The United States entered the twentieth century as a rising industrial power that remained, deliberately, outside the circles of great-power diplomacy. American leaders stood by as the Concert of Europe took shape in 1815, as the revolutions of 1848 swept across the continent, and as the European powers scrambled for African colonies in the 1890s. Given its considerable freedom to maneuver, the United States extended its sphere of influence throughout the Western Hemisphere and its territorial reach across the Pacific Ocean.

Although many saw this rapid expansion as proof of America's "manifest destiny," such progress would not have been possible without a widely recognized balance of power in Western Europe. This contributed to the century of relative calm that followed the Napoleonic Wars (1804–1815), which in turn permitted the United States to focus on its internal state-building efforts and continental expansion. The American dream of permanent isolation from great-power politics proved impossible, however, after Germany's challenge to the balance of power

provoked total war in Europe in 1914. The specter of German domination of Eurasia was rightly viewed as a clear and present danger to American security, and the nation's intervention in behalf of Great Britain
and France finally tipped the scales of that bloody stalemate. In the Second World War the United States was thrust into two distinct theaters of
combat—in Europe and the Pacific—where it fended off simultaneous
challenges from the fascist states of Germany, Italy, and Japan.

The onset of the Cold War coincided with the arrival of the United
States as a great power—not just in the midst of armed conflict but on
a permanent basis. The mid-twentieth century was a propitious time for
the United States to assume this role, given the nation's rapid industrial
expansion, proven military preponderance, and durable political system. Many observers believed that by withdrawing from great-power
politics after World War I, the United States unwittingly had contributed
to the fascist challenges in Europe and the Pacific. Another retreat was
thus unthinkable in the late 1940s, particularly at a time when Joseph
Stalin, the Soviet dictator whose reign of terror and mass murder
exceeded even that of Adolf Hitler, was casting the Soviet Union's long
shadow across Europe. An assertive American response, in the form of a
strategy to contain communism, was in this sense inevitable.

With the two world wars settled in their favor and with the United
States again secure after the Cold War, the American people are facing
the millennium with the same ambivalence about foreign affairs exhib-
ited by their early leaders. The 1990s have been fraught with bloody
regional conflicts, along with the old, unsettled rivalries that resurfaced
after the Soviet Union's collapse. As in the past, many Americans have
turned their energies inward, seeking to resolve domestic maladies and
to allow the convulsions of the "Old World" to work themselves out.
Others, however, have argued that the United States should exploit its
political, economic, and military clout as the "lone superpower" and
assume a leadership role in building a more harmonious and peaceful
world. In short, the new era has revived old controversies about America's role in the system of states—controversies that had been largely dormant while the country bowed to the imperatives of the Cold War.

All this could be considered a harmless, perhaps even an endearing
chapter of America's democratic "experiment" were the stakes not so
immense. The coming decade will likely witness changes of leadership in
Russia, Germany, and Japan, while a post–Deng Xiaoping regime takes
shape in China and a new Labour government, led by Tony Blair,
assumes control in Britain. Regional security arrangements in Western
Europe, the Middle East, and East Asia will be redefined and restruc-
tured. New democracies will be put to the test, along with the claim that
democratic states are by nature peaceful toward one another. Finally, the

United Nations will try to make sense of its global mission, both in peace-keeping and in sustainable development, and historic multilateral arms treaties—including the Chemical Weapons Convention, a ban on nuclear testing, and curbs on conventional arms transfers—will have to be implemented.

As America falls into the patterns of the past, its leaders must recognize that the current period is unique in one critical respect: never before has any single country possessed such immense power in the absence of a formidable adversary. This central fact makes the United States a central *component* of the international system. It no longer is a second-tier state that can take or leave the vagaries of world politics as it did before the world wars. Indeed, American preeminence carries with it an inescapable measure of responsibility.

History demonstrates how timidity by great powers only invites challenges to the status quo which eventually must be confronted at great cost. The rise of Germany in the early 1900s exploited the decline of three empires and the turmoil in revolutionary Russia. Germany's resurgence in the 1930s and Japan's regional conquests were abetted by the false promises of the League of Nations and the disarmament and declared neutrality of the United States. For his part, Stalin quickly seized upon the void in Eastern Europe after World War II, and his successors sought to extend Marxism-Leninism to developing countries recently freed from colonial rule. The lesson is clear that world politics, as nature itself, abhors a vacuum.

REALISM VERSUS MORALISM: THE CURRENT DEBATE

The turbulent international system of the post–Cold War era did not wait patiently for the United States to resolve its latest identity crisis. Upheavals in several regions shattered the widely anticipated "new world order" and forced American leaders to respond in the absence of an overriding redefinition of national purpose (see Chapters 11 and 12). Crises in the Persian Gulf, Balkan Peninsula, central Africa, the Pacific Rim, and Latin America drew varying and inconsistent U.S. responses. But the central question remained: What would be the role of the United States in the post–Cold War world? Anticommunism could no longer serve as a justification for intervention, nor could the bipolar division of power that had compelled the United States to react to nearly every Soviet provocation. Yet a foreign policy based on hemispheric isolation would not be viable in an era of economic integration and global interdependence. Thus, of the two general approaches that vied for supremacy in the 1990s, would realism or moralism prevail?

At one pole were the realists, whose outlook supplanted isolationism and prevailed during the Cold War. They envisioned a United States motivated by consistent and well-defined national interests, rooted in its need for self-preservation in a hostile system of nation-states. In the Cold War's wake, realism guided George Bush to repel Saddam Hussein's threat to the industrial world's vital oil supplies. This sense of realism led the same George Bush, despite his sense of personal horror at the bloodshed in the Balkans, to avoid U.S. involvement because no vital strategic or material interests were at stake.

Realism provides a clear set of orienting principles: the central role of power, the primacy of national interest, the pervasiveness of conflict, and the necessity for self-reliance. But whereas realists can agree on these principles, their prescriptions for American foreign policy often diverge. While most realists oppose the proliferation of weapons of mass destruction, threats to regional power balances, and the rise of another great power in Eurasia, they do not necessarily agree on which country, group, or situation presents a specific threat to American or broader Western interests, let alone on the means to cope with such threats. Thus there are, and always will be, significant differences in policy preferences among realists, who otherwise share certain philosophical views and a sense of prudence and caution about the American role in the world.[1]

The opposing view remains that of traditional moralism, which animated American foreign policy before the world wars and which fueled its sense of destiny. In this view, moral imperatives render American foreign policy distinct from the "power politics" of Old World diplomacy. Its advocates continue to equate the country's national values—individual liberty, religious tolerance, human rights—with universal values. Given America's considerable assets, they believe the United States is in a favorable position to project these values, not simply the country's military power, on the outside world. Such assumptions guided Bill Clinton's campaign of liberal internationalism in 1993 and 1994. They informed William Perry's strategy of "preventive defense," Anthony Lake's "enlargement" doctrine, and Madeleine Albright's concept of "assertive multilateralism." In practice, they led to interventions in Somalia and Haiti and to American support for the UN campaigns of sustainable development and international peace-keeping.[2]

THE CNN REVOLUTION AND FOREIGN POLICY

This moralistic impulse has been driven increasingly by the satellite images conveyed by news networks, many of which feature grisly pictures

1. For an elaboration of this view, see Barry R. Posen and Andrew L. Ross, "Competing Visions for U.S. Grand Strategy," *International Security* (winter 1996–1997): 5–53.
2. See Janne E. Nolan, ed., *Global Engagement* (Washington, D.C.: Brookings, 1995).

of famine, military carnage, and violations of human rights in foreign countries. These images often promote activism in cases that otherwise are only marginally relevant to American interests. During his tenure in the Oval Office, George Bush admitted that he was influenced by television's ability to bring pictures of human suffering and misery into American homes. Such pictures appeared after the victory over Iraq, when Saddam Hussein persecuted the Kurdish minority which had rebelled during the war and sought to secede from the country. The televised footage of more than a million Kurdish refugees, from the very young to the old, fleeing their homes with whatever they could carry and living in the mountains in the bitter winter cold, was wrenching to a global television audience. The subsequent moral outrage created public pressure to act, leading to an American-led relief effort and a declaration that the Kurd-held regions of northern Iraq were off-limits to Iraqi forces.

Televised images of the famine in Somalia also were instrumental in rallying an international response. But when some of the American soldiers sent to Somalia on a humanitarian mission were killed or injured—all before the TV cameras—public and congressional pressure to withdraw became intense. Clinton, in an about-face from his earlier enthusiasm for the UN peace-keeping mission, ordered a hasty retreat. Ironically, then, television brought the United States to Somalia, and television forced it out.

In some respects, this "CNN revolution" has served a vital purpose. Americans have been brought closer to the oppressive and often desperate conditions that exist beyond their shores and have become more sensitive to the roots and consequences of social upheaval. But recognition of human suffering—whether from dictatorial rule, natural disasters, or ethnic violence—does not in itself constitute a sufficient basis for American action. U.S. leaders also must determine the country's stakes in these problems and its capacity to solve them within acceptable political and economic limits. As George Kennan recently observed, "If American policy from here on out, particularly policy involving the use of our armed forces abroad, is to be controlled by popular emotional impulses, and especially ones provoked by the commercial television industry, then there is no place not only for myself, but for the responsible deliberative organs of our government."[3]

PUBLIC OPINION TURNED UPSIDE DOWN

The Balkan crisis raised the most difficult questions about what principles should guide America's post–Cold War foreign policy, especially

3. George Kennan, *At a Century's End: Reflections 1982–1995* (New York: Norton, 1996), 297.

its use of force. For George Bush, the criterion was whether vital inter-ests—that is, strategic or material assets valuable to the United States—were involved. Such interests were a factor in the Persian Gulf; they were not in Bosnia. The stakes in Bosnia were largely humanitarian, as they were in Somalia and Haiti. But in the latter two cases the initial assump-tion was that the United States could satisfy its moral urges at a relative-ly minor cost since UN forces from other countries would take over from the United States after a few months. In Bosnia, moral principles could not be so easily satisfied. The intervention might not be success-ful given the complexity of the conflict and the Balkan's inhospitable ter-rain. But even if it were, it probably would be very costly in lives, dollars, and presidential popularity.

There was a tremendous paradox and irony in this, for the very peo-ple who had opposed going to war against Saddam Hussein were by and large the same people who favored intervention in Bosnia. If only Bosnia had oil, some of them said. That was a very revealing comment since it suggested that the United States would have intervened had there been material interests at stake. For liberals advocating intervention in behalf of the Muslims, however, such intervention was essential precisely because material interests were *not* involved. Neither oil nor strategic position should sully America's cause. What did America stand for if not democracy and human rights?

Thus American foreign policy was turned upside down. After Viet-nam, many liberals rejected John Kennedy's pledge that the United States would "pay any price, bear any burden, meet any hardship, sup-port any friend, oppose any foe to assure the survival and the success of liberty." The war had turned many of them into foes of military inter-vention and pushed many others toward pacifism and isolationism. America's moral standing, in their view, had been irreparably damaged by that conflict. The post-Vietnam problem, then, was not how to con-tain Soviet expansion but how to restrain U.S. power. Most liberals therefore opposed every post-Vietnam use of force until Bush asked the U.S. Congress for authorization to go to war against Iraq—a resolution that passed the Senate by only three votes.

If fighting against Saddam Hussein was not a pure cause, fighting for the Muslims in Bosnia was—one of conscience, unadulterated by geopolitics or material interests. And in such desperate areas as Somalia and Haiti, where political disintegration had produced brutal violence and highly visible human suffering, American military preeminence could, for once, be put to appropriate use. Thus the post-Vietnam doves, overwhelmingly liberal and Democratic, plus a few moderate Republi-cans, transformed themselves into hawks. Humanitarian intervention, at least where it could be achieved successfully at limited cost, was to be the guide in these civil conflicts.

A foreign policy based on moralism has proven difficult to sustain, however. The anti-American backlash in Somalia, fears of "mission creep" in Bosnia, the remoteness of the Tutsi-Hutu rivalry in eastern Africa, and ongoing confrontations with the dictators of Iraq, North Korea, China, and Cuba contributed to the domestic assault on Bill Clinton's variant of liberal internationalism. Human rights and democratization may have been deemed the major concerns of American foreign policy, but the fact remains that not all foreign countries are of equal importance. Nor are all nations equally able to sustain democratic reforms and policies of export-led industrialization. American policy makers increasingly have given priority to maintaining and strengthening relations with the key industrial powers in Western Europe, the Western Hemisphere, and East Asia. In addition, they have sought to consolidate the democratic and market reforms in Eastern Europe and the former Soviet Union, regions where U.S. security interests are most directly involved.

If a government's inhumane treatment of its own people becomes the principal moral cause for U.S. intervention, where will American leaders draw the line? Why not intervene in other areas where ethnic conflicts and attendant cruelties have occurred since the Cold War— Armenia/Azerbaijan, Georgia, Tajikistan, the Sudan, Liberia, Zaire, Tibet, Sri Lanka, or a dozen other places? "Our planet will be filled with barbarism for a long time to come," said one distinguished historian, but "in many cases we must accept the sad necessity of living with tragedies that are beyond our power to control and our wisdom to cure. . . . We cannot right every wrong or reverse each adversity—and . . . there cannot be an American solution to every world problem."[4]

Developments in the 1990s have tested the assumptions of both realism and moralism. The rise of geoeconomics and the growing sense of interdependence do not square with many realist assumptions, while the practical difficulties of resolving deep-seated regional and global problems frustrate moralism. In the absence of an acceptable middle ground, the debates in Washington have grown more polarized and partisan, culminating in bitter political conflicts between Congress and the White House and the paralysis of America's foreign service.

CROSS PRESSURES IN WORLD POLITICS

As the debate over America's mission after the Cold War continues, forces at work in world politics are reshaping its context and the oppor-

---

4. Arthur Schlesinger Jr., "How to Think about Bosnia," *Wall Street Journal*, May 3, 1993.

tunities for American involvement. Some trends were visible long before the Cold War ended; indeed, they were extensions of long-term advances in technology and economic development. Other trends were more closely related to the collapse of the Soviet bloc, to the end of the bipolar balance of power, and to the revival of old antagonisms that had been suppressed by the superpowers. In general, two equal yet opposite forces are at work in world politics, integration and fragmentation— forces that have complicated efforts by the United States to define for itself a coherent foreign policy and world role in the 1990s.[5]

THE PUSH OF INTEGRATION

The long-term process of transnational integration is evident in many aspects of world politics today (see Chapter 12). This process reflects technological advances in communications and transportation along with a growing recognition of problems that cross state borders. In effect, the process of integration has encouraged closer international contact, the melding of the world economy into a single marketplace, a stronger role for nonstate actors, and a higher degree of order and stability within the international system.

New computer technologies and satellite network systems have played perhaps the most critical role in this process of integration. The World Wide Web has made huge amounts of information—from press sources, governments, corporations, and private groups—instantly available. And the Internet has made it possible for citizens in almost any country to communicate cheaply and rapidly with their counterparts overseas. When both aspects of the "information revolution" are taken into account, along with advances in telecommunications, the overall diffusion of information around the world is unprecedented.[6]

On the economic front, similar advances in technology have brought the world closer than ever to the creation of a single economic market, a trend that has well served Bill Clinton's foreign policy based on American economic growth. Multinational corporations have dispersed their research, production, distribution, and marketing operations, confirming "the coming irrelevance of corporate nationality."[7] At the same time, global currency markets have greatly expanded, leading to an estimated $1 trillion in daily exchanges of American dollars, Japanese yen, German marks, and other major currencies. Private investments across national

---

5. For an elaboration, see Benjamin Barber, *McWorld Versus Jihad* (New York: Times Books, 1995).

6. Significantly, the United States took the lead in the computer industry, accounting for three-fourths of the world market. See Daniel F. Burton Jr., "The Brave New Wired World," *Foreign Policy* (spring 1997).

7. Robert Reich, *The Work of Nations* (New York: Vintage, 1992), 136–153.

borders also have multiplied, particularly in developing countries and within the former Soviet bloc, where private flows greatly exceeded foreign aid by the mid-1990s.[8] The creation in 1995 of the World Trade Organization (WTO) provided a single standard for open markets that promised to accelerate the volume of global trade, which already had tripled to nearly $10 trillion in the two decades after 1977. Finally, the annual meetings of the Group of Seven (G-7), composed of the United States, Japan, Britain, Canada, France, Germany, and Italy, which together produce 70 percent of global wealth, have further testified to the interdependence of these countries and to their recognition that no longer does any single country fully control its economic destiny.[9]

The emergence of regional trading blocs may represent a potential threat to global economic cooperation, but the integration of Western Europe into a more cohesive European Union (EU) has brought its members closer together and given them the opportunity to resolve their long-standing *political* differences. In 1992 the twelve EU members ratified the Maastricht treaty, which was designed to move the European Union beyond economic integration, including a single monetary system and currency, toward the creation of a common foreign and security policy. In 1995 three other countries joined the European Union— Austria, Finland, and Sweden—and many others applied for membership. Although internal differences among EU members, and their poor showing in response to the Balkan crisis, raised serious doubts about the prospects for security cooperation, progress made in other areas of Europe's functional integration affirmed the optimistic expectations of early "Europhiles."

Other trading blocs, including the North American Free Trade Agreement (NAFTA) countries and the Asia Pacific Economic Cooperation (APEC) forum, have fewer political strings attached. But they do provide a vehicle for their members to address problems such as environmental decay, immigration, human rights, and the illegal trafficking of narcotics. For example, in May 1997 President Clinton and Mexican president Ernesto Zedillo announced a joint effort to combat the flow of illegal narcotics into the United States. (Mexico had emerged as a "drug superpower" in the early 1990s, and its government was rocked by a series of drug scandals that undermined its criminal justice system.) But it is doubtful that this accord, along with others addressing illegal immigration and additional issues related to the nineteen hundred-mile bor-

8. See the Organization for Economic Cooperation and Development, *Development Cooperation* (Paris: OECD, 1997), A1–A12.

9. The G-7 became the G-8 in 1997 after Russia was accepted as a member, partially as a reward for its acquiescence in the expansion of the North Atlantic Treaty Organization (NATO).

European Union members

Under review in 1997 for future membership

1. SLOVENIA
2. CROATIA
3. BOSNIA
4. SERBIA
5. MACEDONIA
6. ALBANIA

THE EUROPEAN UNION

der between the two countries, would have been reached in the absence of NAFTA.

And not to be overlooked, global integration has been propelled to a large extent by nonstate actors, at both the domestic and transnational levels. For example, the United Nations has assumed a higher profile in confronting global problems such as environmental deterioration and population growth.

THE PULL OF FRAGMENTATION

Greater integration, however, has been accompanied by fragmentation of the international system in many important ways since the Cold War's collapse, a trend that has cast a dark shadow over the emerging international system. Bipolarity was, in a sense, relatively stable because of its very simplicity; it was a system of challenge and response that virtually maintained itself. Watching each other constantly, the superpowers maintained the balance, always aware of the danger of nuclear war and its suicidal potential. As a result, there was no third world war; indeed, after the 1962 Cuban missile crisis there were no comparable crises between the superpowers. And despite tensions, Europe experienced the longest period of peace in this century and one of the longest periods of stability in modern times. The wars that were fought occurred in the developing world, but they never escalated into global conflict.

The breakdown of bipolarity in the early 1990s produced a considerably less peaceful world than was expected in the euphoria attending the Cold War's conclusion. This systemic shift wrought instability in three distinct ways. First, the retreat of the Soviet empire from Eastern Europe revived the nationalist, ethnic, and religious tensions that had accompanied the breakup of the Austro-Hungarian, Russian, and Ottoman (Turkish) empires after World War I and kept Eastern Europe in turmoil throughout the interwar period. The breakup of the Soviet Union into fifteen republics then produced tensions between Russia and Ukraine, open warfare between Armenia and Azerbaijan, the attempted secession and crackdown in Chechnya, civil war in Tajikistan, and the prospect of renewed Russian imperialism across the old Soviet frontiers.

A second consequence was the clear field left for aspirants to regional hegemony to pursue their aggressive designs. It was no longer the case that each superpower, dominant in its own sphere, could restrain its respective clients and prevent local conflicts. Middle powers were now free to act; expansionist rulers were encouraged to fill the power vacuums left by the superpowers. As noted earlier, it is doubtful that Iraq's Saddam Hussein would have invaded Kuwait had the Soviet Union still been a key regional player concerned about avoiding a confrontation with the United States. Similarly, the resurgence of ethnic warfare in Africa coincided with the withdrawal of the great powers.

Finally, the end of the Cold War strongly affected the cohesion of American alliances across the Atlantic and Pacific. Organized to counter the power of the Soviet Union and China, these alliances gave priority to common interests in collective security. With the Cold War over, the raison d'être of NATO became uncertain; at the same time other security arrangements were being created in Europe. The fears of American leaders that NATO would be rendered obsolete explained much of their enthusiasm for its eastward expansion. Meanwhile, in the Pacific the web of multilateral alliances created by the United States had long ceased to exist in any meaningful sense, and the durability of its bilateral ties to nations in East Asia was thrown into question. Although the United States reaffirmed its regional presence by extending its security pact with Japan in April 1996, it is doubtful the emerging "tigers" of the Pacific Rim will indefinitely accept their status as de facto protectorates of the United States.

A RETURN TO FIRST PRINCIPLES

The pattern of global fragmentation just described reveals basic *continuities* in world politics that must not be lost on American leaders. The international system created 350 years ago at Westphalia still provides the essential framework for global political order, and sovereign states remain the system's primary actors. As in the past, their survival ultimately depends on their power resources and diplomatic leverage, not on the canons of international law or universally accepted codes of conduct. To a large extent, the running room for international organizations such as the United Nations and European Union is determined by their most powerful member states, which grant these organizations greater authority only when their own interests are served in the bargain. It must be recalled that the most important international agreements of the post–World War II period—the Treaty of Rome, the SALT and START accords, the Arab-Israeli breakthroughs—were propelled by state leaders, not by international organizations. And the two primary examples of UN "peace-making"—Korea in 1950 and Iraq in 1991—were essentially American operations. In the absence of shared interests among the great powers and international organizations, collective action is not possible.

Amid all the changes in the post–Cold War period, therefore, the essential features of world politics remain intact. While communism has collapsed in the former Soviet Union and has been severely truncated in China, tensions between these major powers and the United States

remain strong, a fact that should give pause to those who believe the
Cold War was primarily an ideological struggle. Ideology may have
informed leaders' perceptions of the Cold War world and defined many
of their long-term goals, but basic conflicts of interest were present as
well. These conflicts, rooted in the structural anarchy of the nation-state
system and the prevailing distribution of power, are not likely to abate
no matter how close we come to the "end of history."

Even in the absence of a threat by another great power, the post–Cold
War world already has affirmed the truth of this proposition: American
military power, whether used (as against Iraq in 1991), threatened (as
against Haiti in 1993, North Korea in 1994, and China in the Taiwan
Straits in 1996), or withheld (as in Bosnia until 1995), is the most crucial
single factor determining the outcome of regional crises today. Similarly, the global economy cannot prosper without the market the United
States provides for the world's industrial and developing nations; the
many technological, industrial, and agricultural products it exports; and
the capital it expends abroad either as foreign investments or development aid. Finally, the United States has lent immeasurable prestige to the
ideals of political freedom, representative government, and constitu-
tionalism—ideals that are now embraced in principle, if not consistently in practice, by an unprecedented number of governments.

It is not enough for any country simply to amass such a considerable
degree of international influence. How such a country *exercises* that
influence—toward greater security and the betterment of its citizens, as
well as those beyond its shores—is the true test of leadership. In this
respect, the United States is uniquely capable of shaping the political,
economic, and social currents of the world. On a more basic level, it can
seek to maintain a degree of stability in the turbulent international system. "Political order is not sufficient to explain economic prosperity, but
it is necessary," observed Joseph S. Nye Jr., a political scientist and assis-
tant secretary of defense in the Clinton administration. "Analysts who
ignore the importance of this political order are like people who forget
the importance of the oxygen they breath. Security is like oxygen—you
tend not to notice it until you begin to lose it, but once that occurs there
is nothing else that you think about."[10]

In bringing the nation's preponderance to bear on the turbulent
world of the late 1990s, however, American leaders must proceed selectively; the United States can neither hide from its global responsibilities
nor seek to resolve every regional crisis that erupts overseas. Only if a
proper balance is struck between these two extremes, and only if the

10. Joseph S. Nye Jr., "The Case for Deep Engagement," *Foreign Affairs* (July–August
1995): 91.

ends and means of its foreign policy are reconciled in practice can America exploit its unrivaled strength, preserve its integrity, and affirm its historic ambitions.

America's success will depend largely on the ability of American leaders to overcome the nation's schizophrenic national style of the past, which has veered between estrangement from the outside world and a penchant for global crusading. Neither course is available to the United States today. As we have seen, the inability of American leaders to agree on a coherent world role after the Cold War invited the political deadlock between the White House and Congress while raising doubts from overseas about the intentions of the United States. If these conditions persist, America will likely continue to lead by improvisation and allow regional crises to dictate its agenda. Such an outcome would be far from optimal, but it would be entirely consistent with the American style of foreign policy.

U.S. Administrations since World War II

Dates	President	Secretary of State	Secretary of Defense	National Security Adviser
1945–1953	Harry Truman	Edward Stettinius James Byrnes George Marshall Dean Acheson	James Forrestal Louis Johnson Robert Lovett George Marshall	
1953–1961	Dwight Eisenhower	John Dulles Christian Herter	Charles Wilson Neil McElroy Thomas Gates	
1961–1963	John Kennedy	Dean Rusk	Robert McNamara	McGeorge Bundy
1963–1969	Lyndon Johnson	Dean Rusk	Robert McNamara Clark Clifford	McGeorge Bundy W. W. Rostow
1969–1974	Richard Nixon	William Rogers Henry Kissinger	Melvin Laird Elliot Richardson James Schlesinger	Henry Kissinger
1974–1977	Gerald Ford	Henry Kissinger	James Schlesinger Donald Rumsfeld	Henry Kissinger Brent Scowcroft
1977–1981	Jimmy Carter	Cyrus Vance Edmund Muskie	Harold Brown	Zbigniew Brzezinski
1981–1989	Ronald Reagan	Alexander Haig George Shultz	Caspar Weinberger Frank Carlucci	Richard Allen William Clark Robert McFarlane John Poindexter Frank Carlucci Colin Powell
1989–1993	George Bush	James Baker Lawrence Eagleburger	Richard Cheney	Brent Scowcroft
1993–	Bill Clinton	Warren Christopher Madeleine Albright	Les Aspin William Perry William Cohen	Anthony Lake Samuel Berger

Chronology of Significant Events

1945   Yalta Conference seeks to organize postwar world.

World War II with Germany ends.

World War II with Japan ends after two atomic bombs are dropped.

President Franklin Roosevelt dies, and Vice President Harry Truman succeeds him.

United Nations is established.

Soviet military forces occupy Poland, Romania, Bulgaria, Hungary, and Czechoslovakia.

1946   United States confronts the Soviet Union over Iran, and Moscow withdraws its troops.

Winston Churchill, Britain's wartime prime minister, delivers "iron curtain" speech at Fulton, Missouri, warning of Soviet threat.

1947   Truman Doctrine commits the United States to assist Greece and Turkey.

Plan for the economic recovery of Western Europe is devised by Secretary of State George Marshall, formerly U.S. chief of staff and architect of victory during World War II.

George Kennan, a Foreign Service officer, provides the government with the analysis that becomes the basis of the containment policy of Soviet Russia.

India becomes independent.

1948   Soviet coup d'état takes place in Czechoslovakia.

Soviets blockade all ground traffic from West Germany to West Berlin and the Western airlift starts.

Vandenberg resolution of U.S. Senate commits American support for the Brussels Pact of self-defense.

Marshall Plan is passed by Congress.

North and South Korea are established.

The state of Israel is established and receives immediate U.S. recognition.

Truman wins upset election.

Stalin expels Yugoslavia's Tito from communist bloc.

1949   North Atlantic Treaty Organization (NATO) is formed.

Soviet Union ends Berlin blockade.

East and West Germany are established.

Soviet Union explodes atomic bomb.

Nationalist China collapses and People's Republic of China (PRC) is established.

U.S. troops are withdrawn from South Korea.

Truman announces Point Four foreign aid program for developing countries.

1950   Soviet Union and communist China sign thirty-year treaty of mutual assistance.

North Korea attacks South Korea by crossing the thirty-eighth parallel.

United States intervenes in behalf of South Korea.

Communist China intervenes after U.S. forces advance into North Korea toward China's frontier.

Sen. Joseph McCarthy begins his attacks on government for treason and "coddling communism."

1951   Gen. Dwight Eisenhower is appointed Supreme Allied Commander in Europe
        and Truman sends U.S. forces to Europe.
        U.S.-Japanese mutual security pact is signed.
        Truman fires Gen. Douglas MacArthur in Korea for proposing that the United
        States attack communist China.
        European Coal and Steel Community (ECSC) is formed.

1952   Eisenhower is elected president.
        Greece and Turkey join NATO.
        Britain tests its first atomic weapon.

1953   Joseph Stalin dies.
        Armistice negotiated along thirty-eighth parallel in Korea.
        Soviet Union intervenes in East Germany to quell revolt.

1954   United States explodes first hydrogen bomb.
        France is defeated at Dienbienphu in Indochina.
        United States threatens to intervene in Indochina.
        Vietnam is partitioned at the seventeenth parallel at the Geneva Conference.
        Southeast Asia Treaty Organization (SEATO) is formed.
        U.S.-Korean pact is signed to prevent a renewal of the war.
        U.S.-Nationalist China defense treaty is signed.
        Central Intelligence Agency overthrows Guatemala's left-wing government.

1955   Communist China shells the Nationalist Chinese (Taiwanese) islands of Que-
        moy and Matsu.
        Formosa resolution authorizes Eisenhower to use force, if necessary, to protect
        Taiwan against a possible communist Chinese invasion.
        Middle East Treaty Organization (Baghdad Pact) is formed.
        West Germany joins NATO, and Soviets establish "their NATO," called the War-
        saw Treaty Organization.

1956   United States withdraws offer to help finance Egypt's Aswan High Dam.
        Egypt nationalizes the Suez Canal.
        Suez War breaks out after Israel attacks Egypt, and France and Britain intervene.
        UN forces are sent to Egypt to keep the peace between Israel and Egypt.
        Soviets suppress Hungarian revolt and almost intervene in Poland.
        Soviet leader Nikita Khrushchev attacks Stalin at twentieth Communist Party
        Congress.

1957   Soviet Union tests intercontinental ballistic missile (ICBM).
        Soviets launch two *Sputniks*, or satellites, into space.
        British test hydrogen bomb.
        Eisenhower Doctrine commits the United States to assist Middle East countries
        that resist communist aggression or states closely tied to the Soviet Union,
        such as Egypt.

1958   United States lands marines in Lebanon, and Britain lands paratroopers in Jor-
        dan after Iraqi revolution.
        Soviet Union declares it would end the four-power occupation of Berlin and
        turn West Berlin into a "free city."
        European Economic Community (Common Market) is established.
        First of several Berlin crises erupts.
        Communist China shells Quemoy and Matsu again.

1959   Khrushchev visits Eisenhower for Camp David meeting over Berlin issue.

Fidel Castro seizes power in Cuba.

Central Treaty Organization (CENTO) replaces the Baghdad Pact.

1960   Soviets shoot down U.S. U-2 spy plane over the Soviet Union.

Paris summit conference collapses over U-2 incident.

The Congo becomes independent from Belgium, causing the first superpower crisis in sub-Saharan Africa.

UN forces sent to the Congo to help resolve the crisis.

France becomes an atomic power.

John Kennedy wins presidential election.

1961   Kennedy launches abortive Bay of Pigs invasion of Cuba.

Kennedy proposes Alliance for Progress for Latin America.

Soviets send Yuri Gagarin into orbital spaceflight.

Kennedy holds summit conference with Khrushchev in Vienna.

Kennedy sends first military advisers to South Vietnam.

Soviets build Berlin Wall.

1962   U.S. sends John Glenn into orbital spaceflight.

In Cuban missile crisis, the United States blockades Cuba to compel the Soviets to withdraw their missiles.

Chinese-Indian frontier conflict erupts.

1963   French president Charles de Gaulle vetoes Britain's entry into the Common Market.

"Hot line" established between the White House and the Kremlin for direct emergency communications.

Atomic test-ban treaty is signed.

President Kennedy is assassinated, and Vice President Lyndon Johnson succeeds him.

1964   Congress passes Gulf of Tonkin resolution, raising the U.S. commitment to the defense of South Vietnam.

Khrushchev falls from power and is replaced by Prime Minister Aleksei Kosygin and Communist Party Secretary Leonid Brezhnev.

1965   United States starts bombing North Vietnam and sends American land forces into South Vietnam.

Protests against the war start.

United States intervenes in the Dominican Republic.

War erupts between Pakistan and India.

1966   People's Republic of China becomes a nuclear power.

France withdraws its forces from NATO's integrated command structure but remains a member of the alliance.

1967   Six-day War between Israel and its Arab neighbors takes place.

Greek colonels seize power in Greece.

1968   Tet offensive in South Vietnam escalates demand for U.S. withdrawal from Vietnam.

Johnson withdraws from presidential race.

Richard Nixon elected president.

Vietnamese peace talks begin in Paris.

Nuclear Non-Proliferation Treaty is made.

Soviet Union intervenes in Czechoslovakia to quell revolt.

1969   Brezhnev Doctrine is proclaimed, asserting the right of Soviet Union to intervene in Soviet sphere to suppress "counterrevolution."

Antiballistic Missile (ABM) deployment is narrowly approved by Senate.

United States tests multiple independently targeted reentry vehicle (MIRV).

Negotiations on Strategic Arms Limitation Treaty (SALT) begin.

"Vietnamization" program starts. South Vietnamese are to do more of the fighting while the United States begins troop withdrawal.

Ho Chi Minh dies.

United States lands men on moon.

Lt. William Calley, Jr., stands trial for My Lai massacre of civilians in South Vietnam by U.S. troops.

First of several Sino-Soviet border clashes occurs.

1970   West Germany, East Germany, the Soviet Union, and Poland conclude treaties recognizing Poland's western border and acknowledging Germany's division into East and West Germany.

Senate repeals Gulf of Tonkin resolution.

U.S. invasion of Cambodia causes widespread student protests, which escalate after National Guard kills four students at Kent State University.

Chile elects a Marxist, Salvador Allende, president.

1971   India and Pakistan go to war over the Bangladesh (East Pakistan) secession effort.

People's Republic of China joins the United Nations.

Four-power Berlin settlement is reached, ensuring Western access to Berlin.

1972   Nixon visits communist China, beginning a process of normalizing relations after two decades of hostility.

North Vietnam invades South Vietnam.

Nixon retaliates by expanding air war against North Vietnam and blockading the harbor of Haiphong.

Nixon visits Moscow for summit conference with Soviet leaders; signs SALT I and ABM treaty.

Watergate affair starts when police arrest five men who had broken into Democratic Party headquarters.

Soviets buy enormous quantities of U.S. grains, raising domestic prices in the United States.

Paris peace talks, close to success, break down, and the United States bombs North Vietnam heavily during Christmas season.

Nixon reelected president in a landslide that carried every state but Massachusetts.

1973   Henry Kissinger is appointed secretary of state while remaining the president's national security adviser.

Vietnamese peace agreement is signed.

United States and China establish liaison offices, or informal embassies, in Washington and Beijing.

Yom Kippur War breaks out in Middle East.

Arab members of the Organization of Petroleum Exporting Countries (OPEC) embargo oil to the United States because of U.S. support for Israel.

Britain, Denmark, and Republic of Ireland join Common Market, increasing
membership to nine countries.

OPEC quadruples oil prices.

U.S.-Soviet Mutual and Balanced Force Reductions talks in Europe start.

West and East Germany exchange recognition and ambassadors, acknowledging
Germany's division into two countries.

Congress passes the War Powers Resolution over Nixon's veto.

Vice President Spiro Agnew resigns and Gerald Ford succeeds him.

Allende is overthrown by military in Chile.

1974 India explodes "peaceful" nuclear device.

Congress asserts right to veto large arms sales to other nations.

Annual Nixon-Brezhnev summit conference further reduces small numbers of
ABMs the United States and Soviet Union are allowed by SALT I.

Kissinger negotiates first agreements between Israel and Egypt and Syria as part
of his "step-by-step" diplomacy intended to achieve a comprehensive regional peace.

Nixon visits Egypt, Syria, and Israel.

Nixon resigns and Ford becomes unelected president; New York governor Nel-
son Rockefeller becomes vice president.

Ford and Brezhnev set Vladivostok guidelines for SALT II negotiations.

1975 Soviet Union rejects American-Soviet trade agreement because of the Jackson-
Vanik amendment.

South Vietnam collapses and a unified communist Vietnam is established.

Cambodia falls to Cambodian communists.

Cambodians seize U.S. merchant ship *Mayaguez,* and the United States reacts
forcefully to free crew and ship.

SEATO dissolves itself.

Helsinki agreements, including Western recognition of Europe's division (and
Soviet domination in Eastern Europe), arrived at by Western and Eastern
states.

Congress passes arms embargo against Turkey.

Lebanese civil war erupts.

Francisco Franco dies and King Juan Carlos starts to lead Spain to democracy.

In Angola three major factions struggle for control as Portugal grants independence.

1976 Soviet-Cuban forces in Angola win victory for Marxist-led faction over pro-
Western factions.

Syrian forces intervene in Lebanon.

Mao Zedong dies.

Jimmy Carter elected president.

1977 Carter announces U.S. withdrawal from South Korea (to be reversed later).

Carter sends letter to leading Soviet dissident, and another dissident visits the
White House.

Soviets denounce Carter's human rights campaign as violation of Soviet sovereignty.

Carter submits new SALT II plan to Soviet Union, which quickly rejects it
because it is not based on Vladivostok guidelines.

Carter halts plans to produce B-1 bomber and instead chooses to deploy air-
launched cruise missiles on B-52 bombers.

United States and Panama sign Panama Canal treaties.

Somalia expels Soviet advisers and denounces friendship treaty with Soviet Union.

Soviet-Cuban military help for Ethiopia grows.

Menachem Begin is elected prime minister in Israel.

Egyptian president Anwar Sadat pays historic visit to Israel, offering peace and friendship. Other Arab states denounce him.

1978 Soviet-Cuban military intervention in Ethiopia's war against Somalia forces latter out of Ogaden.

Soviet-inspired coup occurs in Afghanistan.

Camp David meeting of the United States, Israel, and Egypt arrives at "framework for peace" between two former enemies. Other Arab states denounce framework because it did not provide for a Palestine solution.

Senate approves sale of jet fighters to Israel, Egypt, and Saudi Arabia.

Panama Canal treaties approved by Senate.

Carter postpones neutron bomb (tactical warhead) production.

United States ends arms embargo on Turkey.

Rhodesian prime minister Ian Smith announces "internal solution" to the race problem—the formation of a black-led government.

1979 Shah Mohammad Reza Pahlavi leaves Iran.

United States officially recognizes the People's Republic of China. United States suspends formal relations with Taiwan government and ends mutual defense treaty.

China invades Vietnam to punish it for the invasion of Cambodia.

Shah's regime in Iran replaced by Islamic republic led by Ayatollah Ruhollah Khomeini.

U.S. embassy in Tehran seized and employees held hostage by militant Islamic students after shah is hospitalized in United States for cancer treatment.

United States freezes Iran's financial assets in United States and boycotts Iranian oil.

Oil prices shoot upward as Iranian oil production drops and world supplies tighten.

SALT II treaty signed by Brezhnev and Carter at Vienna summit conference.

Soviets send 80,000 troops into Afghanistan to ensure survival of pro-Soviet regime.

NATO decides to deploy 572 theater nuclear weapons to counter Soviet "Eurostrategic" missile buildup.

1980 U.S. mission to rescue hostages in Tehran ends in disaster before it reaches embassy.

SALT II "temporarily" withdrawn from Senate by Carter after Soviet invasion of Afghanistan.

Carter embargoes shipments of feed grain and high technology to Soviet Union and declares United States will boycott summer Olympic games in Moscow.

Carter Doctrine commits United States to security of Persian Gulf oil-producing states if they are externally threatened.

United States organizes rapid deployment force to back up the Carter Doctrine.

Iraq attacks Iran.

Ronald Reagan elected president.

1981 U.S. hostages released moments after Reagan assumes presidency.

Reagan declares United States will not allow Saudi Arabia to become "another Iran."

Begin reelected in Israel.

Sadat assassinated in Egypt.

Reagan decides on large program to rebuild U.S. military power, including 100 MX missiles and 100 B-1 bombers.

Polish government imposes martial law.

United States imposes economic sanctions on Poland and on Soviet Union, believed to be behind Polish crackdown.

1982   Reagan announces economic assistance plan for Caribbean Basin (the Caribbean and Central America) as he supports El Salvador's government against rebel forces and attempts to isolate the Sandinistas in Nicaragua despite congressional criticism.

Israel invades Lebanon, attempting to destroy the Palestine Liberation Organization (PLO).

U.S. marines are sent into Beirut as part of a multinational peacekeeping force to supervise the PLO's leaving.

China and the United States sign agreement on the reduction of U.S. arms sales to Taiwan.

Brezhnev dies and is succeeded by Yuri Andropov, former head of the Soviet secret police.

Argentina invades the British Falkland Islands, long claimed by Argentina. Britain reconquers the islands.

United States imposes—and later lifts—sanctions on U.S. and European companies selling equipment to the Soviets for building of a natural gas pipeline to Western Europe.

Secretary of State Alexander Haig resigns.

1983   Reagan denounces the Soviet Union as an "evil empire."

Bipartisan Scowcroft Commission recommends deployment of 100 MX missiles and eventual replacement of missiles equipped with MIRVs with mobile, smaller missiles with single warheads. Congress accepts these recommendations.

Catholic bishops in pastoral letter deplore nuclear deterrence for its immorality. French bishops endorse deterrence as "service to peace."

Two hundred forty-one marines killed in suicide truck-bomb attack on their barracks in Beirut.

Soviet Union shoots down Korean 747 jetliner with 269 passengers aboard after it strays into Soviet airspace.

U.S. forces, together with troops from six Caribbean states, invade the island of Grenada. They depose the Marxist government, return Cuban worker-soldiers to Cuba, and withdraw.

United States begins deployment of Pershing II and ground-launched cruise missiles in Europe. Soviet Union responds by breaking off all arms control talks.

1984   Bipartisan Kissinger Commission recommends extensive economic and military assistance to Central America to combat domestic poverty and Soviet-Cuban intervention. Congress critical of administration policy.

Andropov dies and Brezhnev's confidant, Konstantin Chernenko, succeeds him.

Reagan is reelected.

United States pulls marines out of Lebanon.

Napoléon Duarte wins Salvadoran presidency, defeating right-wing candidate.

Congress cuts off all military assistance to the contras in Nicaragua.

Latin American debtor countries meet at Cartagena to discuss the debt problem and repayment.

United States declares Iran a supporter of international terrorism.

1985   Chernenko dies and is succeeded by Mikhail Gorbachev.

Africa, especially Ethiopia, which is engaged in a civil war, suffers from widespread starvation.

Christian Democratic Party, led by Duarte, wins majority in Salvadoran National Assembly.

Various terrorist groups hijack a TWA plane flying from Athens to Rome, seize an Italian cruise ship, and attack Israel's El Al passengers at the Vienna and Rome airports.

Reagan orders limited economic sanctions against South Africa; Congress imposes harsher sanctions in 1986.

Reagan and Gorbachev hold their first summit conference in Geneva, Switzerland.

1986   Ferdinand Marcos in the Philippines and Jean-Claude Duvalier in Haiti are forced to flee their respective countries, and the Reagan administration proclaims its new human rights policy, opposing dictatorships of the left and right.

Congress approves $100 million for the Nicaraguan contras.

The United States attacks Libya for terrorist acts. Syria is shown to be involved in terrorism, and Britain breaks diplomatic relations with Syria after abortive attempt to blow up Israeli airliner.

World's worst nuclear accident takes place at Chernobyl in the Ukraine. Sweden breaks news of radioactivity coming from the Soviet Union.

Reagan and Gorbachev meet in Iceland, and Reagan refuses to trade limitations in Strategic Defense Initiative (SDI) research for deep cuts of Soviet strategic missiles and a mutual elimination of all intermediate-range missiles in Europe.

United States exceeds SALT II limits and declares that the unratified 1979 treaty is no longer "operational."

Iran-contra scandal breaks.

OPEC's oil price falls to $9–$10 a barrel, but then stabilizes at $18 a barrel.

Spain and Portugal join the European Economic Community.

U.S. dollar is allowed to drop substantially against Japanese yen and West German mark to improve U.S. exports and reduce huge trade deficit, but action proves ineffective.

1987   Congressional hearings into Iran-contra scandal raise doubts about Reagan's effectiveness for the remainder of his term.

The United States and the Soviet Union agree to a worldwide ban on short- and intermediate-range missiles, the so-called double zero option, ending years of tension over Soviet SS-20 missile deployment.

The United States reflags Kuwaiti oil tankers in the Persian Gulf and escorts them with U.S. warships to protect them from possible Iranian attacks.

Five Central American presidents devise a plan for peace in their area. The contras and Sandinistas are to negotiate an end to the civil war, and the Sandinista government commits itself to hold general election by spring 1990.

Palestinians in December begin the *intifada*, or uprising, protesting both the continued Israeli occupation of the West Bank and opposition to a Palestinian state, and, more indirectly, the PLO failure to seek a diplomatic solution.

Gorbachev at the seventieth anniversary celebration of Bolshevik Revolution denounces Stalin's historical legacy and defends his program of *perestroika*.

1988   George Bush elected president.

Gorbachev, at first national party conference since 1941, proposes to restructure Soviet government with strong presidency, selected by a more popularly responsive Supreme Soviet.

U.S. Navy shoots down Iranian commercial jetliner with 290 people aboard over Persian Gulf.

Iran and Iraq agree to a cease-fire in their eight-year-long war.

Panama's strongman, Gen. Manuel Noriega, is indicted for drug running by two Florida grand juries.

The right-wing Arena Party wins majority in Salvadoran Legislative Assembly.

PLO and Yasir Arafat declare the right of all states in the region to live in peace with secure boundaries; proclaim a Palestinian state in the West Bank and the Gaza Strip; recognize Israel; and reject terrorism.

The Soviet Baltic republics assert their desire for autonomy, if not independence; ethnic clashes in the southern Soviet Union between Azerbaijanis and Armenians lead to increasing violence.

Gorbachev makes dramatic announcement at UN of unilateral military reductions, including sizable cuts in troop levels and tanks (50,000 and 1,000 respectively), and other offensive weapons of the forces facing NATO.

1989   Gorbachev elected president of the Soviet Union, an alternative base of power to the Communist Party.

Free elections in Poland result in repudiation of the Polish Communist Party. Solidarity forms first noncommunist government in Eastern Europe.

Hungary allows emigration to the West. Mass demonstrations in East Germany protest regime celebrating its fortieth year; cabinet resigns. Hard-line Communist Party leaders are replaced.

Czechoslovakia and Bulgaria follow the reformist path of Poland, Hungary, and East Germany. Only in Romania does government resist and use force, but its leader, Nicolae Ceausescu, is nevertheless overthrown and executed.

Soviet Union withdraws its troops from Afghanistan.

Gorbachev in neutral Finland states that the Soviet Union has no moral or political right to interfere in the affairs of its neighbors. Statement effectively repudiates Brezhnev Doctrine.

The Ayatollah Khomeini dies in Iran.

Huge pro-democracy demonstrations in Beijing are violently suppressed by the communist leadership.

Berlin Wall is opened, beginning process of German reunification.

Panamanian general Noriega voids result of national election. Coup led by Panamanian officers fails. Noriega declares Panama to be in a state of war with the United States, which then invades Panama, overthrows Noriega, and brings him to the United States for trial.

Cuban troops begin withdrawal from Angola based on multilateral agreement under which Namibia achieves its independence.

1990   Lithuanian Communist Party breaks from the Soviet party and speaks for independent Lithuania.

Armenians and Azerbaijanis continue feud while local Communist Party loses control to the Azerbaijani popular front. Gorbachev sends in the Soviet army to restore order and keep the party in power.

Gorbachev, in a revolutionary statement to a plenum of the Communist Party, renounces the constitutionally guaranteed communist monopoly of power and declares his support for an eventual multiparty system as well as private enterprise.

Eastern European free elections in the spring produce noncommunist governments, except in Romania and Bulgaria, where the communists, under a new name, win by large majorities.

Iraqi troops invade neighboring Kuwait, provoking condemnation and economic sanctions by the United Nations.

After East German election in March, East and West Germany begin negotiating reunification. On July 1 they create a financial and economic union. Two weeks later Gorbachev agrees that a reunited Germany can choose to join NATO. On October 3 the two Germanies unify. In November the Conference on Security and Cooperation in Europe endorses Germany's unity. On December 2 elections in both Germanies produce the first postwar all-German parliament.

Soviet Union's two largest republics, Russia and the Ukraine, declare their sovereignty and assert that their laws are superior to those of the Soviet Union. Other republics follow.

Nicaraguan government agrees to free election and loses to rival coalition. The contras disband.

1991   All-German parliament and government are sworn in.

Iraq, refusing to withdraw from Kuwait, is forced out in forty-three days by the U.S.-led UN coalition.

United States and Soviet Union sign a Strategic Arms Reduction Talks (START) agreement, reducing strategic weapons by 30 percent.

Warsaw Treaty Organization formally dissolved. Soviet troops leave Hungary and Czechoslovakia.

Boris Yeltsin, Gorbachev's rival, becomes the first elected leader of the thousand-year-old Russian republic.

Coup against Gorbachev is launched by political opponents. Yeltsin defies the coup attempt and it fails. Gorbachev survives, but his authority declines further as Yeltsin establishes his primacy versus Soviet leaders.

Estonia, Latvia, and Lithuania are granted independence. After efforts to establish a confederation founder, Russia, Belarus, and Ukraine declare the Soviet Union dead and form the Commonwealth of Independent States. Other republics are invited to join.

European Free Trade Association, consisting of Austria, Switzerland, Sweden, Finland, Liechtenstein (neutrals during the Cold War), and Norway and Iceland (NATO members), establishes a common free trade area with the European Community (EC).

Soviet Union dissolves. Gorbachev resigns and cedes Kremlin to Yeltsin.

Slovenia and Croatia secede from Yugoslavia. Serb-dominated Yugoslav army resists secessions by force.

1992   Government of El Salvador reaches accord with Farabundo Marti Liberation Front (FMLN), ending decade of civil war.

U.S. government begins forcible repatriation of Haitian refugees. Establishment of joint military force for Commonwealth of Independent States.

UN peace-keeping troops intervene in Balkans. Voters in Bosnia-Herzegovina approve independence by referendum. European Community and United States recognize Bosnia-Herzegovina along with independent Croatia and

Slovenia. United Nations offers membership to all three countries; Yugoslavia expelled by General Assembly.

Nineteen European states approve European Economic Area (EEA) to create flee-trade zone beyond the borders of the EC.

U.S. Senate and Russian Supreme Soviet ratify START agreement.

France and Germany create 35,000-member joint defense force to serve as nucleus of regional security system for Western European Union.

U.S. and German governments announce G-7 plan to provide Russia with $24 billion in economic assistance upon Russia's entry into the International Monetary Fund.

NATO announces final removal of all ground-based tactical nuclear weapons from Europe.

Asia-Pacific Economic Cooperation (APEC) group announces program of liberalized and expanded trade within region.

Philippine government gains control of Subic Bay Naval Base from United States, ending century of American presence in country.

Bill Clinton elected president on platform of domestic reform.

1993 European Community initiates single market.

United States and Russia approve new START treaty calling for deeper cuts in strategic arsenals; they also sign military cooperation agreement providing for joint exercises and greater consultation in crises.

Terrorist bomb damages World Trade Center, killing six people and forcing the evacuation of 50,000.

North Korean government announces withdrawal from Nuclear Non-Proliferation Treaty (NPT).

United States pledges to accelerate efforts to restore deposed Haitian leader Jean-Bertrand Aristide to power. UN Security Council imposes economic sanctions against military regime.

United States endorses Vance-Owen plan to partition the former Yugoslavia along ethnic lines. United States airdrops relief supplies to besieged Bosnian Muslims. United Nations declares Sarajevo and other cities in Bosnia-Herzegovina to be "safe areas."

Twelve American soldiers are killed in Mogadishu, Somalia. Clinton orders reinforcements and sets timetable for U.S. withdrawal from Somalia.

Israel and Palestinian Liberation Organization sign peace treaty.

U.S. Congress ratifies North American Free Trade Agreement (NAFTA).

South African government approves new constitution, abolishing apartheid and setting agenda for national elections.

1994 United States and Japan reach agreement on future bilateral trade. For China, United States suspends linkage between bilateral trade and that country's behavior in human rights. Trade ties with Vietnam renewed as well.

Assassination of Rwandan president sparks civil war between Hutu and Tutsi tribes, resulting in more than 500,000 casualties.

North Korean government rejects U.S. and UN demands that it allow foreign inspection of its nuclear facilities. Kim Il-Sung dies and is replaced by his son, Kim Jong-Il. After protracted talks, North Korean government agrees to freeze nuclear program in exchange for U.S. economic and technological assistance.

GATT's Uruguay Round concludes. Multilateral trade agreement passed by member states.

Cuban refugees launch new boatlift to Florida coast. U.S. and Cuban governments reach agreement on future emigration levels.

Scandinavian states (except Norway) agree to join European Union.

United States begins "semi-permissive" occupation of Haiti. Military regime yields power to American troops and parliament disbands. Gen. Raul Cédras, leader of the military junta, is exiled to Panama; Aristide resumes leadership.

Iraqi armed forces mass along Kuwaiti border. U.S. forces are deployed to Persian Gulf to deter invasion.

Israel and Jordan sign peace agreement.

United Nations announces plans to withdraw from Somalia by March 1995; cites continuing clan warfare as reason for suspension of efforts.

Midterm elections bring collapse of Democratic majority in U.S. Congress.

1995 Russian troops reclaim control over Chechen capital of Grozny after secession attempt. Chechen rebels retreat to surrounding hillsides and continue fight for independence.

Mexican economy is battered by devaluation of peso. Fiscal crisis results in massive loan guarantees from foreign countries, including $10 billion from United States, to prevent further weakening of Mexican economy.

NATO launches air strikes against Serbian forces after Serbs seize "safe havens" in Srebenica and Zepa and attack civilians in Sarajevo.

U.S. Marines are deployed to Somalia to oversee evacuation of UN peace-keeping forces.

Massacre of Israeli citizens by Islamic terrorists threatens to undermine peace accord between Israel and PLO. Israeli prime minister Yitzhak Rabin assassinated, succeeded by Benjamin Netanyahu of rival Likud Party.

Muslim and Croatian forces launch successful offensive against Serbs, changing balance of power in region. All sides convene in Dayton, Ohio, and agree to cease-fire, temporary NATO occupation, and formation of new Bosnian government.

United States threatens trade war against China over Beijing's alleged violations of international copyright laws.

Republican majority in U.S. Congress promotes "National Security Restoration Act" calling for increased defense spending, cutbacks in foreign aid, and reduced support for UN peace-keeping efforts. President Clinton vetoes congressional measures.

1996 Congress ratifies START II accord with Russia.

Taiwan holds first democratic elections. United States deploys naval forces to region in response to Chinese military provocations in Taiwan Straits.

Control over peace-keeping mission in Haiti transferred from United States to United Nations. Réné Préval elected president in closely monitored but widely boycotted elections.

United States deploys naval forces to free foreign nationals that are trapped in Liberia.

President Clinton and Russian president Boris Yeltsin meet in Moscow together with leaders of Western industrial democracies.

Yeltsin reelected as president of Russia, forming coalition with former general Alexander Lebed to defeat communist leader Gennady Zyuganov. Lebed later fired as national security adviser after challenging Yeltsin's foreign and domestic policies.

Iraq intervenes in Kurdish-held territories considered off-limits by Western powers. United States responds with aerial attacks on Iraqi military installations.

Clinton signs Comprehensive Test Ban Treaty and encourages other states to enter agreement that prevents nuclear testing.

Ethnic violence spreads from Rwanda and Burundi to other parts of Central Africa. Massive refugee population threatens political stability in region.

Clinton calls for NATO expansion by 1999 with likely new members to include Poland, Hungary, and the Czech Republic. Russia declares NATO expansion a threat to its security and seeks separate treaty with alliance.

Muslim leader elected to lead tripartite government in Bosnia. NATO peacekeeping mission extended until June 1998.

Clinton is elected to second term, defeating former senator Robert Dole.

U.S. government, dissatisfied with pace of reform in United Nations, leads effort to prevent UN Secretary-General Boutros Boutros-Ghali from gaining second term. Ghana's Kofi Annan, favored by the United States, is elected secretary-general.

1997   Madeleine Albright is confirmed as U.S. secretary of state, William Cohen as secretary of defense, and Bill Richardson as ambassador to the United Nations. Samuel Berger replaces Anthony Lake as national security adviser. George Tenet is confirmed as CIA director after Lake, Clinton's first choice, withdraws his nomination amid widespread opposition.

Chinese leader Deng Xiaoping dies, leading to uncertain period of political transition.

United States rejects authority of World Trade Organization over threatened U.S. economic sanctions against Cuba. European leaders protest Helms-Burton sanctions but do not retaliate.

Clinton and Boris Yeltsin meet in Helsinki, Finland, and agree to new round of nuclear weapons reductions, labeled START III.

Israel announces plans for new Jewish settlements in East Jerusalem, setting off violent demonstrations by Palestinians and new threats to peace process.

British Labour Party leader Tony Blair replaces Conservative John Major as prime minister.

Congress ratifies Chemical Weapons Convention, previously signed by most other governments.

Zaire's government headed by Mobutu Sese Seko falls to rival forces led by Laurent Kabila. Country becomes the Democratic Republic of Congo, and the new regime is immediately recognized by the U.S. government.

Czech Republic, Hungary, and Poland invited to join NATO. Russian government approves security charter with NATO that calls for consultations and limited security cooperation.

Chinese government assumes control over Hong Kong, a former British colony.

United States grants political asylum to two high-ranking North Korean diplomats after their defection.

NATO troops seize illegal weapons from Bosnian police forces suspected of planning coup against government.

Select Bibliography

All of the entries in this bibliography are books. Readers who wish to keep up with the journal literature on American foreign policy will find the articles in *Foreign Affairs, Foreign Policy*, and *International Security* useful and relevant.

AMERICAN SOCIETY AND STYLE IN FOREIGN POLICY

Almond, Gabriel A. *The American People and Foreign Policy*. New York: Praeger, 1960.

Boorstin, Daniel J. *The Genius of American Politics*. Chicago: Phoenix Books, 1953.

Dallek, Robert. *The American Style of Foreign Policy*. New York: Knopf, 1983.

Elliott, Michael. *The Day Before Yesterday*. New York: Simon and Schuster, 1996.

Hartz, Louis. *The Liberal Tradition in America*. New York: Harvest Books, 1955.

Hofstadter, Richard. *The Paranoid Style in American Politics*. New York: Vintage Books, 1967.

Hunt, Michael H. *Ideology and U.S. Foreign Policy*. New Haven, Conn.: Yale University Press, 1987.

Kennan, George F. *American Diplomacy, 1900–1950*. Chicago: University of Chicago Press, 1951.

Lippmann, Walter. *U.S. Foreign Policy: Shield of the Republic*. Boston: Little, Brown, 1943.

Lipset, Seymour Martin. *American Exceptionalism*. New York: Norton, 1996.

McDougall, Walter A. *The American Encounter with the World Since 1776*. Boston: Houghton Mifflin, 1997.

McElroy, Robert W. *Morality and American Foreign Policy*. Princeton, N.J.: Princeton University Press, 1992.

Morgenthau, Hans J. *In Defense of the National Interest*. New York: Knopf, 1951.

Nichols, Bruce, and Gil Loescher, eds. *The Moral Nation*. South Bend, Ind.: University of Notre Dame Press, 1989.

Osgood, Robert. *Ideals and Self-Interest in America's Foreign Relations*. Chicago: University of Chicago Press, 1953.

Potter, David M. *The People of Plenty*. Chicago: Phoenix Books, 1954.

Stoessinger, John G. *Crusaders and Pragmatists*. 2d ed. New York: Norton, 1985.

Thompson, Kenneth W. *Traditions and Values in Politics and Diplomacy*. Baton Rouge: Louisiana State University Press, 1992.

von Vorys, Karl. *American National Interest*. New York: Praeger, 1990.

Weigel, George. *American Interests, American Purpose*. New York: Praeger, 1989.

AMERICAN FOREIGN POLICY DURING THE COLD WAR

Aron, Raymond. *The Imperial Republic*. Cambridge, Mass.: Winthrop, 1974.

Bell, Coral. *The Diplomacy of Détente*. New York: St. Martin's Press, 1977.

Brzezinski, Zbigniew. *Game Plan*. Boston: Atlantic Monthly Press, 1986.

Cingranelli, David Louis. *Ethics, American Foreign Policy, and the Third World*. New York: St. Martin's Press, 1993.

Dukes, Paul. *The Last Great Game*. New York: St. Martin's Press, 1989.

Fulbright, J. William. *The Arrogance of Power*. New York: Vintage Books, 1967.

———. *The Crippled Giant*. New York: Vintage Books, 1972.

———. *Old Myths and New Realities*. New York: Vintage Books, 1964.

Gaddis, John Lewis. *The Long Peace*. New York: Oxford University Press, 1987.

———. *Russia, the Soviet Union and the United States*. New York: Wiley, 1978.

———. *Strategies of Containment*. New York: Oxford University Press, 1982.

————. *The United States and the Origins of the Cold War, 1941–1947.* New York: Columbia University Press, 1972.

————. *We Now Know: Rethinking Cold War History.* New York: Oxford University Press, 1997.

Halle, Louis J. *The Cold War as History.* New York: Harper and Row, 1967.

Hoffmann, Stanley. *Gulliver's Troubles, or the Setting of American Foreign Policy.* New York: McGraw-Hill, 1968.

————. *Primacy or World Order.* New York: McGraw-Hill, 1978.

Larson, Deborah Welch. *Origins of Containment.* Princeton, N.J.: Princeton University Press, 1985.

Leffler, Melvyn P. *A Preponderance of Power.* Stanford, Calif.: Stanford University Press, 1992.

Leffler, Melvyn P., and David Painter, eds. *The Origins of the Cold War.* New York: Routledge, 1994.

McNamara, Robert S. *Out of the Cold.* New York: Simon and Schuster, 1989.

Mandelbaum, Richard, and Strobe Talbott. *Reagan and Gorbachev.* New York: Vintage Books, 1987.

Moskin, Robert J. *Mr. Truman's War.* New York: Random House, 1996.

Muravchik, Joshua. *The Uncertain Crusade.* New York: Hamilton Press, 1985.

Osgood, Robert, et al. *America and the World.* Baltimore: Johns Hopkins University Press, 1970.

————. *Retreat from Empire?* Baltimore: Johns Hopkins University Press, 1973.

Rodman, Peter W. *More Precious than Peace.* New York: Scribner's, 1994.

Schlesinger, Arthur, Jr. *The Imperial Presidency.* Boston: Houghton Mifflin, 1973.

Schulzinger, Robert D. *The Wise Men of Foreign Affairs.* New York: Columbia University Press, 1985.

Skidmore, David. *Reversing Course.* Nashville, Tenn.: Vanderbilt University Press, 1996.

Smith, Gaddis. *Morality, Reason, and Power.* New York: Hill and Wang, 1986.

Steel, Ronald. *Pax Americana.* New York: Viking Press, 1967.

Tillema, Herbert K. *Appeal to Force.* New York: Crowell, 1973.

Tucker, Robert W. *The Purposes of American Power.* New York: Praeger, 1981.

Wilmot, Chester. *The Struggle for Europe.* New York: Hayes and Brothers, 1952.

Yergin, Daniel. *Shattered Peace.* Boston: Houghton Mifflin, 1977.

AMERICAN FOREIGN POLICY AFTER THE COLD WAR

Art, Robert J., and Seyom Brown, eds. *U.S. Foreign Policy: The Search for a New Role.* New York: Macmillan, 1993.

Brzezinski, Zbigniew. *Out of Control.* New York: Scribner's, 1993.

Callahan, David. *Between Two Worlds.* New York: HarperCollins, 1994.

Chace, James. *The Consequences of the Peace.* New York: Oxford University Press, 1992.

Fry, Earl H. *America the Vincible.* Englewood Cliffs, N.J.: Prentice Hall, 1994.

Gaddis, John Lewis. *The United States and the End of the Cold War.* New York: Oxford University Press, 1992.

Garten, Jeffrey E. *A Cold Peace.* New York: Times Books, 1992.

Garthoff, Raymond. *The Great Transition.* Washington, D.C.: Brookings, 1994.

Gray, Colin. *War, Peace, and Victory.* New York: Simon and Schuster, 1990.

Hogan, Michael J., ed. *The End of the Cold War.* New York: Cambridge University Press, 1992.

Hyland, William G. *The Cold War Is Over.* New York: Times Books, 1990.

Kanter, Arnold, and Linton F. Brooks, eds. *U.S. Intervention Policy for the Post-Cold War World.* New York: Norton, 1995.

Kegley, Charles W., Jr., and Gregory A. Raymond. *A Multipolar Peace?* New York: St. Martin's Press, 1994.

Kennan, George. *At a Century's End.* New York: Norton, 1996.

Kennedy, Paul. *Preparing for the Twenty-First Century.* New York: Random House, 1993.

Lieber, Robert J., ed. *Eagle Adrift.* New York: Longman, 1997.

Maynes, Charles William, and Richard Williamson, eds. *U.S. Foreign Policy and the United Nations.* New York: Norton, 1996.

Mueller, John. *Retreat From Doomsday.* New York: Basic Books, 1989.

Muller, Steven, and Gebhard Schweigler, eds. *From Occupation to Cooperation.* New York: Norton, 1992.

Muravchik, Joshua. *The Imperative of American Leadership: A Challenge to Neo-Isolationism.* Washington, D.C.: American Enterprise Institute, 1996.

Nau, Richard. *The Myth of America's Decline.* New York: Oxford University Press, 1990.

Nolan, Janne E., ed. *Global Engagement.* Washington, D.C.: Brookings, 1994.

Nye, Joseph S., Jr. *Bound to Lead.* New York: Basic Books, 1990.

Payne, Richard J. *The Western European Allies, the Third World, and U.S. Foreign Policy.* New York: Greenwood, 1991.

Rubenstein, Alvin Z., ed. *America's National Interests in a Post-Cold War World.* New York: McGraw-Hill, 1994.

Russett, Bruce M. *Grasping the Democratic Peace.* Princeton, N.J.: Princeton University Press, 1993.

Shuman, Michael H., and Hal Harvey. *Security without War.* Boulder, Colo.: Westview Press, 1993.

Steel, Ronald. *Temptations of a Superpower.* Cambridge, Mass.: Harvard University Press, 1995.

Treverton, Gregory F. *America, Germany, and the Future of Europe.* Princeton, N.J.: Princeton University Press, 1992.

Tucker, Robert W., and David C. Hendrickson. *The Imperial Temptation.* New York: Council on Foreign Relations, 1992.

Yankelovich, Daniel, and I. M. Destler, eds. *Beyond the Beltway.* New York: Norton, 1994.

DIPLOMATIC HISTORIES

Ambrose, Stephen E. *Rise to Globalism: American Foreign Policy since 1938.* 7th ed. Rev. New York: Penguin, 1993.

Bailey, Thomas. *A Diplomatic History of the American People.* 10th ed. Englewood Cliffs, N.J.: Prentice Hall, 1980.

Bemis, Samuel. *A Diplomatic History of the United States.* 4th ed. New York: Holt, 1955.

Clarfield, Gerard. *U.S. Diplomatic History.* 2 vols. Englewood Cliffs, N.J.: Prentice Hall, 1992.

Combs, Jerald A. *The History of American Foreign Policy.* New York: Macmillan, 1975.

DeConde, Alexander. *A History of American Foreign Policy.* 3d ed. 2 vols. New York: Scribner's, 1978.

Ferrell, Robert H. *American Diplomacy.* 4th ed. New York: Norton, 1988.

Fleming, D. F. *The Cold War and Its Origins, 1917–1960.* 2 vols. Garden City, N.Y.: Doubleday, 1961.

Jentleson, Bruce W., and Thomas G. Paterson, eds. *The Encyclopedia of U.S. Foreign Relations.* 4 vols. New York: Oxford University Press, 1997.

Jones, Howard. *The Course of American Diplomacy.* 2d ed. Chicago: Dorsey Press, 1988.

Kissinger, Henry. *Diplomacy.* New York: Simon and Schuster, 1994.

Kunz, Diane B., ed. *The Diplomacy of the Crucial Decade.* New York: Columbia University Press, 1994.

McCormick, Thomas J. *America's Half-Century.* Baltimore: Johns Hopkins University Press, 1989.

Paterson, Thomas G. *Meeting the Communist Threat.* New York: Oxford University Press, 1989.

Pratt, Julius W. *A History of United States Foreign Policy.* New York: Prentice Hall, 1955.

Rappaport, Armin. *A History of American Diplomacy.* New York: Macmillan, 1975.

Schulzinger, Robert D. *American Diplomacy in the Twentieth Century.* 3d ed. New York: Oxford University Press, 1994.

Walker, Martin. *The Cold War.* New York: Henry Holt, 1994.

REVISIONIST INTERPRETATIONS AND DEBATES

Alperovitz, Gar. *Atomic Diplomacy.* New York: Vintage Books, 1967.

Barnet, Richard. *Roots of War.* New York: Atheneum, 1972.

Campbell, David. *United States Foreign Policy and the Politics of Identity.* Minneapolis: University of Minnesota Press, 1992.

Gardner, Lloyd. *Architects of Illusion.* Chicago: Quadrangle Books, 1970.

Johnson, Robert H. *Improbable Dangers.* New York: St. Martin's Press, 1994.

Katzenstein, Peter J., ed. *The Culture of National Security.* New York: Columbia University Press, 1996.

Kolko, Gabriel. *The Roots of American Foreign Policy.* Boston: Beacon Press, 1969.

Kolko, Gabriel, and Joyce Kolko. *The Limits of Power.* New York: Harper and Row, 1972.

Kwitny, Jonathan. *Endless Enemies.* New York: Penguin, 1984.

LaFeber, Walter. *America, Russia, and the Cold War, 1945–1980.* 5th ed. New York: Knopf, 1985.

———. *The New Empire.* Ithaca, N.Y.: Cornell University Press, 1963.

Lens, Sidney. *The Forging of the American Empire.* New York: Crowell, 1971.

Maddox, Robert J. *The New Left and the Origins of the Cold War.* Princeton, N.J.: Princeton University Press, 1973.

Melanson, Richard A. *Writing History and Making Policy.* Lanham, Md.: University Press of America, 1983.

Parenti, Michael. *The Sword and the Dollar.* New York: St. Martin's Press, 1989.

Paterson, Thomas G. *On Every Front.* New York: Norton, 1979.

———. *Soviet-American Confrontation.* Baltimore: Johns Hopkins University Press, 1973.

Sanders, Jerry W. *Peddlers of Crisis.* Boston: South End Press, 1983.

Tucker, Robert W. *The Radical Left and American Foreign Policy.* Baltimore: Johns Hopkins University Press, 1971.

Williams, William Appleman. *The Tragedy of American Diplomacy.* New York: Norton, 1988.

AMERICAN MILITARY STRATEGY

Binkin, Martin. *Who Will Fight the Next War?* Washington, D.C.: Brookings, 1993.

Blight, James G., and David A. Welch. *On the Brink.* New York: Hill and Wang, 1989.

Boll, Michael M. *National Security Planning.* Lexington: University of Kentucky Press, 1988.

Brown, Harold. *The Strategic Defense Initiative.* Boulder, Colo.: Westview Press, 1987.

Caldicott, Helen. *Missile Envy.* New York: Bantam Books, 1986.

Emerson, Steven. *Secret Warriors.* New York: Putnam, 1988.

Flournoy, Michele A. *Nuclear Weapons after the Cold War.* New York: HarperCollins, 1993.

Freedman, Lawrence. *The Evolution of Nuclear Strategy.* 2d ed. New York: St. Martin's Press, 1989.

George, Alexander L., and Richard Smoke. *Deterrence in American Foreign Policy.* New York: Columbia University Press, 1974.

Gertcher, Frank L., and William Weide. *Beyond Deterrence.* Boulder, Colo.: Westview Press, 1990.

Glynn, Patrick. *Closing Pandora's Box.* New York: Basic Books, 1992.

Gray, Colin. *Nuclear Strategy and Nuclear Planning.* Philadelphia: Foreign Policy Research Institute, 1985.

————. *The Soviet-American Arms Race.* Lexington, Mass.: Lexington Books, 1976.

Herken, Gregg. *Counsels of War.* New York: Oxford University Press, 1987.

————. *The Winning Weapon.* New York: Vintage Books, 1981.

Jervis, Robert. *The Illogic of American National Strategy.* Ithaca, N.Y.: Cornell University Press, 1984.

Kaplan, Fred. *The Wizards of Armageddon.* New York: Simon and Schuster, 1983.

Kapstein, Ethan, ed. *Downsizing Defense.* Washington, D.C.: CQ Press, 1993.

Kissinger, Henry A. *Nuclear Weapons and Foreign Policy.* New York: Harper and Brothers, 1957.

Landau, Saul. *The Dangerous Doctrine.* Boulder, Colo.: Westview Press, 1988.

Luttwak, Edward N. *The Pentagon and the Art of War.* New York: Simon and Schuster, 1985.

Nolan, Janne E. *Guardians of the Arsenal.* New York: Basic Books, 1989.

Payne, Keith P. *Strategic Defense.* Lanham, Md.: Hamilton Press, 1986.

Powaski, Ronald E. *March to Armageddon.* New York: Oxford University Press, 1987.

Powell, Robert. *Nuclear Deterrence Theory.* New York: Cambridge University Press, 1990.

Sagan, Scott D., and Kenneth N. Waltz. *The Spread of Nuclear Weapons.* New York: Norton, 1995.

Schwartz, William A., and Charles Derber. *The Nuclear Seduction.* Berkeley: University of California Press, 1990.

Smoke, Richard. *National Security and the Nuclear Dilemma.* 3d ed. New York: Random House, 1992.

Talbott, Strobe. *Deadly Gambits.* New York: Knopf, 1984.

————. *End Game.* New York: Harper and Row, 1980.

Tucker, Robert W. *The Nuclear Debate.* New York: Holmes and Meier, 1985.

Wolfe, Thomas W. *The SALT Experience.* Cambridge, Mass.: Ballinger, 1979.

AMERICAN POLICY IN WESTERN EUROPE

Allin, Dana H. *Cold War Illusions.* New York: St. Martin's Press, 1995.

Calingaert, Michael. *European Integration.* Boulder, Colo: Westview Press, 1996.

Carpenter, Ted Galen. *Beyond NATO.* Washington, D.C.: Cato Institute, 1994.

Cook, Don. *Forging the Alliance.* New York: Arbor House, 1989.

Dean, Jonathan. *Ending Europe's Wars.* New York: Twentieth Century Fund, 1994.

DePorte, A. W. *Europe between the Superpowers.* New Haven, Conn.: Yale University Press, 1985.

Freedman, Lawrence, ed. *Europe Transformed.* New York: St. Martin's Press, 1990.

Gombert, David C., and F. Stephen Larrabee, eds. *America and Europe.* New York: Cambridge University Press, 1997.

Grosser, Alfred. *The Western Alliance.* New York: Vintage Books, 1982.

Harrison, Glennon J. *Europe and the United States.* Armonk, N.Y.: M. E. Sharpe, 1994.

Holborn, Hajo. *The Political Collapse of Europe.* New York: Knopf, 1951.

Jones, Joseph. *The Fifteen Weeks.* New York: Viking Press, 1955.

Kapstein, Ethan B. *The Insecure Alliance.* New York: Oxford University Press, 1990.

Krauss, Melvyn. *How NATO Weakens the West.* New York: Simon and Schuster, 1986.

Laquer, Walter. *The Dream that Failed.* New York: Oxford University Press, 1994.

Mandelbaum, Michael. *The Dawn of Peace in Europe.* New York: Twentieth Century Fund, 1996.

Osgood, Robert E. *NATO.* Chicago: University of Chicago Press, 1962.

Padoa-Schioppa, Tommaso. *The Road to Monetary Union in Europe.* New York: Oxford University Press, 1994.

Sherwood, Elizabeth. *Allies in Crisis.* New Haven, Conn.: Yale University Press, 1990.

Stokes, Gale. *The Walls Came Tumbling Down.* New York: Oxford University Press, 1993.

Tow, William T. *The Limits of Alliance.* Baltimore: Johns Hopkins University Press, 1990.

Treverton, Gregory F. *America, Germany, and the Future of Europe.* Princeton, N.J.: Princeton University Press, 1990.

Tucker, Robert W., and Linda Wrigley. *The Atlantic Alliance and Its Critics.* New York: Praeger, 1983.

Ullman, Richard H. *Securing Europe.* Princeton, N.J.: Princeton University Press, 1991.

AMERICAN POLICY IN EASTERN EUROPE AND THE FORMER SOVIET UNION

Amsden, Alice H., Jacek Kochanowicz, and Lance Taylor. *The Market Meets Its Match.* Cambridge, Mass.: Harvard University Press, 1995.

Bialer, Seweryn, and Michael Mandelbaum. *The Global Rivals.* New York: Knopf, 1988.

———. *Gorbachev's Russia and American Foreign Policy.* Boulder: Westview Press, 1988.

Blaney, John W., ed. *The Successor States to the USSR.* Washington, D.C.: Congressional Quarterly, 1995.

Brown, J. F. *Hopes and Shadows.* Durham, N.C.: Duke University Press, 1994.

Burg, Steven L. *War or Peace?* New York: New York University Press, 1996.

Dawisha, Karen, and Bruce Parrott. *Russia and the New States of Eurasia.* New York: Cambridge University Press, 1994.

Denitch, Bogdan. *Ethnic Nationalism.* Minneapolis: University of Minnesota Press, 1994.

Dobbs, Michael. *Down with Big Brother.* New York: Knopf, 1997.

Dunlop, John B. *The Rise of Russia and the Fall of the Soviet Empire.* Princeton, N.J.: Princeton University Press, 1993.

Goldman, Marshall I. *Lost Opportunity.* New York: Norton, 1994.

Keep, John. *Last of the Empires.* New York: Oxford University Press, 1996.

Midlarsky, Manus I., John A. Vasquez, and Peter V. Gladkov. *From Rivalry to Cooperation.* New York: HarperCollins, 1994.

Remnick, David. *Resurrection.* New York: Random House, 1997.

Rieff, David. *Slaughterhouse.* New York: Simon and Schuster, 1995.

Satter, David. *Age of Delirium.* New York: Knopf, 1996.

Waller, J. Michael. *Secret Empire.* Boulder, Colo.: Westview Press, 1994.

Zimmerman, Warren. *Origins of a Catastrophe.* New York: Times Books, 1996.

Zubok, Vladislav, and Constantine Pleshakov. *Inside the Kremlin's Cold War.* Cambridge, Mass.: Harvard University Press, 1996.

AMERICAN POLICY IN EAST ASIA

Armacost, Michael H. *Friends or Rivals?* New York: Columbia University Press, 1996.

Balassa, Bela, and Marcus Noland. *Japan and the World Economy.* Washington, D.C.: Institute for International Economics, 1988.

Baritz, Loren. *Backfire.* New York: Morrow, 1985.

Barnett, A. Doak. *China Policy.* Washington, D.C.: Brookings, 1977.

Berman, Larry. *Lyndon Johnson's War.* New York: Norton, 1989.

Bernstein, Richard, and Ross H. Munro. *The Coming Conflict with China.* New York: Knopf, 1997.

Buckley, Roger. *U.S.-Japan Alliance Diplomacy, 1945–1990.* New York: Cambridge University Press, 1992.

Carter, K. Holly Maze. *The Asian Dilemma in U.S. Foreign Policy.* Armonk, N.Y.: M. E. Sharpe, 1989.

Cohen, Warren I. *America's Response to China.* 3d ed. New York: Columbia University Press, 1989.

Cumings, Bruce. *Korea's Place in the Sun.* New York: Norton, 1997.

DiLeo, David L. *George Ball, Vietnam, and the Rethinking of Containment.* Chapel Hill: University of North Carolina Press, 1991.

Dower, John. *Japan in Peace and War.* New York: New Press, 1994.

Dulles, Foster R. *American Foreign Policy toward Communist China.* New York: Crowell, 1972.

Fallows, James. *Looking at the Sun.* New York: Pantheon, 1994.

Feis, Herbert. *China Tangle.* Princeton, N.J.: Princeton University Press, 1953.

Frankel, Jeffrey A., and Miles Kahler, eds. *Regionalism and Rivalry.* Chicago: University of Chicago Press, 1993.

Gelb, Leslie, and Richard K. Betts. *The Irony of Vietnam.* Washington, D.C.: Brookings, 1979.

Gelb, Leslie, et al. *The Pentagon Papers.* New York: Bantam Books, 1971.

Halberstam, David. *The Best and the Brightest.* New York: Random House, 1969.

Herring, George C. *America's Longest War.* 2d ed. New York: Wiley, 1988.

———. *LBJ and Vietnam.* Austin: University of Texas Press, 1994.

Hunt, Michael H. *Lyndon Johnson's War.* New York: Hill and Wang, 1996.

Karnow, Stanley C. *In Our Image.* New York: Ballentine Books, 1989.

———. *Vietnam.* New York: Viking Press, 1983.

Kattenburg, Paul. *The Vietnam Trauma in American Foreign Policy, 1945–1975.* New Brunswick: Transaction Books, 1980.

Kihl, Young Whan. *Korea and the World.* Boulder, Colo.: Westview Press, 1994.

Metzger, Thomas A., and Ramon H. Myers, eds. *Greater China and U.S. Foreign Policy.* Stanford, Calif.: Hoover Institution Press, 1996.

Sheehan, Neil. *A Bright Shining Lie.* New York: Random House, 1988.

Spanier, John W. *The Truman-MacArthur Controversy and the Korean War.* Rev. ed. New York: Norton, 1965.

Tow, William T. *Encountering the Dominant Player.* New York: Columbia University Press, 1991.

Tsou, Tang. *America's Failure in China, 1941–1950.* 2 vols. Chicago: Phoenix Books, 1963.

Williams, William Appleman, et al., eds., *America in Vietnam.* Garden City, N.Y.: Anchor Books, 1975.

AMERICAN POLICY IN THE MIDDLE EAST
AND SOUTHERN ASIA

Bill, James A. *The Eagle and the Lion.* New Haven, Conn.: Yale University Press, 1988.

Cohen, Roger, and Claudio Gati. *In The Eyes of the Storm.* New York: Farrar, Straus and Giroux, 1991.

Cordesman, Anthony H. *Perilous Prospects.* Boulder, Colo.: Westview Press, 1996.

Cottam, Richard W. *Iran and the United States.* Pittsburgh: University of Pittsburgh Press, 1988.

Doran, Charles, *Myth, Oil, and Politics.* New York: Free Press, 1977.

Friedman, Thomas L. *From Beirut to Jerusalem.* New York: Anchor Books, 1989.

Gasiorowski, Mark J. *U.S. Foreign Policy and the Shah.* Ithaca, N.Y.: Cornell University Press, 1991.

Gendzier, Irene L. *Notes from the Minefield.* New York: Columbia University Press, 1997.

Golan, Galia. *Yom Kippur and After.* New York: Cambridge University Press, 1977.

Jentleson, Bruce W. *With Friends Like These.* New York: Norton, 1994.

Kux, Dennis. *India and the United States.* Washington, D.C.: National Defense University Press, 1993.

Lenczowski, George. *American Presidents and the Middle East.* Durham, N.C.: Duke University Press, 1990.

McMahon, Robert J. *The Cold War on the Periphery.* New York: Columbia University Press, 1994.

Quandt, William. *Camp David.* Washington, D.C.: Brookings, 1986.

———. *Peace Process.* Washington, D.C.: Brookings, 1993.

Renshon, Stanley A., ed. *The Political Psychology of the Gulf War.* Pittsburgh: University of Pittsburgh Press, 1993.

Roger, Louis, and Owen Roger, eds. *Suez 1956.* New York: Oxford, 1989.

Rubin, Barry. *Revolution until Victory?* Cambridge, Mass.: Harvard University Press, 1994.

Safran, Nadav. *Intifada.* New York: Simon and Schuster, 1989.

———. *Israel: The Embattled Ally.* Cambridge, Mass.: Harvard University Press, 1978.

———. *Saudi Arabia: The Ceaseless Quest for Security.* Cambridge, Mass.: Harvard University Press, 1985.

Sick, Gary. *All Fall Down.* New York: Penguin Books, 1986.

Sifry, Micah L., and Christopher Cerf, eds. *The Gulf War Reader.* New York: Random House, 1991.

Spiegel, Steven L. *The Other Arab-Israeli Conflict.* Chicago: University of Chicago Press, 1985.

Tessler, Mark. *A History of the Israeli-Palestinian Conflict.* Bloomington: Indiana University Press, 1994.

Woodward, Bob. *The Commanders.* New York: Simon and Schuster, 1991.

AMERICAN POLICY IN AFRICA

Alinghaus, Bruce E., ed. *Arms for Africa.* Lexington, Mass.: Lexington Books, 1983.

Anstee, Margaret Joan. *Orphan of the Cold War.* New York: St. Martin's Press, 1996.

Bender, Gerald, James Coleman, and Richard Sklar, eds. *African Crisis Areas and U.S. Foreign Policy.* Berkeley: University of California Press, 1985.

Chester, Edward W. *Clash of Titans.* Maryknoll, N.Y.: Orbis, 1974.

Dickson, David A. *United States Foreign Policy toward Sub-Saharan Africa.* Lanham, Md.: University Press of America, 1985.

Feinberg, Richard E. *The Intemperate Zone.* New York: Norton, 1983.

Giliomee, Hermann, and Lawrence Schlemmer. *From Apartheid to Nation Building.* New York: Oxford University Press, 1990.

Jackson, Henry F. *From the Congo to Soweto.* New York: Morrow, 1982.

Kelly, Sean. *America's Tyrant.* Washington, D.C.: American University Press, 1993.

Layachi, Azzedine. *The United States and North Africa.* New York: Praeger, 1990.

Lemarchand, René, ed. *American Policy in Southern Africa.* Washington, D.C.: University Press of America, 1978.

Packenham, Robert A. *Liberal America and the Third World.* Princeton, N.J.: Princeton University Press, 1973.

Price, Robert M. *U.S. Foreign Policy in Sub-Saharan Africa.* Berkeley: Institute of International Studies, University of California, 1978.

Schraeder, Peter J. *United States Foreign Policy toward Africa.* New York: Cambridge University Press, 1994.

Skinner, Elliott P. *Beyond Constructive Engagement.* New York: Paragon Press, 1986.

AMERICAN POLICY IN LATIN AMERICA

Blasier, Cole. *The Hovering Giant.* Rev. ed. Pittsburgh: University of Pittsburgh Press, 1985.

Coatsworth, John H. *Central America and the United States.* New York: Twayne Publishers, 1994.

Dinges, John. *Our Man in Panama.* New York: Random House, 1990.

Domínguez, Jorge I. *To Make a World Safe for Revolution.* Cambridge, Mass.: Harvard University Press, 1989.

Draper, Theodore. *The Dominican Revolt.* New York: Commentary, 1968.

Duncan, W. Raymond. *The Soviet Union and Cuba.* New York: Praeger, 1985.

Erisman, H. Michael. *Cuba's International Relations.* Boulder, Colo.: Westview Press, 1985.

Gutman, Roy. *Banana Diplomacy.* New York: Simon and Schuster, 1988.

Hufbauer, Gary Clyde, and Jeffrey J. Schott. *Western Hemisphere Economic Integration.* Washington, D.C.: Institute for International Economics, 1994.

Immerman, Robert H. *The CIA in Guatemala: The Foreign Policy of Intervention.* Austin: University of Texas Press, 1982.

Kagan, Robert. *A Twilight Struggle.* New York: Free Press, 1996.

LaFeber, Walter. *Inevitable Revolutions.* New York: Norton, 1983.

Lake, Anthony. *Somoza Falling.* Boston: Houghton Mifflin, 1989.

———. *The "Tar Baby" Option.* New York: Columbia University Press, 1976.

Lowenthal, Abraham F., ed. *Exporting Democracy.* Baltimore: Johns Hopkins University Press, 1991.

———. *Partners in Conflict.* Baltimore: Johns Hopkins University Press, 1987.

Maingot, Anthony P. *The United States and the Caribbean.* Boulder, Colo.: Westview Press, 1996.

Marcella, Gabriel. *Warriors in Peacetime.* Portland: Frank Cass, 1994.

Morley, Morris H. *Imperial State and Revolution.* New York: Cambridge University Press, 1987.

Pastor, Robert A. *Condemned to Repetition.* Princeton, N.J.: Princeton University Press, 1987.

———. *Whirlpool.* Princeton, N.J.: Princeton University Press, 1993.

Rabe, Stephen G. *Eisenhower and Latin America.* Chapel Hill: University of North Carolina Press, 1988.

Schlesinger, Stephen, and Stephen Kinzer. *Bitter Fruit.* Garden City, N.Y.: Anchor Books, 1982.

Shafer, Michael D. *Deadly Paradigms.* Princeton, N.J.: Princeton University Press, 1988.

Sigmund, Paul. *The Overthrow of Allende and the Politics of Chile.* Pittsburgh: University of Pittsburgh Press, 1977.

Smith, Peter H. *Talons of the Eagle.* New York: Oxford University Press, 1996.

Suchliki, Jaime. *Cuba.* New York: Brassey's, 1990.

Walker, Thomas W., ed. *Reagan versus the Sandinistas.* Boulder, Colo.: Westview Press, 1987.

AMERICA AND THE INTERNATIONAL POLITICAL ECONOMY

Baldwin, David A. *Economic Statecraft.* Princeton, N.J.: Princeton University Press, 1985.

Bergsten, C. Fred. *America in the World Economy.* Washington, D.C.: Institute for International Economics, 1988.

Bhagwati, Jagdish. *The World Trading System at Risk.* Princeton, N.J.: Princeton University Press, 1991.

Bhagwati, Jagdish, and Hugh T. Patrick, eds. *Aggressive Unilateralism.* Ann Arbor: University of Michigan Press, 1990.

Block, Fred. *Origins of International Economic Disorder.* Berkeley: University of California Press, 1977.

Destler, I. M. *American Trade Politics.* 2d ed. Washington, D.C.: Twentieth Century Fund, 1992.

———. *Making Foreign Economic Policy.* Washington, D.C.: Brookings, 1980.

Friedberg, Aaron L. *The Weary Titan.* Princeton, N.J.: Princeton University Press, 1988.

Gertcher, Frank L., and William Weide. *The Political Economy of National Defense.* Boulder, Colo.: Westview Press, 1987.

Gilpin, Robert. *The Political Economy of International Relations.* Princeton, N.J.: Princeton University Press, 1987.

Hall, Peter A., ed. *The Political Power of Economic Ideas.* Princeton, N.J.: Princeton University Press, 1989.

Hoekman, Bernard, and Michel Kostecki. *The Political Economy of the World Trading System.* New York: Oxford University Press, 1996.

Hook, Steven W. *National Interest and Foreign Aid.* Boulder, Colo.: Lynne Rienner, 1995.

Hook, Steven W., ed. *Foreign Aid toward the Millennium.* Boulder, Colo.: Lynne Rienner, 1996.

Kapstein, Ethan B. *Governing the Global Economy.* Cambridge, Mass.: Harvard University Press, 1994.

———. *The Political Economy of National Security.* New York: McGraw-Hill, 1992.

Krasner, Stephen D. *Defending the National Interest.* Princeton, N.J.: Princeton University Press, 1978.

———. *Structural Conflict.* Berkeley: University of California Press, 1985.

Kunz, Diane B. *Guns and Butter.* New York: Free Press, 1997.

Lewis, Arthur. *The Evolution of the International Economic Order.* Princeton, N.J.: Princeton University Press, 1978.

Maren, Michael. *The Road to Hell.* New York: Free Press, 1997.

Odell, John S. *U.S. International Monetary Policy.* Princeton, N.J.: Princeton University Press, 1982.

Pollard, Robert A. *Economic Security and the Origins of the Cold War, 1945–1950.* New York: Columbia University Press, 1985.

Reich, Robert. *The Work of Nations.* New York: Vintage, 1992.

Rosecrance, Richard. *America's Economic Resurgence.* New York: Harper and Row, 1990.

Rothstein, Robert. *The Weak in the World of the Strong.* New York: Columbia University Press, 1977.

Spero, Joan, and Jeffrey A. Hart. *The Politics of International Economic Relations.* 5th ed. New York: St. Martin's Press, 1997.

Tucker, Robert. *Inequality of Nations.* New York: Basic Books, 1977.

Tulchin, Martin, and Susan Tulchin. *Buying into America.* New York: Times Books, 1988.

Vogel, Ezra. *Japan as Number One.* New York: Harper and Row, 1979.

DOMESTIC POLITICS AND AMERICAN FOREIGN POLICY

Allison, Graham T. *Essence of Decision.* Boston: Little, Brown, 1971.

Barnet, Richard J. *The Rockets' Red Glare.* New York: Touchstone, 1990.

Blechman, Barry. *The Politics of National Security.* New York: Oxford University Press, 1990.

Caldwell, Daniel. *The Dynamics of Domestic Politics and Arms Control.* Columbia: University of South Carolina Press, 1991.

Charles-Philippe, David. *Foreign Policy Failure in the White House.* Lanham, Md.: University Press of America, 1994.

Crabb, Cecil V., Jr., and Pat M. Holt. *Invitation to Struggle.* 4th ed. Washington, D.C.: CQ Press, 1992.

Crabb, Cecil V., Jr., and Kevin V. Mulcahy. *Presidents and Foreign Policy Making.* Baton Rouge: Louisiana State University Press, 1986.

Darling, Arthur B. *The Central Intelligence Agency.* University Park: Pennsylvania State University Press, 1990.

Destler, I. M., Leslie H. Gelb, and Anthony Lake. *Our Own Worst Enemy.* New York: Simon and Schuster, 1984.

Dumbrell, John. *The Making of U.S. Foreign Policy.* New York: Manchester University Press, 1990.

Franck, Thomas M., and Edward Weisband. *Foreign Policy by Congress.* New York: Oxford University Press, 1979.

Graves, Ernest, and Steven A. Hidreth. *U.S. Security Assistance.* Lexington, Mass.: Lexington Books, 1985.

Halperin, Morton H. *Bureaucratic Politics and Foreign Policy.* Washington, D.C.: Brookings, 1974.

Henkin, Louis. *Foreign Affairs and the Constitution.* New York: Norton, 1972.

Hinckley, Barbara. *Less than Meets the Eye.* Chicago: University of Chicago Press, 1994.

Hughes, Barry B. *The Domestic Context of American Foreign Policy.* San Francisco: W. H. Freeman, 1978.

Janis, Irving L. *Groupthink*. 2d ed. Boston: Houghton Mifflin, 1983.
Jeffreys-Jones, Rhodri. *The CIA and American Diplomacy*. New Haven, Conn.: Yale University Press, 1989.
Jervis, Robert, and Jack Snyder, eds. *Dominos and Bandwagons*. New York: Oxford University Press, 1991.
Johnson, Loch K. *America's Secret Power*. New York: Oxford University Press, 1989.
Lindsay, James M. *Congress and the Politics of U.S. Foreign Policy*. Baltimore: Johns Hopkins University Press, 1994.
Lord, Carnes. *The Presidency and the Management of National Security*. New York: Free Press, 1988.
McNaugher, Thomas L. *New Weapons, Old Politics*. Washington, D.C.: Brookings, 1989.
Mann, Thomas E., ed. *A Question of Balance*. Washington, D.C.: Brookings, 1990.
May, Christopher. *In the Name of War*. Cambridge, Mass.: Harvard University Press, 1989.
Nathan, James A., and James K. Oliver. *Foreign Policy Making and the American Political System*. 2d ed. Boston: Little, Brown, 1987.
Pastor, Robert A. *Congress and the Politics of U.S. Foreign Economic Policy*. Berkeley: University of California Press, 1980.
Richelson, Jeffrey T. *The U.S. Intelligence Community*. Cambridge, Mass.: Ballinger, 1985.
Ripley, Randall B., and James Lindsay. *Congress Resurgent*. Ann Arbor: University of Michigan Press, 1993.
Rosati, Jerel A. *The Carter Administration's Quest for Global Community*. Columbia: University of South Carolina Press, 1987.
———. *The Politics of U.S. Foreign Policy*. Fort Worth: Harcourt Brace Jovanovich, 1993.
Rubin, Barry. *Secrets of State*. New York: Oxford University Press, 1985.
Shuman, Howard E., and Walter R. Thomas. *The Constitution and National Security*. Washington, D.C.: National Defense University Press, 1990.
Sobel, Richard, ed. *Public Opinion in U.S. Foreign Policy*. Lanham, Md.: Rowman and Littlefield, 1993.
Tivnan, Edward. *The Lobby*. New York: Simon and Schuster, 1987.
Tucker, Robert H., Charles B. Keely, and Linda Wrigley, eds. *Immigration and U.S. Foreign Policy*. Boulder, Colo.: Westview Press, 1990.
Warburg, Gerald. *Conflict and Consensus*. Cambridge, Mass.: Ballinger, 1989.
Wittkopf, Eugene R. *Faces of Internationalism*. Durham, N.C.: Duke University Press, 1990.

MEMOIRS AND BIOGRAPHIES OF AMERICAN LEADERS

Acheson, Dean. *Present at the Creation*. New York: Norton, 1969.
Ambrose, Stephen E. *Eisenhower*. 2 vols. New York: Simon and Schuster, 1983 and 1984.
———. *Nixon*. New York: Simon and Schuster, 1992.
Andrianopoulos, Gerry A. *Kissinger and Brzezinski*. New York: St. Martin's Press, 1991.
Baker, James A., III. *The Politics of Diplomacy*. New York: Putnam, 1995.
Bill, James A. *George Ball*. New Haven, Conn.: Yale University Press, 1997.
Brands, H. W. *The Wages of Globalism*. New York: Oxford University Press, 1994.
Brinkley, Douglas, ed. *Dean Acheson and the Making of U.S. Foreign Policy*. New York: St. Martin's Press, 1993.
Brown, Harold. *Thinking about National Security*. Boulder, Colo.: Westview Press, 1983.
Brzezinski, Zbigniew. *Power and Principle*. New York: Farrar, Straus and Giroux, 1983.
Bullock, Alan. *Hitler and Stalin*. New York: Knopf, 1992.
Bundy, McGeorge. *Danger and Survival*. New York: Random House, 1988.
Byrnes, James F. *Speaking Frankly*. New York: Harper and Brothers, 1947.
Cannon, Lou. *Reagan*. New York: Random House, 1981.
Carter, Jimmy. *Keeping Faith*. New York: Bantam Books, 1982.
Conquest, Richard. *Stalin*. New York: Viking, 1991.

Dallek, Robert. *Franklin D. Roosevelt and American Foreign Policy, 1932–1945.* New York: Oxford University Press, 1979.

Dobrynin, Anatoly. *In Confidence.* New York: Times Books, 1995.

Eisenhower, David. *Eisenhower at War.* New York: Random House, 1986.

Eisenhower, Dwight D. *Mandate for Change.* New York: New American Library, 1965.

———. *Waging Peace.* New York: Doubleday, 1965.

Feis, Herbert. *Churchill, Roosevelt, Stalin.* Princeton, N.J.: Princeton University Press, 1957.

Ferrell, Robert H. *George C. Marshall.* New York: Cooper Square Publishers, 1966.

Gates, Robert M. *From the Shadows.* New York: Simon and Schuster, 1996.

Guhin, Michael. *John Foster Dulles.* New York: Columbia University Press, 1972.

Hoopes, Townsend. *The Devil and John Foster Dulles.* Boston: Atlantic/Little, Brown, 1975.

Immerman, Richard H. *John Foster Dulles and the Diplomacy of the Cold War.* Princeton, N.J.: Princeton University Press, 1990.

Isaacson, Walter. *Kissinger.* New York: Simon and Schuster, 1992.

Isaacson, Walter, and Evan Thomas. *The Wise Men.* New York: Simon and Schuster, 1986.

Johnson, Lyndon B. *The Vantage Point.* New York: Popular Library, 1971.

Kalb, Marvin, and Bernard Kalb. *Kissinger.* Boston: Little, Brown, 1974.

Kearns, Doris. *Lyndon Johnson and the American Dream.* New York: Harper and Row, 1976.

Kennan, George F. *Memoirs.* Boston: Little, Brown, 1967.

Kennedy, Robert F. *Thirteen Days.* New York: Norton, 1971.

Kissinger, Henry A. *The White House Years.* Boston: Little, Brown, 1979.

———. *Years of Upheaval.* Boston: Little, Brown, 1982.

McCullough, David. *Truman.* New York: Simon and Schuster, 1992.

McFarlane, Robert C., with Zofia Smardz. *Special Trust.* New York: Cadell and Davies, 1994.

McLellan, David S. *Cyrus Vance.* Totowa, N.J.: Rowman and Allanheld, 1985.

Miscamble, Wilson D. *George F. Kennan and the Making of American Foreign Policy, 1947–1950.* Princeton, N.J.: Princeton University Press, 1992.

Nixon, Richard. *RN.* New York: Grosset and Dunlap, 1978.

———. *Seize the Moment.* New York: Simon and Schuster, 1992.

Parmet, Herbert S. *Eisenhower and the American Crusades.* New York: Macmillan, 1972.

Pogue, Forrest C. *George C. Marshall.* New York: Viking Press, 1987.

Rusk, Dean, as told to Richard Rusk. *As I Saw It.* New York: Norton, 1990.

Schlesinger, Arthur M., Jr. *A Thousand Days.* New York: Crest Books, 1967.

Schulzinger, Robert D. *Henry Kissinger.* New York: Columbia University Press, 1989.

Sherwood, Robert E. *Roosevelt and Hopkins.* New York: Harper, 1948.

Smith, Gaddis. *Dean Acheson.* New York: Cooper Square Publishers, 1972.

Sorensen, Theodore C. *Kennedy.* New York: Bantam Books, 1966.

Stoessinger, John. *Henry Kissinger.* New York: Norton, 1976.

Truman, Harry S. *Memoirs.* 2 vols. New York: New American Library, 1965.

Vance, Cyrus. *Hard Choices.* New York: Simon and Schuster, 1982.

Weinberger, Caspar W. *Fighting for Peace.* New York: Warner, 1990.

Yeltsin, Boris. *The Struggle for Russia.* New York: Times Books, 1994.

Select World Wide Web Sites

Readers may find this list of sites on the World Wide Web helpful in following foreign policy-related developments in the United States and other countries. All sites offer further linkages. Each URL should be preceded by http://.

U.S. GOVERNMENT: EXECUTIVE BRANCH

White House (www.whitehouse.gov)
Secretary of State (www.state.gov)
U.S. Agency for International Development (www.info.usaid.gov)
U.S. Arms Control and Disarmament Agency (www.acda.gov)
U.S. Information Agency (www.usia.gov)
Secretary of Defense (www.dtic.mil/defenselink/osd)
Joint Chiefs of Staff (www.dtic.mil/jcs)
U.S. Army (www.dtic.mil/armylink)
U.S. Navy (www.navy.mil)
U.S. Air Force (www.af.mil)
U.S. Marine Corps (www.usmc.mil)
Secretary of Commerce (www.doc.gov)
Central Intelligence Agency (www.odci.gov/cia)
National Security Agency (www.nsa.gov)
U.S. Mission to the United Nations (www.undp.org/missions/usa)
U.S. Trade Representative (www.ustr.gov)

U.S. GOVERNMENT: LEGISLATIVE BRANCH

Library of Congress (www.loc.gov)
U.S. Senate (www.senate.gov)
Senate Armed Services Committee
    (www.senate.gov/committee/armed_services.html)
Senate Foreign Relations Committee
    (www.senate.gov/committee/foreign.html)
U.S. House of Representatives (www.house.gov)
House International Relations Committee
    (www.house.gov/international_relations)
House National Security Committee (www.house.gov/nsc)

INTERNATIONAL GOVERNMENTAL ORGANIZATIONS

Asia-Pacific Economic Cooperation (www.apecsec.org.sg)
European Union (europa.eu.int)
North Atlantic Treaty Organization (www.nato.int)
Organization of American States (www.oas.org)
Organization for Economic Co-operation and Development (www.oecd.org)
United Nations (www.unsystem.org)
World Bank (www.worldbank.org)
World Trade Organization (www.wto.org)
International Finance Corporation (www.ifc.org)
International Monetary Fund (www.imf.org)

Select World Wide Web Sites

INTERNATIONAL NONGOVERNMENTAL ORGANIZATIONS

Amnesty International (www.amnesty.org)
Green Cross International (www.gci.ch)
Greenpeace (www.greenpeace.org)
Human Rights Watch (www.hrw.org)
International Chamber of Commerce (www.iccwbo.org)
International Committee of the Red Cross (www.icrc.org)
World Wildlife Fund (www.wwf.org)

Index